THE THEATRE OF TIMBERLAKE WERTENBAKER

Sophie Bush is a writer-researcher specialising in contemporary theatre history and the processes of playmaking. Her doctorate, on the work of Timberlake Wertenbaker, was awarded by the University of Sheffield in 2011. She is a Lecturer in Performance at Sheffield Hallam University, and has previously taught at the Universities of Sheffield, Huddersfield and Manchester Metropolitan. She maintains an involvement with practical theatre-making, as director and devisor.

THE THEATRE OF TIMBERLAKE WERTENBAKER

Sophie Bush

Series Editors: Patrick Lonergan and Erin Hurley

B L O O M S B U R Y

LONDON • NEW DELHI • NEW YORK • SYDNEY

Bloomsbury Methuen Drama
An imprint of Bloomsbury Publishing Plc

50 Bedford Square	1385 Broadway
London	New York
WC1B 3DP	NY 10018
UK	USA

www.bloomsbury.com

Bloomsbury is a registered trademark of Bloomsbury Publishing Plc

First published 2013

British Library Cataloguing-in-Publication Data
A catalogue record for this book is available from the British Library.

ISBN: HB: 978–1-4081–8964–1
PB: 978–1-4081–8479–0
ePub: 978–1-4081–8409–7
ePDF: 978–1-4725–2068–5

Library of Congress Cataloging-in-Publication Data
Bush, Sophie.
The Theatre of Timberlake Wertenbaker / Sophie Bush.
pages cm
Includes bibliographical references and index.
ISBN 978-1-4081-8479-0 (pbk.) -- ISBN 978-1-4081-8964-1 (hardback) --
ISBN 978-1-4725-2068-5 (ebook (epdf) -- ISBN 978-1-4081-8409-7 (ebook
(epub) 1. Wertenbaker, Timberlake--Criticism and interpretation. I. Title.

PS3573.E74Z55 2013
812'.54--dc23

2013013876

Typeset by Fakenham Prepress Solutions, Fakenham, Norfolk NR21 8NN
Printed and bound in Great Britain

CONTENTS

Acknowledgements   vii
List of Illustrations   viii
Introduction: Timberlake Wertenbaker's Floating Identities   1

1 'Good enough to go on': The Beginnings of a Playwright   23

2 'They never went on quests': The Gender of Identification   63

3 'To speak in order to be': On Language and Identity   97

4 *Our Country's Good*: Three Professional Perspectives   143
   Creating *Our Country's Good*: Collaborative Writing   143
   Practice and Political Ideals at the Royal Court in
   the 1980s
   Sarah Sigal

   Our Country's Good in Melbourne   161
   Roger Hodgman

   Our Country's Good in the Classroom   167
   Debby Turner

5 'The longing to belong': On Cultural Genealogies   181

6 'Landscapes with figures in them': On Pity and Tenderness   232

Conclusions   266

Contents

Notes and References   273
Chronology   310
Bibliography   314
Notes on Contributors   323
Index   325

ACKNOWLEDGEMENTS

This project was made possible by the support and guidance of Critical Companions series editor Patrick Lonergan; Mark Dudgeon and Emily Hockley at Bloomsbury Methuen Drama; Maureen Barry, Chris Hopkins and Chris Wigginton at Sheffield Hallam University; Frances Babbage, Steve Nicholson and Bill McDonnell at the University of Sheffield; Richard Boon; Timberlake Wertenbaker; the British Library; the V&A Reading Room at Blythe House; Angela Bush and many other valued colleagues, friends and family members, too numerous to list.

For SJD

LIST OF ILLUSTRATIONS

1. Melbourne Theatre Company's *Our Country's Good*. Set designed by Tony Tripp. Photography: Jeff Busby, 163

2. Melbourne Theatre Company's *Our Country's Good*. Photography: Jeff Busby, 166

INTRODUCTION
TIMBERLAKE WERTENBAKER'S FLOATING IDENTITIES

Izena duen guztiak izatea ere badauke
Everything with a name exists
(Basque saying)

'I think the whole thing about being a writer is that you have a floating identity', Timberlake Wertenbaker told the journalist Hilary de Vries.[1] Suzie Mackenzie gained a similar impression of the playwright: 'In a sense, she might say, she has no country, no class, no culture. No language even. Or, to put it another way, what she has in the way of cultural inheritance, she has determined for herself.'[2] This book proposes that the fluidity and mutability of identity embraced by Mackenzie's statement and Wertenbaker's concept of a 'floating identity' has been a continuous feature of the playwright's life and work, both of which have resisted labels. This unwillingness to be categorised has, arguably, had an impact on the way Wertenbaker and her plays have been understood and critiqued, both in academic circles and amongst the press, with whom she has had, at best, an ambiguous, at worst, a fraught, relationship. This antagonism is another thread that runs through this book. Mackenzie's willingness to accept Wertenbaker's non-definitions is unusual, contrasting with some journalists' specific, almost objectifying descriptions of 'an attractive young woman of mixed French, English and American blood',[3] 'a striking, dark-haired woman'[4] or 'a mature girl of warmth and grace who happens to be a playwright'.[5] Such remarks, which seem to present Wertenbaker's profession as secondary to her nationality, even to her appearance, may explain, in part, her desire to self-determine.

Wertenbaker's career has spanned more than three decades, yet she has received far less scholarly attention than many of her

1

contemporaries. While her 1988 play *Our Country's Good* has been almost canonised through its wealth of awards, popularity with amateur and professional companies all over the world and long-standing inclusion on school and university syllabuses, many of her plays have not attracted the consideration they merit. This book attempts to counteract this phenomenon, highlighting the extent and quality of Wertenbaker's oeuvre, while still giving detailed analyses of her best-known plays. It provides a comprehensive overview that foregrounds the development of the work, drawing extensively on archive materials, and maintaining a constant focus on issues of production and reception.

Wertenbaker is anxious that scholarship on her work should not impose false limitations on its potential meanings. This, she suggests, is 'always a problem', 'because I don't write political plays as such. [...] *Three Birds* – it's not a feminist play, and *After Darwin* [...] touches on colonialism, but it's not [purely] about that. [...] [S]ometimes people don't like it, because it's not saying what they want me to say'. She hopes that her work does not fit into rigid parameters and we agreed that her plays might benefit from more open examination. [6] Consequently, I avoid reading the work according to potentially restrictive theoretical frameworks, instead grouping plays chronologically to foreground Wertenbaker's career as a developing process that has both waxed and waned, in terms of critical commendation, if not in terms of quality. While I offer thematic links across the groupings, these are intended to retain a sense of fluidity, imbuing this structure with the same sense of mutability that is crucial to Wertenbaker's plays.

Chapter One explores the largely undocumented earliest stages of Wertenbaker's career and the plays she drafted before 1980. An account of the process by which she gained entry to the theatre industry, which reveals a series of opportunities and pitfalls, is followed by textual analyses of the unpublished (and frequently unperformed) pieces that date from this period. I split these works into three categories: those dealing predominantly with the personal and containing limited social or political reference ('The Third' and 'The Vigil'), those that are the most overtly political of Wertenbaker's career, addressing topical issues such as the threat from nuclear power and the excesses of the Western, capitalist world ("This is No Place for Tallulah Bankhead', 'Near Miss', 'Act for Our Times', 'Breaking Through' and 'Second Sentence'), and a third group of three unfinished pieces ('Monads', 'Don Juan's Women' and 'Agamemnon's Daughter'), which begin to show the successful combination of the personal and political, and the playful interaction with the literary canon, for which many of Wertenbaker's later plays are known.

Chapter Two focuses on the years 1980 to 1985: a transitional period for Wertenbaker, during which she began receiving commissions, rather than always having to tout her work around 'on spec'. The majority of these productions were relatively small-scale and low-profile and she was often frustrated by having to tailor her writing to the specific requirements of certain companies. Towards the end of this period, she established stronger links with London's foremost new writing theatre, the Royal Court, and began to gain increased public recognition. I suggest that it was during this time that Wertenbaker's work was most focused on exploring gender and its relationship with identities, and I examine her persistent interest in 'women on quests'.[7] Issues of production and reception are discussed alongside textual analyses. I consider how far Wertenbaker identifies as a 'feminist', or 'woman playwright', and the relationship between this and her representation in the media. The key texts discussed are *New Anatomies* (1981), *The Grace of Mary Traverse* (1985), and the unpublished works 'Variations' (c.1981) and 'Inside Out' (c.1982).

The year 1988 was an important one for Wertenbaker, with almost simultaneous premieres of what remain her two most frequently performed plays (*Our Country's Good* and *The Love of the Nightingale*) by two highly regarded British theatre companies (the Royal Court and the Royal Shakespeare Company, respectively). In the years that followed, Wertenbaker received constant requests to sit on panels and committees and to be interviewed by everyone from broadsheet journalists to sixth-form students. She was commissioned for lucrative film and television work as well as plays, and was in such demand that she had to turn work down on a number

3

of occasions. Chapter Three focuses on this period in Wertenbaker's career, and her two plays of 1988, focusing on the dangers of the loss of 'voice', and the potential to regain it, which Wertenbaker links to self-expression through engagement with the alternative 'language' provided by the arts.

In Chapter Four, three contributing scholars and practitioners offer a range of international and professional perspectives on *Our Country's Good*. Firstly, playwright and academic Sarah Sigal discusses the challenges and rewards of the research, development and writing process employed by Wertenbaker and director Max Stafford-Clark in 1988. Secondly, theatre director Roger Hodgman recounts his experience of directing the play in Melbourne, considering the play's significance to Australian audiences. Finally, experienced teacher Debby Turner explores the play's educational value, offering a range of practical and reflective exercises for teachers and students. These essays highlight and begin to explain this play's far-reaching influence (in both geographical and interdisciplinary terms), throughout the theatre industry and the education system.

Chapter Five is concerned with Wertenbaker's turn-of-the-century plays: *The Break of Day* (1995), *After Darwin* (1998), *Credible Witness* (2001) and *The Ash Girl* (2000). All these texts have discussions about cultural identities at their core, raising questions concerning the effects of voluntary and forced cultural relocation, and the values and problems associated with remembering, discovering, abandoning or creating cultural histories. Alongside these recurrent concerns is a parallel strand that engages with ideas of reproduction and genealogy; Edward Said's theories of filiation and affiliation are valuable in illuminating the potential conversations between these two elements of the work.

Chapter Six discusses Wertenbaker's most recent work. After a brief consideration of *Arden City* (2008), *Jenufa* (2007) and 'The Laws of Motion' (2004), I focus on *The Line* (2009). I argue that this text positions the visual arts as a synecdoche for the arts in general and Wertenbaker's own practice of playwriting in particular. As this is a device Wertenbaker also employs in *Three Birds Alighting on a Field* (1991), I consider these two 'art plays' alongside each other.

This chapter begins to draw conclusions about Wertenbaker's oeuvre as a whole, her most pronounced and long-standing concerns, and the fluctuating shape of her career. Most visibly consistent amid her changing themes and styles is her optimism: a hope for the future, which she connects sometimes to the beauty of the natural world and sometimes to the human imagination and our capacity for pity and tenderness.

Into the Archive Alone

[A]lthough I love working with actors and talking to them, in the end I have to write from my own insights and puzzlement; walk into the labyrinth alone.[8]

Wertenbaker's extensive, uncatalogued and barely discussed archive contains a wealth of research materials, including typescripts, press-cuttings, photographs and handwritten notes. Wertenbaker claims to have 'never rewritten a play less than 4 times. [...] To me a play was like a prey one stalked. The writing and the rewriting was a closing circle around the play.'[9] The many stages of this process are clear from the multiple versions of her plays, which often change significantly over the course of their creation. The first chapter of this book, which discusses ten unpublished plays from the late 1970s, relies entirely on these drafts. Subsequent chapters are more focused on the 'final' published versions of texts, but make frequent consideration of the development and genesis of these plays.[10] A notable example of the value of such material is the existence of an article ('Women ex-prisoners: out of the closet and on to the stage') and an unpublished play ('Second Sentence') from 1979/80, which explore modern-day prejudices towards the prison community, foreshadowing sentiments expressed in *Our Country's Good* and demonstrating that this later play was a result of long-standing concerns, rather than a straightforward response to the publication of Thomas Keneally's novel *The Playmaker*.

Wertenbaker's professional correspondence is another valuable resource, which reveals much about her career development and collaborations. As Judy Simons has noted, the 'expression [...] of anxieties that beset writers over the processes of production informs our understanding of the genesis of a text and the problems surrounding it'.[11] The sequences of letters that flew between Wertenbaker, her agents, and potential producers and collaborators, disclose a succession of hopes, disappointments, successes and failures, discussed throughout the book. They also offer significant and, at times, unique insights into what Wertenbaker felt about her plays and those who produced them. When the academic Susan Carlson sent a draft of her book *Women and Comedy* (for which Wertenbaker had been interviewed) for Wertenbaker to approve, her assistant replied that Wertenbaker 'would like you to change *the* women's group to *a* women's group and she would like the word "suicidally" removed and replaced by *in despair*'.[12] These tactful alterations refer to the account Wertenbaker had given Carlson of her fraught relations with the Women's Theatre Group. Referring to the published text of Carlson's book, one can see that Wertenbaker's request was followed to the letter. The extremity of Wertenbaker's original statement has only resurfaced because a draft of the letter sent to Carlson is now accessible through the archive. Such correspondence reveals far more about the material conditions and political machinations behind artistic production than a published text or staged production can.

Despite the archive's potential, it is not a complete or authoritative documentation of Wertenbaker's career. While letters provide tantalising details about working conditions and inspirations, as a record they are manifestly incomplete. Additionally, we must remember that, to an extent, the letter is another category of performative writing. Julia Swindells considers that 'all autobiographical statements show some process of mediation between the subject and the author' and Simons suggests that 'the more we read others' diaries, the more we become aware of the diaries' fictive quality, and of the creation of a central character, established through an act of imagination as powerful as those responsible for stimulating writers' published works'.[13] Despite these caveats, Wertenbaker's archive retains great value for scholars, highlighting the essentially collaborative and communal nature of theatrical production. The way playwrights are treated, or believe themselves to have been treated, by those with whom they work is something that often goes unrecorded by formal sources. Published texts give simple production credits, revealing nothing about the pleasures or difficulties of creation. Any traces of discontent or frustration are edited out of press releases and, if at all possible, out of the performances audiences and critics attend. Even theatrical histories, such as Carson's, often present tactfully edited accounts. In contrast, archival sources can appear tantalisingly uncensored. Yet uncensored they are not, certainly not in the case of a living writer who has chosen to include or withhold every element of this record. Once this acknowledgement has been made, the playwright's active role in the creation of that archive can be seen, not as a drawback, but a boon: another injection of their presence, shaping and breathing life into our picture of their profession.

Timberlake Wertenbaker

Wertenbaker was born in New York in the mid 1940s to Charles Wertenbaker, a foreign correspondent for *TIME* magazine, and Lael Tucker Wertenbaker, also a journalist. The couple returned to work in France with Timberlake and her elder brother shortly after her birth. The family lived in a small fishing village called Ciboure in the Basque region of France. Wertenbaker paints an idyllic picture of a childhood spent roaming the picturesque Basque countryside and buried deep in adventurous books, her favourite of which was Dumas's *The Three Musketeers*. 'I always had a hankering for adventure', she remembers, 'I identified with d'Artagnan, I liked the friendships he had.'[14] As discussed in Chapter Two, such literature had a deep impact on Wertenbaker, particularly when she realised that adventures were often limited to male characters. Although she initially learnt to read and write in English, she began to read in French at the age of four and briefly spoke Basque.[15] She appears to have identified as Basque, rather than French or American, during this period and recalls that it 'was a shock to find out that I was not Basque'.[16] She was deeply affected by the political situation of the Basque people, attributing a life-long fear of being silenced to having witnessed the suppression of the Basque language and culture by the French government: 'The threat of the loss of language is one of the greatest threats. I grew up in the Basque country of France where the language was systematically eroded and destroyed so I feel very strongly about language.'[17] Wertenbaker admits that she was not fully aware of this suppression at the time, and found her village 'a great place to be', because of its lively culture, which was another source of influence. 'Basque country was theatre in itself, because it's a very verbal culture', she explains, 'you knew what was going on in the village, so there were endless stories and gossip.' Although too young to appreciate 'to what extent the Basques had an oral culture and how much poetry there was', she believes that 'even if you're in touch with that culture, you must sense that'.[18] Perhaps these early experiences of the theatrical as part of an intangible, living culture may have shaped Wertenbaker's desire to create plays that cannot be easily pinned down or defined.

Wertenbaker's continental schooling was another factor through which she 'got very hooked on theatre, because there really is a lot of theatre in French education'.[19] Her Basque surroundings, while theatrical in themselves, did not offer much opportunity for playgoing, but she 'read a lot of plays' from an early age. 'I don't know why', she recalls, 'I mean, [they were] just something that was in the library.'[20] This off-hand statement is typical of the way Wertenbaker describes many of her life and career choices. This habit gives the impression that she is keen to resist the idea that she was somehow 'born' to be a playwright, and perhaps demonstrates the same distaste for determinism that appears in much of her work.

In 1955, Wertenbaker's father died of cancer, a process graphically documented in her mother's 1959 book *Death of a Man*.[21] The family subsequently relocated to New York, a move with which Wertenbaker felt ill at ease. She describes her first experience of American life as 'terrible. Terrible and I hated it.' Torn from the freedom of a rural childhood and subjected to the pressures and confinements of a major city, her sense of dislocation was profound. 'For me', she recalls, 'childhood is a world full of hope which does crack. For me it cracked when we left the Basque country.'[22] On a more positive note, New York offered far greater access to cultural events and the first two plays Wertenbaker remembers seeing there were *The King and I* and a French language production of Genet's *Deathwatch*. She recalls being 'absolutely fascinated' by the latter,[23] which she claims 'influenced [her] immensely'.[24] She has even suggested, with an uncharacteristic sense of determinism, that 'it's what made me a playwright. Or [...] the combination of the musical and that, made me a playwright',[25] although she 'didn't think of going into [theatre], until much later'.[26] There is little about the style or content of either of these pieces that could be cited as a direct influence on Wertenbaker's playwriting, although *The King and I* does contain the trope (frequently used by Wertenbaker) of the play-within-the-play. What seems to have made the impact was rather her realisation of the power of the theatrical experience.

Aged 15, Wertenbaker returned to reading and writing in English. As with her physical relocation, she was not immediately comfortable with this change. 'I felt ill at ease in America with its brave, male, woodsman prose', she remembers, 'and didn't feel at home again until I discovered *Women in Love*.'[27] This comment suggests that the tone of the American novels, rather than their language, alienated Wertenbaker. Her bilingual upbringing ensured her comprehension of English texts, but she suffered a similar discomfort to Procne in *The Love of the Nightingale*, who is aware that even for those who 'speak the same language', '[t]he words are the same, but point to different things'.[28] The sense of trauma connected to the experience of cultural and linguistic dislocation is a recurrent theme in Wertenbaker's work, appearing prominently in *New Anatomies*, *Our Country's Good*, *Three Birds Alighting on a Field*, *The Break of Day*, *After Darwin*, and receiving its fullest treatment in *Credible Witness*. This theme, and the accompanying idea that hope and possibility can spring from these same dislocations, are discussed in Chapter Five.

Like many of her displaced characters, as a young adult Wertenbaker became, if not settled in, at least acclimatised to, her surroundings. She remained in the United States to attend St John's College in Annapolis, which she describes as an institution 'run mostly by Germans who had left during the war. It was based on the philosophies of Plato. It was very odd.'[29] Much of Wertenbaker's work shows a great awareness of philosophical systems; '[I]t was Plato I really liked', she admits, citing the direct influence of 'the Meno in *Our Country's Good*. Elsewhere, she is reluctant to suggest specific links between philosophical concepts and particular plays. 'I think all it did was to give me the courage to approach a difficult subject matter', she explains, 'a subject matter I didn't know very well, like when I was doing *After Darwin*. I mean, the theory of evolution is not that simple [...], and I was a bit nervous of it, so it helped me to think about that.' However, she is also keen to highlight that 'everything [she] read had an influence'.[30]

Having gained her first degree, Wertenbaker began a Masters course in Russian at the University of Georgetown, before abandoning it as a 'waste of time'.[31] Lael Wertenbaker suggested her daughter become a diplomat, but Wertenbaker did not feel she had the required tact.[32] Having a talent for writing, she worked instead as a researcher for Dumbarton Oaks, before moving to Time-Life Books and a job as a caption writer. By the end of her twenties she was, in her own words, 'upwardly mobile in a well-paid, prestigious New York job'.[33] But while this employment kept her in 'beautiful clothes and expensive meals', after five years she was beginning to wonder whether there might be 'some other reason for being than producing captions at a snail's pace'. Frustrated with her profession, she struggled with the knowledge that she would never 'in the least be missed at my job', and that 'crowded tube, shops, streets, stores and offices all said that I was inessential'. These factors contributed to a general sense of dissatisfaction: 'I was suffering from a malaise common to people, like me, in their mid twenties [...], who had a "good job", a "good life", all the external trappings of happiness [...], without actual happiness'.[34] This situation has some parallels with that of Judith in Wertenbaker's 1978 play 'This is No Place for Tallulah Bankhead', but where Judith's malaise leads her to suicide, Wertenbaker's prompted a more positive course of action.

With the approach of her thirtieth birthday, Wertenbaker's restlessness pushed her to embark on an adventure she described as 'partly unjustifiable'. In 1975, she gave up her comfortable New York existence to become a stable-hand in Somerset. She had previously enjoyed a fortnight's holiday at these stables and had taken riding lessons in London and New York, but still lacked experience and justified her impulsive decision in distinctly irrational terms: 'I believe very much in fate and the intricate patterns it makes of our lives always fascinate me.'[35] Before finalising her plans, she 'consulted instead [of common sense] supernatural forces', which included her astrologer ('a lovely woman who had been my advisor in many things') and her Jungian analyst (who 'thought it would do me good and bring [me] in touch with an instinctive part of myself I did not know').[36] These comments reveal an interest in the mystical, reflected in a number of Wertenbaker's works, most notably 'Monads' and 'The Vigil' (discussed in Chapter One).

Working as a stable-hand proved a life-changing experience for Wertenbaker, which she began to write a book about. These drafts of 'A Year on Exmoor' contain further evidence that Wertenbaker was developing ambitions to write more than captions. They reference an unspecified novel that was rejected by an agency during this time, and a gothic novel about a girl working as a stable-hand, which Wertenbaker used to vent some of her grievances against her employer's more draconian attitudes.[37] However, there is no mention of Wertenbaker attempting dramatic writing at this stage and her Exmoor experience is presented as fulfilling in an aesthetic and practical sense, rather than a cerebral or cultural one. She describes being 'so off thinking and writing', a feeling that lingered into her return to city life. 'I went to the theatre last night', she records, 'I liked it. Could equally well have done without it. Was glad to leave.'[38]

Wertenbaker was keen to retain her Exmoor mentality and not 'fall back into the old person: slightly lethargic, lost'.[39] She complained that in city life 'we are not even confronted with ethics' and considered that 'when the glittering layers of life in a city are taken away, it reduces itself to Greed and passing the time'.[40] Expanding on what she termed 'the exhaustion of cities', she decried being surrounded by so much ugliness. A constant blocking of the mind, wishing to be somewhere else. Hence the exhaustion. [...] How much damage to the soul, but to the body as well, does ugliness cause. As much damage as smoking, breathing chemicals. It corrodes the spirit, eventually the body. Plato was right. One must live with beauty. [...] More so, it seems, than love.[41]

The importance of appreciating the natural world is a theme in several of Wertenbaker's plays, and is discussed in more detail in Chapter Six. I suggest that it was on Exmoor that Wertenbaker rediscovered the importance of the freedom and beauty she had enjoyed as a child in the Basque Country.

After a brief return to New York, Wertenbaker embarked on another journey, moving to the Greek Island of Spetse by the end of 1976. Here, Wertenbaker earned her living teaching French, but enjoyed a leisurely lifestyle of 'swimming, having all the time I wanted to write'.[42] In February 1977, she recorded being 'in Greece working on [the Exmoor book] and on some plays we are putting on here'.[43] This comment and the first draft of her play 'The Third' (dated 16 December 1976) are the earliest archived records of Wertenbaker's writing for the stage.

A Backdrop of British Theatre

Wertenbaker's earliest theatrical writings and the first productions of her work occurred on Spetse, but London has been home to the vast majority of her professional career, and its theatrical climate has been the major force with which she has had to contend during the last forty years. She began establishing herself as a London playwright in the late 1970s, a decade after theatre censorship had been famously abolished. It is unrealistic to suggest that there were no longer restrictions on the playwright's craft: internal censorship imposed by the governing boards of subsidised institutions was still, in some cases, as restrictive as the Lord Chamberlain had been and 'market pressure' exerted further influence. However, as Dominic Shellard has recognised, the end of censorship was a catalyst for other advances:

[T]he fact that writers no longer had to submit scripts for time-consuming vetting introduced a revolutionising spontaneity to seventies drama. Productions could be mounted immediately, small collaborative groups were formed [...] and new venues such as pubs, community centres, 'arts labs' and working men's clubs began to spring up to cater for the increasing demand. Whereas in London there were approximately half a dozen such venues in 1968, by the late seventies there were over a hundred, including the King's Head pub in Islington, the Half Moon in Aldgate, the Bush [...], the Mall of the Institute for Contemporary Arts (ICA) and the Royal Court's Theatre Upstairs.[44]

Of these five venues, all but the Bush were crucial stepping stones in Wertenbaker's career.

In terms of opportunities for women, while Shellard comments that it 'would be hard to argue that during [the 1970s] female playwrights achieved the breakthrough they deserved in terms of widely acknowledged success',[45] the British theatre had begun to shift away from the 'male-dominated club'[46] it had been during the 1960s.[47] Caryl Churchill, whose first professional stage play *Owners* was produced in 1972, had by the end of the decade written some of her best-known works, including *Light Shining in Buckinghamshire* (1976), *Vinegar Tom* (1976) and *Cloud Nine* (1979). Pam Gems also gained public recognition in this decade, producing her most famous work *Piaf* in 1978. Alongside these high-profile writers, the 1970s saw an increase in all female or women-centred companies, such as the Women's Theatre Group (est. 1973), Monstrous Regiment (est. 1975), Gay Sweatshop (est. 1975), Siren (est.1979) and Clean Break (est. 1979), all of which offered increased opportunities for female playwrights. Wertenbaker has emphasised how important it was to have female role models:

Playwrights need models, and not just historical, but contemporary ones. I also believe women playwrights are helped by women models. Caryl Churchill has broken new ground for women by extending the boundaries of subject, Louise Page has reached previously undefined areas of memory and feeling. I have left these plays encouraged and thrilled and I am not the only writer grateful to the Court for having put them on.[48]

As well as the collectives whose principle motive was to challenge gender prejudices, other groups with alternative and/or ensemble working methods appeared around this time. One of the most notable was Joint Stock, established in 1974 by William Gaskill, David Hare, David Aukin and Max Stafford-Clark. The 'Joint Stock method', whereby cast, director and writer underwent several weeks of workshops to research and develop a text, has been much discussed and frequently emulated, not least by Stafford-Clark's subsequent company Out of Joint. There has been some criticism that these methods, particularly as employed by Max Stafford-Clark during his tenure as Artistic Director of the Royal Court, disadvantaged writers by acting as an 'implied attack on an old-fashioned model of the playwright writing a play and the theatre putting it on'.[49] Wertenbaker, however, enjoyed a strong relationship with Stafford-Clark and produced some of her most successful work in this way, as highlighted by Sarah Sigal's essay in Chapter Four on the development of *Our Country's Good*.

Despite its gradual democratisation, the theatre of the 1970s was still dominated by white men. All major theatres, including the Court, the Royal Shakespeare Company (RSC) and the National were run and programmed by men, a situation that Wertenbaker considered forced women playwrights 'to fight odds'.[50] The work of David Hare, Howard Brenton, David Edgar, Howard Barker, Trevor Griffiths and John McGrath defined a generation of British 'political' theatre (the narrowness of this definition perhaps contributing to the neglect of some of the politically engaged work of female playwrights, including Wertenbaker, in the next decade).

Outside feminist collectives, the position of women was rarely a prominent theme; the troubles in Northern Ireland, the questioning of 'British' national identity, the threat (and actuality) of terrorism, and the backlash of reductions in civil liberties (including internment without trial) provided much material for the subsidised sector, perhaps reaching their peak in Howard Brenton's controversial *Romans in Britain* (1980). Meanwhile, according to Billington, 'the best West End plays of the period revolved around one particular quality: *the emotional detachment of the English male* [*sic*]'.[51] As the decade ran into further trouble with the start of recession in 1974, strikes and rising unemployment contributed to a general sense of disillusionment and uncertainty, which permeated large swathes of dramatic writing.

In 1975, theatre subsidy had been frozen (meaning, as inflation rose, a reduction in real terms). This was a shock for many in the subsidised sector, who had lived through a decade of year-on-year grant increases. National institutions such as the RSC and the National Theatre had always required high levels of government funding, but as the overall budget dwindled, began to consume even larger shares. The Royal Court suffered from this, its difficulties reaching crisis point in 1983/4, when the Arts Council threatened to withdraw its subsidy altogether. Wertenbaker was among those who petitioned the Arts Council on its behalf and a national outcry, led by industry heavyweights such as Laurence Olivier and David Hare and the critic Nicholas de Jongh, contributed to the Court's reprieve.

While the 1970s had seen something of a move towards individualism, materialism and free market values, these ideas were pushed to breaking point during Margaret Thatcher's 1980s. Under what Billington describes as a 'culture of greed and social Darwinism' (elements of which Wertenbaker would explore in her 1998 play *After Darwin*), subsidy was reduced, not merely through financial necessity, but because the whole concept of government funding for the arts was questioned by those in power.[52] As Shellard describes, 'the stress on private enterprise and self-help meant that the notion of the state funding theatrical activity would be viewed largely with suspicion'.[53] The extent of this was revealed in 1987 when the Tory Arts Minister Richard Luce remarked that 'the only test of our ability to succeed is whether we can attract enough customers'.[54] Cuts were not administered on an ad hoc basis, with particularly punitive measures taken on 'politically provocative companies such as Joint Stock and 7:84 [...] that interrogated the administration in power'. In 1985, the government stated openly that 'the paucity of the drama grant had been partly due to the public opposition to its policies by [theatre] professionals such as Peter Hall', who was running the National Theatre at the time.[55] When, in 1986, the *Sunday Times* ran an article misleadingly alleging that Hall and Trevor Nunn (who was then running the RSC) had benefited improperly from the transfer of publicly funded productions to the commercial sector, Hall was suspicious that the attack 'might have been politically motivated, given his open hostility to government policy'.[56] At the very least, the incident demonstrated the power of the pervasively right-wing media.

While small political companies and regional theatres suffered the worst of the cuts, nowhere escaped unscathed. The Royal Court's Theatre Upstairs and even the National's Cottesloe went dark for months at a time. In 1986, the Cork Report discovered that large sections of British theatre only survived by being 'run like a glorified sweatshop'. Since 1971, both new work (considered risky) and classical revivals (that required large expensive casts) had declined, often being replaced by musicals or 'one set, small cast plays'. The report's modest recommendation that theatre subsidy could be supplemented with a tiny amount of the BBC licence fee was dismissed with 'patronising contempt' by Tory Arts Council Chairman Sir William Rees-Mogg.[57]

The commercial theatre, which had failed to create work to rival that of the subsidised sector in the previous decade, came into its own in the 1980s with a series of large-scale, home-grown musicals, designed to capture the growing tourist trade and appeal to the desire for escapism generated by the increasingly depressing social climate. Even large-scale subsidised institutions reached for a share of this business with epic adaptations (*Nicholas Nickleby*, RSC,

1980) and revivals of play cycles from Shakespeare (*The Plantagenets*, RSC, 1988), the Greeks (*The Greeks*, RSC, 1980 and *The Oresteia*, National Theatre, 1981) and elsewhere (*The Mysteries*, National Theatre, 1985). While it was hard for new writing to compete in this 'market', a number of playwrights challenged the tide of selfishness and acquisitiveness that characterised the decade. These included Caryl Churchill (*Top Girls*, 1982 and *Serious Money*, 1987), Sarah Daniels (*Masterpieces*, 1983), David Hare and Howard Brenton (*Pravda*, 1985). Additionally, new voices emerged to highlight the extremes of poverty and hardship that were the underside of 1980s materialism and Thatcherism, notably Jim Cartwright's *Road* (1986) and Andrea Dunbar's *The Arbour* (1980) and *Rita, Sue and Bob Too* (1982).

Several of Wertenbaker's most successful plays were produced in the 1980s, and the visibility of female playwrights continued to increase, particularly at the Royal Court, where Max Stafford-Clark (artistic director between 1979 and 1993) believed that 'it just happens that the most exciting and vital work is being written by women'.[58] As well as Daniels, Churchill, Wertenbaker and Dunbar, the 1980s saw significant contributions from Louise Page, Bryony Lavery, Charlotte Keatley, Winsome Pinnock, Clare McIntyre, Kay Adshead and April de Angelis, although this list should not disguise the fact that plays programmed, written, directed and reviewed by men still dominated British theatre.[59]

Several (male) critics have exaggerated the perilous condition of new writing at the end of the 1980s. Michael Billington records that, during this decade, 'although the stubborn and tenacious older writers nagged, criticised and questioned, the well [of new writers] looked in danger of drying up'.[60] Graham Whybrow, who became literary manager at the Court in 1994, remembers that 'by the beginning of the '90s there [was] widely perceived to be a crisis in new writing in the theatre'.[61] Although in the introduction to *State of Play* (a collection of papers drawn from David Edgar's playwriting conferences at Birmingham University), Edgar admits that 'reports of the collapse of new theatre writing in Britain had been greatly exaggerated', he praises the 'upsurge' he felt took place in the 1990s. The 'main reason' Edgar cites for this increase perhaps reveals the attitude behind other critics' dismissal of new writing in the 1980s. Edgar claims that 1990s 'writers found a subject' in the form of 'masculinity and its discontents'. He considers 'the decline of the dominant role of men – in the work place and in the family' as 'probably the biggest single story of the last thirty years in the western countries'.[62] The confidence with which Edgar presents the male response to female empowerment as a subject of much greater importance than the progress made by women is quite remarkable. As the subjectivity of male experience is emphasised, that of women is almost denied, reduced to a phenomenon that (male) society must react to, as it would to the aftermath of a world war or political regime change. Wertenbaker spoke out against this male-centric approach to theatre history at one of Edgar's own playwriting conferences: 'When lazy theatre commentators say there was no theatre in the 1980s, they mean there was very little male theatre. In fact the 1980s saw an explosion of writing from women.'[63]

Contrastingly, new writing in the 1990s, particularly at the Royal Court, was 'dominated by a very defined male presence'.[64] Wertenbaker describes an influx of 'male violence [and] homoerotica', which made the decade 'not the most welcoming moment for women'.[65] Drama with openly gay themes had been growing in visibility since the formation of Gay Sweatshop in 1975, gaining higher profile with their 1979 production of *Bent*, starring Ian McKellen. The 1990s saw a noticeable increase in such work, including Kevin Elyot's *My Night with Reg* (1994), Jonathon Harvey's *Beautiful Thing* (1994) and Mark Ravenhill's *Shopping and Fucking* (1996). That Milton Shulman could respond to this trend with an article in the *Evening Standard* entitled 'Stop the plague of pink plays'[66] shows how necessary this work was, something of which Wertenbaker, who invested five hundred pounds in *My Night with Reg*, was surely aware. However, as her comments suggest, these plays focused predominately on the male experience of homosexuality.

Politically, the 1990s were an uncertain time. The anger of the poll tax riots turned into elation at Thatcher's resignation (1990), soon tempered by continuing recession, the first Gulf War (1990 to 1991) and the unexpected re-election of another term of Conservative government (1992). Meanwhile, the collapse of Eastern European communism exacerbated the sense of doubt among British socialists and war ravaged former Yugoslavia. According to director James Macdonald, this last issue 'was a subject no British writer was tackling' until Sarah Kane's now legendary *Blasted* hit the Royal Court stage in 1995. Subsequently labelled 'in-yer-face' theatre, the play, which explores shocking and sexually violent themes and images, caused a storm of (largely negative) publicity but has since been recognised as a seminal work. Macdonald, who directed the play, claims it changed the rules of theatre, allowing writers to access 'the political entirely through the personal'.[67] While this may sound similar to the 'personal is political' mantra developed by feminist movements in the 1960s and 1970s, what Macdonald cites seems more akin to the individualisation and social fragmentation of Thatcher's 1980s. Stephen Daldry, the Court's artistic director during this period, saw the development as evidence of a more pluralist theatre in which '[o]pposition was going to come from a variety of different voices that might not be coherent'.[68] However, Graham Whybrow's description of '"gesture" plays, not "argument" plays', and their 'sceptical, angry, frustrated, disempowered' writers, reveals the impotence of such postmodern angst.[69] Billington summarises the mood of this generation of playwrights, for whom 'there were no ready-made Utopias and no grand narrative schemes. The best that we could hope to do was construct our own private dreams and tell each other stories.'[70] Wertenbaker was not immune to this atmosphere, commenting in 1991 that there was 'something intellectually despairing in the world, as if solutions no longer exist. [...] [H]ow easy it is to block threat or compassion by increased cocooning of the senses and the mind'.[71] However, Wertenbaker's plays repeatedly sought to resist these trends, presenting art's ability 'to show, in detail, a few people with their aspirations and their frailties' as a vital antidote to such cocooning.[72]

If, by the 1990s, the left were struggling to envisage a better future, the right were more backward-looking than ever, viewing 'the arts' through the distancing frame of the newly created Department of National Heritage.[73] Although the introduction of National Lottery grants in the mid 1990s proved useful to theatres long overdue a renovation, these funds were restricted to capital projects and did not benefit production work. This exemplifies the phenomenon, identified by Shellard, whereby 'the British nation prefers to invest in buildings rather than people'.[74] Wertenbaker recognised these ironies when she wrote to the Arts Council, asking them to consider a similar investment in playwrights:

> When, however, theatres are hoping – as they all are and the money is there – to get £2 million or more for new or refurbished buildings, the playwright becomes puzzled. It is like being given the money to buy silverware, with no money to spend on food. I understand the need to separate subsidy from lottery, but the playwright, who is neither a producing venue nor bricks and mortar, is rather forgotten in all this. Every year, fewer playwrights manage to survive on writing plays alone. [...] I feel that if the Arts Council does not do something imaginative soon, in ten years [...] you may have to call on lottery funds to instigate a search for the last surviving member of that rare species, the living playwright.[75]

After the initial euphoria of Labour's 1997 election victory, the theatre community was disappointed by no immediate increase in subsidy. It was not until the 2000 Boyden Report's revelation of the dire condition of the industry that things began to improve, particularly in the much beleaguered regions. Some institutions saw funding doubled, trebled or even quadrupled during the first five years of the twenty-first century. A greater emphasis was placed on inclusion, from increased funding for community arts, to the introduction of cheaper tickets at the National Theatre through the Travelex sponsored scheme. Theatre created by and for the United Kingdom's increasingly diverse communities also rose dramatically, with plays by Kwame Kwei-Armah, Debbie Tucker Green, Gurpreet Kaur Bhatti, Tanika Gupta and many more gaining public recognition.

The decade saw a resurgence of explicitly political theatre, partially in response to the so-called 'War on Terror'. Verbatim theatre became an increasingly popular medium, perhaps suggesting the desire to capture the 'truth' behind events many felt the government and media attempted to disguise. While this could be seen to challenge the authority of the individual playwright more significantly than the collective script development of the 'Joint Stock method', some major playwrights adapted the trend, combining recorded speech with their own imaginings. Sometimes labelled 'docudramas', notable examples include David Hare's *The Permanent Way* (2003), *Stuff Happens* (2004) and *The Power of Yes* (2009), and Lucy Prebble's *ENRON* (2009).

Another dominant trend in post-millennial theatre has been towards immersive and site-specific theatre by companies such as Punchdrunk, Grid Iron and Zecora Ura/Para Active. Often heavily reliant on visual imagery and multi-media and frequently devised by an ensemble, rather than a single playwright, these practices have enchanted some critics and left others uneasy. Billington is among the sceptical. Having built his career around the 'belief that the health of the British theatre over the past sixty years has depended heavily on its dramatists and their ability to reflect the state of the nation', his concern is for the future of the straight play in a culture increasingly saturated by multiple media, many of which offer extremes of experience and/or participatory elements.[76] In an ideal world, the contemporary theatre could welcome all such projects, but with the current financial and political climate threatening a return to the conditions of the 1980s, the fear that site-specific or immersive spectacles will divert attention and funding from the less overtly dazzling craft of playwriting is understandable. In the Arts Council's 2011 funding review, Punchdrunk were one of the few organisations to receive a dramatic increase in funding.

Throughout the last four decades, Wertenbaker has remained committed to the 'straight' play, the theatrical medium and, specifically, to British theatre. After leaving Spetse, all her original stage plays premiered in the United Kingdom, the majority starting life in London and others first appearing in Brighton, Edinburgh,

Stratford, Birmingham, Leicester, Ipswich and Bath. Having fought her way into the male-dominated theatre scene of the 1970s, she came into her own during the beleaguered 1980s – producing, in 1988's *Our Country's Good*, a play which seemed to speak on behalf of the battle-weary theatrical community – only to fall out of fashion during the angry 1990s. The impression this somewhat simplified narrative creates is that, while Wertenbaker has embraced the concept of a 'floating identity' in both her work and her public profile, her dominant ideological concerns have fluctuated less obviously than the prevailing trends of the periods she has lived through.

CHAPTER 1
'GOOD ENOUGH TO GO ON': THE BEGINNINGS OF A PLAYWRIGHT

I have had many ambitions as a writer, but only two have been all consuming. The first, at the beginning, was to write a play I felt was good enough to go on [...][1]

Of the plays Wertenbaker drafted between 1976 and 1980, all are unpublished and the majority remain unperformed. Some are no more than a few loose scenes or a synopsis that was never developed. Wertenbaker claims to have been happy to 'forget about' these works, asserting that 'they didn't really matter'.[2] But, although these early plays may seem unimportant more than thirty years later, and following the success of many later works, they are of great significance to the study of the development of the writer and the interplay of themes and concerns throughout her career. Crucially, these formative works reveal the first things that Wertenbaker felt compelled to write about. While it is possible to view some of these concerns, or the treatment of them, as immature or of their time, other scripts and fragments of text reveal the genesis of ideas that resurface throughout her later writing. Furthermore, a number of these plays contain rich and engaging characters, devices and narrative elements, and some are so well developed as to present a real opportunity for future staging.

Wertenbaker did not receive her first commission until 1980. Although writing for commission offers more financial security than writing 'on spec', Wertenbaker has complained about having to write 'things for other people', because 'it's not exactly what you want to do'.[3] In contrast, her earliest pieces allowed her more freedom: the opportunity to be as didactic or as obscure, as experimental or as traditional, as she wished. In this light, her early plays gain increased significance. For the purposes of my analysis, I divide these plays into three categories. The earliest ('The Third' and 'The Vigil', 1977) were written while Wertenbaker was still living on the Greek island of Spetse. It appears that Wertenbaker had been attracted to this island at least partially because of its connections to John Fowles's novel *The Magus* (1966).[4] Letters from this period reveal that Wertenbaker shared Fowles's interest in mysticism and the psychoanalytic practices of Carl Jung, and these influences are evident in her own writing. The plays Wertenbaker wrote on Spetse are chiefly concerned with personal and romantic relationships and contain limited social or political discussion. They are not naturalistic, follow non-linear narratives and, despite modern references, seem to exist in an uncertain temporal dimension.

A slightly later group of plays ('This is No Place for Tallulah Bankhead', 1978; 'Act for Our Times', c.1978; 'Near Miss', c.1979; 'Breaking Through', 1980 and 'Second Sentence', 1980), written after Wertenbaker left Greece, are situated more firmly in the modern West. They are, in some respects, the reverse of the Spetse pieces, being the most didactically political of Wertenbaker's career. They deal directly with topical concerns such as the threat from nuclear power and the excesses of Western capitalism. With the exception of 'Breaking Through', the pieces operate within real-time, one-location conventions and suggest a naturalistic performance style.

Outside these groupings are three unfinished plays ('Agamemnon's Daughter', c.1978; 'Don Juan's Women', c.1979 and 'Monads', c.1979) that set a precedent for Wertenbaker's later, more sophisticated works. These plays begin to show the successful combination of the personal and the political that define Wertenbaker's greatest plays, as well as demonstrating, as their titles suggest, the beginnings of her long-standing preoccupations with canonicity. It is not possible to locate all these works precisely as many drafts are undated, and it is sometimes difficult to tell if they have been developed over weeks, months, or even years. There is no record as to whether these texts began life on Spetse, but in the case of 'Monads', which is set on the island, the continued influence of this place and culture on Wertenbaker is clear.

Wertenbaker remembers her first experience of playwriting as an almost accidental step, which quickly had a huge impact:

> I was in Greece, and I was with some people in the theatre. [...] [W]e were just sitting around actually, and just sort of decided to write this little play together, just for fun. I mean, it was just one of those afternoons. And I did then go home and [...] sort of write this kind of monologue, and it just felt [...] right, you know, it really did. And I've used that image before – I don't know if I've ever told anyone, but just like putting a hand in a glove. I mean, I just liked it.[5]

On Spetse, Wertenbaker's playwriting took two distinct strands. One she described as 'children's plays for the Greek kids: political: there's no water on the island because the tourists drink it all type of thing'.[6] There is little evidence of these plays in the archive. For adults, she wrote two one act plays, 'The Third' and 'The Vigil', which both premiered on Spetse in 1977:[7]

> There were some actors, [...] I mean it was semi-amateur... and we put on the plays and there was a little audience – in English – there was a kind of ex-pat community there and that was great. And on the basis of these two short plays I sort of thought I was a playwright, you know, came to London waving my plays around, and that was it really.[8]

After leaving Spetse, Wertenbaker spent time in New York and the United Kingdom, before making a more permanent move to London in 1979. Correspondence between Wertenbaker and her first agents (the London -based Anthony Sheil Associates Ltd) shows that this move coincided almost exactly with her resolve to become a professional playwright.

In May 1978, Wertenbaker received her first staging outside Greece, when the King's Head Theatre Club produced 'This is No Place for Tallulah Bankhead' as a lunchtime production. This was not a huge break for Wertenbaker and attracted little attention in the press. *The Stage*, although not overtly negative, thought the play 'would probably appear a more bitter indictment of a society which has produced both the CIA and napalm in the country of the author's origin'.[9] This comment highlights the play's status as the first work of an unknown playwright, still situated as an outsider to British theatre: someone yet to prove herself or be 'accepted'. The play does give away Wertenbaker's American background, with references to walking on Fifth Avenue and going for a milkshake.

Like many young artists, Wertenbaker was unable to earn a living from writing alone and had to support herself with a job at the Camden Plaza cinema. She writes that she was 'undergoing the most severe crisis of confidence I've had yet in my work. Very severe, rather cracking me, I feel very fragile, shattered, but – one goes on.'[10] Fortunately, she gained support from Verity Bargate, then director of the Soho Poly. Wertenbaker looked up to Bargate and valued her opinion, writing, 'how happy and excited I felt after seeing you and how grateful I am for your encouragement'.[11] Bargate found Wertenbaker valuable collaborators, such as Liane Aukin, who helped her develop 'Happy Ending' (later 'Case to Answer') and directed a rehearsed reading of it with the Half Moon Theatre Workshop. 'It went incredibly well', Wertenbaker reported to Bargate, 'It was extraordinary intuition on your part to have put me in touch with Liane – I like her very much and she was so helpful.' However, it was Bargate's help that Wertenbaker really needed, and the possibility of a production at the Soho Poly. '[O]bviously I keep hoping it will finally be done', she wrote, 'we had such a good time with the reading – but that play was written so much with your help and refusal to accept the early sloppiness that I feel it "belongs" to the Soho Poly. It's not just that of course, it's also the best theatre.'[12] Bargate's declining health was a temporary stumbling block for Wertenbaker's ambition. In March 1979, Wertenbaker's agent advised her to send the play elsewhere as the Soho Poly was 'in chaos' due to Bargate's absence. 'I know this is awfully unfair to you after waiting so long', she added.[13] However, a year later, the Soho Poly did produce the play (directed by Aukin) and Wertenbaker is adamant about the importance of Bargate's role in her career: 'I didn't have any belief, and to have Verity Bargate suddenly [...] say, "I'm interested in this and I'm discovering you". I mean, she was wonderful. She had that kind of enthusiasm.'[14]

Alongside Bargate's interest in 'Case to Answer', other small encouragements allowed Wertenbaker to keep faith in the fact 'that I'd sort of found something, not that I could do, but might lead... I don't know – I gave it a year.' This has become a recurrent practice for Wertenbaker:

[E]very year I thought about giving it up. I mean, every year I've continued to think of giving it up. So it's not an easy life being a playwright. I mean, maybe it is for some playwrights, but it hasn't been for me particularly. [...] I thought I'll give it a year, and then I thought I'll give it another year, and something happened, and then [...] there was always just enough to keep going, just enough.[15]

The Half Moon reading of 'Happy Ending'/'Case to Answer' had been attended by members of the Brighton Actors' Workshop, who subsequently decided to produce 'Second Sentence'. Billed as Wertenbaker's first fully professional production, the play premiered in March 1980, directed by Faynia Williams. Wertenbaker recorded that the play sometimes brought in 'sixty people in a theatre that seats thirty five and usually attracts eight. Some people went back to see it twice'.[16] *The Stage* was impressed, praising Wertenbaker's 'ability to grasp the attention of an audience so quickly and maintain it so confidently'. 'The strength of the play lies in the rounded reality of the characters and the living quality of their dialogue', concluded their reviewer.[17]

Within months, Wertenbaker received the long-awaited Soho Poly 'Case to Answer' (May 1980), an American production of the same play (June 1980), and the British premiere of 'The Third' at the King's Head (July 1980). Until this point in her career, Wertenbaker had combined journalism and playwriting. Now her agent recommended that, as she was 'having more and more success with [her] plays', but was 'finding it increasingly difficult to sell [her] articles', she 'should bow out' of the latter.[18] Wertenbaker agreed that 'journalism, as with everything else, requires much more effort than I am willing to give it at the moment: it doesn't seem to be any longer something one can do part time'.[19] It is therefore possible to consider 1980 as the year in which Wertenbaker embraced playwriting as a full-time professional career.[20]

Personal Politics

'The Third' is the earliest dated stage play in Wertenbaker's archive.[21] It charts a romantic relationship from desire-fuelled, heady beginnings, through arguments and resolutions, to an almost happy settlement. The piece explores the complexity of negotiating another human being, showing how its characters 'groped for one another, each trying to sort out what the other was. And were baffled.'[22] Innovatively, Wertenbaker presents this process from the perspective of the slightly manipulative, mischievous and self-indulgent relationship itself. The play's first draft is a short monologue for the androgynous character of 'the relationship', but later drafts define this presence as male (albeit ambiguously so) and give him a name: '*The role of the third, call him* **Dominic** *for convenience, must be played by a youthful man with soft movements and a melodious voice. He conveys airiness, agility, and something not quite human.*'[23] As the drafts progress, Wertenbaker adds the roles of the couple, Simon and Helen, first as a silent presence, then with speech of their own. They are not presented in a naturalistic manner and never converse with one another. They appear as if controlled by Dominic, having '*at the beginning of the play movements that suggest a slight trance*', which '*gradually disappears by the end*'. '*[W]hen they speak, it is as if at* **Dominic**'s *bidding*'.[24]

Of the two human characters, Wertenbaker paints a more vivid picture of Helen:

> She [...] was what the moderns label a feminist and mistakenly think the ancient Greeks called an Amazon.

Actually, the Greeks would have dubbed her an Antigone. A sociologist – and you know that can mean anything – she was an independent, individualistic girl, forging her way in the world with definite ideas, some ideals, and a will to trample anything in her way. Literate, rebellious, a so-called free spirit. Now, my experience has shown me that these [...] independent women are the most fragile. But they are also resilient. Whatever breaks in their emotions, they mend with their intellect, so that however many times they capitulate, they challenge again.[25]

She was advised that Helen's character was 'much better developed than the man', and it was suggested that she look at literary precedents, such as Chekhov's male characters or Stanley in *A Streetcar Named Desire*, to capture some of the insecurity and helplessness missing from the part of Simon.[26] *The Stage* felt similarly that, while 'Helen [...] is given dialogue which rings very true, [the writing] does not really add a full dimension to the photographer Simon'.[27] Much later in her career, Wertenbaker declared it 'easier for me to write a male character, because I have an infinite number of models, than possibly it is for some [male] playwrights to write female characters, because they don't have them down the line of history'.[28] This assertion seems to echo Hélène Cixous's claim that 'today writing is woman's' because 'woman admits there is other. [...] It is much harder for man to let the other come through him'.[29] However, it seems that at the start of Wertenbaker's career, before she had studied the 'infinite number of models' available to her, she too found it easier to create convincing characters that shared her gender identification.

Perhaps because of the vitality of Helen's role, reviewers identified a feminist influence within 'The Third'. *Spare Rib* concluded favourably that Wertenbaker 'writes about women, relationships and what she calls "personal politics". Her work is sensitive and feminist without strident, soapbox tones'.[30] 'The Third' certainly alludes to the compromises women can feel compelled to make in romantic relationships:

Helen [A]s usual, I held back the many books read, the degree in sociology, the odd thoughts, and presented him with the dull, bland front I hang around myself like an ill-fitting costume. He probably didn't notice I wasn't stupid, or didn't care, and despised me for being so easy.[31]

The term 'personal politics' is, however, apt, as the play does not move its examination of Helen's subjective female experience into broader social or political arenas. Slightly more far-reaching, but still focused on personal relationships, is Wertenbaker's next play, 'The Vigil', which examines a man's desire to become a monk, and the distress this causes his loving wife.[32] Its setting is described as '*Now. Late at night*' and a note specifies that the stage is '*bare but has a religious tone: an icon on a wall, a tall candlestick*'. The atmosphere of religiosity is crucial. An earlier draft calls for the '*music of a Russian Orthodox evening service*' and the to-ing and fro-ing of monks and priests to accompany the action. By the final draft, these elements are gone, but Christian theology has a strong presence in the text. The man, Alexis, speaks largely in lines '*taken from the Psalms*', which '*must be said with a slight suggestion of recitation*'.[33]

'The Vigil' is subtitled 'a play in four moments' and its four short scenes have the quality of the separate movements in a piece of music. They do not follow naturalistic conventions or a linear narrative. In the first, the female character, Martha, speaks about her relationship with Alexis, revealing that he saved her from the sadness of a previous, damaging relationship, which she describes in some detail. Although Martha seems to be speaking to Alexis (she refers to him as 'you', not 'he'), Alexis does not acknowledge her, speaking only in psalms. This creates the impression that Martha is speaking to the audience in a confessional manner. In the second scene, Martha tells the audience about Alexis's religious conversion (now speaking of him in the third person) and her failure to share it:

[H]e began to believe. Grace. Faith soothed the rattling of his mind. Not so, mine. [...] These priests, who move with such grace, have awkward minds. Call women unclean, fear contamination. [...] However could I confess my young girl's lust to a virginal old man? […] The truth is, I do not want to love God. I love a man, my husband. I thought our marriage was blessed.[34]

The third 'moment' reveals Alexis's back story. He also invokes the damage caused by a previous relationship, in which he impregnated a very young girl (Felicity) and convinced her to have an abortion. The details of this account echo a draft novel found in the prose section of Wertenbaker's archive. Entitled 'Rites of Entry', this novel details the struggles of its teenage characters to navigate this complicated transition in their lives. The 'rites' referred to in the title are those the teenagers 'have devised for themselves, madness and sexual *laisser aller*'. In a synopsis, Wertenbaker writes:

> I would like to pick up the theme of the 'rites', and make a slight allusion to more primitive societies where these rites are organised: the walkabouts of the Australian aborigines, the temple prostitutes, the divine madness, all the rites designed to mark the passage from childhood into adolescence. The need for these has remained and adolescence now finds its own rites to mark this passage.[35]

The novel's fourteen-year-old narrator Tess embarks on a relationship with an older boy (Percy), very similar to that described by Alexis. Both texts feature an incident in which the girl becomes jealous while her boyfriend is talking with his friends in an intellectual manner from which she feels excluded. Both couples resolve this altercation by consummating their relationships and, in both cases, pregnancy, abortion and trauma follow. In 'Rites of Entry', Tess goes through many further losses of childhood/innocence, including prostitution and drug abuse, before eventually reclaiming her life at college. 'The Vigil' borrows elements from the first half of Tess's story to create Felicity (the girl Alexis impregnated as a teenager, but who does not appear as an onstage character) and draws on its second half to provide a back-story for Martha.

In 'Rites of Entry', Percy eventually succumbs to a self-induced madness. This is one of the 'rites' Wertenbaker alludes to, aligning it with systems of primitive spirituality and shamanism: 'Madness, according to Percy, went further than death. It was going beyond life, what was considered life at least, and yet remaining alive to see the results. It meant going into another world while keeping one's body in this one.'[36] Percy is institutionalised by his family but escapes and is found dead in a remote cave. This is echoed in an earlier draft of 'The Vigil', in which Alexis explains, 'I took on my own expiation. I left for a year, went to a cave of Lower California, and went through hunger, fear, thirst, filth. I took drugs, I tried to go mad but I have too clean a grip on the world.'[37] In the final draft of 'The Vigil', the psychological trials Alexis recalls are reduced to a 'little psychoanalysis to warn against excessive guilt and concentrate rather on my parents' damages'.[38] However, this is positioned as an inadequate way of dealing with trauma, which, the play suggests, has almost certainly contributed to his new-found religious fervour. 'The Vigil' blurs the boundaries between religion and insanity, and this intersection is even more apparent in Percy's madness:

When it was dark, around eight in the evening, we began the vigil. Percy called it the vigil. It was not always the same, but it did always have the feel of a vigil, the waiting for something, watching the night go by, preparing for a day that never seemed to come.[39]

Alexis's desire to take orders evokes the idea that human beings (particularly adolescents) need some sort of meaningful spirituality that is often missing from contemporary society. This concept is also present in a synopsis Wertenbaker wrote for a play that would be titled 'The Upper World' (based on 'Orpheus and Euridice in reverse'). It describes a young woman's attempts to extricate her lover from a psychiatric hospital. He agrees to go with her

if she will first follow him into his 'hell', if he can reconstruct with her the journey to his 'madness' [...], a series of rites he devised in his late adolescence (17) with which to go from the world of childhood into that of adulthood, the kind of rites common in primitive societies.[40]

Wertenbaker wrote:

> I don't want to get into a lot of psychiatry, although I'll use a bit of Jung and the archetypes. The rites are the boy's own, a meeting with his own ghosts for his passage into the normal adult world. But given lack of guidance and the instability of that adult world, he has become stuck in the rites themselves, the underworld. And perhaps in the end, he's better there, although I don't want to raise those questions, just present the opposition of two worlds. By the way, I haven't seen Equus,[41] but I don't think this repeats, at least I hope not. What interests me about this play is the [...] very poetical mythology that lies just beneath ordinary life and an ordinary relationship, the poetry primitive rites recapture and sometimes the East.[42]

Tess also describes her relationship with Percy as 'a night in the underworld, the confrontation with the spirits of Hades. But this time it was Orpheus who was imprisoned down there and Euridice who sought him. We tried to get out.'[43] The many similarities between the short play 'The Vigil', the draft novel 'Rites of Entry' and the synopsis for 'The Upper World', show how much the theme of missing outlets for human spirituality occupied Wertenbaker at this stage in her career. This theme expands the scope of these texts beyond their surface preoccupation with personal and romantic relationships; perhaps we might even read it as the earliest articulation of the need to find new or alternative 'languages' that offer an escape from dominant and repressive structures and ideologies, an idea which resurfaces frequently in Wertenbaker's work and is discussed throughout this book.

Some of the similarities between Tess's and Felicity's stories, particularly the theme of premature sexual experiences and the physical and emotional fall-out from them, are repeated in other fragments of Wertenbaker's early writing. Other recurrent themes include infidelity and motherhood. These concerns align the texts discussed in this section with the 'personal is political' mantra

33

embraced by many feminists of this period.[44] At a later stage in her career, Wertenbaker would resist such categorisation and champion the need for women to write more ambitiously about subjects often deemed 'outside' female experience. Yet even at this early stage, alongside these plays of personal politics, Wertenbaker was developing another strand of writing, more strident in its political tone.

The New Marxist Timberlake?

Wertenbaker's youth seems to have been somewhat politically ambivalent. In 'A Year on Exmoor', she comments that among her friends she is 'considered extremely conservative'[45] and in 'Learning to live with the English', she claims to identify as 'Feminist, yes, but left wing in a country which quickly eradicates the vague and trendy left means a card carrying communist. On the other hand, I didn't think of myself as right wing.'[46] However, in the late 1970s, her political consciousness increased notably, as is evident from the sceptical tone of this letter from a friend:

> I'd be very interested to see the new Marxist Timberlake – Are you really converted? Or is it a possible whim? Don't get upset my love I'm only joking. I do know what a serious person you are as well as I know how impossibly reactionary you can be just for the fun of it.[47]

Wertenbaker's response shows a thoughtful and questioning attitude to her changing ideas, which foreshadows the subtlety of her later plays:

> As for the politics, it is serious, although I don't know what they are. I mean I am not a Marxist because I haven't read enough Marx and there are some things I disagree with anyway. I am very wary of a fast emotional conversion. All I am doing is reading when I can and talking with this Marxist theatre group I've joined. I don't particularly like the kind of

plays they do but I like our discussions. Dan and I also talk a lot, one source of argument as he is a real Marxist and would like me to agree and I won't. [...] [A]ll I know is that I see a lot I didn't see in Spetse and before and that I avoid more and more people of my so called class because I can no longer accept their assumptions. It's changed my writing, I think [...]. I wish I were clearer, that there was a line of action. It's not enough to be 'politicised' when you don't do anything with it and it's difficult to know exactly what to do. I suppose I can use the theatre and write more and more political plays, but then you have to deal with the limits of theatre, although that's a challenge in a way. Very muddled all this.[48]

This final comment provides the perfect summation of the complicated issues Wertenbaker was beginning to mull over. Her refusal to agree wholeheartedly, either with 'Dan' or with the assumptions of her 'so called class', is reminiscent of the well-considered scepticism with which she approaches multi-layered concerns in her work. This lack of certainty ensures Wertenbaker avoids fundamentalism and maintains a healthy level of self-interrogation.

'This is No Place for Tallulah Bankhead' (King's Head, 1978)[49]

This one-act play is the dramatisation of a séance: Judith has killed herself and her ex-husband (Michael), current lover (Jamie), and best friend (Janet) visit a medium to try and discover why. As the séance begins, the medium 'becomes' Judith; that is, she

changes her appearance and gestures: (She can take off a scarf from her head, shake out long hair, turn the scarf into a shawl. Or undo a few buttons from her blouse so that her movements are loose and seductive. There is something teasing in her voice and manner as she slides past the other three in her speeches.)[50]

This touch of metatheatricality is the only stylistic aspect of this play that takes it beyond realism. Prompted by questions, 'Judith' launches into a series of monologues that tell of harassment from starving women, burnt Vietnamese children and tortured South American exiles, all of whom pronounce her 'guilty' and drive her to her own (self)execution. Gradually, the idea emerges that, in a world of pressing political issues, there is no place for women like Judith (or Tallulah Bankhead):

> I am, I said, a woman, I am beautiful and witty. Such women have always existed. They were not wives, they were not politicians. They were simply beautiful and entertaining. They gave much pleasure and caused some pain. I enjoy being this. I am good at it. Why can't you let such as we be? The beautiful, the exotic, the luxurious women? [...] Hadn't I noticed, they asked, that these women [...] were already, as they had to be, superseded?[51]

Elements of Judith's life, particularly the 'inessential' nature of her career (a researcher for an encyclopaedia on food), resonate with Wertenbaker's pre-Exmoor existence. Janet had harangued Judith that 'with honours in philosophy', she 'could do better than research Tabasco sauce', but unlike Wertenbaker, Judith accepted mediocrity.[52] She dealt with the trauma of her visitations by having 'another good lunch, discussing the country's need for our encyclopaedias and wondering whether our readers would understand the word panache'.[53] This line reads like a joke at the expense of Wertenbaker's former employers at Time-Life or Dumbarton Oaks.

Most of Judith's 'executioners' are foreigners suffering from Western excess and disinterest: the victims of famine, torture and war. However, one stands apart from these: a Western girl of about thirteen, who Judith describes as smelling of 'milk and adolescence'. Her complaint is against Judith's failure to join the feminist cause:

> They've asked us to do an essay, she said, on our ambitions. I have so many. I want to be in politics. But before that I want to deepdive off Antarctica. I wouldn't mind working on a

space programme to learn about the universe. I am very good in maths and physics. And I would like to follow a Saharan salt caravan. But, she continued, as I wondered why I never had or never allowed myself such dreams, but I have no chance. No chance, she said, unless you help [...]. You're a woman [...]. I want to start with a chance already there. I don't want to use up my intelligence, my energies, my emotions just fighting. You must fight and create my chance.[54]

That Wertenbaker gives this figure an equal status to victims of famine and torture demonstrates the importance that she attached to the situation of Western women at this time.

'Act for Our Times' (c.1978)[55]

In this rather nihilistic piece, two women chase each other into an underground station, one (Nicole) having just burnt down her pursuer (Vicky)'s bookshop. When Nicole removes the hood that covers her face, the women realise they were once best friends. Now in their mid-fifties, they have not seen each other for fifteen years. Cultural references place these women in approximately the same generation as Wertenbaker, but because they are about twenty-five years older than she was when she wrote the play, its setting is futuristic. No specific date is given, but the women recall attending 'consciousness-raising' during the 1970s as something long past. Statements such as, 'I thought the 70s were an aberration, but the 80s proved it. The past twenty years have been static', place the play in, at least, the 1990s and possibly as post-millennial.[56] Some of Wertenbaker's setting appears rather naïve (the colonising of other planets is mentioned and stage directions refer to advertisements that '*show fashions of a later age with angular shapes, shiny materials, spaceship influence*'),[57] but other elements are prescient; the currency is Eurodollars, prices have rocketed, and the condemnation of the 1980s, quoted above, foreshadows many that were made in retrospect.

Like most of the plays discussed in this section, 'Act for Our Times' employs a realistic style, with a single locale and real-time progression of events. However, it contains elements that – like the medium's embodiment of Judith in 'This is No Place for Tallulah Bankhead' – show Wertenbaker experimenting with more overtly theatrical techniques. When the women first recognise each other, Vicky is reluctant to believe that Nicole is the friend she remembers. To convince Vicky of her authenticity, Nicole plays out the memory of their first encounter as a knowing, almost metatheatrical, role-play:

> **Nicole** *is agile and an excellent mimic. She strikes an adolescent pose, shoulders hunched: a girl smoking a cigarette [...]. The mimicry must be exaggerated, a mockery. [...]* **Nicole** *now changes into a shy, more innocent looking adolescent and with quick little steps edges up to* **Vicky**. *[...] She plays both roles, switching her voices and the poses.*[58]

After some encouragement, Vicky takes over her own role and together the women act out their adolescent selves, before sliding their reminiscences into the past tense. The theatricality of this episode bears some resemblance to the way Philomele uses theatre to reclaim her identity and tell her story in *The Love of the Nightingale*. In theatrical terms, it allows the play to slip into an expositional tone, while avoiding the heavy-handedness of flashback.

Eventually, the women turn from their shared past to the missing fifteen years. It transpires that Nicole burnt Vicky's bookshop as part of an organised movement for random destruction, which she joined after losing her daughter to leukaemia. Nicole describes the organisation as 'the most modern of movements. The most logical of this century. It adheres to senseless violence.'[59] At the heart of this play is a debate between the idea that there is so much horror, pain and violence in the world that we might as well give up and join in, and the idea that there is still hope to be found in friendship and the search for knowledge and understanding. Speaking from the former perspective, Nicole (who considered writing a book called 'History Abandons the World') thinks history, as a progressive force, ended in '1968, or before': 'I'm old, it sighs, I'm tired, I've had enough. And it turns its back on the whole mess and leaves.'[60] Vicky, who highlights recent progress made by women, maintains a more positive argument:

Vicky You forget women. […] We're changing things.
Nicole A few nerve twitches in the general paralysis.
Vicky No, Nicole. It's just done with less pomp and drama.
Nicole Tragedy is the only truth.
Vicky Changes here and there. Subtle.
Nicole Imperceptible.
Vicky Modest, but real.[61]

Where Wertenbaker's own perspective fits into this spectrum of debate is unclear from this play. Vicky's hopeful outlook has just enough strength to win over the world-weary Nicole, who agrees to spend some time recuperating with her. However, this potential endorsement of Vicky's optimism is challenged when, having swapped clothes with Nicole to allow her to escape the police, Vicky is shot dead in her place. One reader's report complained that this went 'against [the play's] more eloquent passages'[62] and, in a later draft for radio, Wertenbaker tempered this negativity by having Vicky wounded instead of killed, and allowing the two to escape together to an uncertain fate.

Wertenbaker made several attempts to get this play produced on stage or radio, but none proved successful. In 1980, both this play and 'Case to Answer' (then called 'Happy Ending') won a competition to be produced in the Central Casting Theatre's New Playwrights Festival in Ithaca, New York. Both plays went into rehearsal under the direction of Caissa Willmer, but 'Act for Our Times' was called off when one of its actresses broke her contract to take a role elsewhere. Later, Willmer wrote to Wertenbaker with several criticisms of her writing, including that the play 'strains credulity', is 'a lengthy debate, not an interplay of character and situation' and that she had been 'continuously assailed by a sense of lack of integration of elements and effects. I'm afraid that I am tempted to be bloody presumptuous and suggest that you study

Ibsen a bit more closely!!'[63] While this play is not as dramatically sophisticated as Wertenbaker's later works, Willmer's criticisms are unnecessarily harsh and somewhat misguided. Her complaint that the play 'could leave the audience with three totally different final perspectives' (which Willmer called 'a weak shrug' and a 'great shame') could be considered a positive attribute. In Willmer's view, the play presented 'an impasse that has shown no way to growth or development out of terrible dilemma. We are left with no conclusion, [which is needed] if the debate is to become a play.' However, looking at this absence of a neatly resolved conclusion with hindsight tells us that Wertenbaker was experimenting with what would become a trademark feature of her most successful plays. As Wertenbaker has commented, 'Stories don't end, you simply take them through different transformations. I like to leave people's lives open, characters' lives open'.[64] Wertenbaker is by no means the only exponent of such opinions and, by 1980, the open-ended drama was commonplace, making Willmer's comments appear rather old-fashioned.[65] One might even be presumptuous enough to suggest that *she* study a dramatist such as Beckett more closely.

'Near Miss' (c.1979)

Wertenbaker initially intended to turn her drafts of 'Near Miss' into a television play, but abandoned this project early in its development. [66] While she was visiting the USA in March 1979, there was an accident at a nuclear power facility in Harrisburg, Pennsylvania. 'All's well here except for that terrifying nuclear accident', she wrote, 'I don't know how much you've heard about it over there, but besides two days of radiation leaks, they didn't know until today whether the whole thing might not blow up. What a country!'[67] A couple of months later, she decided to base a play on 'an incident similar to Harrisburg',[68] transposing these events to rural Somerset.

The play depicts a couple (Robert and Marina) who have escaped to the countryside after becoming disillusioned with political activism, but are forced to rethink their attitude when visited by an old acquaintance (Nigel) with frightening information about leakage from a nearby nuclear power station. As the play continues, the situation worsens and the plant threatens meltdown. A synopsis states that the play ends with a 'substantial but not catastrophic release of radiation',[69] but a full draft ends inconclusively with the characters expecting to die as the meltdown begins. Wertenbaker describes her interest in this subject as lying largely with 'the unbelievable contradiction of a world progressing and at the same time toying with suicide (this is hard to express, but I don't want to write a let's all go back to the land play, all technology is bad, etc, I think it's much more delicate)'.[70] Essentially, the play is about whether or not to take action, for what cause and in what form, asking whether violence is ever justifiable. Nigel defines his cause as a 'war' in which casualties are expected, but Robert, who was once involved in an incident that killed a guard and his young daughter, finds such categorisation problematic. 'Yes. That was our language', he remembers, 'But the guard and his daughter didn't know it was a war.'[71]

In the pasts they are trying to forget, Robert and Marina were involved in a range of political causes, but as the play progresses, it is concern for the environment that emerges as paramount. As Nigel argues, 'it is the primary issue. If we're not careful we won't even have an earth on which to worry about other problems.'[72] The impact of this argument is increased by the play's deceptively idyllic rural opening. In a passage that echoes some of Wertenbaker's accounts of riding on Exmoor, Marina extols

[t]he moors, the grey day, the slight rain. I couldn't see the channel, but I could smell some of the salt. There is so much beauty around, don't you agree? (*Pause*) You find it in your work, I know, but the earth. The earth has such beauty. I wanted to embrace it all, the moment, the rain, the heather on the moors.[73]

Environmental concerns are not always so explicit in Wertenbaker's plays, but they remain an underlying presence in many (as discussed in Chapter Six). 'Near Miss' links the appreciation of the natural world with motherhood. Before Nigel arrives, Marina asks Robert, 'Would you mind if we had a child? Today I feel like passing on the beauty of the world. To the next generation: I offer you the earth.'[74] This connection between hopefulness and the desire to procreate is a recurrent trope in Wertenbaker's work.[75] The theme is expanded when Nigel arrives with his cousin Cathy, who is pregnant, young and idealistic. Cathy's pregnancy has changed her outlook. 'I feel an urge, no a passion, a madness to live, to have my child live', she explains, 'It's strange. Before [I was pregnant], I probably wouldn't have cared that much.' At times, Cathy's ideals ('I want my child to have friends, to be kind. It's all so simple') sound naïve, but she argues with clarity and humility against Nigel and Robert's aggressive political surety:

> **Robert** You have to look beyond your small desires.
> **Cathy** Why? If everybody had kept to their small desires, we wouldn't be where we are. Oh, things wouldn't be as efficient, but destruction wouldn't be as efficient.
> **Nigel** You want to go backwards, that's sentimental and impossible.
> **Cathy** Don't you have a simple minded notion of what it means to go forward? [...]
> **Nigel** We can't go back. It's just a matter of controlling the greed and carelessness of certain people.
> **Cathy** I wish you wouldn't always call it going back. To ask for a little less, to use less, to be less demanding of life, or of comfort, that is not going back. To live in villages rather than hideous cities, to ride rather than drive cars.[76]

Cathy blames men for the world's problems, feeling that '[w]omen would have done better'.[77] Wertenbaker would explore this idea more rigorously in her next tranche of plays, most notably *The Grace of Mary Traverse* (1985). The concept receives less interrogation in 'Near Miss', but is endorsed somewhat towards the end of the play. Marina (who is revealed to be infertile) and Cathy bond over the suggestion that Marina could help Cathy when she becomes a single parent. This palpable sense of shared future and companionship creates, albeit briefly, the most positive atmosphere of the play. This is broken by the return of the men, who have been listening to the car radio, with news of the imminent meltdown. Although the men are not personally responsible for this terrible occurrence, there is symbolism in the image of female solidarity destroyed by a male intrusion that signals destruction.

'Second Sentence' (Brighton Actors' Workshop, 1980)

'Second Sentence' examines the relationships between three women in an Italian-English family, after the elder sister (Giulietta) returns home from prison.[78] Her mother (Maria) wants to 'decide those three years didn't happen' and curtails any conversation about them. When an ex-cellmate telephones to wish Giulietta well, Maria insists she 'shouldn't be friends with women who've been to – who've been in There'. This attitude troubles Giulietta, who recognises that 'those three years…they've made me what I am'.[79] Her teenage sister (Luisa) is moderately pleased to see her, but more interested in boys and make-up, and Giulietta is dismayed by her apparent lack of ambition or sense of social responsibility. The drama comes to a head when Luisa's boyfriend cancels a date because he has found out about Giulietta's past. Luisa is devastated and verbally attacks Giulietta, calling her a criminal and chastising her for all the family suffered after her sentencing became public. As Luisa shouts and Maria weeps into her ruined dinner, Giulietta slips quietly away from the family she no longer belongs to, having accepted 'that's what I am and that's what I'll always be, isn't it? A woman who's been to prison'.[80]

Giulietta's 'crime' was her involvement with a group of political activists who stole documents from a company they wanted to expose as corrupt. This moral basis for her actions challenges preconceptions about criminality. Giulietta speaks with conviction about the unjust nature of sentencing and the degrading treatment of prisoners. Many of her opinions are reminiscent of arguments that Wertenbaker would develop in *Our Country's Good*:

I just assumed people who went to prison were born that way, that it was some sort of genetic deformity. Most people think that. And then, once you're in there, you realise it's not like that at all. It's almost always such a little thing. But it's too late to tell those out there that. You're silenced, forgotten. [...] And there are other women like me still in there, women you call monsters, but they've done, believe me, such little things.[81]

Giulietta accuses the penal system of trying to convince inmates they are 'bad' by placing a negative interpretation on everything they do or want. 'If you asked to go to the church it was because you wanted to steal out of the collection box', she explains.[82] Several of these arguments echo an article Wertenbaker wrote after interviewing women from Clean Break Theatre Company: 'Women ex-prisoners: out of the closet and on to the stage', which discusses prejudice towards (ex)prisoners and the frequent embarrassment of their families. Despite gaining many negative experiences of the penal system, company-founder Jenny Hicks claims to have 'nothing but praise for the education system, particularly Holloway. If anything rehabilitated me into society, it was that.' There is a clear link between these ideas and those expressed in *Our Country's Good*, and it is interesting to note that Wertenbaker was thinking about these things in 1979/80. While it may be tempting to think of *Our Country's Good* simply as an adaptation of Thomas Keneally's *The Playmaker*, these sources reveal that Wertenbaker held similar concerns almost a decade before the novel's publication.

'Breaking Through' (Women's Theatre Group, 1980)

Wertenbaker's first commission from the Women's Theatre Group (WTG) was the youth show 'Breaking Through'.[83] Because of the WTG's ideological background and the fact that the project was Theatre in Education for a teenage audience, this is one of Wertenbaker's most didactic plays. Its central message is a protest against the nuclear power industry (a concern Wertenbaker held prior to this project), dealt with from a feminist perspective.

In the play's opening scene, we meet Si and Phy, two beings from an alternative, but recognisable, universe called Allo. Research materials contained in the archive show that Wertenbaker had been exploring the concept of utopia, and Allo was her attempt to create one. In Allo, people value access to green space, continually explore how to make life better, and minimise sexual difference. While Si has spent a long time studying Earth, Phy knows little about it: a conceit that allows Si to explain things in a way that makes the familiar appear strange. For example, Phy's confusion at the earth dwellers' clothes prompts the following lesson:

They seem to think that little difference of the sexes is terribly important. They turn it into a kind of mystery. On earth, the organs are always emphasised, remember that when we meet humans. I'll walk around like this – (She struts, sticking out her breasts.) And you must walk like this. (Walks, caressing an imaginary cock.) [...] One sex has all the power and the other, the female sex, has to emphasise its submission. As you see, I can hardly walk.[84]

Si and Phy travel to Earth to warn its inhabitants about the danger of the nuclear industry. They befriend Julie, a disaffected school-leaver, and Angelina, a Portuguese immigrant who has developed cancer from cleaning rail tracks after a spillage of radioactive waste from Windscale (now Sellafield). The first difficulty is one of communication, as speaking directly to the girls causes them to assume Si and Phy are insane. To get around this they play music, which subliminally reveals the necessary information to the girls, as if they were recalling the plot of a half-forgotten film. The use of music (or other forms of artistic expression) to communicate when words fail is a trope Wertenbaker returns to in later plays, such as *The Love of the Nightingale* (1988) and *Credible Witness* (2001). Convincing the girls that they can and should act proves equally challenging. Julie (who we first meet on the way to an exam she is already convinced she has failed) has no confidence in her ability. When Si and Phy suggest that she asks her class to join their cause, she protests, 'I'm one of the stupidest in the class. And a girl, I can't speak to them'.[85] By showing Julie make the journey from disenfranchised apathy to engaged action, the piece argues that the girls in its target audience could do the same.

Once Julie has been convinced to act, her path is blocked at every turn by a succession of officials. Each encounter makes a feminist point: while a nuclear official patronises them ('women don't always understand how important it is to kill off enemies. [...] You remind me of my daughter'), a medical expert refuses to be a whistle blower: 'we must be scientific, we can't act like hysterical women, particularly those of us who are women. If I made an outcry they'd say I was proving that women were too emotional and couldn't hold this sort of job'.[86] Each figure defers responsibility, sending the girls onwards and upwards until they finally meet the 'multinational'. This 'character' does not appear, but is represented by a sinister, disembodied voice:

I am –
I am. I own.
I am hungry.
I am – everywhere, in every county. I own, everything, everywhere. I own.[87]

Realising that no authority will help them, the girls plan their own resistance: a sit-in protest to block the tracks every time a train carrying nuclear waste passes through. The play ends with Angelina (already dying from cancer) throwing herself in front of a train that refuses to stop. Despite her death, an element of hope is created from the idea that small-scale, grass-roots protests can affect policy making. In earlier drafts, the play ended with a galvanising chorus of examples from around the world, and its final words emphasised the impact the play was intended to have on life outside the theatre: 'If you're a girl, if you're young, if you think you can't understand these things, or can't do anything about them you're wrong – You don't have to be violent – just determined.'[88] The final text left audiences with a didactic feminist statement, as Si and Phy discuss why the earth has developed so poorly in comparison to their own planet:

> **Si** It hurts me to see a Universe come to this – and humanoids. Waste everywhere, no hope, and the danger of a war that will destroy everything. I don't understand, how does it happen?
> **Phy** Remember that domination lesson? I wonder if it's not because one sex is so much more powerful than the other. There's no equation, it's all out of balance.[89]

Wertenbaker was aware that this play lacked subtlety and, although proud of the project, was keen not to be labelled a Theatre in Education writer:

> I'd like it to be at the bottom of the pile because it's a youth show, I mean it isn't exactly subtle, and although it's been incredibly rewarding to watch 80 15-year-olds, including the National Front contingent, get involved in it despite themselves, I don't want to write many more of them, at the moment.[90]

Dancing with Herstories

The final section of this chapter examines three unfinished plays that begin to combine the political consciousness of the plays discussed in the previous section, with the talent for storytelling and theatricality recognisable from Wertenbaker's later works. What sets these works aside from the rest of Wertenbaker's early writing is their employment of historicisation and/or mythical themes and narratives. In later years, Wertenbaker commented that all her work was 'a delving into the past in order to talk about the present'.[91] 'If you write things in the past you free them from people's prejudices', she explained, 'You can be more poetic. You tend to be less poetic when it is a contemporary play. You can be more imaginative in the past.'[92] Poeticism is certainly more visible in this final grouping of texts than in those discussed in the previous section. Of the three more fully developed pieces, two use historico-mythical settings: mythical Greece for 'Agamemnon's Daughter' and a fictionalised seventeenth-century Spain for 'Don Juan's Women'. The third, 'Monads', has a contemporary setting, but is enriched by its relationship with Greek mythology and with John Fowles's highly theatrical novel *The Magus*. In all these texts, Wertenbaker combines this increased theatricality with her previously demonstrated talent for creating strong female characters. Around this time, many feminist writers were rediscovering or reinventing the stories of women excluded from traditional historical narratives or the literary canon: a practice coined 'herstory' by feminist scholar Robin Morgan in her 1970 anthology of Second Wave radical feminist writings *Sisterhood is Powerful*.[93] Very much in this vein, Wertenbaker's titles – 'Agamemnon's Daughter' and 'Don Juan's Women' – play with and question the ownership of well-known stories, relocating the driving force of their narratives within female subjectivity.

'Agamemnon's Daughter' (c.1978)

'Agamemnon's Daughter' revisits the ancient Greek legend, familiar from Sophocles' *Electra* and Aeschylus' *The Libation Bearers*.[94] Wertenbaker examines this story through the eyes of its female characters: Agamemnon's murderous wife Clytemnestra and their vengeful daughter Electra. In 1977, hoping to receive a commission from the Soho Poly, Wertenbaker wrote to Verity Bargate that the idea for this play 'interests me more than all the others'.[95] Tellingly, the character of Electra continued to fascinate Wertenbaker long after this project was abandoned. In 1990, she wrote of the 'dark and vengeful Electra, the great image of the dispossessed woman, dispossessed even in her tragedy because no one ever knows what happens to her. The furies don't pursue her, she is not judged, and therefore never integrated into the State. This still bothers me.'[96] 'Agamemnon's Daughter' offers a feminist perspective on these events, particularly through Clytemnestra's detailed account of the motivations behind her regicide.

Wertenbaker claimed her character was 'based on a theory

of [Robert] Graves that the myth of Clytemnestra represents a shifting of power from matriarchy to patriarchy'.[97] Consequently, Wertenbaker's Clytemnestra is both frightened and enraged:

In former times, not so long ago, queens ruled. Queens chose their kings, and when those kings had ceased to serve a purpose, they were discarded and replaced by new kings. I come from those queens. We ruled the lands. But it changed, we noticed too late. They started talking, quietly at first, about war heroes. There have always been wars, that's not new, but suddenly the men started to become heroes. This made the sons important and the daughters and the women were left out. They couldn't be war heroes.[98]

Clytemnestra sees the Trojan War as male plot to create a narrative to advance 'these ideas of heroism [and] honour [with which] men have slowly taken the power from the women'.[99] This alternative ideology challenges received conceptions of the legend of Troy, demonstrating that traditional myth-making has not simply excluded women from its narratives, but vilified them:

And then, they invented stories. That it was a woman who caused all the evil in the world. And now, that it's a woman that caused the war, not their own greed and the glitter of Troy's wealth. It's another woman who caused the terrible fight between Agamemnon and Achilles which caused more deaths. Not Agamemnon's pride and his insistence he was the best commander. And now, because a queen rightfully rids herself of a king who ruled badly, who lost all his men, they look at her with horror and say she is a murderess.[100]

Despite the strength of Clytemnestra's defence, the play does not position its audience exclusively on her side. In her dialogue with Electra, our sympathies switch constantly between the two. If we are encouraged to forgive Clytemnestra's murder, her treatment of her daughter is harder to justify. Clytemnestra 'blames Electra for being part of the new generation that accepts these myths and accepts subserviency [*sic*]'.[101] She bitterly implicates Electra in her grievances: 'Yes, they've taught you well to judge your own mother, to condemn a queen.' Electra responds simply, 'Why didn't you teach me?'[102] Electra's concerns are less political than her mother's, allowing Wertenbaker to explore 'the personal grief of the unloved child, the bafflement this causes and the eventual anger'.[103] Electra recalls a childhood spent waiting for a sign of her mother's love: 'An occasional word, a look, like a quick sliding ray on a piece of ground that for a moment is lit, and exists. No. No such moment for Electra'.[104]

Clytemnestra's lack of interest in Electra seems partially motivated by grief over Agamemnon's sacrifice of Iphigenia (and consequently, rooted once again in the masculine war that necessitated this act). Electra feels this sorely, bemoaning, 'Iphigenia. What magic in that name. How ugly, by comparison, Electra. [...] [W]ere all the tears shed for Iphigenia? No care left in the mother's heart for a mere Electra.'[105] While Clytemnestra's anguish is humanising, her refusal to grasp any of the olive branches Electra offers is not. Electra begs her mother to see 'it's still not too late. If you would only speak to me, just once, and be gentle', but her pleas fall on deaf ears.[106] Most poignant of all, is an exchange that occurs once Electra has been compelled to marry a peasant (her stepfather's plan to humble her):

> **Electra** When a girl is to marry, her mother tells her of the rites and secrets of marriage.
> **Clytemnestra** The women will do that. [...] Send me word when your first child is born. [...]
> **Electra** From a mother to a daughter, a word of farewell.
> **Clytemnestra** I'm tired.[107]

This vivid depiction of the mother–daughter relationship, and the psychological and ideological context for its breakdown, produces a drama that is thought-provoking and engaging on a political and a human level.

Framing the central scene of mother–daughter confrontation are two shorter scenes, in which two peasant women wash clothes. In dramatic terms, these episodes provide something of the combined function of the Chorus and the 'messenger' character common to many Greek tragedies. That is, in the first scene, they provide the back story and, in the final one, they report the dramatic denouement, avoiding the need to depict it on stage. 'I can still hear her screams', recalls one woman, 'I'm your mother, she cried. And Electra just laughed.'[108] Their comment on the action preserves elements of the tragic Chorus, but is anachronistically contemporary. The women's dialogue shows a Brechtian influence: contextualising the lives of great mythical figures against a backdrop of the ordinary people who lived alongside them. The older woman's fatalistic view that their lives will continue in the same way, regardless of their own actions or those of the royal house, is challenged by the young woman's belief that change is achievable:

> **Young woman** [...] [S]he talked to us. About how we could fight. How it would be better if we didn't accept everything, if we fought. [...] She said they were no different from us. It was our fault if we believed that and were so afraid of them.
> **Old woman** They pretend to like us. But they never stay. They go back up there. Where they belong. Who can resist fate? [...] And we stay down here. It's always been that way. What did she change for you your Electra with all those words, what did she change? [...]
> **Young woman** It changed something. [...] She made us stop crying for all that we'd lost in the war, she made us stop crying for all the men. She said we could do things ourselves. Even the women. She said her own mother had said that. [...] Yes, it's changed.
> **Old woman** She left.
> **Young woman** [...] Maybe she shouldn't have done that. But Pylades, he must have been handsome. We won't forget. You'll see. We'll change things. [...] I don't know what we are going to do. But we'll do something.[109]

Wertenbaker would explore a similar choric device in *The Love of the Nightingale* and, to some extent, with the role of the Aborigine in *Our Country's Good*, as well as in her latest, as yet unpublished, stage play 'Jefferson's Garden'.[110]

It is unclear why Wertenbaker abandoned 'Agamemnon's Daughter', which she marked as 'unsuccessful'.[111] There are no letters to suggest it was rejected by, or even sent out to, theatres. Several decades later, she would return to tell Electra's story, but as a more direct translation of Sophocles (*Elektra*, 2010).

'Don Juan's Women' (c.1979)

Similar in its re-evaluative stance is 'Don Juan's Women', two drafts of which (written between March and October 1979) are contained in Wertenbaker's archive.[112] Wertenbaker's motivation for this play stemmed partially from her identification of a potentially unexplored area. 'I was [...] rather discouraged to find there have been about 600 plays written on Don Juan', she wrote, 'but, none on his women'. Although she saw this oversight as a travesty, it also presented an opportunity: 'Male chauvinism offers certain compensations.'[113] Wertenbaker wanted Don Juan's women to reclaim their own stories, empowering them further by having them put Don Juan on trial. This was to be 'an accurate inquisition scene, but run by women'.[114] However, Wertenbaker was apprehensive about the way her gendered perspective might be received. The play begins with a prologue delivered by a female 'clown' and, in the earlier draft, this included the lines

> Don't groan. This is not a feminist manifesto. And although our playwright is a woman, she has no blind pity for her sex. Rather, from a natural, even biological, identification with the seducees instead of the seducer, she was driven to investigate their characters.[115]

The later draft bears its feminism less apologetically, even using terminology created by the feminist movement:

I am a student of herstory. I search for the women history has hidden from us and bring their actions to light. It's an ungrateful job. Dig and dig and it's rarely beauties I uncover. There are the tragic victims and the heroines, yes, a few. But usually, it's not so simple. Unlike historians, we are not drawn to simple minded conclusions; we are more subtle.[116]

Explaining that the Arts Council 'no longer allows for [the] extravagance' of presenting all Don Juan's 2,064 seducees,[117] Wertenbaker characterises three: the highly intelligent noblewoman Dona Anna, the disgraced nun Elvira, and the peasant girl Zerlina. These women present three different models of female subjectivity. Dona Anna is exceedingly well-read and shows great interest in philosophy and language. She references Aristotle, Socrates, Thrasymachus, Plato and Descartes, and is always struggling to achieve good rhetoric. 'Of course, metaphors are relatively easy', she admits, 'Metonymies are more difficult, not to mention allegory, irony, antithesis.'[118] She resents the unfavourable position of women in her society and, during the 'trial' scene, recognises that her grievances go beyond Don Juan:

Dona Anna A woman's day is so dull and her life a hypocrisy.
Clown Order. That's a general complaint.
Dona Anna To understand the particular one must first understand the general. I'm sure Aristotle said that.
Clown You accuse?
Dona Anna The world first of all[119].

Anna reveals that, contrary to received accounts of her seduction, it was she who lured Don Juan, and many men before him. 'I have the blood of conquerors in me', she explains, 'what can a woman conquer from behind the windows of an elegant house? Only the men who pass by below.'[120] The image of an intelligent woman with a hankering for adventure, stuck behind 'the windows of an elegant house', is reminiscent of Mary Traverse and her rival in grace, the 'girl at number fourteen', who sits 'at her window, staring at everything'.[121] Despite Anna's awareness of her gender subjugation, she aspires to convey a traditional ideal of femininity. In order to maintain this ideal, she is happy to describe herself as Don Juan's victim, explaining that 'it's so convenient to be a victim. It allows you to do what you want'.[122] When Elvira insists that her own righteous pursuit of Don Juan is not a sign of insanity, Anna concludes, 'frankly, I'd let them think I was mad. It's more acceptable. To be ridiculous just isn't feminine.'[123]

Determined to save other women from Don Juan, Elvira shows great strength of purpose. It is she who calls the women together and drives their course of action. She recognises that existing legal procedures exclude women from justice. '[W]e can't rely on a real tribunal, a tribunal of men', she explains, 'We must make our own. *We* must bring him to trial.'[124] Elvira sees the benefit of female solidarity, insisting that the three women 'must stay together. We are women. We are the same': a claim that horrifies the snobbish Anna.[125] However, like Anna, Elvira's subjectivity is diminished by her desire to be defined as a victim.

To some extent, it is the unrefined and uneducated Zerlina who most fully embodies the rejection of female passivity that Wertenbaker was keen to explore. Handwritten notes accompanying this text reveal Wertenbaker's interests: 'Dishonour [...] – hint at position of women as victims – take it for granted that they are objects – passive – have to realize later that they [need not] necessarily be passive – that they must be responsible for themselves'.[126] Zerlina's character changes significantly between the two drafts. In the earlier one, she asks, 'What's a victim?'[127] and 'What does it mean to have forty six men?'[128] (to which, Elvira replies, 'It means to be a victim forty six times'). Later Anna has to explain sexual intercourse to her:

Dona Anna [I]t euh – grows and springs out. Now. That (*mimics*) goes in – into your – hole.
Zerlina You mean it's detachable?[129]

Zerlina's naivety is similar to Procne's in *The Love of the Nightingale*, who reveals how woefully unprepared for marriage she is with the statement 'I haven't seen one yet, but that's what they told me to prepare me. They have sponges. [...] Getting bigger and smaller and moving up and down. [...] I think most of it you can do on your own. The sponge, I think it detaches.'[130] The consequences of Zerlina's ignorance emerge when she is raped by Don Juan, while acting as bait in a plan formulated by the other two women and barely understood by her. 'You didn't tell me Don Juan would – would do what he did', she bewails, 'He forced me. He was so quick. It hurt!'[131] By indicating that Zerlina has been treated expendably, particularly by Anna, Wertenbaker touches on the controversial issue of social class within feminist movements. However, this ending fails to demonstrate women's ability to resist the status of victim as effectively as the later draft, which ends with Zerlina's continued and unconsummated desire for Don Juan. 'I'm not a victim', she states flatly, not only refusing to be the victim of men, but also resisting falling prey to her upper class 'sisters'.[132] Throughout this version, Zerlina is more confident and more knowing, answering Anna's obsession with rhetoric with the smart retort 'I'm the one he's interested in. I don't have to be a metaphor.'[133] The developments across these two versions of the text suggest that Wertenbaker's desire not to present women as victims grew over the drafting of this play. This concern continued into much of her later work, and is a theme discussed more thoroughly in Chapter Two.

'Monads' (c.1979)

First called 'One Evening', then 'That's the Way I Like it', I refer to this play by the title it assumes for most of its development: 'Monads'.[134] The number of revisions this text underwent suggests that it was once very important to Wertenbaker. In 1980, she wrote to the Arts Council, requesting a six-month bursary to develop the work (by then referred to as 'Greek Adventure' or 'Return to Greece'). In 1981, an article in *The Stage* mentioned that she was still working on a play 'about tourism, set on a Greek island [...], for which she has received a bursary from the Arts Council'. This article reported that Wertenbaker believed tourism to be 'the 20th century's new colonialism, an insidious underminer of cultures and economies'[135] and, while this is not the play's primary theme, its basic premise is the clash of cultures on a small Greek island, which becomes inhabited by tourists every summer.[136] These nuances are carefully drawn and were no doubt informed by Wertenbaker's experience of living on Spetse. The play has two sets of characters: 'natural' ones, around which the narrative revolves, and 'symbolic' ones, who help establish setting. At the play's opening, the symbolic characters read out varying impressions of Greece and the Greeks, which range from romantic ('discovery of yourself'), to racist ('concepts of democratic process and of individual rights are not understood') and patronising ('The Greek knows how to live with his rags').[137]

The central 'natural' character (Claire) is a young British archaeologist in search of an ancient Greek statue she believes is buried on the island. She begins this 'adventure' in a level-headed, almost clinical frame of mind, which Alice (a Greek who befriends her) attributes to her cultural background: 'what you English call being human is having no passions, control at all times. Nothing in excess'. Alice warns Claire that 'no one has found a god and remained unscathed', but Claire refuses to be influenced:[138]

> For centuries people thought of that statue as a god. They feared it, worshipped it, and in some way it did affect them. But when I find the statue, I'll study it, put a date on it, write an article and forget it. (Pause.) That's what I like about this century. We don't pretend that ordinary feelings are anything but ordinary. No more tragedies.

Alice believes that Claire's refusal to fear the 'gods' leaves her vulnerable:

Alice What about Claire? Has she ever been mad?
Claire Never. I'm supremely rational.
Alice Hubris. Be careful. In Greece we believe that when you say something like that, the gods punish you.[139]

According to Alice, the Greek psyche, with its appreciation of the sacred, tragic and irrational, is better able to withstand the vagaries of life. 'We don't have your rigid Anglo Saxon divisions between madness and sanity', she explains, 'We can go quite mad and function at the same time.'[140] The dichotomy between Greek and English, passion and reason, abandonment and restraint, is constantly re-established throughout the play. This is linked to the mythical and philosophical concept of Apollonian and Dionysian man, which represents the conflicting rational and irrational sides of human nature and the interplay of logos and mythos. The play's setting reinforces this: '*Two canopies come out from the backstage wall: each has the name of a café. One is called DIONYSUS, written in Greek and Greek-type lettering. The other café is called APOLLO, same lettering.*'[141] Alice thinks Claire would benefit from succumbing to some Greek passion, wanting her 'to experience a touch of wildness', which might loosen her 'frigidity of the spirit'.[142] Initially, Greece does have a positive effect on Claire, who embraces its beauty: 'I only want to live this moment. […] Every smell, every sound touches me. […] I'm aware of every layer, the world outside, the surface of my body touching it, the inside of my body. I've never felt so well.'[143] Her enchantment with Grecian life changes her work ethic dramatically. Abandoning her previous desire to study, date and forget the statue, she reveals:

I put the statue back in the earth and buried my lunch with him. A small offering. [...] What is the price of a god behind bars? Trapped by the archaeologist, teeth examined by the anthropologist, gaped at by the tourist, and peanuts thrown by the academics […] – not for him such humiliations. […] Not on me the crime of tearing him limb from limb.[144]

Claire seems to have understood Alice's lessons about the gods, but in other areas she begins to take her advice too far. Despite having once called the 'search for romance' 'distorting',[145] she falls obsessively in love with local boy Adonis. Another English woman tries to reassure Alice that 'Claire is a sensible English girl', but this is no comfort for Alice, who realises Claire is 'Too sensible. That's where the danger lies.'[146] Once Claire has unlocked the capacity for irrational passion, she lacks fore-knowledge of how to regulate it. She refuses to accept that her affair with Adonis is temporary and will end when his Greek fiancée returns. She is driven so far from her rational self that she causes Adonis's death by sabotaging his moped. Like Caryl Churchill's and David Lan's *A Mouthful of Birds* (1986), this episode was intended to evoke *The Bacchae* of Euripides: 'When she's caught by this unjustifiable passion for a Greek boy, Claire can only be destroyed by it and although Adonis is not Dionysus and she is not a maenad, the results are the same.'[147]

Alongside its reworking of Greek mythology, 'Monads' has inter-textual links with John Fowles's *The Magus*. In this novel, a young Englishman (Nicholas Urfe) travels to a fictionalised Spetse (Phraxos) to teach English at a grand but isolated boarding school. This school is also referenced in 'Monads', where we meet its English master Hugh, who shares Claire's love of reason. 'I don't like the [Greek] alphabet', he complains, 'I feel I lose my bearings. I don't like that. I don't like losing control.'[148] Nicholas also relies on reason. During the course of the novel he falls prey to a series of mind games, designed by fellow islander Maurice Conchis, in an attempt to shake him from his logical grasp of reality. One of Conchis's fellow schemers tells Nicholas that this experiment may be designed to communicate '[t]he place of mystery in life. Not taking anything for granted. A world where nothing is certain. That's what he's trying to create here.'[149] Later, in a passage similar to Claire's discussion of her god statue, Conchis describes

> a conflict in me between mystery and meaning. I had pursued the latter, worshipped the latter as a doctor. As a socialist and rationalist. But then I saw that the attempt to scientize reality, to name it and categorise it and vivisect it out of existence, was like trying to remove the air from the atmosphere.[150]

Other thematic elements link this novel to 'Monads' and other of Wertenbaker's plays. Conchis likens the charades he devises for

Nicholas both to theatre and psychiatry. He explicitly refers to 'meta-theatre' and invokes Greek tragedy with the word 'catastasis'.[151] The novel has a number of false endings, in which Nicholas is led to believe his ordeal is coming to an end. When, at one such point, he plays on the metatheatrical atmosphere Conchis has engendered by suggesting 'A quick curtain?' Conchis's response sounds like a mantra for Wertenbaker's playwriting: 'No real play has a curtain. It is acted, and then it continues to act.'[152]

Conchis voices ideas about masculinity and conflict, which resemble those explored in 'Agamemnon's Daughter', 'Near Miss' and later works, such as *The Grace of Mary Traverse*:

I should like you to reflect [that these] events could have taken place only in a world where man considers himself superior to woman. In what the Americans call 'a man's world'. That is, a world governed by brute force, humourless arrogance, illusory prestige and primeval stupidity. [...] Men love war because it allows them to look serious. Because they imagine it is the one thing that stops women laughing at them. In it they can reduce women to the status of objects. That is the great distinction between the sexes. Men see objects, women see the relationship between objects. [...] It is an extra dimension of feeling we men are without and one that makes war abhorrent to all real women – and absurd. [...] War is a psychosis caused by an inability to see relationships. Our relationship with our fellow men. Our relationship with our economical and historical situation.[153]

Also reminiscent of Wertenbaker is the way Conchis deliberately evades being categorised by factors such as nationality:

I took a breath; for once he was avoiding my eyes.
'You must have been born somewhere.'
'I have long ceased to care what I am, in those terms.'
'And you must have lived in England.'
[...] 'Does your appetite for invention never end?'

'At least I know you have a house in Greece.'
[...] 'I have always craved for territory. In the technical
ornithological sense. A fixed domain on which no others of
my species may trespass without my permission.'
'Yet you live very little here.'
He hesitated, as if he began to find this interrogation tedious.
'Life is more complicated for human beings than for birds. And
human territory is defined least of all by physical frontiers.'[154]

Wertenbaker signposts the connection between 'Monads' and *The
Magus* by having her characters acknowledge their island's status as
a site of literary tourism. Catherine Hardy-Clover, an English snob
who has settled on the island, refers to 'that horrible man' and his
'dreadful novel', which has caused the island to be 'invaded with
tourists. Hippies, and other unspeakable types'. While this fictional
novel is not *The Magus*, but 'Plant of Madness', it seems to share
characteristics of Fowles's work: 'The plot is very complicated. But
the idea comes from a legend connected with the island. It's believed
that in the hills there grows a plant. When it flowers, the people go
mad.'[155] In addition to its discussion of rationality and madness,
'Monads' has gendered points to raise. Asked if she is a feminist,
Claire replies, 'I don't really know what that means. I belong to
these times, that's all. I care about my work. I try to be as human as
possible.'[156] This statement compares very closely to Wertenbaker's
comment, 'I don't know what feminism means. I mean, I live my
life in feminist terms, I earn my own living, I'm independent.'[157] In a
note accompanying one draft of 'Monads', Wertenbaker asserts that

Feminists, as part of the last modern political movement,
face the same shadow [as previous ideological movements]:
women believed liberation would bring happiness, but the
little liberation that has been achieved has not brought
proportional happiness. Claire is a highly civilised, rational
woman who's managed to circumvent any kind of oppression
or pain to become one of life's tourists [...]. Alice's warnings
are to us as well as to her, if we don't reintegrate that element

of the tragic, irrational which we've buried so well in sociological and psychoanalytical cement, we'll inevitably destroy
ourselves and others both privately and politically. We'll
remain very nasty tourists.[158]

The need to 'reintegrate that element of the tragic, irrational which
we've buried' is recognisable from 'Rites of Entry', 'The Upper
World' and 'The Vigil', but linking this concept to a debate about
feminism is thought-provoking and potentially controversial. In
2001, Wertenbaker gave a paper called 'The Voices We Hear' at
the Archive of Performances of Greek and Roman Drama.[159] In it,
she outlined her theory that, while the men of classical tragedy are
involved in a constant struggle for self-knowledge, the women are
often characterised by irrationality and a refusal to justify their acts,

> portraying the terrifying possibility that maybe the human
> being was not someone to whom you could say 'know
> thyself', but someone to whom you would have to say: 'you
> are unknowable'. [...] [T]hose characters [...] remained
> incomprehensible, blinded to themselves, irrational and
> forever unresolved, haunting the rational mind.[160]

From 'Monads' it is apparent that Wertenbaker held the germ of
this idea 25 years before she made it public. In 'The Voices We
Hear', Wertenbaker by no means suggests that women are essentially
irrational beings, but she does court controversy by celebrating their
potential to engage with something that male-identified logocen-
trism has tried to eradicate. Such an argument is contentious, in so
far as it sets women at a distance from the centre of a culture that
privileges empirical knowledge and, by implication, undermines
the possibility of women's integration within this. Implicit in this
article and in 'Monads' is a critique of the privileging of logic and
reason and the subsequent exclusion of alternative ways of knowing
based on intuition and emotion. However valid this criticism,
the association Wertenbaker makes between irrationality and the
female sex is something with which many women (now and in

1980) would take issue. Perhaps knowledge of this contributed to Wertenbaker's abandonment of this play, with which she was never satisfied. 'Sometimes I feel that if I worked very hard on it I could get something interesting', she confessed to her agent, 'sometimes I don't. The problem is, there's also another play I'm very keen to write.'[161] This new idea would become *The Grace of Mary Traverse*, which, as we will see in the next chapter, proved a more fruitful project.

Conclusions

Unsurprisingly, Wertenbaker's earliest plays are extremely varied, as the young writer floated her identity over a number of themes and styles, until she began to develop her own voice. So we have it that, almost simultaneously, Wertenbaker was writing the least political and the most didactic plays of her career. On both sides of this spectrum, we see a tendency towards strong female characterisation, sometimes at the expense of male characters. Almost certainly connected to this is an awareness of the need to hear female voices. Recognition of this need provoked a richer strand of plays concerned with reassessing traditional narratives from a female viewpoint, and questioning typical models of women as passive 'victims' and men as active 'heroes'. These plays demonstrate that Wertenbaker was well acquainted with many feminist arguments. However, even at this stage, her consciousness of the complexity of gender issues made her reluctant to affiliate herself fully with any one movement. We also see the beginnings of more controversial ideas about women's access to irrationality. These ideas did not receive public exposure until the paper delivered over twenty years later, but they do relate, in part, to a theme that dominates several of her next plays: the tendency for women seeking liberation from traditional definitions of femininity to appropriate a version of 'maleness', rather than redefine 'femaleness' on their own terms.

CHAPTER 2
'THEY NEVER WENT ON QUESTS':
THE GENDER OF IDENTIFICATION

D'Artagnan's rashness. D'Artagnan's loyalty. I wanted to be him. I've often wondered about the gender of identification. At some point, I must have realised that I was a girl reading instead of some neutral thing that could become d'Artagnan, because I embarked on *Les Petites Filles Modèles* by La Comtesse de Ségur. [...] Moving from the musketeers to *Les Petites Filles* was as painful as the scene in Strindberg's *Dance of Death* when Alice tells her step daughter Judith to let down her dress and put up her hair and start taking smaller steps. Alice is not just demanding a physical change, but a confinement of the mind.[1]

Wertenbaker has a shrewd understanding of the interaction between identities, gender and literature. Far from the ideal of the floating identity, the above quotation implies that women's identities are physically and mentally constrained, and that literature can challenge or reinforce those limitations. Wertenbaker's own plays, particularly up until 1985, interrogate the interplay of gender and identity through the perspectives of strong-willed female protagonists. This chapter discusses the possibilities available to women who seek definition beyond patriarchal ideals, as depicted in *The Grace of Mary Traverse* (1985), *New Anatomies* (1981), and the unpublished 'Variations' (c.1981) and 'Inside Out' (c.1982). Textual analysis is supported by the consideration of archive sources and reviews, which illuminate issues of production and reception and give insights into socio-political attitudes in the early 1980s. Although Wertenbaker described the 1980s as 'a terrific time because you could see the work of other women playwrights', as opposed to the 'slightly more reactionary' 1990s,[2] many contemporaneous responses to her 1980s plays (particularly *The Grace of Mary Traverse*) were tinged with sexism. These nuances must be carefully weighed when attempting to judge the success or significance of these works.

New Anatomies (Women's Theatre Group, 1981)

The nineteenth-century traveller, writer and cross-dresser Isabelle Eberhardt is the subject of *New Anatomies*. An uncompromising woman who sought to redefine her gendered and cultural identities, Isabelle roamed the Sahara, dressed as a Qadria Marabout. She spurned offers of Western 'civilisation', favouring the company of Arab travellers. Her lifestyle met with resistance from Europeans, many of whom attempted to dissuade her from her 'unnatural' existence, and force her to follow their prescriptions for the feminine ideal.[3] Wertenbaker's text illustrates how vehemently Isabelle resisted these deterministic forces. Its opening lines introduce an atmosphere of order and instruction: 'Lost the way. Detour. Closed. (*Pause. As if an order to herself*) Go inside.'[4] Equally aware of the danger of being *post*-determined, Isabelle is suspicious of her 'chronicler' Séverine, accusing her of 'stealing' her story, but equally resentful if not being recorded: 'Why aren't you writing all this down, chronicler? Duty to get it right, no editing. (*Burps.*) Edit that.'[5]

Isabelle's characterisation reflects Wertenbaker's desire not to depict women as 'sugar and spice and everything nice', or bow to 'feminine/(ist) notions of what women should be'.[6] Thus, twenty-seven-year-old Isabelle first stumbles onto the stage with '*no teeth and almost no hair*', demanding, 'a fuck'.[7] The role of Isabelle challenges the performer to embody a mixture of the graphically real and the theatrically grotesque. Occupying the stage almost continuously, the actress who plays Isabelle is the only performer who does not take multiple roles, and the part requires a depth of character that is absent from the play's more transitory figures.

Alongside the desire not to be edited, Isabelle presents Séverine with the problem of a constantly changing story. Isabelle recalls growing up in St Petersburg, until Séverine reminds her she has previously said Geneva. She claims not to have any brothers, but when prompted by a mention of Antoine, '*[m]akes a gesture for fucking*'. This revelation of incest is immediately countered by a denial, which, in turn, becomes a confirmation: 'Didn't. Would have. Nasty little piece got her claws into him first. No, did.'[8] It is as if, by constantly changing the details of her story, Isabelle hopes to prevent anyone 'fixing' or defining her life in retrospect, as much as she resists definition in the present.

In Act I, sc. ii (in Wertenbaker's non-linear narrative, the beginning of Isabelle's story), we learn that Isabelle's ability to imagine alternative existences began in childhood. With her effeminate older brother Antoine, she creates Siberian wildernesses, Crimean lemon groves and Saharan expanses for their adventures. Their mother worries about the lack of fairy stories her anarchist husband allowed his children, but this has not damaged their imaginations. Arguably, the suppression of fairy tales may have enabled the children to develop their imaginings outside the archetypal ideals of masculinity and femininity present in such stories. Standing in opposition to this lack of restriction is Isabelle and Antoine's sister Natalie, who follows convention so rigidly that they see her efforts to make them behave '[l]ike Swiss clocks. Tick tock'.[9] An unconventional upbringing has given Isabelle a sense of freedom, but Natalie yearns for a family that follows expected social structures:

> In a family you first have a mother who looks after her children, protects them, teaches them [...]. A mother who teaches her children how to behave and looks after the house and cooks meals [...]. And secondly in a family a brother is a brother, a boy then a man, not this snivelling, delicate half girl.[10]

Natalie's subscription to prescriptive gender models highlights Isabelle's deviation from them, and her language articulates the social forces seeking to determine Isabelle. When Natalie speaks of 'duty', Isabelle hears the '[w]ords of a Swiss preacher, song of the rain on the cultivated fields', and vows never to be cultivated or preached to. Natalie sees no other choice than obedience, but Isabelle recognises that as long as 'obedience comes not from direct fear, but fear of the rules', there is always an alternative. Isabelle appreciates that the systems restraining individual desires, rather than the desires themselves, may be 'unnatural'. When she asks Natalie if the gardener they want her to marry grows cactus plants, Natalie replies, 'They're the wrong plants for this climate'. Isabelle corrects her, 'It's the wrong climate for the plants.' Natalie warns, 'You'll need a roof over your head', but again Isabelle upturns her logic, insisting, 'No rain in the desert, no need for a roof.'[11]

Prescriptive notions of gender are not confined to female characters. Antoine, described as *'frail and feminine'*,[12] suffers the same predetermining forces as Isabelle, but does not show her strength in resisting them. The irony of this is reinforced throughout the play by the fact that Antoine is played by a woman. By Act I, sc. iv, he is married and working in the army. Isabelle returns to the metaphor 'Tick tock, a Swiss clock, the needle that crushes the dreams to sleep' to describe the stifling determinism of his monotonous job. He has already decided that 'Life isn't what we dreamt', but Isabelle has kept faith that '[i]t could be'. Antoine believes he 'see[s] how things are now', but Isabelle rebukes him, 'What dictionary are you using? The Swiss clockmaker's or the poet's?'[13] When this line is compared to Aristotle's maxim, 'the historian describes the thing that has been and the poet the kind of thing that might be' (which Wertenbaker quotes elsewhere), it becomes clearer that Isabelle's ability to create multiple possibilities for her existence arises, at least partly, from the 'poet's dictionary' she has at her disposal.[14] The imagination is, Wertenbaker suggests, central to our ability to self-determine.

Act I, sc. iv provides Isabelle's first experience of intentionally dressing as a man. Prior to this, although she has resisted performing the expected model of femininity, she has not sought to identify as male. In Act I, sc. ii, she appears *'dressed in a man's shirt and a skirt much too big for her'*: a combination which implies handed-down clothes more than transvestism.[15] Likewise, in Act I, sc. iv, although Antoine's wife (Jenny) condemns Isabelle's smoking as vulgar and unfeminine, there is no suggestion that Isabelle engages in this supposedly 'masculine' activity because she has any sense of gender dysphoria, rather she likes to do as she pleases. In contrast to these almost accidental performances of masculinity, Isabelle's first intentional moment of cross-dressing is heavily signposted. The other actions of the scene recede into the background in order to ritualise and focus in on Isabelle's moment of (self)discovery: '**Isabelle** *takes a jellaba and puts it on, slowly, formally. Freeze while she is doing this.*'[16] Once dressed in the man's jellaba, Isabelle instantly sees increased possibilities. Natalie tells her that a 'woman can't go out by herself at this time of night', but Isabelle realises that 'in these… I'm not a woman'.[17] This line is telling: Isabelle does not say 'in these… I'm a man', but 'in these… I'm not a woman'. In other words, she longs to lose the identity of woman, not necessarily gain that of man. In Act I, sc. v, she expands on the new-found freedom of male dress:

If a voice pursues me: foreigner, European – I'll not turn around. If the voice says: you, woman, yes, woman – I'll not turn around […]. But if it hails me: you, you there, who need vast spaces and ask for nothing but to move, you, alone, free, seeking peace and a home in the desert, who wish only to obey the strange ciphers of your fate – yes, then I will turn around, then I'll answer: I am here.[18]

The characteristics (of being 'alone, free, seeking peace and a home') with which Isabelle wishes to identify are not (or should not be) gender specific. Again, she is not professing a desire to identify as male, but to identify as free, and in order to do this she decides she must dress as a man. Tellingly, it is as crucial to her to lose the prescriptive label 'European' (with its connotations of fixed abodes and monotonous occupations) as it is that of 'woman'.

The possibilities provided by male dress are expanded on in Act II, sc. i, set in a fashionable Parisian salon where several women discuss their motivations for cross-dressing. Like Isabelle, they cite the increased opportunities provided by male clothing, rather than feelings of gender dysphoria. Male impersonator Verda Miles admits to being 'the most womanly woman' offstage, but was drawn to the 'hundreds of exciting roles before me' when she first put on a man's costume. Salon hostess Lydia enjoys the silk and lace of women's clothes, but finds them a distraction, acknowledging, 'when I dress as a man, I simply begin to think, I get ideas'. Séverine identifies as a lesbian woman, not a man, but has learnt that male dress means 'I can take my girlfriends to coffee bars without having men pester us.'[19] Although a seemingly progressive group of women, all their statements reinforce the social constructs that restrict their lives. Verda will play male roles, rather than create new, more interesting ones for women; Lydia remains convinced that femininity stands in opposition to rational thought; Séverine re-enacts a tradition that requires women to be owned by men, or at least accompanied by them when occupying public space. Thus, the 'freedom' presented by male dress is positioned as tenuous and limited.

Likewise, although Isabelle takes her transvestism further than the salon women, the freedom she seeks through cross-dressing is never fully realised. Rather, she is eventually restricted by it. Although she never expresses the desire to *be* a man, her conviction to pass for one in public requires her to behave and dress as one. By the end of the play, the stress of living this pretence or duality takes its toll, and Isabelle appears confused and disorientated. She describes 'many young men of great beauty' at a monastery she visited, and implies homosexual activity, admitting, 'I couldn't join. They would know I was not completely a man.' Her straddling of genders leaves her belonging to neither and excluded from both. She has lost the self-surety and determination of earlier scenes. 'Suddenly my destiny: forgot the script', she muses, miserably admitting that, after all her efforts, she has still not found the wisdom she sought. She evokes the desire for another change of direction, showing pleasure at the rain she once detested as a symbol of European culture: 'Get clean that way, wash the traces and the letters. Fresh sand, new letters.'[20] Isabelle's premature death prevents her exploring any new possibilities and her life ends with the same sense of paradox with which it was lived: in a flash flood, in the desert.

Adding perspective to the published text of *New Anatomies* are several drafts and a radio adaptation. In the third draft of the stage play, the scene in which an Arab man is tried for the attempted assassination of Isabelle (Act II, sc. iii of the published text) is preceded by a note: 'the following scene, the most important scene in the play, is by no means written as it will be, and must be read for content only'. Knowing that Wertenbaker considered this scene pivotal to her work prompts those working with the finished text to take particular care when interpreting it. Another draft frames the whole play with a trial scene, but here it is Isabelle who stands accused of 'offences against men and offences against nature'.[21] At the end of this draft, Isabelle is pronounced guilty. The trial scene that appears in the published text makes this point more subtly, using a number of pointers to communicate that it is Isabelle, not her attempted murderer, who is on trial. A strong visual statement is made by the transition of the murderer from the previous scene into the judge, both parts being played by the same actress. This doubling is no coincidence, but occurs explicitly, while the actress speaks lines that begin as a confession ('An angel appeared to tell me the Marabout of the Qadria, Si Lachmi, would be proceeding to El-Oued accompanied by Miss Eberhardt') and end as reported speech ('This, Miss Eberhardt, is what the accused has to say in his defence'). The first accusation against Isabelle – that her behaviour is 'un-Christian' – appears in the next line. The judge cross-examines Isabelle for a page and a half, before coming to the verdict that she 'would be safe in Europe'. This is followed by several more judgements:

Judge You are European.
Isabelle No, I am not –
Judge Were you lying when you told us you were born in Switzerland?
Isabelle No.
Judge You are a European, Miss Eberhardt. You are also a young woman.
Isabelle No I am not.[22]

The judge chooses to define and condemn Isabelle based not on 'what I am doing' but on 'what I am'. In contrast, her self-definition comes almost solely from what she does:

Judge May I point out, Miss Eberhardt, that a man was recently sent to prison in London for a much lesser offence than yours.

Isabelle What? He took a walk on the beach?

Judge This Mr Wilde had a perversion of inclination. You, Miss Eberhardt, have perverted nature.

Isabelle Nature defined by you, confined by you, farmed by you to make you fat.[23]

Assuming that the desert-dwelling Isabelle is ignorant of the circumstances of Oscar Wilde's trial, her first retort ('What? He took a walk on the beach?') seems less a sardonic quip, more a genuine attempt to define a 'lesser offence' than her wish to travel the desert. This, not her habit of wearing male dress, is the 'desire' that she assumes the judge is referring to: further evidence that cross-dressing is not a deep-rooted part of Isabelle's identity, simply a means to an end.

Isabelle's second retort twists the meaning of the judge's reference to her personal 'nature', linking the male hegemony's 'farming' of women (which requires women to conform to the sort of desires considered 'natural') with their farming of lands. This alludes to the colonisation of other nations, which make men like the judge 'fatter' and richer. Further parallels are drawn by the lack of respect shown to women and to Algerian natives by characters such as Captain Soubiel, and the more enlightened attitude Colonel Lyautey takes towards both. The linking of disenfranchised women with subjugated nations is a recurrent trope in Wertenbaker's writing and is discussed in detail in Chapter Three.

Wertenbaker's attraction to the 'trial scene' is evident from several other plays. While drafting 'Don Juan's Women', she wrote: 'I hesitate a little to use a trial as it seems to be an obsession of mine and I use it a lot.'[24] However, this did not stop her including the device in that play, in 'This is No Place for Tallulah Bankhead' (1978) and in 'Case to

Answer' (1980). None of these 'trials' feature actual courtrooms, and all have an element of vigilantism about them: the 'victims' judge and sentence the accused. Another recurrent motif requires the accused to participate in their own condemnation. In 'Case to Answer', Niko must unwittingly define himself guilty; in 'This is No Place for Tallulah Bankhead', Judith must carry out her own execution. Some later plays emphasise miscarriages of justice: Jack's death sentence, compared to Lord Gordon's pardon, in relation to the Gordon Riots in *The Grace of Mary Traverse*; the muteness of Philomele's accusations against Tereus in *The Love of the Nightingale*. In *Our Country's Good*, the trial of Liz Morden has a more positive outcome, one that not only saves her life, but reaffirms the power of theatre.

Wertenbaker writes of her interest in the trial, 'It is said [...] that the origins of the theatre are in religious ritual [...] but drama has another heredity and it seems to me a more obvious and vital one: the bringing of judgement. Every play, worth its salt, is a trial in thicker or thinner disguise.' She goes on to suggest that 'the function of theatre as a court has been better understood in England than anywhere else', pointing to the fact that the Royal Court is often referred to simply as 'the Court'. If we see the whole process of theatre as a metaphorical trial, the effect of putting more literal trial scenes into that structure works similarly to the device of putting a play into a play; while metatheatre draws our attention to the theatricality of the whole, the trial scene highlights the judicial aspects of the medium. Wertenbaker argues strongly that it is never the playwright's job to deliver a verdict, merely to present the evidence. 'It is always for the jury to make that pronouncement', she insists, clearly positioning the audience in this vital role:

> Citizens are required by law to do jury duty – that is, we're asked to decide on the guilt or innocence of one person. In the theatre, we are asked to decide on the guilt or innocence of our society, our lives, and to take responsibility for it. Surely to shirk that duty is, if not a legal crime, a moral crime, a crime that is not against the state, but against our own humanity.[25]

Perhaps it is no coincidence that in her more recent play *Credible Witness*, we are left not with the result of a trial, but with the promise that the case will be 'reopen[ed]'.[26]

By necessity, the radio play of 'New Anatomies' differs considerably from the stage version.[27] From specific moments, such as the murderer's transition into judge, to the constant device of women playing men, multi-roling gives the stage play its defining theatricality. If the play makes a point about women's need to cross-dress in order to access more interesting roles (on stage or in life), it does so as much through the device of actresses dressing as men to play the roles in the play, as through direct discussion. If a writer wishes to complicate preconceived ideas of gender, what complicates more than having women playing women, women playing men, and women playing women who choose to dress (and sometimes behave) as men, all on stage at the same time? As Carlson notes, the device 'echoes characters' concerns about sex roles' and 'demonstrates how the power of casting against traditional gender expectations has become a central tool in women's remapping of comedy'.[28] It is the visceral, bodily nature of the theatrical medium that allows these devices to function. The same effect could not be achieved by female voices in a radio play, and all the ritualistic foregrounding of dress, achieved by changing role and costume in full view of an audience, would be entirely lost. Thus 'New Anatomies' becomes far more conventional as a radio play. Its female parts are voiced by women, and its male ones, by men. It is less interesting structurally, following Isabelle's 'life much more closely, chronologically and simply than the stage play'.[29] One point of interest is an additional scene in which Isabelle, having been forced to return to France, is living with Antoine and Jenny. She works on the docks to save the money required to return to the desert and Antoine worries that this uncouth occupation attracts the attention of the neighbours. He suggests prostitution as an easier way to make money, arguing, 'You're a woman, why don't you use that? Even Jenny would find your doing that more acceptable than working on the docks.'[30] This assessment echoes those made by the judge in the stage play; society can accept perversions of inclination, which result in undesirable but accepted professions such as prostitution, but cannot accept the perversion of nature it sees in a woman carrying out a job that is perceived as essentially masculine.

Perhaps because the Women's Theatre Group was recognised as a feminist collective, a larger than average proportion of those reviewing the original stage production of *New Anatomies* were women. Most looked favourably on the play's foregrounding of gender themes, praising both production and writing that 'works powerfully and humorously as protest against patriarchal oppression',[31] 'reaches successfully beyond historicism, to consider much wider questions of sex and gender',[32] and 'works towards a brave new anatomy indeed'.[33] Carole Woddis, who interviewed Wertenbaker at this time, described her as someone who wished to be considered a 'writer first and feminist second',[34] and reviews suggest the 'question of feminism arose as something natural from the play rather than something imposed'. Wertenbaker maintained that Isabelle was not a 'mouthpiece for feminist statement' but a 'woman leading her life the way she chose; [...] active rather than passive, and with a definite quest'.[35] During this period, Wertenbaker frequently returned to the theme of a woman 'with a definite quest', which echoes earlier, unfinished pieces such as 'Agamemnon's Daughter', 'Don Juan's Women' and 'Monads', and anticipates *The Grace of Mary Traverse*. The concern can be traced as far back as Wertenbaker's childhood and the alienation she experienced upon realising she was a gendered reader. Isabelle Eberhardt provided Wertenbaker with a historical example of a woman on a quest (at other times, she claimed that 'to find a woman of historical significance, I had to invent her'),[36] which enabled her to explore the question of 'why women feel they have to take on male characteristics to survive in the world'.[37] Both these elements are equally crucial to her next published play, *The Grace of Mary Traverse*. Before turning to this text, I discuss two unpublished pieces that continue to focus on historical examples of women who found opportunities for transgression through transvestism.

Variations on a Theme of Cross-Dressing

In the introduction to her first volume of collected plays, Wertenbaker explains;

> *New Anatomies* was originally going to be one act of a play about three women who dressed as men. I was intrigued by the mental liberation in the simple physical act of cross-dressing. The other two women were George Sand and Ono Kamachi, a Japanese poet and courtesan. Eventually the fascinating Isabelle Eberhardt [...] took up a whole play to herself.[38]

What Wertenbaker does not record here is that the stories of George Sand and Ono Kamachi (or Komachi) also expanded to fill plays of their own. The Komachi legend became 'Inside Out', a piece for four actors, first performed by the Rodent Arts Trust (RAT) at the 1982 Edinburgh Fringe; George Sand is the subject of a one-woman show, 'Variations'.[39] Although unpublished, both plays can be found in Wertenbaker's archive. Like *New Anatomies*, these texts make a central dramatic feature of the act of cross-dressing. In 1981, Wertenbaker recorded:

> For about a year I have been fascinated by the question of why a woman should choose to dress as a man and what happens to her when she does. It seemed to me that when women in history threw off their female clothes and therefore gestures, walk, physical restrictions, they rid themselves at the same time of a whole set of conventions, a way of looking at the world and actually became something else, spiritually, mentally. I was intrigued at the notion of showing that transformation on stage, someone becoming other, beginning with the clothes, then the movements and suddenly the words changing as well.[40]

In 'Variations', the stage is set with a *'dummy or clothes hanger with different clothes and hats; delicate shoes, boots, sandals'*. The only other properties are '*a small desk with ink, feathered pens, papers, and other instruments of the nineteenth century writer*', emphasising Wertenbaker's intention to focus on Sand's identities as writer and cross-dresser.[41] The play sets itself up as a re-evaluative portrayal of Sand, opening with a babble of previous judgements: 'She's not a women, she's a man. Women attract, she repels. She's generous, an artist, therefore she's a man', 'The French Byron', 'The most womanly of women', 'That boring Sappho', 'Goethe's sister', 'An ink pisser', 'Mother of the Russian novel', 'A graveyard of men'. Many of these terms reflect the misogyny Sand has been subjected to, others ('Goethe's sister', 'The French Byron') demonstrate the tendency to define women in relation to men (see next section for reviews of *The Grace of Mary Traverse*, which refer to a female Faust, a female Tom Jones and a female 'Rake's Progress'). Sand asks us to dispel such preconceptions. 'Do you prefer fables or the truth?' she challenges, 'Are your myths fixed or can they be cracked? Am I to be buried under your judgements or will you hear my plea?' She invokes the trial motif, discussed in the previous section: 'Don't you know I have already condemned myself, to death, and there is little time left?'[42]

The piece is overtly theatrical, with Sand frequently breaking from her own narration of events to embody and voice important figures from her life. At times this seems more than just a dramaturgical device, reflecting the way Sand actually sees the world:

[W]hen [my father] comes before you, you'll see not an ancestor, not even a father, but more, myself, in larger, brighter traits. [...] When my father comes and speaks, it is myself, or sometimes, by a strange shift, my son, also called Maurice. I am his mother, his daughter, I am him, his self.[43]

Sand's extreme identification with her father and son is offset by a troubled and distant relationship with her mother and daughter. The privileging of male relations is a trait shared with Isabelle Eberhardt (and with Electra in 'Agamemnon's Daughter'), although Wertenbaker does not connect this tendency explicitly to the desire to cross-dress. Sand also shares Isabelle's vivid childhood imagination. 'I have a fantasy', recalls Sand, 'I grow wings, I fly over the vast plain of snow and I find the army. […] I brandish a flaming sword and drive the Cossacks out of Paris.' [44] Perhaps this capacity allows both characters to envisage alternative adult lives.

As with Isabelle, Sand's first experiences of cross-dressing are practically, rather than ideologically, motivated:

> Deschartres has prescribed more exercises for my condition and takes me shooting with him. But it's impossible. Skirts these days are made so narrow at the bottom I leave half of them on the brambles. Deschartres says one of the local noblemen used to take his daughters out dressed as boys. This count thought it was criminal to put adolescent girls in dresses when they needed the most freedom of movement. Yes. So. Off with these tubes, I have a smock, gaiters, a cap. That's better. I can jump brooks, I can crawl through bushes, I can run![45]

At first, male clothing provides physical freedom, but this soon leads to psychological effects. 'The trouble is, now that I'm in trousers Deschartres is convinced my mind has improved and is inflicting me with ten times more Latin', she explains.[46] This idea is similar to that expressed by Lydia in the salon scene of *New Anatomies*. Again, it is for the sake of convenience that Sand returns to masculine dress in adulthood:

> My one dress drags in the mud. I feel I'm skating on ice in these ridiculous shoes and they break in two days. And the hats, walk under a gutter and that's it. It came to the point where I couldn't go out anymore and I'd watch all my friends run from literary and political events to museums, the opera, the theatre. […] Then I had this coat made for me, and with a tie, a hat (*puts them on*), no one knows I'm not a student. And my boots, look, at last I'm secure on the pavements, I can fly from one side of Paris to the other, sit in the cheap seats in the pit of the theatre, and no one bothers me, no one even sees me.[47]

Sand's realisation that men will not bother what appears to be a single man, echoes Séverine's reasons for cross-dressing in *New Anatomies*. Although Sand's initial motivation for transvestism is more practical than ideological, she does not only struggle with female dress, but with the characteristics she has been taught to associate with women. Having read widely from the canon of male authors, she has come to 'love Montaigne best of all, but his opinion of women is a problem. Indeed, the opinions of all the philosophers, not to mention fathers of the church on women, is a problem. "Vain, impure, nervous, childish, chatty, perfidious, lazy...".' Attempting to reconcile these pronouncements with her own gendered experience, she does not know which side of this contradiction to fault. 'I know I am not vain. My total lack of grace and coquetry has despaired my grandmother. I long for truth and beauty. My will is strong, stoical blood runs in my veins. Am I not a woman then?' Sand concludes that the qualities assigned to women must be 'a question of education? Surely, we're not born morally inferior?'[48] While this comment offers women the possibility to 'improve' themselves, it condemns their current state, and is based on the ideals of male philosophers. Sand challenges the misogynistic labelling of women but, in the same breath, legitimises the privileging of the masculine:

Am I a coquette, is my name frailty, or am I a woman of sensibility? Am I mediocre or superior? Have I spirit or am I a little slut with no common sense? [...] [D]id I never, dimly, strive for more? Those male virtues I dreamt of, noble deeds, excellence. [...] Am I a frivolous woman or a serious soul?[49]

Likewise, she favours the company of men:

Men, always men in this woman's life, is that what you're saying. It's true. I have not liked the company of women very much. It bores me. Because their horizons are so narrow, it's the fault of their education. I find women are always telling me the story of storms in teacups with the emotion of tragedy, and at the end I feel cheated.[50]

Sand would rather distance herself from women than attempt to re-establish what being a woman can mean. She recognises that male hegemony disadvantages women, but accepts that, partially because of this, most women *are* inferior companions. The only exceptions she allows are the other 'artists, like me', who have 'forced the boundaries'.[51] This acknowledgement hints at the ability to value people for what they do, as opposed to what they are. It also re-establishes the idea that Sand's identity is constructed as much by her status as a writer, as by her transvestism.

'Inside Out' (Rodent Arts Trust, 1982)

In 1981, Wertenbaker attended Clive Tempest's 'New Theatre Workshop' in Cumbria, where she formed links with the director Pat Trueman and the actor Peter Sykes, founder of the Rodent Arts Trust (RAT). The three began collaborating on a play about the legendary Japanese courtesan Ono Komachi. This became 'Inside Out', opening in the Herriot Watt Theatre at the 1982 Edinburgh Fringe Festival.[52]

Legend tells us that the incomparably beautiful Komachi once challenged a suitor (Shosho) to journey to her garden for one hundred nights, in order to earn her as a lover. As the nights progressed, Komachi became infatuated by Shosho's persistence, and both waited eagerly for the promised consummation. On the ninety-ninth night Shosho died and Komachi was left to wander the land in despair.[53] In Wertenbaker's version, we first meet the aged, haggard Komachi, relentlessly counting under her breath. She appears to have wandered all the way into our world, much to the confusion of a young girl who encounters her. With the help of a single Chorus figure 'in a tidy modern suit a business man might wear', we are transported to Komachi's youth. This detour seems intended to emphasise the contemporary nature of the play's theme over the specifics of its setting. As the Chorus explains:

First: where are we? Ninth century Japan. Or anywhere, anytime. Desire has no race. In the rules of this play, past and present intermingle: no prejudice: so far, so unnatural, so oriental? Well, it was civilised, that's important. Other than that, don't take Japan too literally.[54]

As the time period changes, the role of Komachi is transferred to a different actor. Unlike *New Anatomies*, in which an all-female cast take a multitude of male and female roles, 'Inside Out' draws on the Noh tradition of male actors playing female roles. In the RAT production, Peter Sykes played both Shosho and old Komachi (who appears in the play's opening and closing scenes). However, Noh convention was not upheld throughout, as two actresses (Jenny Howe and Katrin Cartlidge) played the young girl (who, as we move back in time, morphs into Komachi's servant Li) and young Komachi. This being so, the decision to use cross-gendered casting in the role of old Komachi cannot be seen simply as an attempt to recreate the authenticity of a Noh production. Rather, as in *New Anatomies*, it suggests a deliberate device, intended to draw attention to issues of gender and performance. Yet, while *New Anatomies* enables women to assume conventionally male roles, 'Inside Out' gives its most interesting and complex woman's role to a man.

At first glance, it appears odd that Wertenbaker chose to employ a device that is rooted in a tradition that has sought to exclude women from public and performance space. It is possible that the decision was out of Wertenbaker's control; Peter Sykes was heavily involved in the genesis of this play and may have influenced his double casting, perhaps wishing to create a vehicle through which to demonstrate his skill as an actor. His high status within the triumvirate responsible for the production is evident from publicity materials, upon which his name is displayed as prominently as Wertenbaker's. A letter from Jenny Howe makes gently teasing remarks, which suggest Sykes gave off an air of self-importance. She reports that he 'waffles on about being a "Physical Actor"', and comments, 'Even Peter in his limited way is open to suggestion for small changes.'[55] However, Wertenbaker recorded that Sykes was 'very pleasant to work with, very positive', suggesting the collaboration was a constructive one, in which decisions were made mutually.[56]

If casting a man as old Komachi invokes a tradition that excludes women from theatre, Wertenbaker undercuts this by blurring gender boundaries throughout the play. In the first scene between the young Komachi and Shosho, Komachi (who is bored by Shosho's lack of poetry) instigates a cross-gender role-play in which she portrays Shosho (as seen through her eyes) and vice versa:

> *She plays with the cloth and then suddenly catches* **Shosho** *with it and wraps him in it.*
> **Komachi** Now you can be Komachi. [...] (*She imitates* **Shosho**'*s manner, and voice.*) Lady, open your legs.
> **Shosho** (*getting into the game and imitating* **Komachi**) But I only open my legs to the poetic.[57]

This game, which does not feature in the limited accounts of the Komachi legend, is of Wertenbaker's invention. During it, Komachi is pleased to 'find this pursuit and aggression amusing. Better than being still, always the rampart to be assaulted'. This episode returns the play to more familiar territory: a woman's discovery of the varied and interesting roles made available through the act of cross-dressing. It also allows Komachi to voice more serious revelations about the masculine view of 'courtship':

> **Komachi** (*Imitating* **Shosho**.) Woman, I could rape you, but that would be a brief release. I want to improve myself, I seek a pleasure more refined.[58]

Additionally, this scene enabled Wertenbaker to challenge a central element of misogyny within the Komachi legend: the fatal cruelty inherent in her excessive test of Shosho's endurance. The limited accounts of this story give her request a hard-heartedness, vanity and lack of motivation, which Wertenbaker's play attempts to undo. By placing the request within this role-play, Wertenbaker has Shosho voice it as he pretends to be Komachi. Komachi questions the extent of the challenge, and even gives Shosho the chance to reduce it. This is reiterated at the point of Shosho's death, when Komachi (still played by an actress) wails, 'Komachi had no right to ask for a hundred nights. But I didn't, it was Shosho, remember, it was Shosho: an act equal to a poem, his words, his promise. [...] His voice was soft, like mine – my voice. I – I was Shosho... Yes. And she laughed.' Here, the blurring of gender boundaries is emphasised by Komachi's inconsistent use of the first and third person, as well as her acquisition of several physical and verbal manifestations of Shosho:

> (**Komachi** *brandishes the knife, with a strength reminiscent of* **Shosho**.) She drove me to it. Too much desire. She was the cause, she must be punished. I'll have my revenge. Komachi, let me go to her.[59]

At this point, the actress leaves the stage (still impersonating Shosho) and the actor playing the dead Shosho becomes Komachi again. In the final version of the text, the exact technique for this transition is not explained, but the first draft specifies that Komachi '*takes off her layers of silk. They wrap* **Shosho** *in it. His hair, which is long, loosens.* **Komachi** *takes his sword*'.[60] In the final scene, as in the opening one, this actor's role switches constantly between Shosho and old Komachi, often on a line to line basis.

In the earliest drafts of 'Inside Out', a further incidence of role-play occurs. In this version, it is Komachi who sets Shosho his challenge and when we next see him, he has already started to resent her. He begins to parody Komachi: 'make yourself interesting, Shosho, make yourself poetic. [...] I have grace, I am beautiful, wit to bury you, worship me from afar, and be grateful.' He then '*sits on the bench, as a beautiful woman would, in a pose*', but his mockery soon leads to realisation:

> This stillness gets tedious. [...] Why has no one come by? I'll go look for them, but no, that would crease the perfect repose of my beauty. It would be suspicious, it would show signs of fear, even age. [...] It isn't easy, this waiting, not always pleasant. (*Silence*) Let me be Shosho again. I don't like this.

(*He* (*as* **Komachi**) *struggles with this* (*as in a dream, difficulty of making the first move to wake up*)). [...] I would not want to be like her. Poor Komachi.[61]

This moment of recognition mirrors the discoveries Komachi makes through cross-gender role-play, demonstrating that men too have something to learn from such experiences. Shosho's 'act' may begin, traditionally, as a mockery or parody of women, but it ends with empathy. Perhaps then, Wertenbaker's one exploration into the realm of male to female transvestism can be read as progressively as her more frequently used device of women playing men.

Like Isabelle Eberhardt and George Sand, Ono Komachi was a writer: considered one of the six best *Waka* poets of Heian period Japan.[62] Wertenbaker uses several tropes and phrases from Komachi's work, drawing her title from the following verse:

When longing for him
Tortures me beyond endurance,
I reverse my robe –
Garb of night, black as leopard-flower berries –
And wear it inside out.[63]

Just as 'Variations' emphasises Sand's identity as a writer, 'Inside Out' highlights Komachi's literary prowess. Introduced (by the Chorus) as 'a courtesan, young, beautiful and accomplished', Komachi interjects, 'I made verses.' The Chorus dismisses this, hinting at the struggle women face to be recognised as artists:

Chorus Don't be put off by the verses. It was like knowing how to ride a motorbike, an extra, for the male frisson.
Komachi I was famous for my verses.
Chorus A beautiful woman, and men gathered, mothlike.[64]

Despite Komachi's protestations, the play foregrounds her desirability over her poetry. One of the issues Wertenbaker hoped the play would raise was 'the rather pertinent question of how morally responsible a woman is for the desire she provokes',[65] and her piece challenges the misogynistic tendency to blame women for male lust and sexual abuse.[66] However, 'Inside Out' is equally reluctant to deny women agency in these matters. When Shosho asks Komachi, 'Why isn't it enough that I want you so much', she explains it is because she has 'no part in it'.[67] As in many of the plays examined in the previous chapter, Wertenbaker is keen to depict women as active participants in, rather than mere victims of, the processes of seduction.

Wertenbaker's 'three women who dressed as men' each represent the actual historical figure that inspired them in very different ways. 'Variations' is the closest to a bio-play. Its one-woman structure places focus firmly on the character of Sand, and although other figures are mentioned (and momentarily brought to life), they are only seen through Sand's eyes. Additionally, Wertenbaker's frequent employment of Sand's own words creates a subjective, but intimate, picture of the woman. Wertenbaker appears keen to dispel previous mythologisation of Sand and to explore more authentic possibilities. In contrast, her portrayal of Komachi is myth incarnate. While this is partially necessitated by the lack of historical records about this ancient woman (in comparison to the many accounts of Sand and Eberhardt), there is evident artistic motivation too. Komachi is of less interest as a psychological character than as a representative or symbolic one that facilitates the theme of Wertenbaker's piece. The play explores the process of myth-making on a number of levels, from the way a story becomes corrupted to form a range of different versions, to the means by which ideologies (such as the tendency to blame women for provoking male desire) are constructed. Thus, it is only natural that the play's central figure should be characterised along mythic lines.

New Anatomies sits somewhere between these two models. The play allows its audience to piece together an idea of Isabelle's character from numerous, at times contradictory, sources. While none of these seem as distant as myth, neither do they fix Isabelle as securely as the character of Sand is constructed. Isabelle is a puzzle, a patchwork of varied impressions, which build on, or challenge, those made previously. Even when we are given Isabelle's own accounts of her life, we are swiftly reminded that she is not a reliable narrator.

All three plays reveal how the stories of their protagonists have been constrained and corrupted by previous (predominately male) tellers. We hear these accounts from the voices that vie to define Sand at the opening of her play and the Chorus who dismisses Komachi's poetry to emphasise her desirability. The fear of them is implicit in Isabelle's distrust of Séverine's position as her 'chronicler'. These plays provide three alternative ways of subverting such misrepresentations. In 'Inside Out', by immersing herself in the myths themselves, Wertenbaker metatheatrically highlights the way they are created; in 'Variations', she allows the mythologised subject to speak for herself, dismantling the words of others; in *New Anatomies*, she blurs the boundaries between our ideas of fact and fiction, destabilising all pre-existing accounts in the process.

The Grace of Mary Traverse (Royal Court, 1985)

The Grace of Mary Traverse has been labelled a 'female *Faust*',[68] a female 'Rake's Progress',[69] and a 'female equivalent of Tom Jones'.[70] Such resonances were not unintended; an early synopsis for the play (originally called 'Grace Note') proposed a 'female variation on the Faust legend'.[71] However, the comparisons highlight the absence of female protagonists comparable to Wertenbaker's (anti)heroine, and this lack of precedent motivated the work:

I think: the greatest deprivation of women has not been economical but mythological. They have no Don Juan, Faust, Peer Gynt or even Percival. They never went on quests, or we've never heard of them. Along those lines: when women write about women, instead of writing about physical virgins and whores, they write about spiritual virgins only: the temptation of making all women victims of [male chauvinist pigs] or circumstance. Well I'd like to write about a rake, a woman, who went through corruption – but on a quest like Don Juan or Faust. In all of literature, there's only Moll Flanders who even approaches that, and then she was a capitalist, not a hero.[72]

Wertenbaker was interested in female corruption. In an early draft of the play, two unnamed characters discuss how to tempt women. They discount the lure of 'sex' and the male character's suggestion of 'wealth' is vetoed by the female. Finally, they settle on 'knowledge', the acquisition of which requires a more active engagement on the part of the 'temptee'.[73] For Wertenbaker, this was crucial:

That is: what would the *Rake's Progress* be if the rake were a woman. Female corruption has always been understood as prostitution, which is passive. It would be intriguing to improvise with actresses – and actors – around the theme of non-passive female corruption: women on quests of one sort or another, whether mental, material or sensual.[74]

Wertenbaker cites improvisation here, because she was applying to take part in a 'New Theatre Workshop' run by Clive Tempest. Notes, taken by another workshop participant, reveal that Wertenbaker did indeed develop the premise for her play here:

exploration of the decision to go down into depravity – v strong use of music ... difference between male and female tempter – we saw the questor making that decision to go down... to explore corruption... the closing of the eyes... [...] – we were all on a high – Timberlake went away to write.[75]

Wertenbaker's finished play involves Mary in an array of 'corruptions', including sexual promiscuity, incest, cruelty, gambling, blackmail and political manipulation. However, we first meet her attempting to converse with an empty chair, under the watchful gaze of her father. Defined by his reproaches ('You are not here to express your desires but to make conversation') and her own self-censorship ('No, that's a direct question', 'No, that's too enthusiastic'),[76] she justifies her first rebellious step – leaving the house with her servant Mrs Temptwell – in terms of complying with her father's ideals: 'It'll only improve my conversation and Papa will admire me.'[77] When the experience fails to fulfil these expectations, Mary is disappointed, until her interest is grabbed by witnessing male behaviour. Hypnotised by the rape of another woman (Sophie), Mary finds she 'couldn't stop looking. (*Pause.*) It's not like the books.'[78] Mary is struck by the wealth of opportunities available exclusively to men. Although she knows she could hold her own among the wits conversing in a coffee house, her entry is barred on account of her gender. 'I have no map to this world', she bemoans, 'I walk in it as a foreigner and sense only danger.'[79] Mrs Temptwell suggests Mary 'could be like [them] if [she] wanted to', drawing her into a Faustian pact.[80]

Mary's first task is to experience lust and sex from a masculine perspective, not by prostituting herself, but by hiring the services of Mr Hardlong. When Mary shows reticence, Hardlong chastises her for clinging to an ideal of female sexual passivity: 'Perhaps you want me to seduce you and let you remain irresponsible? [...] Or are you waiting for a declaration of love? Let romance blunt the sting of your need, mask a selfish deed with selfless acquiescence?' This scene can be read as a reversal of traditional depictions of the 'male gaze'.[81] Stage directions specify that, in contrast with the prevalence of female nudity in late-twentieth-century media, '*Mary is fully dressed. Mr Hardlong is naked.*' In addition to this image, Hardlong's speech (particularly the repetition of the command to look) and name draw attention to his body in a distinctly voyeuristic way:

No, open your eyes. Look at me. The neck is beautiful, Mary, but doesn't require endless study. Look down. The arms have their appeal and the hands hold promise. The chest can be charming, the ribs melancholic. Look down still. They call these the loins, artists draw their vulnerability, but you're not painting a martyrdom. Look now.[82]

Left unsatisfied by brief pleasure with Hardlong, Mary struggles to behave as a man. She refuses Mrs Temptwell's offer to find her another lover, having decided she 'like[s] this one'. Perturbed, *'Mary eats pensively, but nonetheless grossly.'*[83] Viewed in relation to her previous observation that men 'stuff food into their mouths with no concern for their waists',[84] this act demonstrates Mary's abandonment of the ethereal ideal of the weightless woman she was attempting to perfect in the play's opening scenes.[85] However, gluttony leaves her equally unsatisfied, still feeling 'a void in the pit of [her] stomach'.[86]

In the next scene, Mary participates more confidently in the masculine space of the gambling den. When fellow gambler Mr Manners suggests that the skill to discard wisely 'is more in man's nature', Mary replies that 'nature is simply a matter of practice'.[87] She appears determined to maintain her male-identification; when Mrs Temptwell urges her to '[b]urst into tears' to avoid paying her debts, Mary mocks the suggestion: 'What? Turn female now?'[88] However, not all the possibilities provided by Mary's sex can be rejected so easily. By Act III, she is pregnant: a gender-specific condition that highlights biological, as well as societal, limitations on Mary's quest for masculine autonomy. Consequently, Mary shuns any identification with motherhood: 'Damn this leech in my stomach, sucking at my blood, determined to wriggle into life.'[89]

Despite her resolve, Mary (like Isabelle Eberhardt) fails to gain fulfilment from participating in the world as a man. 'This isn't experience', she rails, 'this is another bounded room. You promised more.' Searching for 'more', Mary realises that she has yet to explore the political power men wield. 'They let their imaginations roam freely over the future', she comprehends, 'yes, they think about the country, and then they rule the country.'[90] Initially motivated by the ideal of liberty for all, Mary soon learns from Mr Manners the thrill of manipulation: power, not to do good, but purely for power's sake.[91] This introduces one of the central questions of Wertenbaker's text: 'a question a lot of women face today: if they're going to throw themselves into the world, the running of the world, which means knowledge and power, are they going to have to become as horrible as men'.[92] The play remains ambiguous about this issue. In one draft, Mary is ennobled by her assertion that she, not the 'rabble', should be arrested for the Gordon Riots. (In answer, she is patronised, 'Nonsense. A woman will make the mob seem hysterical. We want them to look dangerous').[93] In the published text, she is less honourable, merely stating, 'Who will listen', when she is begged to speak out against the injustice of the arrests.[94] However, although Mary adopts something of Mr Manners's corruption, the horror that her actions generate is not assuaged by his appalling reassurance, 'There is nothing so cleansing as massive death.'[95] Recognising, at last, the barbarity of the world she has tried to force her way into, Mary attempts to retreat, but discovers knowledge and experience are even harder to lose than to gain. Entirely disillusioned, she becomes nihilistic and considers killing her child, an action associated with the abandonment of maternal, and by association feminine, instincts.[96] In earlier drafts, this act is explicitly linked to Mary's (here called Ann Sophie) recognition of the limited potential for a girl child:

> **Ann Sophie** Do you want her to grow up to be a poor creature like you, taking in other children not to starve herself. Or is she to become a whore, or a woman of the kind they are bringing into the new factories.
> **Nurse** She's your daughter, my lady. She can become like you.
> **Ann Sophie** Like me? Do you know what you're saying? Yes, she can grow up in innocence and ignorance, confined in the stupidity of her own imagination, thinking of the world as a benign place waiting only to receive her. What's in that? Stupidity, narrowness and finally, misery.[97]

In the published text, Mary's hopelessness extends to the whole of humanity: 'I would like to pour poison down the throat of this world, burn out its hideous memories. A white cloud to cancel it all. How? I don't know. But I can start here. I can look after what I've generated. Stop it.'[98] Because Ann Sophie has a specific complaint against the lack of possibilities open to women, she is able to dispell it by embracing a vision of 'a different world where she can live and learn'.[99] Mary's all-encompassing nihilism needs a greater act of imagination to conquer it, yet she too is dissuaded from infanticide by the intervention of her servant Sophie. Mary Kate Trotter, who played Mary in a Canadian production of the play, interpreted this to mean that the 'turning point [for Mary] is the purity, the very femaleness of her friend Sophie [...]. Sophie shows her that there is heart [...]. Together, they can survive.'[100] While Sophie does represent a certain type of 'femaleness' within the play, Trotter's interpretation of this is misleadingly idealistic. The antithesis of Mary's active descent into male vice, Sophie embodies several stereotypes of female passivity. In Act I, sc. iii, she is raped and in Act II, sc. iii, she is forced into prostitution. Men desire Sophie because she 'will serve [their] luxury' and 'ask for nothing in return'. Mrs Temptwell explains that 'Sophie has no desires' and Mary recognises that this 'causes desires in others'.[101] In the first two acts of the play, she speaks barely more than a few words together and struggles with abstract notions of thought and feeling. However, there are signs that Sophie's passivity is less complete than these comments suggest. She is raped because she has the courage to challenge the attempted rape of Mary (a courage and a favour that Mary does not return), and she protests, albeit briefly, at having to prostitute herself to pay, in kind, for Hardlong's services to Mary: 'Mrs Temptwell, you didn't tell me...'.[102] During the third act, Sophie grows in voice and confidence, eventually gaining the strength to challenge Mary over killing her child. Thus, at times, Mary's performance of gender appears favourable to Sophie's but, at others, this is reversed, creating a shifting impression of female identities. The play does not preach a 'correct' way for women to behave or identify, but interrogates two extremes in order to juxtapose their rewards and drawbacks.

Like Isabelle Eberhardt, Mary is a woman on a quest. She seeks to redefine herself in opposition to societal expectations and, in the absence of models for female transgression, follows examples of male corruption. As with Isabelle, the rejection of established ideals of femininity is only deemed achievable by the espousal of established ideals of masculinity. Mary and Isabelle change sides, so to speak, but do not challenge the status quo of the gender binary or create new, female-derived concepts of femininity. Crucially, neither woman finds the happiness and freedom she seeks, nor do they achieve such things for others. This highlights the naivety of the assumption that women would run the world more successfully than men, if they continued to run it along patriarchal lines. Martha Ritchie has pointed to the similarities (and shared initials) between Mary Traverse and British Prime Minister Margaret Thatcher. '[F]or Wertenbaker', Ritchie suggests, 'the idea of a female leader is always an illusion, a contradiction in terms: in a female organisation, a leader would not be necessary; in a male structure a woman would lead like a man, and on behalf of men.'[103] She had been influenced in this by 'the hidden structure'[104] of the Greenham Common Women's Peace Camp (begun in 1981), which she described as 'the most extraordinary event', 'so moving and special':[105] 'no leaders, things happen, people communicate, but you wouldn't know how. No symbols of power'.[106] Thus, Wertenbaker's texts hint at the potential for progress, only if different systems are embraced, and women are positioned as crucial agents in these processes as their disenfranchisement from current systems makes them better able to recognise the need for change. As Wertenbaker asserts, 'It is really the women who are beginning to take up, not the running of the world necessarily, but the questions about the world.'[107] Wertenbaker's twentieth-century plays highlight that these questions were as difficult to answer in the 1980s as they were for her eighteenth- and nineteenth- century characters. Early drafts of *The Grace of Mary Traverse* seem to provide more definite answers. 'I don't intend to renounce the world, I intend to live in it [...]. I'll go to the country and fight against despair. I'll bring up my child to do the same. We'll look at the world and take part in it, in a way never done before. [...] We won't despair',[108] resolves Mary. The published play remains more cautious. Sophie, Mary and her daughter (Little Mary) sit reconciled with Mary's father in his sunlit gardens. The scene endorses an appreciation of the natural world, our attempts to understand our place in it, and a belief in the future, symbolised by the act of raising a child. This scene is the closest Wertenbaker comes to envisioning a viable alternative to the world Mary wished to 'pour poison down the throat of'. Its idealism has been criticised as 'optimistic but preposterous [...] a note of lyrical but dotty hope',[109] yet this ideal is no more 'preposterous' than that of the graceful, weightless woman we were presented with at the start of the play. Wertenbaker would not claim to have answered the impossible question of the alternative feminine ideal, but her final scene's brief exploration of one possibility reminds us of the need to keep searching.

Staged at the Royal Court's Theatre Downstairs, *The Grace of Mary Traverse* was Wertenbaker's first high-profile commission and received attention from all the major papers. Reviewers were predominantly male and several demonstrated intolerance towards Wertenbaker's concerns. Michael Coveney sneered, 'Feminism is at the gates. And the gates are locked', before grudgingly conceding, 'For all its gnawing limitations and passages of automatic rant, the play does light up from scene to scene.'[110] He dismissed the scene in which the previously chaste Mary discovers, through Hardlong's tuition, her body's potential to desire, as 'one of the silliest scenes ever enacted even in Sloane Square'. Martin Cropper described the play as 'a clotted, uneven alloy of Shavian comedy and feminist wish-fulfilment', but failed to identify which feminists might 'wish' to follow the same harrowing path as Mary.[111]

Antithetically, Suzie Mackenzie was inspired to conclude that Janet McTeer, who played Mary, 'convinced me of Wertenbaker's central thread – that as women we do indeed live in an inviolable state of grace'.[112] Ironically, this was the sort of idealistic assumption that Wertenbaker's piece intended to challenge. Wertenbaker was concerned that men 'may write from stereotypes', but also that

women are falling into the same trap: the tendency is to be forced to write a woman either as victim or as superheroine. If you write anything else you're accused (by yourself if not by others) of being mean to women. This is actually a serious problem and one I'd very much like to discuss because just as women are freeing themselves enough from convention to actually write plays they're falling into a more insidious trap of feminine/(ist) notions of what women should be, should write, and I think we've remained much closer to 'sugar and spice and everything nice' than we realise. That's why I want to explore this notion of corruption.[113]

Michael Billington's review offered the most complex reading of the play, asserting that Wertenbaker had found 'a highly original metaphor for women's experience', which seemed to suggest 'that women who cross sexual frontiers [...] and play by masculine rules must expect to end up battered if tenuously optimistic'.[114] This appreciation of both the hope and trauma of Mary's experience certainly shows greater insight than John Peter's blunt assessment:

Ms W [*sic*] was seized with an Idea and then went in search of a Form to enable her to deliver a matching Message [...]: a corrupt, male-dominated world breeds its own nemesis in the shape of an avenging angel. [...] [T]he Eternal Feminine draws us on alright, but it also lets us down.[115]

Equally unwilling to engage was Milton Shulman, who called the piece a 'sardonic feminist tract', which 'specifically blames the male sex for spawning humanity's most corrupt social values'.[116] This comment seems particularly at odds with a play intended as 'a kind of Eighteenth Century study in corruption from the female point of view. That is: what would the Rake's Progress be if the rake were a woman'.[117] However, Shulman was not the only reviewer to see both the attack on men and the championing of the ideal of 'woman' that Wertenbaker was expressly trying to avoid. Wertenbaker recognised this tendency:

There was an interesting reaction because in the second act when Mary gets up on a soapbox and says all these things about freedom for this and that, I remember one critic saying, 'The play was fine until Wertenbaker started spouting all this feminist business.' Now, the quotes Mary was using were directly from Tom Paine, but the fact that a woman was saying that, and I think unconsciously the fact that I was a woman playwright, turned it all into something feminist. It was feminist, but it was the eighteenth century and it was Tom Paine. I remember spotting that and thinking if it had been a man saying those things, or a male playwright, that criticism would not have been made.[118]

The reductive approach of reviewers towards perceived feminism goes some way towards explaining Wertenbaker's distaste for such labels. She has spoken out against the assumption that women write about 'women's issues', suggesting 'we all just write about humans',[119] and has sometimes resisted the term 'feminist', stating this is simply 'because I don't like labels'.[120] It is telling that the gendered themes present in both *New Anatomies* and *The Grace of Mary Traverse*, received largely positive criticism when presented through the feminist mouthpiece of the Women's Theatre Group and reviewed largely by female journalists, but were greeted with hostility by predominately male journalists in the more mainstream setting of the Royal Court. Although the early 1980s provided increased opportunities to see the work of female playwrights, it seems there were still critics who felt women's voices need only be tolerated within certain frameworks: that by having feminist companies such as the WTG, these voices could be segregated, marginalised and, ultimately, avoided. Perhaps then, it is more worthwhile for a playwright seeking to re-evaluate notions of gender, to receive negative reviews that show the work is reaching those it is intended to challenge, than positive comments from journalists already sympathetic to such concerns. Wertenbaker was pleased that, although *The Grace of Mary Traverse* received a mixed response, 'it had serious reviews, which is what you want. Whether they liked it or not, they took it quite seriously.'[121] Contemporary scholars who use reviews to inform their understanding of these productions must take these distinctions into consideration, and judgements about a work's critical 'success' must carry an awareness of such nuances.

Conclusions

While Wertenbaker has questioned the application of the term 'feminist' to herself and her work, many of her plays, particularly in the period 1980 to 1985, deal explicitly with problems facing women. Although these plays adopt historical or mythical frames, all discuss issues of contemporary relevance, such as stereotyping and predetermination, both in the everyday lives of real woman and for women from the literary canon. Wertenbaker sought to challenge what she perceived as a literary tradition to portray women as passive victims, denied opportunities for activity and adventure, and showed a persistent interest in 'women on quests'.[122] These did not follow masculine notions of a hunt for wealth or treasure, but were quests nonetheless: Isabelle's search for wisdom in the dunes of the Sahara; Sand's desire for personal freedom and literary recognition; Komachi's desperate hunt for the status of her youth; Mary's pursuit of experience, understanding and, finally, 'Grace' in eighteenth-century London. Experimenting with male dress and/ or behaviour initially promises to lead towards these characters' goals but, to varying degrees, eventually proves disappointing, alienating and confusing. By this, Wertenbaker seems to imply the need for women to derive their own routes to freedom, success and happiness, without merely adopting the same methods men have used to achieve these ends. There is, perhaps, a parallel to be made between Wertenbaker's own reluctance to be labelled and her early career explorations of these models of female creativity that could not be easily accommodated within the existing order.

Many of the concerns discussed in this chapter re-emerge throughout Wertenbaker's writing but, after this stage in her career, gender issues are often less dominant than in these earlier plays. While it might be tempting to deduce that Wertenbaker had been dissuaded from continued exploration of feminist issues by the sexism of the press, the evidence points towards a more complex set of factors. For example, much of her later work was produced in more mainstream environments, by companies with male-dominated hierarchies, such as the Royal Court, the RSC and

Out of Joint, rather than by the small companies and female collectives with whom she collaborated in the early 1980s. Additionally, between *The Grace of Mary Traverse* and Wertenbaker's next original plays (*Our Country's Good* and *The Love of the Nightingale*, 1988), she suffered the loss of her partner (the RSC actor John Price), an experience that changed the way she thought and wrote about gender:

> I think I had a fairly callous feminist view that men are pretty awful and they always do well. But when you experience someone's death, you realise the fragility of the human being. [...] I could never be angry with men again in a blanket way. I had lived with men and found them interesting, but not interesting as a gender. And that stopped. I think that's it. I stopped dividing the world into gender.[123]

Rather than signalling a major shift of focus, or abandonment of the feminist cause, it is more accurate to describe a developing continuum. Perhaps the best way to demonstrate this is with reference to another play from this period: 'Case to Answer' (1980).[124] Wertenbaker describes this piece as 'essentially about politics versus personal politics and women not being able or allowed to talk'.[125] It explores the relationship of a young couple (Sylvia and Niko) and their failure to communicate with one another, despite their relationship seeming to bear all the traits of political and social enlightenment: an 'equal' partnership that shares chores and wage-earning. This play has a clear feminist underpinning, which became more explicit over the course of the writing process.[126] However, the gender debate is not the only one within the play.

Like Caryl Churchill's *Cloud Nine* (1979), 'Case to Answer' establishes a series of connections between male colonialist attitudes to women and to other countries.[127] With a characterisation that echoes the position of colonised peoples, Sylvia has lost confidence in her voice after years of her husband devaluing her speech. 'It was not overt', she admits, 'Just the occasional wince. And the force of your eloquence'.[128] This process is demonstrated by Niko's frequently dismissive lines, such as 'Sylvia, what are you babbling about?'[129] and 'What's all this gibberish?' that imply Sylvia's speech is nothing more than unintelligible noise.[130] Niko, Sylvia claims, has not only eroded the patterns of speech she did have, but gradually replaced them with his own: 'Having frozen my language, you substituted yours, thereby transmitting your values, beliefs, convictions and thoughts. Since I had no means of questioning you, I had no way of resisting the power of your convictions'.[131] Wertenbaker ensures that we do not fail to notice the colonial parallels of this loss of identity stemming from a lack or substitution of voice by having Sylvia question Niko about the French and Spanish governments' deliberate efforts to eradicate the Basque language:

> **Sylvia** What about language? Not allowing someone, a country, its own speech. Does that ever happen?
> **Niko** All the time. Franco did it with the Basques. The French are more subtle, they insinuate French is so superior a language only a savage wouldn't want to speak it and they transmit their values that way.
> **Sylvia** What do you call that?
> **Niko** Oppression. Cultural imperialism is oppression.[132]

Sylvia then spells out the connections between the political and the personal: 'You've just said there's a worse kind of suffering. People who feel they're not worth listening to. People with no culture, no language, people who are always ignored. Can't you see I'm one of those?'[133] These links between the oppression of women (a concern that had motivated much of Wertenbaker's writing to this point) and the oppression of whole nations (a concern that forms the basis of many more recent works) are highly relevant. They highlight the presence of a continuum, which finds its midpoint in the plays discussed in the next chapter. As we will see, Wertenbaker suggests that it is through our relationship with, and access to, language that these connections are most clearly revealed.

CHAPTER 3
'TO SPEAK IN ORDER TO BE': ON LANGUAGE AND IDENTITY

[W]atch a child working out her first sentence [...]. [I]t is beyond the need to survive, you can survive with a few words and a lot of crying. It is a sentence, I believe, that is usually a descriptive sentence and inevitably communicated to someone. It is the beginning of dialogue. [...] The inevitable need to speak in order to be.[1]

Here Wertenbaker echoes Descartes's famous pronouncement on consciousness and being, repositioning language as the essential condition for existence. This makes explicit a concern that is frequently addressed in her playwriting. Susan Carlson has highlighted Wertenbaker's 'attention to language, a focus which is most obvious in her characters' self-consciousness about words'. Carlson suggests that 'Wertenbaker's own self-consciousness is clear in her building of extra-textual relations between her plays and other texts, and in her sensitivity to the conscriptions of language by those persons or institutions with power.'[2] We have seen these devices in many of the plays already discussed, but Wertenbaker returns to them with increased urgency in *Our Country's Good* and *The Love of the Nightingale*. These works, both premiered in the autumn of 1988, are the focus of this chapter.

The only new work Wertenbaker had staged between *The Grace of Mary Traverse* (1985) and her two plays of 1988 was her 1986 translation of Ariane Mnouchkine's *Mephisto* for the RSC. She also started work on an adaptation of Ovid's *Metamorphoses* – a mammoth undertaking, begun as early as 1985/6 and eventually pared down into *The Love of the Nightingale*[3] – and a preliminary version of *After Darwin*, which contained the roots of her 1998 play of that name, but differed considerably in form and content. In the introduction to her first volume of collected plays, Wertenbaker describes this draft as 'a play about a man with a terminal illness on a sea voyage. It had singing whales and wise tortoises and has remained comfortably in a drawer.'[4] It was while Wertenbaker was developing these works that her partner, John Price, died unexpectedly, after which she had difficulty regaining the impetus to write. As Sarah Sigal discusses in the next chapter, she took some persuasion to accept Max Stafford-Clark's commission to write *Our Country's Good* because it 'was a bleak time [...] of deep mourning', and she 'didn't think [she] could do it'.[5] This bereavement had a thematic, even ideological, impact on Wertenbaker's work. Her belief that she 'stopped dividing the world into gender'[6] at this point is borne out by the two versions of *After Darwin*, between which Sara Freeman has discovered an 'overall shift [...] from an emphasis on gender to a focus on culture'.[7] Freeman's findings fit closely with my own, supporting my decision to study the plays grouped in Chapter Five (including the finished version of *After Darwin*) through the frame of cultural identities.

This chapter begins by examining *The Love of the Nightingale*; developing my conclusions concerning Wertenbaker's perception of the need for women to find original routes out of oppression, I suggest that this play and 'Case to Answer' establish metaphors that extend these ideas beyond gendered contexts. I then consider whether *Our Country's Good* advances these arguments, paying particular attention to the many varying interpretations the play has received. This discussion continues in Chapter Four, which offers three complementary articles from contributing scholars and practitioners, who offer a range of international and professional perspectives on Wertenbaker's best-known play.

The Love of the Nightingale (RSC, 1988)

The Love of the Nightingale was first performed by the RSC at The Other Place, Stratford, in 1988. Its narrative is loosely based on the myth of Philomela (Philomele in Wertenbaker's version) and Tereus, found in Book Six of Ovid's *Metamorphoses*. The play begins in the palace of the Athenian king Pandion and his daughters, Philomele and Procne, and the story is set in motion when Procne is given in marriage to Tereus, king of Thrace. Procne feels isolated and lonely in faraway Thrace and sends Tereus to fetch her sister. During his return voyage, Tereus becomes infatuated with Philomele, rapes her, and cuts out her tongue to prevent her from disclosing his crime. Several years later, Philomele devises a way to reveal her abuse. In the Ovidian narrative, she achieves this by weaving her story into a tapestry, but Wertenbaker's play replaces the private art of weaving with the very public device of a puppet play-within-the-play. This is performed during the only opportunity for Thracian women to monopolise public space: the festival of Bacchus. Here, Philomele is reunited with her sister and the two women enact their revenge on Tereus by killing his (and Procne's) son Itys. Tereus, in turn, attempts to kill the sisters, but they are spared this fate by the metamorphoses of the three central characters into birds.[8]

At first glance, the subjugation of women, specifically the issue of rape, appears to dominate *The Love of the Nightingale* and, unsurprisingly, many academic analyses of the play foreground feminist readings. Jennifer A. Wagner's interpretation draws on the work of feminist scholars such as Lizbeth Goodman, Helene Cixous and Linda Walsh Jenkins and describes Wertenbaker's 'revisionary procedures' as 'feminism informed'.[9] Sheila Rabillard proposes that 'Wertenbaker's self-conscious transformation of narrative myth into drama emphasises the need for feminist readers to "overread" the myth', and that 'the need for the feminist critic' can be seen in the character of Procne and her response to Philomele's puppet play.[10] Anne Varty reads the play as 'a story about how men take action to silence articulate women, and about how women may fight back', in which 'men abuse the consensus about what words mean [...] as a means of abusing women, and women are deprived of speech altogether'.[11] Joe Winston writes that the play 'immediately identifies the destructive forces within society as emanating not from expressions of female sexuality but from acts of male violence',[12] and Laura Monros-Gaspar describes Wertenbaker's perspective as 'gender-biased'.[13]

Such assessments do not point towards the first new play by a writer who had recently 'stopped dividing the world into gender'.[14] While some thought the ancient story had been 'used, brilliantly, as a template on which to mount a discussion on the roots of male violence and rape',[15] others criticised Wertenbaker for 'using male characters schematically, [so that] her feminist bias is too nakedly revealed'.[16] Most stated a gender focus as fact ('Wertenbaker presumably sounds a modern warning that women will, or must, respond violently to violent male lust';[17] 'her real subject is rape as a constant in male–female relations'; 'silence is an emblem of sexual oppression'),[18] some adopting a dismissive tone: 'All Wertenbaker has to say is "It was Tereus's fault. Aren't men beasts?"'[19] Whether it aroused sympathy or suspicion, the majority took it as given that Wertenbaker's focus was sexual politics, and it is not difficult to see why. A feminist influence is apparent from the play's opening. Two soldiers fight, taking turns to insult one another. As the insults worsen, Wertenbaker highlights how much of our derogatory vocabulary is derived from misogynistic views of women. First we hear the commonplace insult 'You son of a bitch'. This is intensified by the more unpleasant 'You son of a bleeding whore', before both are ridiculed and questioned by the crowning insult: 'You son of a woman!'[20] This escalation creates a *verfremdungseffekt* that scrutinises the acceptance of more commonly used misogynistic terms.

Like Wertenbaker's women-centred, re-evaluative versions of *Don Juan* and *Electra*, the play foregrounds the experiences of its female characters. Philomele and Procne have a far greater presence in Wertenbaker's version than in Ovid's, both in the number of scenes/ episodes that feature them, and in the way they are portrayed during these. In Ovid, Philomela does not appear until Tereus has returned to Athens to request her presence in Thrace. She is presented as object rather than subject of the story. She has no speech and there is no narration of her thoughts or feelings. She is described only in terms of her outward appearance – her beauty and her actions – as observed by an onlooker: 'Philomela entered, attired in rich apparel, but richer still in beauty.' Contrastingly, Tereus' thoughts and feelings are expressed by phrases such as ''Tereus was inflamed', 'his own passionate nature', 'His impulse was to [...]' and 'His heart could scarce contain the fires that burnt in it'.[21]

Wertenbaker's play deviates greatly from this. Instead of focusing on public, male-controlled events, her second scene draws us into an intimate exchange between Philomele and Procne. As well as establishing the play as a story of female experience, this scene reverses the concept of the male gaze. During it, the sisters' voyeuristically observe a soldier, who is unaware of their gaze and to whom the audience is never introduced. Throughout the scene, Philomele's language foregrounds her body as a place of feeling and sensation: 'I feel such things, Procne, such things. Tigers, rivers, serpents, here, in my stomach, a little below. [...] I want to run my hands down bronzed skin'. While drawing attention to the subjectivity of her own body and its desires, her words place the male body in a more objectified position: 'he's so handsome. [...] Look at the sweat shining down his body.'[22] Wertenbaker recognises female desire as central to the concept of women as active protagonists, understanding and driving their own stories. 'Desire', she explains, 'is a move towards something. And possibly I have resisted the idea that women don't desire.'[23] To advance this idea, she invents a romance between Philomele and the captain of Tereus' ship. Through these episodes, Wertenbaker challenges the tendency to see rape as a violation of chastity and virginity, rather than simply a violation of a woman's right to choose her sexual partners.

One of Wertenbaker's greatest deviations from Ovid is the way in which Philomele reveals her rape. Wertenbaker's choice of a puppet play over Ovid's account of tapestry-weaving creates a more theatrical scene, but there are ideological, as well as stylistic, motivations. Philomele's act is stronger than Philomela's because it subverts both the traditionally male art of performance and the traditionally male arena of the public square. This works against the tendency for classical texts to suggest 'public life is the property of men and women are relegated to the invisible private sphere'.[24]

Without question, some of the most disturbing and theatrical moments of *The Love of the Nightingale* (the rape and its revelation) are crucially connected to issues of gender. However, there is good reason to discuss the play here, rather than in the previous chapter. Firstly, Wertenbaker has resisted one-dimensional gendered readings of this play. 'Although it has been interpreted as being about men and women', she acknowledges, 'I was actually thinking about the violence that erupts in societies when they have been silenced for too long.'[25] Pre-empting the public ('mis')interpretation of this theme, the Male Chorus of Wertenbaker's play muse: 'This one, you will say, watching Philomele, watching Tereus, watching Philomele, must be about men and women, yes, you think, a myth for our times, we understand. / You will be beside the myth. If you think of anything, think of countries, silence.'[26] Although these lines seem to make the play's intended focus explicit, on their own they do not weigh as heavily as the multiple scenes that appear to foreground gender issues. However, Wertenbaker re-emphasises the need to 'think of countries' in a number of subtler ways. A monologue, given by Philomele's nurse Niobe, includes the simile 'Countries are like women.' The speech occurs as the rape is happening offstage and is punctuated with Philomele's screams. The brutality of this is juxtaposed with Niobe's dispassionate account of her native island's failed attempt to withstand Athenian invasion. Niobe compares the futility of their resistance to that of Philomele against Tereus: 'She should have consented. Easier that way. Now it will be all pain. Well I know. We fought Athens. Foolish of a small island but we were proud. [...] Power is something you can't resist.'[27] In paralleling Philomele's rape with the invasion of a country, and the power of a man over a woman with that of a stronger nation over a weaker one, Wertenbaker's play allows an alternative or complementary reading to emerge through the frame of postcolonial theory.[28]

Crucial to a postcolonial reading of this play is the second element of the Chorus's instruction. We must not only think of countries, but of silence, and its antithesis: language. In his seminal work *Black Skin, White Masks*, Frantz Fanon recognised that, beyond language's communicative value, 'to speak means [...] above all to assume a culture, to support the weight of a civilisation'. Consequently, the erosion of a people's language meant an erosion of their culture and, ultimately, of their identity. Fanon recognised this practice as a key element in the process of colonisation: 'Every colonised people – in other words, every people in whose soul an inferiority complex has been created by the death and burial of its local cultural originality – finds itself face to face with the language of the civilising nation.'[29] This concept was equally central to the postcolonial theorist and writer Ngugi wa Thiong'o. Born in colonial Kenya, Thiong'o was educated at English-speaking Kenyan schools and attended Leeds University. His early works were written in English but, in 1986, he wrote *Decolonising the Mind: The Politics of Language in African Literature* as a 'farewell to English'. In it, he outlined his reasons for returning to the native Kenyan languages of Gikuyu and Kiswahili. 'The choice of language and the use to which language is put', Thiong'o asserts, 'is central to a people's definition of themselves in relation to their natural and societal environment, indeed in relation to the entire universe.'[30]

Both Wertenbaker and Thiong'o have written about the use of native language suppression as a weapon, or means of control, for colonising forces. Wertenbaker explains:

the French [...] told everybody who spoke Basque, 'if your children speak Basque they will be stupid'. I mean, they literally said that. And they said that to the schools, [...] 'any child who speaks Basque in school much be punished'. So that even now, when you speak to that generation, they say, 'oh, you know Basque, it's so backwards' [...]. So that's how they did it, you know, by making people ashamed of their language.[31]

Wertenbaker's account, particularly its emphasis on the potential for such abuse to be delivered through an education system, echoes Thiong'o's descriptions of his experience of colonial Kenya. As Thiong'o contends, 'The night of the sword and the bullet was followed by the morning of the chalk and the blackboard. The physical violence of the battlefield was followed by the psychological violence of the classroom' and 'the domination of a people's language by the language of the colonising nations was crucial to the domination of the mental universe of the colonised'.[32] Thiong'o's comments highlight that, for long-term colonial enterprises, linguistic or 'psychological violence' became equally important as (if not more important than) acts of warfare or physical punishment. Likewise, Wertenbaker has emphasised the success of the French government's coercive devaluation of the Basque language, in comparison to the Spanish regime's more overtly punitive measures. This suggests that, while conventional violence may strengthen the identities of those determined to resist it, cutting people off from their language has a disastrous effect on their sense of agency. After Philomele's silencing, Niobe muses, 'The silence of the dead can turn into a wild chorus. But the one alive who cannot speak, that one has truly lost all power.'[33] Viewed through this lens, we can read Philomele's rape as the initial act of physical violence – 'the night of the sword and bullet' – and the cutting out of her tongue as the subsequent act of linguistic suppression. (Although this act carries as much physical violence as the rape, its symbolic value is that of linguistic or psychological violence). Crucially, it is this second violation that is most damaging to Philomele's identity. After the rape, Philomele is devastated, but not subjugated. She is able to rebuke Tereus with all her previous wit, articulacy and strength of character.[34] However, after she is silenced, much of her identity appears lost. No longer able to speak for herself, she must be defined by the voices of others. When asked who Philomele is, Niobe answers, 'No one. No name. Nothing. A king's fancy. No more.'[35]

Even Procne questions the authenticity of the silent Philomele: 'perhaps you're not Philomele. A resemblance. A mockery in this drunken feast. How can I know?'[36] Her resistance is motivated both by Philomele's voicelessness, and by what she has, nonetheless, been able to voice. Procne does not wish to accept Philomele's revelation of Tereus' crimes, but more importantly, she is furious with Philomele's inability to be the articulate sister she prized. Procne places great value on verbal communication. In the height of her loneliness, she consoles herself with memories of her sister's articulacy. 'How we talked', she recalls, 'Our words played, caressed each other, our words were tossed lightly, a challenge to catch.'[37] Even after she believes Philomele is dead, Procne continues this practice, telling Itys how his aunt 'could speak with the philosophers' and 'was bold and quick'.[38] When she is reunited with a very different sister from the one she idolised, Procne would rather question the authenticity of this altered, flesh and blood Philomele than the one fixed in her memories. In several of her plays (including *After Darwin*, *Credible Witness* and *The Ash Girl*), Wertenbaker depicts the inability to adapt to changing people and circumstances as a character flaw, while the potential to evolve is presented as a source of hope. Here, Procne seems to inhabit the former category. Likewise, her refusal to engage with, and attempts to silence, the Thracian women are catalysts for the play's tragedy. Procne struggles with the Thracians' rich metaphorical discourse, which is very different from her rational Athenian one. Rather than attempt to understand their speech, she is dismissive of its value, telling her attendants to '[b]e silent' and using devaluing phrases such as 'What are you women muttering about this time?'.[39] While Procne is not an unsympathetic character, an audience is encouraged to retain a sense of critical judgement when viewing this role.

Niobe's denial of Philomele's identity is positioned differently from Procne's. It expresses a mixture of contempt and a genuine loss of purpose. To Niobe, Philomele had been a mistress whose wishes she was duty-bound to follow. Once silenced, as Niobe explains, 'She can no longer command me. What good is a servant without orders?'[40] Like Procne, Niobe demonstrates a failure to adapt to changing roles and circumstances, although this can be blamed, in part, on the Athenians' treatment of her. Forced to see her relationship with Philomele through the dynamic of servant and master/mistress, she lacks the language to translate it into other terms. Unable to relate to a silent Philomele, she denies her altogether. There is also an echo of Mrs Temptwell's desire to see Mary Traverse ruined. Niobe does not possess the doting, maternal nature of traditional nurse figures in Greek tragedies such as

Antigone and *Hippolytus*. Rather, she is characterised by bitterness and resignation, a result of her enslavement by Philomele's people. Some bond of duty (or financial bribe) keeps her body in Philomele's service, but Philomele's muteness allows Niobe to abandon the linguistic respect she was once obliged to show.

As well as reading Philomele's silencing as an act of linguistic violence, it is possible to view the rape itself in these terms. Tereus justifies his actions by referring them to those of Phaedra in the play-within-the-play: 'I am Phaedra. I love you. That way.'[41] Philomele has previously defended Phaedra's feelings to Tereus, telling him, 'love is a god [...] you cannot control' and 'must obey'.[42] Later, Tereus appropriates these lines, twisting their meaning (crucially their definition of 'love'): 'Who can resist the gods? Those are your words, Philomele. They convinced me, your words.' By assuming her voice to justify his act, Tereus implies that Philomele is to blame for what has befallen her. Secondly, Tereus dismisses Philomele's protesting voice with the words 'Then my love will be for both. I will love you and love myself for you.' When Philomele insists that she must consent, he replies, 'It would be better, but no, you don't have to.'[43] By vetoing Philomele's right to give or withhold consent, Tereus overrules the agency of her language, replacing her dissenting voice with his consenting one.

Anne Varty suggests that Tereus' disregard for Philomele's words shows that 'the men who rule society do so partly by dictating how language is to be used. The male hegemony deploys words to its advantage and to the disadvantage of women, hardly even allowing them the access of use.'[44] However, the play does not present the practice of silencing as exclusively masculine. After the rape, but before the mutilation, Niobe attempts to curb Philomele's protestations, telling her to 'grovel', 'keep silent' and, ironically, to 'hold back [her] tongue'. While Niobe's advice could be seen as practical, even desirable, in light of what follows, Wertenbaker does not encourage this interpretation. It is hard to sympathise with recommendations that include 'Smile. Beg. [...] He might still be interested. That would be excellent.'[45] Although the ability to adapt to new circumstances is something Wertenbaker's writing often seems to endorse, this is always presented as a subtle process of compromise and fusion that keeps elements of the old, but invigorates them with something of the new. The debasement that Niobe suggests to Philomele would require, not an adaptation, but a complete reversal of Philomele's identity and, consequently, cannot be given a positive gloss.

Wertenbaker states that 'if a culture loses its language, it loses its tenderness.'[46] The word 'tenderness' appears in a number of Wertenbaker's plays, and is a key concept in *The Line* (2009) and *After Darwin* (1998). Wertenbaker seems to use the word to mean something akin to human compassion, and it is very telling that she correlates this with access to language, providing the reverse of the connection she establishes between silence and brutality. In *The Love of the Nightingale*, Philomele makes the same equation with her line 'When you love you want to imprison the one you love in your words, in your tenderness'.[47] While it is possible to deliver this line to imply that 'words' and 'tenderness' are two separate things in which one could imprison one's love, a more fitting interpretation would have Philomele using the words synonymously: clarifying the first with the latter. Later in the play, Tereus does use words to 'imprison' Philomele but, in doing so, rips them from their tenderness, distorting their meaning.

Tereus' extreme lack of tenderness may come, in part, from a lack of words. This possibility is signalled early on. When Pandion asks Tereus about the theatre in Thrace, Tereus replies that they 'prefer sport'.[48] The inadequacy of such a substitution is clear. An activity that (according to Phillip in *Our Country's Good*) requires 'attention, judgement, patience, all social virtues',[49] and (according to Robert in *The Break of Day*) demonstrates our faith in 'a future with language',[50] is hardly matched by one in which the importance of physical prowess renders language almost unnecessary. Later in the scene, Tereus tells Philomele they have 'no theatre or even philosophers in Thrace', further emphasising the absence of language and debate within his country. Tereus' lack of linguistic sophistication is apparent in his curt sentences (often containing no more than two or three words) and his simplistic reading of the play-within-the-play (*Hippolytus*). When the character of Phaedra asks the Athenian audience for pity, Tereus barks, 'Why should we pity her? These plays condone vice'.[51] That Tereus has no capacity to pity others becomes increasingly apparent throughout the play.[52]

In Tereus' next scene, his presence induces a stultifying effect on conversation, as he himself remarks, 'You were talking easily enough [before]'.[53] When Philomele attempts a natural enquiry into what her sister talks about, Tereus dismisses it ('What women talk about') and tries to instigate a completely false topic: 'Talk to me about the night.' Unsurprisingly, this provokes a complete impasse. Tereus fails to grasp the reciprocal nature – the fluidity and malleability – of conversation. Instead, he tries to control and order it, as he would his army. As the play progresses, his linguistic weakness is highlighted again and again. In sc. xi, Philomele ignores his calls five times, maintaining her own conversation to Niobe (almost a page of dialogue) throughout. In the two pages of text that precede her mutilation, Philomele makes lengthy and eloquent speeches, into which Tereus struggles to squeeze more than a couple of words at a time (all attempts to silence her). Because his interjections are so desperately ineffective in the face of her articulacy, his only alternative is brutality.

While Wertenbaker is no apologist for Tereus, by hinting that linguistic inadequacy has spurred him to his crimes, she avoids creating a pantomime villain. The whole culture of Thrace is shown to be guilty of reproducing the oppressive tendencies that contribute to the play's tragedy, and this is nowhere more apparent than in the scenes which feature Itys. Although only a child, Itys already demonstrates many of his father's domineering characteristics, his linguistic weakness and his lack of tenderness. When Procne tells him he would have liked his aunt Philomele, Itys dismisses her, 'I have uncles. They're strong.'[54] He states a preference for war over peace and, in the penultimate scene, attacks Philomele, shouting, 'I'll kick you. Kill you all. Cut off your heads. Pick out your eyes.'[55] The sense that Itys must be sacrificed because he represents the continuation of his father's line, and its accompanying attitudes, is apparent. In earlier drafts, this was made clearer by the addition of

'Cut out your tongues' to Itys' list of threats. Procne makes this point explicit by revealing Itys' body to Tereus with the words 'If you bend over the stream and search for your reflection, Tereus, this is what it looks like.' This shows the process of filiation as a means of directly reproducing oppression. With Tereus' response, 'I loved my country. I loved my child',[56] this is linked to concepts of nationalism, as in many of the plays discussed in Chapter Five.

The Love of the Nightingale features two choruses: one male, one female.[57] While watching the play-within-the-play, the Queen tells its audience that the 'playwright always speaks through the chorus'.[58] It is unclear whether Wertenbaker intends this statement to be viewed with irony, but in a newspaper article published at the time of the play, she refers to

> a freedom I envy very much in the contemporary novel, that the narrative can stop and you suddenly have three pages of, say, Salman Rushdie thinking about this or that. In drama we are so bound by the naturalistic idea that the real meaning should emerge from the subtext, that there is increasingly little text left. We have even lost the soliloquy. In one way, I was attracted to the idea of the chorus because it enables you to embody thought on stage without having to put it inside a character.[59]

If Wertenbaker does intend her audience *without* to follow the Queen's instructions to the audience *within*, there is a further question as to which Chorus should be heeded. In order to propose an answer, it is necessary to examine the nature of both.

The Male Chorus have no clear identity, either individually or as a group. Indeterminate in number, name and character, they sometimes seem to inhabit a different temporal dimension from the rest of the play but, at other points, are positioned in the quintessentially masculine roles of soldiers or sailors in Tereus' employment. In the original production, members of the Male Chorus doubled as characters specifically referred to as soldiers, reinforcing this association. Although female characters have a strong subjective presence in this work, the more authoritative, narrative voice is retained by the Male Chorus throughout most of the play. They seem to speak as the voice of history, telling us, confidently, 'We choose to be accurate, and we record'.[60] Their lack of characterisation occasionally gives the impression that Wertenbaker *is* speaking through them, for example, in sc. viii:

> **Male Chorus** What is a myth? The oblique image of an unwanted truth, reverberating through time.
> **Male Chorus** And yet, the first, the Greek meaning of myth, is simply what is delivered by word of mouth, a myth is speech, public speech.
> **Male Chorus** And myth also means the matter itself, the content of speech.
> **Male Chorus** We might ask, has the content become increasingly unacceptable and therefore the speech more indirect? How has the meaning of myth been transformed from public speech to unlikely story?[61]

This kind of semantic discussion is frequently present in Wertenbaker's writing.[62] The repetition of this motif suggests that the meaning of words is something that interests Wertenbaker herself, rather than merely one of her characters. A few lines later, the Chorus speak the line that tells us to think of the play in terms of countries and silence, rather than men and women, but should we accept this statement as Wertenbaker's own view? The similarity between this line and other statements Wertenbaker has made (for example, in her introduction to this play) suggests so. However, in sc. x, Wertenbaker disrupts the possibility of viewing the Male Chorus as her own narrative voice by placing them on opposing sides of a debate:

> **Male Chorus** Questions. The child's instinct suppressed in the adult.
> **Male Chorus** For the sake of order, peace.

Male Chorus But at what price?
Male Chorus I wouldn't want to live in a world that's always
shifting. Questions are like earthquakes.[63]

As the play progresses, Wertenbaker distances herself further from
this chorus. Directly before the scene in which Tereus tells Philomele
the lie that her sister is dead, the Male Chorus tell us, 'We asked no
more questions and at night, we slept soundly, and did not see.'[64]
That these voices report not to have witnessed an event Wertenbaker
depicts means that they are lying, or that the story is detached from
their perspective. Either way, they can no longer be seen as reliable
narrators, let alone as vessels through which authorial voice will pass.
In this way, Wertenbaker undermines the idea that the clearest or
most authoritative voice is the most trustworthy.

In contrast to these figures, Wertenbaker positions another group,
consisting of Procne's ladies-in-waiting. Because Wertenbaker labels
these Thracian women a 'Female Chorus' and their speech has a
poetic, choric feel to it, the temptation is to view these figures as
another indistinct group. Sheila Rabillard does this when she refers
to them as 'a *uniformly* unsympathetic audience for their foreign
queen' [my emphasis].[65] However, the Female Chorus is no such
homogenous mass, but is made up of five individually named
women, with definable character differences. For example, Hero
seems to lead the group. She has the most speech and her lines,
usually statements rather than questions, take on a greater air of
authority than those of the others. Iris is the friendliest and most
welcoming to Procne, repeatedly trying to engage with her. Helen
seems anxious throughout, with recurrently fearful and pessimistic
lines. June appears bitter and hostile towards Procne and is always
limiting the potential for dialogue: 'Best to say nothing. Procne?
May we go now?' Finally, Echo's short repetitive lines give her a
child-like otherworldliness. She also tries to reach out to Procne,
answering her statements with echoes of her own words.[66] Rabillard
has argued that the Thracian women are guilty of linguistically
excluding Procne. However, on a number of occasions, we see one
or all of them reach out to her, only to be dismissed:

111

Iris We speak the same language, Procne.
Procne The words are the same, but point to different things.
[...]
Hero We offered to initiate you.
Procne Barbarian practices. I am an Athenian.[67]

Rabillard also accuses these women of seeing 'no attraction in the play of language and philosophical enquiry', an assessment that seems to carry the same assumptions about what constitutes linguistic sophistication as her article elsewhere disparages.[68] The Thracian women may not 'play' their language by the same rules as the Athenians (the rules of logic), but these are not necessarily the only, or even the best, rules.[69] Ultimately, both sisters find their rules fail them. After her rape, Philomele finds no solace in logic, desperately searching for the cause of an event she knows 'isn't reasonable'.[70] Procne expresses the same disillusionment when Tereus' crimes have been revealed: 'the justice we learnt as children [...]. Where is it?'[71] These instances demonstrate that, within oppressive regimes, conventional ideas of language (those based on logic and reason) can fail, be subverted or entirely denied certain members of society. In such a world, it is surely advantageous for the disenfranchised to be able to access other, subtler systems of self-expression and communication that are harder for dominant forces to control. This would seem to be the practice of the Thracian women. In this passage, in which they try to warn Procne of Philomele's danger, it is clear that their linguistic sophistication is greater than hers:

Hero The sky was so dark this morning...
Procne It'll rain. It always rains...
Hero I was not talking meteorologically. Images require sympathy.
Echo Another way of listening.[72]

In Procne's rational experience of language, a dark sky signals nothing but rain. She does not have the 'sympathy' Hero knows is necessary to see beyond the literal and perceive subtler implications.

This inadequacy means Procne fails to hear their warnings, and this contributes to the play's unfolding tragedy. While Procne cannot comprehend the way her attendants use language, they seem to understand her without difficulty. We should therefore see their poetic, metaphorical speech as evidence, not of a failure to comprehend logic, but of a subtle understanding of its limitations, and a means of self-protection.

As introduced in the previous chapter, the practices of psychological and linguistic oppression are also explored in Wertenbaker's unpublished play 'Case to Answer' (1980), which establishes connections between male colonialist attitudes to women and to other countries. Although its protagonist Sylvia resents the way her husband Niko has devalued her voice, she feels forced to abandon it in order to communicate with him, adopting instead the politico-legal discourse in which she knows he is fluent:

> Count one, Statement of offence: theft of language. The particulars of the offence are that by continually ignoring my language, you made me feel it was inadequate. By making me doubt its value, you took it away from me. Count two. Masculine cultural imperialism.[73]

This practice echoes the way that independence movements of colonised countries were forced to negotiate with their colonisers in the Europeans' languages. Sylvia later attempts to shoot Niko with his own gun, demonstrating the ability of the colonised to adopt, not only their colonisers' language, but also their means of violence and aggression. Similarly, in The *Love of the Nightingale*, Philomele and Procne kill Itys with his own sword.

Margarete Rubik has argued that the 'employment of the very methods used for their own victimisation also betokens women's tragic inability to think or act along radically new lines'.[74] She believes that there is an 'absence of a genuine female voice' in *The Love of the Nightingale* as '[w]omen merely perpetuate their submission to old concepts of femininity, or they imitate their male oppressors by reacting with identical forms of behaviour'.[75] These arguments correspond with those I proposed in the previous chapter, in relation to *New Anatomies*, 'Variations' and *The Grace of Mary Traverse*. However, although Rubik's thesis is eventually borne out by the murder of Itys, Philomele's initial attempt to regain her lost voice does not adopt the voice, or the violence, of her coloniser/oppressor. Rather, she employs the highly original practice (or 'radically new line') of re-enacting her story with puppet dolls. Neither does she attempt to communicate directly with her coloniser/oppressor, but addresses her own people (if we extend the woman/colonised nation metaphor, we can read other women as Philomele's compatriots) at the all-female Bacchic festivities. This course of action is successful in its aims of reuniting Philomele with Procne, and communicating the crimes of Tereus. It is at this point that Philomele abandons the more creative and positive line of action represented by the puppet play and adopts the violence of infanticide. Although Sheila Rabillard has argued that, through Procne's response to Philomele's play, Wertenbaker stages the 'need for the feminist critic', I contend that Procne's influence represents a more corruptive force, especially when this episode is considered alongside Procne's silencing of the Thracian women.[76]

The extreme actions of Sylvia, Philomele and Procne justify Wertenbaker's warning that 'Silence leads to violence'.[77] 'Without language', she maintains, 'brutality will triumph'.[78] She links these ideas to her Basque experience and to 'the violence in certain [other] countries where people are denied freedom of speech; it was when all the horrendous upheavals were taking place in South Africa'.[79] This process can be witnessed, on a smaller scale, closer to home. In a 1990 article about Blundeston Prison's production of *Our Country's Good*, Nicholas de Jongh quoted one prisoner's view that 'If I could not express myself [through drama], I would express myself in violence.'[80] Wertenbaker does not fail to acknowledge the tragedy that it is often the suppressed and colonised peoples themselves who suffer all the more from their employment of such methods of resistance. Although Joe Winston argues that Itys' murder can be viewed as 'a model of female violence which is grounded in political resistance',[81] the endings of *The Love of the Nightingale* and 'Case to Answer' do not appear to endorse the adoption of such strategies. Most tellingly, in both plays, the women's revenge backfires dramatically. In 'Case to Answer', the gun, originally aimed at Niko, in fact wounds Sylvia. In *The Love of the Nightingale*, the sisters' murder perpetuates a cycle of violence and revenge, which would result in Tereus killing them both, but for their transformation into birds. This metamorphosis is not presented as a thing of wonder, but of necessity. When Itys asks Philomele if she likes being a nightingale, her response is disillusioning: 'not much, I never liked birds, but we were all so angry the bloodshed would have gone on for ever. So it was better to become a nightingale. You see the world differently.'[82] The fantastical nature of Philomele's mythical route out of cyclical violence makes the need for an alternative accessible to real-life victims of brutality all the more apparent. How, Wertenbaker asks, are they to 'see the world differently', without the view of the nightingale?

Both *The Love of the Nightingale* and 'Case to Answer' seem to advocate the need for their female subjects to find alternative routes out of oppression, which do not simply appropriate the methods of violence they have suffered from. This follows the same trajectory as my previous assertion that Wertenbaker suggests women who seek to expand their access to knowledge, power and freedom, should not do so by aping masculine patterns of behaviour. However, the metaphorical associations that these plays establish between women and whole countries or oppressed peoples, such as the Basques, extend these ideas beyond the gender focus of plays such as *New Anatomies* and *The Grace of Mary Traverse*. All these plays reveal such alternatives to be elusive. In 'Case to Answer', Sylvia's last lines acknowledge, 'When that land comes into its own, battered and uncertain, it ceases to be a place of ease and sunshine. It may even cease to be desirable. (*Pause*) My act of courage was not aiming the gun and risking murder or suicide. (*Pause*) Admire me now.'[83] The final stage direction reads '*She turns to Niko and looks at him, uncertain. He keeps his head down and doesn't look at her.*' This ending gives us hope in Sylvia's new found voice, but emphasises the couple's ongoing communicative struggles, reflective of those faced by newly independent nations. Similarly, in the final scene of *The Love of the Nightingale*, Philomele encourages Itys to ask questions, but when these prove difficult to answer, has to resort to song instead of speech:

> **Itys** What does wrong mean?
> **Philomele** It is what isn't right.
> **Itys** What is right?
> *The Nightingale sings.*
> Didn't you want me to ask questions?[84]

Perhaps this musical ending should not be viewed as an easy way out of communication, but as yet another possibility for it. Perhaps, as a nightingale, Philomele learns not only to see the world differently, but to speak it differently too. Song is, after all, as much a use of voice as speech. It may, although not necessarily, be a less direct form of communication, but it shares, perhaps exceeds, speech's self-expressive qualities. The language of the Thracian women shares some of these features, described by Jennifer A. Wagner as an 'idiomatic speech full of metaphor and images, often as compressed as poetry, that expresses the darker truths of intuition and emotion as precisely, if more obscurely than Procne's language expresses reason and logic'.[85] This description resembles the concept of a distinctly feminine discourse, controversially outlined by feminists such as Helene Cixous and Luce Irigaray. In the late 1980s, some feminist theatres were exploring these ideas and Sue Ellen Case's *Feminism and Theatre* (published the same year as *The Love of the Nightingale*) describes such a language in similar terms to Wagner's:

> [E]lliptical rather than illustrative, fragmentary rather than whole, ambiguous rather than clear and interrupted rather than complete. [...] Without closure, the sense of beginning, middle and end, or a central focus, it abandons the hierarchical organisation principles of traditional form that served to elide women from discourse.[86]

However, it seems unhelpful to suggest that such a language would be the exclusive property of female speakers. In fact, both Wagner's and Case's descriptions bear a significant resemblance to Thiong'o's accounts of Gikuyu:

> We [...] learnt to value words for their meanings and nuances. Language was not a mere string of words. It had a suggestive power well beyond the immediate and lexical meaning. Our appreciation of the suggestive magical power of language was reinforced by the games we played with words through riddles, proverbs, transpositions of syllables, or through nonsensical but musically arranged words. So we learnt the music of our language on top of the content. The language, through images and symbols, gave us a view of the world, but it had a beauty of its own.[87]

In drawing connections between women, previously colonised non-Western nations and a language that privileges expression over logic, one risks reinforcing the binaries of Male/Female, West/East and Logos/Mythos, which many feminist and postcolonial theorists find deeply unhelpful and restrictive. However, I suggest that Wertenbaker offers the possibility of a language that is not exclusive to women, or to non-Western nations, but which specifically benefits the suppressed. By deliberately eluding logic, such a language might allow its speakers to avoid the subjugating labels and oppressive linguistic appropriations they suffer under the dominant culture. It offers a source of hope, available through a more imaginative use of voice, which provides an indirect route towards communication. In later works, Wertenbaker continues to distance such a 'language' from its association with particular genders or races, presenting it as a communicative ideal that anyone can strive toward. For example, as discussed in Chapter Five, the asylum seekers in *Credible Witness* share an uneasy relationship with language, but find certain 'rituals' involving food and music, which recapture and express their troubled identities. In *Our Country's Good*, it is a production of George Farquhar's *The Recruiting Officer* that allows a diverse group of disenfranchised convicts to rediscover and redefine their own voices, by temporarily borrowing those of their characters.

Our Country's Good (Royal Court, 1988)

Our Country's Good remains Wertenbaker's best-known work. It has been widely translated and professionally performed around the world, from Roger Hodgman's Melbourne production, detailed in Chapter Four, to others across Europe and the United States. As Debby Turner highlights in the next chapter, it is also a long-standing staple of university and school classrooms, as well as a favourite with amateur theatre companies. Wertenbaker based the play on the twentieth-century Australian writer Thomas Keneally's 1987 novel, *The Playmaker*, and on factual accounts of the first British transportation to, and settlement of, Australia, such as Robert Hughes's *The Fatal Shore*. Her focus is the rehearsal of a convict production of the Irish playwright George Farquhar's (1677–1707) *The Recruiting Officer* (an event that is historically documented, but the details of which have been re-imagined by herself and Keneally). As Sigal explores in the following chapter, the play was developed collaboratively with director Max Stafford-Clark and a group of actors. A note that Wertenbaker made near the start of this process records her early emphasis on the topic of theatre:

> The argument
> the theatre is a waste of time and resources, pointless, silly, corrupting, evil, dangerous
> the theatre is pleasurable, good for the mind, good for the body, enriching, humanising.[88]

While (as its title suggests) the theatrical process drives the narrative of *The Playmaker*, Keneally's novel is also about the wider colonial enterprise. Relations with the aborigines are an important theme and Governor Phillip's 'friendship' with the captured and 'civilised' Arabanoo is a major sub-plot. These storylines are absent from

Wertenbaker's text, with the aboriginal experience represented by a solitary figure who speaks only a few sentences over the course of the play. This led some critics to accuse Wertenbaker of marginalising the aboriginal voice,[89] and even Hodgman describes the part as 'underwritten'. Early notes and drafts show that, initially, Wertenbaker had attempted to dramatise the aborigines more comprehensively. Her archive contains several pages of research on the first encounters between natives and settlers, and her first list of scenes included 'meeting the natives/the capture of Arabanoo' and 'Arabanoo's illness'.[90] There are early drafts of a scene called 'the encounter between the original Australians and the English as recounted by each',[91] or 'Communication'.[92] These are written with the conceit that the two groups cannot understand each other, but have almost identical lines, such as 'We must speak to them like children.'[93] Arabanoo is present in an early list of Wertenbaker's characters, with the super-objective 'Arabanoo: wants to go home'. This desire, shared by many characters, links Arabanoo to one of the play's central motifs. However, as the play developed, these elements were reduced or omitted for a number of reasons. Crucially, Wertenbaker realised that, although she could adapt existing aboriginal accounts of the First Fleet's arrival to create the short monologues that appear in her final text, she did not 'have the language' to create truthful dialogue for the aboriginal voice.[94] Additionally, there was the practicality of condensing the novel to stage time, and the decision to foreground metatheatrically the play-within-the-play. Wertenbaker's original character list had also featured the convict woman Goose, who does not appear in the final play.[95] Like Arabanoo, Goose has a substantial role in Keneally's novel, but not in relation to its 'playmaking' plot. It is apparent that this is the common feature of all characters and plot elements lost during Wertenbaker's drafting process. Conversely, hardened convict Liz Morden does not appear in *The Playmaker* and was largely generated from an interview Linda Bassett (who first played Liz) conducted with a contemporary woman (see Sigal's essay in Chapter Four).

Although not as literal in its depiction, *Our Country's Good* is as concerned with the loss and reclamation of voice as *The Love of the*

Nightingale. This was a driving force from the earliest stages of the play's development, when Wertenbaker's notes record her desire to explore the 'theme of language' through the juxtaposition of formal English, canting slang and aboriginal languages.[96] At the start of the play, the convicts are a brutalised and wretched bunch; many have adopted silence, either to escape notice, or through a lack of faith in the value of speech. Some, such as Mary Brenham, are so introverted that they barely speak at all. In Act I, sc. v: 'An Audition', Mary allows her friend Dabby to communicate to the play's 'director', Second Lieutenant Ralph Clark, on her behalf:

> **Dabby** You asked to see Mary Brenham, Lieutenant. Here she is.
> **Ralph** Yes – the Governor has asked me to put on a play. (*to* **Mary**) You know what a play is?
> **Dabby** I've seen lots of plays, Lieutenant, so has Mary.[97]

The stage directions attached to Mary's first lines (the single words 'Yes' and 'No') require them to be delivered '*inaudibly*'.[98] Full of shame and self-loathing, Mary struggles to re-imagine herself in terms of the play. 'How can I play Sylvia?' she bemoans, 'She is brave and strong. She couldn't have done what I've done.'[99] Although Mary, it transpires, has *done* very little, her shame lies in what she has not prevented being done to her: a shame of passivity, rather than action. But as Mary's involvement with the part of Sylvia grows, she finds drive and identification through the role. 'I like playing Sylvia', she discovers, 'She's bold, she breaks rules out of love for her Captain and she's not ashamed.'[100] This strength is something Mary can transfer to life outside the 'rehearsal room', using her performance of Sylvia as a way into her courtship with Ralph. When she starts to drop her head after kissing him – a sign of her former reticence, even of shame – Ralph gently admonishes her, 'Don't lower your head. Sylvia wouldn't.'[101] In the play's final scene, Mary has reached a level of linguistic confidence, which allows her to speak not only for herself but on behalf of others. When Wisehammer stammers, 'There's – There's –', Mary intervenes, 'There's his prologue':[102] a complete reversal of the audition scene, in which Dabby speaks on behalf of Mary. Mary also speaks out to ensure herself a centre stage position for the curtain call:

> **Arscott** I'll be in the middle. I'm the tallest.
> **Mary** No, Arscott. (**Mary** *places herself in the middle.*)[103]

This shows not only the confidence to speak but to counteract the speech of another: a remarkable change in Mary's verbal assurance. Furthermore, her ability to create a place for herself in linguistic space consequently enables her to create a place for herself in physical space.

Mary's journey from silence to speech is relatively straightforward. Others, such as Liz Morden, have a more complex relationship with language. Initially, Liz shows greater linguistic sophistication than Mary, at least among her fellows. At the start of Act Two, she has a lengthy and eloquent monologue in canting slang. However, this language fails Liz when she is positioned against the colonial forces of law and order. When she is accused of stealing food from the colony's stores, Liz refuses to speak in her own defence. A number of reasons for this are suggested, from Captain Ross's simplistic 'She won't speak because she is guilty', to Ralph's more sympathetic 'She won't speak [...] because of the convict code of honour. She doesn't want to beg for her life'.[104] When Liz finally explains her motivations, even Ralph, it transpires, has failed to understand her:

> **Phillip** Why wouldn't you say any of this before?
> **Ross** Because she didn't have time to invent a lie.
> **Collins** Major, you are demeaning the process of law.
> **Phillip** Why, Liz?
> **Liz** Because it wouldn't have mattered.
> **Phillip** Speaking the truth?
> **Liz** Speaking.[105]

Liz did not, like Mary, lack the confidence *to* speak, but the confidence *in* speech, seeing no value in language within the society and situation in which she is living. That is, a society that discounts the speech of women and convicts as easily as Tereus discounts Philomele's non-consent. What then causes Liz to change her mind and regain some faith in humanity? The last lines before Liz chooses to speak appear to make it almost crudely apparent that 'the play' is her motivation:

Phillip The play seems to be having miraculous effects already. Don't you want to be in it Liz?
Ralph Morden, you must speak.
Collins For the good of the colony.
Phillip And of the play.[106]

What is not clear from the '*long silence*' before Liz delivers her next line ('I didn't steal the food') is *how* the play affects this decision. The officer's lines are phrased in a way that leads one to assume that Liz has chosen to speak 'for the good of [...] the play', that she values the experience and understands her commitment to fellow cast members enough to see a point in continuing her own existence. However, just because this is what the officers' words imply, does not mean this *is* why Liz speaks. Perhaps by reminding Liz of the play, the officers remind her of the value her speech is accorded during its rehearsal. In Act I, sc. xi: 'The First Rehearsal', Liz objects to Ralph cutting her off before she has finished a speech. Her rebuke, delivered with an exclamation mark, suggests the aggression we expect from Liz. The surprise comes when Ralph, instead of flogging her for talking back to him, replies courteously, 'You're right, Morden, please excuse me.' This is such a change from the way the convicts are used to being spoken to that Liz's next line is specified as '*embarrassed*': 'No, no, there's no need for that, Lieutenant. I only meant – I don't have to.'[107] This exchange might appear unremarkable to the modern ear, but what Ralph does, in affording Liz's speech the same respect as his own, is almost revolutionary (especially when we consider that Ralph is first seen counting the lashes Sideway is receiving for 'answering an officer').[108] Evoking the play that prompted this incident may give Liz just enough faith to trust those around her to value her language.

Liz's decision to speak literally saves her life, but language and theatre are used in equally powerful ways throughout the play. Earlier in this chapter, I argued that Philomele's puppet play attempts an act of non-violent resistance. Ann Wilson has suggested that the same is true of certain performance acts in *Our Country's Good*. Act II, sc. v: 'The Second Rehearsal' is disrupted by the sadistic Major Ross, intent on maintaining the convicts' humiliation. He forces Sideway to reveal the scars of his lashes and makes Dabby beg like a dog as she did to obtain food during the long sea voyage. Finally, he turns to the more fragile Mary, requesting that she lift her skirt to reveal an intimate tattoo. At this point, recognising Mary's intense distress, Liz and Sideway start acting across Ross's interrogations. Wilson considers that this 'act of non-violent resistance through the performance of Farquhar's text marks the success of the project'.[109] Wertenbaker chooses to interrupt Ross's violence with Farquhar's line 'What pleasures I may receive abroad are indeed uncertain; but this I am sure of, I shall meet with less cruelty among the most barbarous nations than I have found at home.'[110] Whether Sideway should seem to appreciate the pertinence of this line is a choice Wertenbaker leaves for director and actor. Therefore, although at this moment Farquhar's text provides a means of resistance, both through its function as a performance act, and through its content, it is the former that is of greater importance, as this is where we can be sure the resistance is deliberate and knowing.

As we have seen, language is embraced by Sideway and Liz as an act of non-violent resistance to oppression, by Liz as a means of obtaining justice, and by Mary as a quiet but firm statement of her right to a place in the world. Beyond these highly theatrical moments, the use of language as everyday conversation develops significantly throughout the play. The final scene, in which the convict actors prepare backstage for performance, drops in and out of a number of conversations, from mundane enquiries about the location of shoes, to heartfelt condolences to Duckling over the death of her lover Harry. What is remarkable about this easy babble of voices is its distance from the play's opening scene, in which four convicts speak out, but do not acknowledge each other.

These internal monologues are as far removed from the dialogue of the final scene as the individual speech acts of Mary and Liz are from their initial silence. The sense of self-worth, camaraderie and confidence the convicts gain through this process is underlined by the celebratory mood as the play ends '*to the triumphant music of Beethoven's Fifth Symphony and the sound of applause and laughter from the First Fleet audience*'.[111]

Its exhilaratingly '*triumphant*' ending made *Our Country's Good* instantly popular with audiences. One reviewer described a performance at which 'after three curtain calls and the houselights up, the audience still obstinately refused to stop applauding until a fourth and much delayed call was made'. 'This is the very stuff of the theatre', he enthused.[112] Stafford-Clark remembers this unprecedented response: 'Three standing ovations at the end of a play is difficult, it's never easy in England, it's not a tradition in this country. There were standing ovations every night at the end of *Our Country's Good*.'[113] When the Court revived the production in 1989, the company were so used to taking four curtain calls per performance that Show Reports record the exceptions: 'A three-curtain-call audience (i.e. the usual screaming adulation to which we have become accustomed was not quite there tonight!)'.[114]

The play was equally popular within the theatre industry, where, as Stafford-Clark recognised, it 'struck a big chord [with those] under considerable stress and quite demoralised after ten years of fighting a government which had no sympathy with it'.[115] Sara Freeman agreed that the play's 'redemptive message was both a balm to the battered sensibilities of the British artistic community and a political statement of opposition against the policies of a conservative government'.[116] When reprised in 1989, the twin productions of *Our Country's Good* and *The Recruiting Officer* were the most lucrative of the Court's financial year, later transferring to the West End.[117] The play's success did not end there as Wertenbaker's text spoke to communities all over the world. Unsurprisingly, the first to pick it up were the Australians. When the Royal Court's own production toured to Sydney in 1989, the last performance 'had a curtain call like the end of a Judy Garland concert'.[118] Soon after, places as disparate as the USA, Romania and Israel were keen to acquire performance and translation rights. Anthony Vivis's review in *Bucharest EUROPE* referred to '[f]requent laughter and applause' that he felt 'confirmed that many lines had a special political significance to post-December Romania'.[119] Wertenbaker also considered the Romanian production a particular success, suggesting that the play had a heightened appeal to those who had recent experience of an oppressive regime.[120]

As Turner's essay in the following chapter recognises, the play's celebration of self-empowerment through language and theatre has made it popular with educational establishments, whether schools or prison theatre projects. Many educators wrote to Wertenbaker to explain what her text meant to those who studied or produced it and her archive is full of letters from students and teachers wishing to interview her or have her speak at their institutions. These requests surged in the aftermath of *Our Country's Good*, until, in 1993, she was forced to stop 'giving any interviews to anyone', due 'to pressure of time'.[121] Among these letters, the most revealing are those that demonstrate an active engagement with Wertenbaker's text: a teacher from a further education college in Sheffield who sent additional scenes a young woman in her class had been inspired to create;[122] a school teacher in London who forwarded a whole class's alternative prologues;[123] the Venturers Drama Group for the visually impaired who wrote to thank Wertenbaker for her interest in their production of the play.[124] These sources seem to demonstrate that Wertenbaker's play is capable of providing a similarly inspirational learning process to the fictional one it depicts: an assertion supported by Turner's experience as a teacher.

Perhaps it was to be expected that such success would provoke a backlash. For *Our Country's Good* this came from the academic community. Some critics argue that, counter to the celebratory atmosphere of the play's final scene, the convicts do not reclaim an original or authentic voice but, like Philomele and Procne (in *The Love of the Nightingale*) and Sylvia (in 'Case to Answer'), merely adopt the voice of the oppressive, colonial force to which they have been subjugated. First to voice this concern was Ann Wilson in a 1991 article for *Modern Drama*. Despite identifying 'act[s] of non-violent resistance' only made possible by the project,[125] Wilson maintains that 'the production of *The Recruiting Officer* is an act of colonising because it is the imposition of one culture on another' and the convicts' participation within it 'amounts to the adoption of cultural values of the dominant community'. She complains that 'the image of England which is evoked by the production is not John Wisehammer's nor Dabby Bryant's [...] but one which belongs to the educated'.[126] After applying Edward Said's theories on culture and imperialism to Wertenbaker's play, Peter Buse came to similar conclusions that, at best, the play 'obscures the link between culture and imperialism for the sake of a feel good ending'.[127] Even Susan Carlson, a very positive critic of Wertenbaker's work, identifies problematic elements within this text:

> So while one might recognise the regenerative power of language in this play, another way to understand [it] is to see that those with institutional power control language, and that the only way to challenge such power is to become fluent in the very language which oppresses you.[128]

Carlson's analysis sounds familiar. Are the convicts' journeys as problematic as those of Philomele, Procne, Sylvia and Mary Traverse? Do they simply adopt the language of the oppressor, and if so, why does the play end in a celebration that can seem to eclipse other underlying uncertainties and questions in the text?

In order to make accusations of cultural imperialism, Wilson and Buse make a number of assumptions about the 'ownership' of culture. They take it as given that the process of putting on a play, and the play itself, are manifestations of a culture imposed on the convicts by those of a higher social standing. I argue that both these assumptions are flawed to varying extents, and begin by discussing the ownership of the cultural *artefact* that is the *The Recruiting Officer*, before moving on to consider the ownership of the cultural *tradition* of creating theatre.

The son of an Irish clergyman of modest means and standing, George Farquhar fell into worse fortune after a financially ill-advised marriage to a widow with children. He dropped (or was thrown) out of college and worked variously as an actor, playwright and recruiting officer. None of this biography points to a man of high social status and accordingly, although some officers in *Our Country's Good* uphold him as an example of high culture, there may be just as much reason for the convicts to claim him as one of their own. Additionally, far from being chosen as a vehicle for the dissemination of particular cultural values, *The Recruiting Officer* is produced simply by virtue of it being one of the few 'odd play[s]' transported to Australia.[129] In an earlier draft of Act I, sc. iii: 'Punishment', Collins reveals that the fleet's 'entire supply of literature consists of 30 copies of the gentleman's magazine, four bibles, one copy of *Lady Jane Grey* and two copies of *The Recruiting Officer*.[130] These material circumstances, rather than any ideological ones, lead to the uptake of Farquhar's text. In fact, some of the more draconian officers express concern that the play may 'teach [...] insubordination, disobedience [and] revolution',[131] because 'it makes fun of officers, it shows an officer lying and cheating [and] shows a corrupt justice'.[132] Equally, an element of subversion is highlighted in Ross's response to what is now considered a great work of 'English' literature: 'An Irishman! I have to sit there and listen to an Irishman!'[133] Perhaps Farquhar, like Wertenbaker, can be seen as a writer with a floating identity.

Wertenbaker is dubious about using plays to spread specific polemics, claiming that 'was the dream of one generation in the sixties and seventies. Worthy, idealistic, I was there at the end of it [...]. And then, I learnt some modesty.'[134] In *Our Country's Good*, she communicates this scepticism by giving the ineffectual Reverend Johnson (described as 'an ass')[135] ridiculous lines, such as 'The play doesn't propagate Catholic doctrine, does it?' and 'It sanctions Holy Matrimony then?'[136] As noted by Christine Dymkowski, the 'problem of a play's content is one to which Wertenbaker returns throughout *Our Country's Good*: she is careful to distinguish between the dramatic text per se and the collective experience of theatre-making and theatre-going'.[137] In other words, Wertenbaker presents the *process* of theatrical involvement, rather than the cultural artefact of the play text, as the transformative and redemptive force at work. Dymkowski believes the play 'locates this capacity in rehearsal more than in performance'[138] and Stephen Weeks explains that while '[r]ehearsal tends towards an open ended and dialogical process emphasising choice and agency; performance tends towards fixity and the insertion of the actor into a larger structure generative of meanings far beyond the range of individual choice'.[139] These interpretations are endorsed by the fact that *Our Country's Good* details the convicts' rehearsal process (highlighting this in the titling of a number of scenes: 'An Audition', 'The Women Learn their Lines', 'The First Rehearsal', 'The Second Rehearsal'), but ends this journey as the performance begins, avoiding the 'fixity' and disenfranchisement described by Weeks.

If we accept that *Our Country's Good* accords greater value to theatrical process than theatrical artefact, we must ask whether there is anything innately 'colonising' or culturally imperialistic about rehearsing a play. Wertenbaker's text does not appear to suggest so. From the start, it is made clear that theatre is not an alien art-form to the convicts. Dabby claims that she and Mary have 'seen lots of plays', and although one might question the authenticity of her boast, it seems to hold weight when she explains insightfully that 'in all those plays, there's always a friend. That's because a girl has to talk to someone and she talks to her friend'. Robert Sideway shows his appreciation of 'the pinnacle, the glory of the day: Drury Lane. The coaches, the actors scuttling, the gentleman watching, the ladies tittering.' Again, any suspicion that his interest is purely motivated by the availability of handkerchiefs at such events is tempered by a sense of genuine knowledge, concerning 'Mr Garrick, the lovely Peg Woffington. (*Conspiratorially*) He was so cruel to her. She was so pale.'[140] Even far removed from these London scenes, Irishman Ketch has been bitten by the theatre bug: 'Some players came to our village once. They were loved like the angels, Lieutenant, like the angels. And the way the women watched them – the light of a spring dawn in their eyes. [...] Lieutenant – I want to be an actor.'[141]

Related to the assumption that the theatre is not the cultural property of the convicts is the supposition that it *is* the cultural property of the officer class. Once again this presumption does not sit comfortably with evidence from the text. The majority of officers fall into two positions on theatre: those who think it socially and morally dangerous and those who show no interest. The first position is voiced by Ross, who believes 'order will become disorder' as 'theatre leads to threatening theory', and the Reverend Johnson, who upholds the cliché that 'actresses are not famed for their morals'. In the latter camp are the scientist Dawes, who sees no point in a play as it 'won't change the shape of the universe', but no harm in it '[a]s long as I don't have to watch it', and the ever-practical Captain Tench, who argues that 'if you want to build a civilisation there are more important things than a play'.[142] Of the few officers who support the play, Ralph is initially motivated entirely by his own desire for self-advancement. This is clear in Harry's surprise ('I didn't know that Ralph') when Ralph asks him to tell Governor Phillip how much he likes theatre.[143] Even Captain Collins, who is in favour of the project as a social experiment, says little about theatre itself and is largely motivated by his dislike for Tench and Ross.

From this evidence, it would seem that the production of *The Recruiting Officer* is less a high cultural dictate imposed upon the convicts by their superiors, than something the convicts desire very much and is very nearly suppressed by opposition from above. This model fits closely to the stories of modern-day prisoners with whom Wertenbaker communicated. All speak glowingly of the benefits of theatre projects. One writes of 'drama as a refuge against the hopelessness of prison life [...], turning us, as individuals, into better human beings' and helping 'to dispel the preconceived notions which society has of the prison community'.[144] Yet many also record significant opposition to such work:

This production has had a couple of setbacks; there was a riot here a few weeks ago (none of my group were involved) and the governor seized the play they were rehearsing and hoping to perform (Snoo Wilson's 'THE GLAD HAND') and completely vetoed it. As they had been working on the play for three months without a director this was an enormous test of their patience and again, they impressed me by their reaction.[145]

Anyway alls going well and then one of the actress [sic] bought in as a birthday present for one of the bloke a glass frames picture, someone jealous person grass's, security finds out end of play. The poxy excuse they come up with was it was glass. Big deal I can go down the canteen and buy a bottle of tomato sauce, no difference, glass is glass they just wanted an excuse [sic].[146]

There is also evidence that the appetite for theatre within contemporary prisons extends to those wishing to watch rather than act. Joe White, who played Ralph Clark in the first prison production of *Our Country's Good* and went on to work in the professional theatre, has criticised the 'perception by the prison authorities of prisoners being intolerant towards serious theatre'. He considers that 'such audiences have proved to be the most receptive and appreciative [...] one could hope to perform to'.[147] The desire for theatre-making among both real-life and Wertenbaker's fictional convicts at the very least complicates Buse's and Wilson's charges of cultural imperialism. However, it is also important to consider the way culture is consumed during these projects.

Much of the critical debate concerning the convicts' interaction with Farquhar's play has focused on the character of Liz Morden. Liz is a particularly hardened convict, described by Phillip as 'lower than a slave, full of loathing, foul mouthed, desperate', and consequently central to his social experiment: 'To be made an example of [...], by redemption'.[148] By the play's penultimate scene, Liz has learnt the value of participating in her masters' language. She demonstrates this by speaking to defend herself and with her response to Phillip wishing her well for the play: 'Your Excellency, I will endeavour to speak Mr Farquhar's lines with the elegance and clarity their own worth commands.'[149] Some critics interpret this speech positively:

Theatre, it seems, can empower women with some degree of linguistic franchise. The ability to command many voices and to play many parts [provides] survival strategies for women. Those women, ostensibly powerful, who lack linguistic versatility [...], appear dramatically weak. While those who can switch linguistic codes according to context enjoy greater power whatever their status.[150]

However, others suggest that the line shows Liz's capitulation to a language, and model of civilisation, that is not her own. If, as critical theorist Theodor Adorno proposes, '[d]efiance of society includes defiance of its language', then Liz's capacity for resistance is surely reduced by this remark.[151] Yet several critics recognise the ambiguity in this moment of the play:

Language has reclaimed her; she has succumbed to the discipline of playmaking rather than the discipline of the scaffold. Yet her reclamation is a form of dispossession, for she has acquired a language that does not allow her any determination of self.[152]

When Liz speaks the King's English, there is inscription: the moment confirms a degree of consent to the captain's essentially colonial vision [but] because the ratification is performative it is fundamentally ambiguous. Sincerity or irony? The dignity of class position, expressed in well-balanced sentences, or its mockery?[153]

This recognition of the performative nature of Liz's statement is crucial. If we accept that Liz is performing this line (role-playing *within* the role), it can be read as a demonstration of her knowing appropriation and manipulation of certain elements of her masters' language to serve her own purpose. We already know Liz is intelligent and articulate in her own dialect (canting slang). That she could subconsciously absorb the language of the play and naturalise it to this extent seems unlikely; rather, we should assume she has consciously interacted with it. This is further evidenced by the difference between the fluency and appropriateness of this remark, and her stilted delivery of lines she has learnt, but does not understand, at the first rehearsal. Finally, in her remark to Phillip, Liz does not quote the play, she creates her own words 'in the style of' the play: a very active engagement with the source text. The range of critical interpretations of this moment reflects the subtlety of Wertenbaker's writing and, in performance, decisions made by actors and directors can affect its impact significantly.

Liz is not the only convict to engage creatively with Farquhar's text. Wisehammer uses the play as a starting point for his own writing: appropriating and reinterpreting it to generate greater meaning for himself and his fellows. Sideway is so inspired by the project that he endeavours to set up his own theatre company once he has earned his freedom, an aim realised by the historical figure on which his character is based.[154] These ventures give the characters a reason to see Australia as a new beginning, rather than an end to their lives. Although they benefit the authorities, who need the convicts' rehabilitation to successfully colonise Australia, they also give hope to the convicts. While the play quells some of the convicts' rebelliousness, it does so by gradually improving their quality of life, making it hard to argue that their continued misery would be preferable. Furthermore, not all the convicts are pacified in this way. Dabby, who is left planning her escape in the final scene, is certainly not:

> **Arscott** When I say my lines, I think of nothing else. Why can't you do the same?
> **Dabby** Because it's only for one night. I want to grow old in Devon.[155]

Wertenbaker does not shy away from the reality that some never find the play an adequate means of self-expression. Wisehammer enjoys the project as a whole, but recognises that *The Recruiting Officer*'s formal prologue 'won't make any sense to the convicts'.[156] Dabby faults the play more generally for failing to represent the people she knows. 'I want to see a play that shows life as we know it', she complains, questioning Mary's identification with Sylvia: 'She hasn't been poor, she hasn't had to survive, and her father's a Justice of the Peace. I want to play myself.'[157] By presenting dissenting voices alongside those that prize the play, Wertenbaker avoids the naivety of which her work has sometimes been accused. Even the final, triumphant scene, charged with obscuring 'the link between culture and imperialism',[158] contains several disruptions to this mood; Ralph tells Mary they will name their baby after his wife, and (despite Hodgman's assertion that the Aborigine in his production developed 'a rapport and empathy with the convicts, whom he recognised as being oppressed by the same group and class that was invading his country') Sideway hopes selfishly that the Aborigines, who gather round the camp because they are dying of smallpox, 'won't upset the audience'.[159] As Carlson has discussed, productions can emphasise the play's problematic moments or its celebratory ones, and these decisions have considerable influence over whether an audience is left in critical thought or on an emotive high.[160] Wertenbaker claims her intention was to create a 'dark play that had some jokes in it', admitting that in subsequent productions she has seen the 'danger that it becomes much lighter. Obviously I wanted to celebrate something, but it is not a happy play. It ends well for a moment but there is some doubt about it. In reality, it isn't a happy end.' Perhaps the harshest reminder of this ambiguity is the real-life suicide of 'Josie', the Clean Break member, whose interview contributed so much to the character of Liz Morden. Wertenbaker acknowledges the tragedy of this, but also the triumph that 'for one part of her life she had regained a sense of self because of a teacher at Holloway'.[161]

The historical circumstances of the original production shed much light on the company's desire to present a celebratory view of theatre. By 1988, British subsidised theatre had been starved by almost a decade of Margaret Thatcher's Conservative government. Repeated funding cuts forced theatres further towards compromising sponsorship deals and commercial viability, often at the expense of experimentation and provocation. In 1988, a 'Theatre in Crisis' conference was held at the University of London and, in 1989, Max Stafford-Clark feared that 'a debate about the future of the Royal Court cannot be long postponed. It seems unlikely that we can continue to operate for much longer in the manner we have for 32 years. Our funding is no longer sufficient.'[162]

Not only the professional theatre was threatened; prison education departments, responsible for rehabilitative theatre work with contemporary convicts, were also being cut or reduced to barely operable levels. Prisons were expected to emphasise punishment over rehabilitation and Wertenbaker remembers hearing government ministers voicing Captain Tench-like sentiments about innate criminality:[163]

There was a lot of talk when I was writing about 'born' criminals, just as there had been in the eighteenth century. It was the beginning of the Michael Howard era, although he wasn't home secretary then. [...] I'm not sure if that wasn't also the beginning of the idea that you were genetically criminal. I just found that so distasteful and so familiar. I mean, we've been there before. [...] It was also the beginning of the devaluation of education [...], the idea that you couldn't educate certain people, that it was hopeless.[164]

As Jim Davis recognised, the play was 'as much a response to the Britain of the late 1980s as to Keneally's novel' (which, Sigal suggests, has much to do with the Joint Stock method of its creation).[165] This is apparent from Wertenbaker's determination to track down the quotation from Rosenthal and Jacobson's *Pygmalion in the Classroom*, which prefaces the play text:

The quote I'm looking for would be from a student who said something like, When I was on that side, or treated like that, this happened to me. [...] In my play [...] a group of convicts totally brutalised by their treatment is suddenly humanised and given hope through the rehearsal of a play. It's partly about the humanising nature of theatre, but also, simply, about these people suddenly being asked to do something and treated accordingly. I need a modern reference.[166]

Notes from the workshop phase reveal that Wertenbaker was also keen to find contemporary parallels for her eighteenth-century characters:

An abused child – now – Duckling
A scab – now – Ketch
A hardened thief – now – Linda
[?] – Sideway
A failure + neurotic – Harry
A [?] + neurotic – Ralph
A shamed – Mary[167]

Tellingly, Wertenbaker's interest in the redemption of prisoners through drama predated the publication of Keneally's novel by almost a decade. Initially, she was influenced by Clean Break Theatre Company (est. 1979), who provide female ex-convicts with gainful employment and a sense of self-worth. While working as a freelance journalist, Wertenbaker interviewed founder members Jenny Hicks and Jacqueline Holborough, and quoted many of their endorsements of the rehabilitative power of theatre in her subsequent unpublished article. From her own experience of prison, Hicks realised that even 'if a person is violent it doesn't help to treat him like an animal. The brutality of prison only leads to more brutality. [...] What you really need is caring people in the establishment, people who believe in rehabilitation.' Her words are echoed in Phillip's view of Liz Morden: 'I am speaking of redeeming her humanity. [...] If we treat her like a corpse, of course she will die. Try a little kindness, Lieutenant.'[168] Hicks's description of 'all ages, all backgrounds and political leanings, but all working together on this one production' is paralleled by the coming together of the initially disparate and hostile group in *Our Country's Good*. Finally, Hicks's account of seeing 'women who had been told all their lives they couldn't or shouldn't do anything suddenly gain confidence working with other women', sets a precedent for Mary Brenham's journey.[169]

As well as interviewing members of Clean Break, the company attended a production of Howard Barker's *The Love of a Good Man* at HMP Wormwood Scrubs. This proved a pivotal moment; 'incredibly moving and relevant', wrote Wertenbaker, 'We then understood why we were doing this play',[170] 'they confirmed everything that we felt; that theatre is dignifying, that it is important and that it is fun'.[171] Since its second edition (1991), a selection of correspondence from inmates who benefited from such productions has been published with the playtext. Wertenbaker saw these letters as a vital addition and 'felt very strongly about having them published [as] it gives another dimension to the play when people put it on elsewhere'.[172] One inmate, Billy Reid, comments:

> I'm glad I took the plunge into Drama when I did. Initially I joined to refine my speech and learn how to communicate with other people. Those reasons must come across really stupid to someone like yourself who knows a lot about the theatrical world, well wotever I got a lot-lot more than wot I'd expected. That wasn't all down to the acting side of it but more down to O.C's.G. and the part of Harry. I got so much out of that play.[173]

It is revealing that Reid cites the desire to refine his speech, which could be considered colonising under Buse's or Wilson's arguments, as his motivation for taking up drama. Perhaps this was influenced by authorities, but even so, he records having 'got a lot-lot more' from the project. Thus, Reid, like many of Wertenbaker's fictional convicts, surpassed the bounds of the civilising experiment, making it his own. Such ownership was vital to Wertenbaker's conception of her play. She insisted that it was 'because the characters discovered [the value of theatre] for themselves' that *Our Country's Good* 'ended up an up note'.[174] In the next chapter, Hodgman describes the equally transformative results of 'playmaking' with a group of juvenile prostitutes in Vancouver's West End. These real-life endorsements of the transformative power of theatre give further justification to Wertenbaker's largely positive articulation of this theme.

Reviews of *Our Country's Good* provide a revealing counterpoint to these discussions. The play's themes of redemption and humanity were remarked upon by many. One reviewer spoke of the convicts' discovery of the 'latent humanity within themselves',[175] another of 'their own natural intelligence', enabling 'their spirits [to] arise, phoenix-like, from the ashes of their own despair'.[176] Such recognition of the recovery of humanity already possessed, rather than the imposition of something new, is the key distinction between conservative and liberal interpretations of this text. Stafford-Clark reported that 'Timberlake's thesis is that theatre has a power – not the power of redemption, but the power to change people's lives, the power to bring out the best in people.'[177] Other critics have understood the play's position within the nature/nurture debate that was dominating discussions of criminality: 'convicts double as officers just by putting on a wig, making explicit the play's point that in every one there is a myriad of qualities and faults that ignorance and poverty or education and wealth can either kill or swell'.[178] However, several reviewers (often writing in Conservative publications) read the play differently, or revealed underlying prejudices in their choice of vocabulary. *The Spectator*'s Christopher Edwards described the convicts as 'pickpockets, whores, murderers and fraudsters', and defined the theatrical project as one to 'introduce the convicts to the possibility of assuming an identity that is not criminal'.[179] Milton Shulman, who referenced the 'civilising nature' of theatre, began his review with the comment 'Of all the desperate proposals that have been made to deal with the hooligans and violent elements in British society, no one has yet suggested that amateur dramatics might help alleviate the problem.'[180] Not only was Shulman misinformed (as highlighted by the company's research into modern-day prison theatre), his analogy carries an implicit disdain for contemporary convicts, as well as those from the seventeenth century, whom he referred to as 'barbarous' and 'savage'. In contrast, he pronounced Phillip and Ralph 'enlightened'. In America, several journalists made equally reactionary assessments. Adele Gaster described the prisoners' 'low moral fiber', concluding crassly, 'even the dregs of society can achieve miracles, the play seems to say. We need to treat even the despicable with kindness to bring out their humanity.'[181]

The most extreme example of morally censorious opinion, believing itself reflected by the play, is Chris Pudlinski's review in *The Register Citizen*. Pudlinski used the word 'evolution' to describe the convicts' journey, implying that the convicts are somehow primitive – less than human – to begin with. This contempt is reinforced by his account of the 'contrast between the well-meaning [Ralph] and the obnoxious inmates'. That Pudlinski had trouble shoe-horning the play into his deeply conservative world-view is evident in his discussion of Act I, sc. ix: 'Ralph Clark Tries to Kiss his Dear Wife's Picture'. This scene is highly charged with repressed sexuality, and often directed to imply (or explicitly present) an element of masturbation.[182] Pudlinski, however, read it as a 'private moment of suffering', 'rudely interrupted' by Ketch, who 'rambles on about his troubles' before admitting that he 'only wants to be in the play'. That Ralph's 'moral struggle is regrettably played down' and he 'succumbs to his lustful passion' for Mary (usually viewed as a positive sign of Ralph's acceptance of the convicts' humanity) is similarly condemned. Pudlinski's closing words voice the very assumptions that concern Buse and Wilson:

It is for the good of England that these convicts are shipped to Australia. It is for the good of Australia that the convicts learn life's refinements by rehearsing a play. The argument of nature versus nurture forces us to ask: Will proper upbringing and education prevent crime or should we just fill the room with a hangman's noose? The play argues for leniency.[183]

Pudlinski reverses almost every element of ideology in my reading of *Our Country's Good*, imbuing it instead with his own moral and political convictions. However, that it is possible for him to do this, shows that, as Wilson and Buse have argued, such culturally imperialistic sentiments can be drawn from the play. Studying both the text itself and its surrounding narratives of real-life prison theatre may lead us to a fairly safe conclusion that Wertenbaker would not endorse a conservative reading of her text but, as Buse explains, 'one of the strengths of the play is the way in which it presents many different voices without privileging any single one'.[184] Joe White describes *Our Country's Good* as 'the "correct" play – one which would satisfy the-powers-that-be', but also one in which 'we had found our voice'.[185] While this duality is a strength, it is also a danger. Wertenbaker resists telling her audience what to think and, consequently, even if there is no deliberate conservatism or cultural imperialism within her text, some have been able to find its latent presence. This is almost a reversal of the process by which many feminist, post-colonial or working-class scholars have been able to read against conservative, patriarchal and hegemonic texts to assert their own interpretations.[186]

It is unlikely that this possibility was unforeseen by Wertenbaker. Returning briefly to *The Love of the Nightingale*, we find another play-within-a-play: Euripides' *Hippolytus*. Extracts of this play-within are accompanied by a constant commentary from its audience of characters from the play-without. Early on, King Pandion states, 'I find plays help me think. You catch a phrase, recognise a character. Perhaps this play will help us come to a decision.'[187] It is no coincidence that Pandion goes to the theatre to make decisions; Wertenbaker is emphasising theatre's role as a place of thought and interrogation. However, it is also no accident that several unfortunate decisions are made in this way. The play's characters relate their own lives to the story of Hippolytus in a number of problematic ways. Pandion likens Tereus to the obsessively chaste Hippolytus, an association that may help Tereus mask his intention to rape. Philomele thinks that the play argues that human beings must obey the gods of love, a view that Tereus twists to justify rape. An audience sees the irony of taking such literal interpretations from a playtext, and thus, by showing her characters misinterpreting the play-within, Wertenbaker warns her audience against misin-terpreting the play-without. As Dymkowski asks, if an 'audience cannot be sure of the meaning of the Greek play, how can it be sure of the meaning of the present one?'.[188] Yet as soon as the real-life audience begins to think it is cleverer than the onstage audience, there is another shift. Pandion takes the line 'I rage against the gods who sent you far away, out of your father's lands to meet with such disaster' to justify his decision that Philomele should not leave *her* father's lands. Philomele's rational response, 'But, Father, I'm not Hippolytus. You haven't cursed me. And Tereus isn't Phaedra', seems to fit with the sceptical view that Wertenbaker has encouraged her audience to take.[189] However, this agreement is juxtaposed with the realisation that Pandion's decision is, in fact, the right one, however superstitiously he arrived at it.

The only overall 'message' it is possible to take from this series of fluctuating contradictions is that it is impossible for theatre to make comprehensively didactic statements; there are always myriad interpretations of any given work. Of course, this is the case with any art form, but it is particularly apparent in theatre, because, as well as the multiple viewpoints an audience brings, the text receives several interpretations prior to its public consumption: those of directors, designers, actors, promoters and the like. Furthermore, although *Our Country's Good* is much more than an adaptation of *The Playmaker*, this source text provided its underlying narrative and influenced many of its characterisations. Thus, it could be argued that Wertenbaker's play resists elements of cultural imperialism contained within Keneally's novel but, although partially successful, is not able to entirely eradicate their presence in her play.[190]

Susan Carlson and Jim Davis have both discussed how the atmosphere generated during different productions of *Our Country's Good* can have a significant effect on our reading of the play. Davis, for example, argues that Wertenbaker presents the empowering possibilities of theatre with a certain irony, but that the original Royal Court production failed to highlight this. Consequently, he proposes that the 'fact that neither the Royal Court production nor the critical response to the play recognised this possibility suggests that Wertenbaker herself was ultimately disempowered – exiled [...] from her own language – by the colonizing power of the theatre itself'.[191] If Davis's assessment is correct, the Royal Court's staging of *Our Country's Good* could have contributed significantly to Buse's and Wilson's reservations. Like these critics, Sara Soncini considers the convict production to be an 'imperialist venture' and maintains that the only way to enjoy the celebratory atmosphere of the play's finale is by adopting 'a temporary forgetfulness of the contradictions inherent in the situation'.[192] However, she argues that Wertenbaker knowingly manipulates her audience in this way, in the hope that critical thought will set in once the curtain is down. If, as Davis suggests, these after-thoughts are to be generated, at least partially, by an underlying sense of irony, and if that sense of irony failed to materialise in the Royal Court production, one can see how the text may have appeared more conservative than it does on the page. Such analyses emphasise that those staging plays must consider their ideological, as well as their aesthetic, responsibilities to a text. Equally, academics must bear in mind that the book on their desk is not a complete or definitive text, nor is any one realised production they may use as a case-study. This difficulty is voiced by Philip Gaskell, who asks:

what is the text of [a] play? Is it the words written down on the pages of the author's script, or of the company's prompt-book, or of the published reading text, words which each reader has to interpret for himself? Or is it perhaps a tape-recording of the words spoken aloud by actors [...]? Or is it a videotape [...] from which the viewer can experience the play as a completed work of art, but with his view limited by what the actors, the director, the camera crew, and the sound recordist make of that particular performance?[193]

Perhaps it is most helpful to see the text as a complex web of all these things, constantly reconfiguring itself from each attempt to define it. As Gaskell describes, 'what we get in theatre is a living art: works that are dynamic and developing, not static and completed; plays which evolve with the ideas of the author and are fashioned by the interpretation of the company; performances which are continually affected by the reactions of their audiences'.[194]

Conclusions

In Chapter Two, I suggested that 'Case to Answer', *The Grace of Mary Traverse* and *New Anatomies* demonstrate the need for women to resist patriarchal ideals of the feminine, without simply appropriating patriarchal ideals of the masculine. In *The Love of the Nightingale*, we find similar recommendations for women to 'fight' the physical, sexual and psychological violence of men, without resorting to male tactics of aggression. However, both this text and 'Case to Answer' establish a metaphorical connection between oppressed women and colonised nations or races, which encourages us to extend this reading beyond gender and see if it may apply to other subjugated peoples. *Our Country's Good* shows one such group of disenfranchised convicts, who also take on a new language to survive. There has been some debate over what this new language is. Ann Wilson and Peter Buse have argued that it is a colonial, patriarchal language belonging to the officer class and partially responsible for the convict's subjugation. I contend that it is something more constructive: the language of theatre or of the arts, and a possible example of the alternative discourse that Wertenbaker's earlier plays urge us to seek. This would go some way towards explaining why the convicts' theatrical project is presented in a largely positive way.

In Chapter Five, we will see Wertenbaker move further towards envisioning alternative languages, including those that are no longer linguistic. Such processes demonstrate that, while Wertenbaker believes human beings share an 'inevitable need to speak in order to be', she offers multiple sources of hope to those who have lost their voices, providing they look to original and imaginative solutions, and do not simply assume the tactics of those who silenced them. First, however, we will pause to consider *Our Country's Good* from a wider range of perspectives.

CHAPTER 4
OUR COUNTRY'S GOOD: THREE
PROFESSIONAL PERSPECTIVES

This chapter provides a range of international and professional perspectives on *Our Country's Good*, authored by three experienced practitioners and scholars, who have had a close association with the play. In the first piece, Sarah Sigal discusses the research, development and writing process employed by Wertenbaker and Stafford-Clark, drawing on her wider research into such models of creation. Next, veteran theatre director Roger Hodgman recounts his experience of directing the first Australian production of the play. Finally, Debby Turner provides a scheme of practical and reflective exercises, designed to aid students and teachers in their exploration of Wertenbaker's text.

Creating *Our Country's Good*: Collaborative Writing Practice and Political Ideals at the Royal Court in the 1980s
Sarah Sigal

Our Country's Good is not only one of Timberlake Wertenbaker's best-known plays, the process through which it was developed serves as an important example of an approach to writer–director collaboration designed to develop a play through research-driven workshops. The application of the Joint Stock workshop process to the adaptation of Thomas Keneally's *The Playmaker* not only enabled Wertenbaker and director Max Stafford-Clark to come to a mutual understanding of the nature of the play they were creating, but also encouraged the company to draw parallels between the politics of crime and punishment in the 1780s and the 1980s, carving political metaphor out of historical narrative. The collaborative process that Wertenbaker and Stafford-Clark employed allowed the two to engage with eighteenth-century history, as well as the political issues of the time, through the flexible framework of the Joint Stock method. This essay will examine the process that was used to develop *Our Country's Good*, and in doing so, reach a conclusion about the relationship between Wertenbaker and Stafford-Clark, their own preoccupations that were inherent in the development of the project and the extent of the creative agency of the performers who participated in the process.

In the autumn of 1987, Stafford-Clark, who was, at the time, the Artistic Director of the Royal Court, commissioned Wertenbaker, whose work he knew from previous Royal Court productions, to adapt *The Playmaker* for the stage. Stafford-Clark wanted to perform the adaptation of *The Playmaker* in repertoire with a production of George Farquhar's *The Recruiting Officer* during the summer of 1988.[1] Although Wertenbaker was initially interested in the project, soon after Stafford-Clark approached her, her partner John Price died suddenly from a stroke, leaving Wertenbaker in a state of grief and causing her to turn the project down.[2] Stafford-Clark persisted, encouraging Wertenbaker to consider the project, insisting that she would be fully supported (both professionally and emotionally) throughout the process. Wertenbaker reconsidered, eventually seeing what was to become *Our Country's Good* as an opportunity to write about the redemptive, 'humanising' aspects of theatre and theatre-making. Wertenbaker explains how Stafford-Clark persuaded her to write *Our Country's Good* and participate in the workshops:

Max said, '[. . .] No one will tell you what to write. No one will interfere with the script [but] the actors will do a lot of research for you.' He put no pressure on getting a play at the end because I didn't think I could do a play. I'd pulled out of the workshop at some point before we had started. [. . .] I'd panicked, and I was in quite a state, and that's when he said, 'Just come and try it. Just spend two weeks.'[3]

Stafford-Clark wanted Wertenbaker to understand from the beginning that the approach to developing the script would be structured in order to aid her in researching the history of the period (and, indeed, any aspect of the project) as well as discovering theatrical possibilities for adapting Keneally's novel, rather than dictating the focus of the play. He understood the difficulty of writing and researching a historical play, having workshopped and directed several previously, such as David Hare's *Fanshen* in 1975 and Caryl Churchill's *Cloud Nine* in 1979. Although Wertenbaker had already written one play set in the eighteenth century (*The Grace of Mary Traverse* in 1985), Stafford-Clark hoped the Joint Stock process would give Wertenbaker the freedom to think laterally about the play without having the burden of doing all the historical research on her own, but it would also engender a feeling of community within the company and deepen the working relationship between himself and Wertenbaker. Stafford-Clark remarked that in creating a new play, especially when using a research and development process, that the relationship between the writer and director is 'crucial', comparing it to 'a two-handed trans-Atlantic voyage in an open boat', an uncertain and difficult endeavour necessitating clear communication.[4] Stafford-Clark wrote that, although he had worked with writer Caryl Churchill using the Joint Stock method several times, and they had 'evolved a close understanding', 'it was some years since I had attempted the same relationship with anybody else'.[5] It was important for Stafford-Clark to cement his working relationship with Wertenbaker not only in order to understand her tendencies as a writer and for her to understand his approaches to working as a director, but also to engender trust between the two during such a difficult time in Wertenbaker's life.[6]

The Workshop

In applying the Joint Stock process to *Our Country's Good*, Stafford-Clark was returning to a way of working that he had developed with director William Gaskill (Artistic Director of the Royal Court from 1965 to 1972) while creating such plays as *The Speakers* (1974), *Fanshen* and Howard Brenton's *Epsom Downs* (1977). The Joint

Stock Theatre Company (1974–89) was established by Stafford-Clark, William Gaskill, David Hare and David Aukin, but was later run solely by Stafford-Clark. By the time Stafford-Clark worked with Wertenbaker, Joint Stock had defined the notion of 'workshop' within British theatre as a means of helping a commissioned writer research and develop a script by drawing from the responses of performers to research, discussion and structured improvisation, and of helping the company as a whole to develop an understanding about the themes of the play. The director and performers assisted the writer in researching the subject matter of the project by conducting interviews, reading, going on research trips and improvising around various themes for three or four weeks, allowing the writer to become aware of the theatrical possibilities of what would otherwise have been dense, complex material. The writer was then given nine or ten weeks alone to write the play that resulted from this research.[7] At the end of this period, the writer would produce a draft script that would then be refined during the director-led rehearsal process.[8]

The Joint Stock process provided a system for working with writers in a way that established a balance of power between the creative autonomy of the writer and the director; the director choosing the subject matter and the direction of the workshops, and the writer having the freedom to write the play alone. This was also a process that was achievable within a limited time frame and on a restricted budget, while still facilitating a significant research and development period. Stafford-Clark notes that one of the most important achievements of the company was its ability to produce epic dramas using a versatile, mid-sized cast of nine or ten, exploring an event 'through the eyes of a range of people', often playing multiple roles with cross-gender and cross-racial casting.[9] This process allowed the company to investigate the subject matter first intellectually, through research and discussion, and then performatively, through the improvisations with which they experimented in order to embody the more conceptual, subjective elements of the material, all the time feeling a sense of creative agency about the group process. This is not to say that the process was ever an easy one, as the writers were required to 'surrender a certain degree of autonomy' and leave their work open to the criticisms of the group, and the performers and director were committed to staging a script before it existed.[10] The Joint Stock process relied heavily on the trust developed among the participants: trust that the writer would produce a script that would satisfy the director and performers, and trust that the director and performers would help the writer fulfil his or her vision. Stafford-Clark felt that working within an ensemble, even for only a single production, was the most productive and collaborative approach to making work.[11]

The *Our Country's Good* workshop was designed primarily to provide Wertenbaker with the information she needed to write the play, but also served to give Stafford-Clark and the cast a sense of the history behind *The Playmaker* and a deeper understanding of the different socio-economic backgrounds of its characters. As the cast was researching and rehearsing *The Recruiting Officer* at the same time that it was workshopping *Our Country's Good*, the company had the benefit of the combined research for both projects. This included an examination of a full spectrum of Georgian society: the landed gentry of early-eighteenth-century Shrewsbury (the setting of Farquhar's play, which Stafford-Clark and the cast visited) and the working poor and 'criminal classes' of the late eighteenth century, who would have been those transported on the First Fleet. In developing both projects simultaneously, the performers gained an understanding of the tastes of eighteenth-century Britons, the acting and writing styles of the period and the challenges the settler-convicts might have faced while attempting to mount a production of Farquhar's play. The company read *The Fatal Shore* by Robert Hughes, about the settlement of Australia from the 1770s to the 1840s; Henry Mayhew's *London Labour and the London Poor*, an investigative journalistic piece about London's underclass during the mid-Victorian period; and also the diary of Lieutenant Ralph Clark, the Marine officer upon whom Keneally based *The Playmaker*'s main character.[12] Company member Linda Bassett commented that this historical research had a great impact on the group in terms of understanding the misery, hopelessness and brutality their characters would have experienced, and how different the performers' own lives were from a convict's life in the 1780s.[13] She added that the strange and unintended side-effect of this immersive research process was that, for a brief period, it coloured their interpretation of *The Recruiting Officer*, a Restoration comedy, turning it into a darker play by embedding their emotional responses to the research on brutality and convict life into their interpretation of Farquhar's script.[14]

The process of developing *Our Country's Good* began with a two-week workshop involving Wertenbaker, Stafford-Clark and ten performers, researching material individually or in small groups, sharing it with the company and participating in improvisations, status games, mock debates and hot-seating inspired by the material.[15] Stafford-Clark was aware of the potential hazards of the kind of unfocused research that can often occur when working without a script, so was careful to be as precise as possible in choosing the exercises and source materials used in the process in order to maintain a semblance of focus.[16] For example, improvisation was not employed to devise material that would provide Wertenbaker with the content of the play, but rather to explore a concept inherent in the subject matter; particular areas were investigated in order to fulfil Wertenbaker's specific needs and interests. One technique – which Stafford-Clark had used previously on productions such as Caryl Churchill's *Serious Money* in 1987 – was for a couple of performers to interview someone, gain an understanding of that person, and then allow themselves to be interviewed as that person by the company in the rehearsal room. Wertenbaker comments that this process was particularly helpful for her as a writer because it gave her distance from the subjects interviewed, but allowed her to engage with their personalities and behaviours through the performers' varied interpretations of them.[17]

The workshops were designed to allow the company not only to explore the information that was essential to the themes of the proposed adaptation, but also to understand the characters through different perspectives, creating modern parallels to eighteenth-century situations through improvisations guided by Stafford-Clark. In his study guide to *Our Country's Good*, the director instructs:

Any production set in the past has to discover the differences between now and then [. . .] What are the similarities?
What has changed? [. . .] no exercise or improvisation can be
detailed unless you have absorbed the information first. [. . .]
Wertenbaker's play is essentially fictitious, but a study of that
particular time span is essential to [. . .] place the events of
the play in context.[18]

While some subjects were more concrete and easily researched, for
example, the backgrounds of convicts transported on the First Fleet,
others, such as the concept of brutality, were more elusive. Both
Wertenbaker and performers note this as having been a particularly difficult aspect of the lives of the characters to embody, as the
backgrounds and experiences of the characters were so far removed
from those of anyone in the company. In these situations, Stafford-
Clark combined historical research with games and structured
improvisation in order to help Wertenbaker and the performers get a
sense of what they were trying to understand in a more visceral way.
For example, in order to help the group understand criminality and
survival, the director set up an exercise called 'The Transportation
Game' (outlined in more detail by Turner), in which the performers
were told they had twenty pounds each, but needed forty pounds
to survive. Each 'character' was given a playing card with a different
number denoting his or her level of criminality: how far his or
her character would be willing to go to get forty pounds.[19] The
performers reflected that structured, goal-oriented improvisation
allowed them to explore the criminal mentality more thoroughly
than through research alone. Other exercises used playing cards to
explore topics such as cruelty, social status and politics and to investigate different characters' responses to them.

What became apparent to Wertenbaker during the workshop
was that although the group was beginning to understand the penal
system of the eighteenth century and the backgrounds of those
convicted, it was important to understand Keneally's characters from
a more immediate, contemporary perspective. One of Wertenbaker's
goals was to discover what circumstances might lead someone to

become a criminal in Britain in the late eighteenth century, but also in the late twentieth century. Part of her interest in adapting *The Playmaker* stemmed from a production she saw by Clean Break, a company that makes work with women in the criminal justice system and with those at risk of offending or re-offending.[20] Wertenbaker said that she was so impressed with their work that she met with them and wrote an article about the company (discussed by Bush in Chapters One and Three) for a magazine, who then refused to publish it on the grounds that it was 'too political'; she stated that, 'I was angry at the time and also felt I owed Clean Break something for their honesty and generosity, so there was some unfinished business there.'[21] Wertenbaker explained that during the late 1980s, under Thatcher's Conservative government, 'the prevailing ethos was hard punishment' and, 'that anybody who had committed a crime was unredeemable', a concept that she wanted ardently to disprove.[22] Wertenbaker felt strongly that education in general and the arts in particular were essential in enriching the human experience; in adapting *The Playmaker*, a novel about the struggle of a group of convicts to put on a play in the face of adversity, she could clearly and imaginatively illustrate the human potential for transformation, counteracting the then-popular belief that criminality was innate.[23]

After reading Mayhew's book on poverty in Victorian London, the performers each chose an example of one of the people detailed by Mayhew, and took on what that individual's persona might be, being interviewed by the group, fleshing out their histories and backgrounds, and explaining how they had entered a life of crime.[24] Stafford-Clark would ask the performers to cut from one character to another in order to hear the contrasts between voices but also so that the performers could feed off each other's energy and choices in their improvisations. The director wrote: 'The overlapping gave great drive and energy to the session and prevented the actors either from being too self-conscious or from planning too carefully. It meant they began to work more from instinct.'[25] With these historically researched personas as a starting point, Wertenbaker asked the performers to engage with contemporary stories of poverty and criminality, looking for ways to make the history of Georgian convicts putting on a play relevant to a contemporary audience. Two of the performers interviewed Josie, a woman who had been in Holloway Prison and who was now a member of Clean Break, and recounted her story to the group through an improvised character study.[26] This moment was one of the major turning points in the process, as it allowed the company to see the commonalities between the backgrounds of the criminals in Keneally's book and those currently serving sentences in Thatcher's Britain and that criminal behaviour was not innate but rather a product of a society with a dramatically unequal distribution of income and little chance for those at the bottom of the economic spectrum to advance. This moment embodied what Stafford-Clark felt was one of the greatest advantages of the Joint Stock process for writers; he explained that, 'For the writer [. . .] the focus on meeting people and on the sheer unexpectedness of real life seems to lead to a closer encounter with truth than the theatre often provides'. [27] The flexibility and versatility of the research and development process enabled Wertenbaker to find a way of incorporating the 'encounter' with Josie into Keneally's story, colouring the adaptation with a subtle contemporary feel and endowing the historical research the company had done with a political sensibility. Later on in the process, the group went to Wormwood Scrubs Prison to see a production of Howard Barker's *The Love of a Good Man*, afterward speaking to the prisoners and staff about the impact of the rehearsal process, as a contemporary parallel to the convict production of *The Recruiting Officer* that they were researching. Stafford-Clark noted that, 'We had learned from our evening at Wormwood Scrubs and there was no apology for the passion and commitment with which the actors prepared for their performance.' [28]

Writing and Adaptation

After the workshops, Wertenbaker went away for two months and wrote a draft of the script, while the company continued to rehearse *The Recruiting Officer*. The effects of the two-week workshop can be seen in the script, which Wertenbaker says changed the book 'quite radically'. [29] She noted that when she began 'to write the play in May, everything went in: personal memories, things said and done in the workshops by [Stafford-Clark] and the actors, research and even current events. [. . .] Personal memories tangle with research and fact in ways that are not immediately clear.'[30] By the time Wertenbaker faced writing the first draft of the script, *Our Country's Good* had become more than simply a stage adaptation of *The Playmaker*, intended as a kind of companion piece to *The Recruiting Officer*, it had taken on a life of its own, incorporating the research from the workshops as well as Wertenbaker's and Stafford-Clark's political convictions. After such an immersive research process devoted to the play, it was inevitable that Wertenbaker would write a script that reflected not only her interpretation of *The Playmaker* but also her experience of the workshops and conversations with the company. As Maya E. Roth wrote: 'isn't it reductive to repeatedly refer to *Our Country's Good* as based on *The Playmaker* if we do not in the same breath also acknowledge the play's radical transformation of that novel, and the playwright's equally rigorous work with other source materials'.[31] One of the transformations that Wertenbaker achieved was creating a metaphor from the narrative of *The Playmaker* to demonstrate the redemptive nature of theatre-making for convicts (such as the production's lead Mary Brenham) as well as for those who are emotionally adrift in the world (such as Lieutenant Ralph Clark). She explained that, 'art is redemptive and the theatre is particularly important because it's a public space. That's the crucial element.'[32] From her contact with the members of Clean Break and the prisoner-performers in *The Love of a Good Man* at Wormwood Scrubs, Wertenbaker came to understand that these people valued their experiences with theatre-making because it allowed them to experience a world outside the criminal justice system, where they could express themselves creatively, and was passionate about endorsing and dramatising their experiences. As a result, *Our Country's Good* had turned Keneally's book, which had been focused primarily on Ralph Clark's journey, into an epic play that gave equal credence to all the characters' experiences. The ensemble nature of the play gave the impression that the perspectives of the convicts, the Marines, the officers and the upper-class colonial administrators had equal weight, sending the message that the experiences of the prisoners who had suffered the eight-month-long journey to Australia as well as lifetimes of deprivation were just as significant as the more refined, wealthier and more 'respectable' characters in Farquhar's comedy of manners. In a letter to Wertenbaker, Joe White, one of the convict-performers who had been in the performance the company had seen at Wormwood Scrubs, wrote: 'Reading through the play, there were moments of ghostly familiarity, uncanny likeness.'[33] Wertenbaker explained why she chose to address the issue of incarceration in the form of a history play, rather than writing directly about the inmates at Wormwood Scrubs or the members of Clean Break: 'If you write things in the past you free them of people's prejudices. You can be more poetic [. . .] more imaginative in the past'.[34] Wertenbaker felt it would be easier not only for her to write a more interesting, original play, but also for audiences to focus on the characters in an unfamiliar time period, setting aside (and perhaps later even questioning) their political convictions by watching a play set in the eighteenth century rather than set in the 1980s.[35] In an article on Wertenbaker, John Mahoney wrote that her 'idealism always betrays undercurrents of agnosticism; her political message is invariably tinged with uncertainty'; Wertenbaker felt that in writing a period piece rather than a play about characters with immediately identifiable contemporary parallels, she could be not only more imaginative but also more indirect, allowing audiences to draw their own conclusions about the message (or messages) of the play.[36]

Our Country's Good also embraced a more feminist view of the experiences of the first transported convicts of New South Wales than *The Playmaker*, altering aspects of the novel to make the female characters more dynamic and their roles in the narrative of the production more prominent. For example, Wertenbaker turned the 'beautiful and mysterious' character of convict Nancy Turner, who plays Melinda in *The Recruiting Officer*, into Liz Morden, a more realistic, hardened criminal. In order to make this transformation, Wertenbaker drew on 'hotseating' exercises that arose from the interview between the performers and the former prisoner Josie.[37]

Wertenbaker used this experience from the workshop particularly in the monologue in Act II, sc. i, in which Morden has a chance to give an account of herself and how she came to be involved in various criminal activities, whereas Keneally does not go in depth into Nancy Turner's background or reasons for criminal acts. Performer Linda Bassett (who played Liz Morden) noted that this choice of Wertenbaker's was also the result of the chapter the company read in *The Fatal Shore* about the 'Lizzies', the women who were strong enough to survive transportation and life in the Australian colony. This made the entire company realise that, in reality, any female convict who was able to survive the eight-month voyage on the First Fleet would have to be represented as a more resilient character in the play.[38] This choice is also another example of how Wertenbaker adapted the play as an episodic, ensemble piece that focused on the histories and experiences of everyone involved in making *The Recruiting Officer*, whereas Keneally's book was a more focused narrative that told the story mostly from the perspective of Ralph Clark, choosing to give a narrower context to the convict production.

Although Stafford-Clark maintained that the structure for the play was the same as the novel's, the structure used in *Our Country's Good* altered that of *The Playmaker* significantly.[39] *The Playmaker* is almost exhaustive in its recounting of historical details and use of period language, giving the reader a relatively realistic impression of the experience of the First Fleet. *Our Country's Good* is far more stylised in its epic structure, moving quickly from one setting to another, some scenes being as long as eight pages and others as brief as four lines. The position of being a writer on attachment to an ensemble with a shared purpose encouraged Wertenbaker to create a script which combined rich characterisations drawn from company members' research and improvisations in the workshop, and contributed to the episodic structure of the play. In Wertenbaker's notes from the workshop period, she details the objectives of each character, an approach to characterisation that mirrors Stafford-Clark's.[40] As in previous productions of his, Stafford-Clark used the Stanislavsky-based approach of breaking down the characters' intentions line by line, so as to gain clarity in terms of each character's objectives from moment to moment and scene to scene, as well as their overall journey throughout the play.[41] In addition to the research the company did throughout the workshop, this tendency of Wertenbaker's (which, perhaps, originated from Stafford-Clark) to clarify each character's objectives served to make *Our Country's Good* more character than narrative driven.

As Wertenbaker asserted, the play was not intended to be a 'play about history' (as it was, after all, a fictionalised account loosely based on real events) but rather a 'metaphor' for the resilience of the human spirit.[42] This multi-voiced, character-driven approach to adapting Keneally's novel facilitated the creation of this metaphor, allowing the audience to get to know each character and his or her motivations individually. Roth explained that Wertenbaker 'de-centres the narrative's authority' through 'shifting frames of narrative style' that convey several possible meanings in the 'gaps, tensions and fissions' within the text.[43] For example, the first chapter of *The Playmaker* details Ralph Clark's attempts to find convicts to perform in *The Recruiting Officer*, slowly introducing us to different characters, already settled in the colony, establishing Ralph as the main character around whom all others in the book orbit in a relatively straightforward fashion.[44] In the first scene of *Our Country's Good*, we are shown the convicts in the hold of the ship on the voyage to Sydney, one of whom is being punished by flogging while Ralph Clark counts the lashes. Another recounts his fear of the sea around him and his desire for the female convicts, another muses on his insatiable hunger, and Mary Brenham tries to explain why she committed the crime that led to her transportation; we are given an overview of the horrors of the experience of living in the dark, cramped hold of a ship for eight months, and the human reactions to them.[45] This scene not only establishes the play as an ensemble piece, but allows us to follow different characters throughout the play, deciding for ourselves whose experiences and perspectives we find most relatable, sympathetic and/or provocative. This visceral introduction to the world of the play also gives the audience a context within which to understand the significance to the characters of the rehearsals for *The Recruiting Officer* and how they provided a temporary respite from their suffering. In one of the later scenes of rehearsal, one of the convict-performers John Arscott says, 'When I say Kite's lines, I forget everything else. I forgot the judge said I'm going to have to spend the rest of my natural life in this place getting beaten and working like a slave. [. . .] I don't have to remember the things I've done [. . .]. I'm Kite. I'm in Shrewsbury.'[46] These lines provide a stark contrast to the first scene in which Arscott details the extreme hunger he has been suffering on board the ship, deepening the metaphor of the production of Farquhar's play as an act of hope for the convicts.

Rehearsal and Redrafting

Throughout the rehearsal period, the company would rehearse Wertenbaker's draft script with the director in the mornings while Wertenbaker developed new scenes or rewrote old ones at home. In the afternoons, Stafford-Clark and the performers would show Wertenbaker what they had achieved that morning and then had the chance to work with Wertenbaker's rewrites. After the first read-through of the text, the company felt confident on the whole, but thought that some of the characters were underdeveloped. [47] Stafford-Clark felt that there was no 'through line' holding the play together and wondered if the narrative strand of the romance between Ralph and Mary was a strong enough framework to hold the whole play together.[48] Paradoxically, although Stafford-Clark had specified to Wertenbaker that it was not necessary to achieve a final draft of the play before rehearsals began, in order to take the pressure off her, the process of redrafting during rehearsal was challenging for the whole company. Wertenbaker recalls the burden of having to write new scenes and redrafts of old ones in the early hours of the morning and then come into rehearsal in the afternoon in order to see how the rest of the script was developing, and was under considerable pressure to make the (sometimes extensive) changes to the script demanded of her on a daily basis in order to make the play more coherent.[49] However, this working structure posed a conundrum in that, as Wertenbaker was not present for the first half of the day, the company could not make changes to script until she arrived in the afternoon, but in the afternoon they would also be faced with the task of working with the new material the writer had written that morning.[50] Wertenbaker was exhausted from getting up early every morning, Stafford-Clark felt the strain of trying to balance serving her vision and directing a play that would stand up to critical and audience scrutiny, and the performers found the constant inflow of new drafts of scenes necessary but often stressful.[51] As company member Ron Cook explained, 'It was a difficult process. We had a lot of rewriting, right up to the wire, and during the preview we were still changing it. It was like being in the tube—you come up to street level to find out where you are.'[52] It was not only important for the director and performers to achieve a consistent vision for the play, but also for the writer to continue to edit old scenes and write new ones: two goals which did not always sit well together. As Cook noted, Wertenbaker would not be able to understand whether a scene was working or not until she saw it performed in rehearsal, but the performers would not necessarily be able to perform their roles to full effect until they had a comprehensive understanding of the direction and tone of the play as a whole. It is important to note that this rehearsal period followed that of *The Recruiting Officer*, with only a short break for the technical rehearsal, previews and opening of the latter, so the performers were faced with the task of rehearsing *Our Country's Good* during the day and performing Farquhar's play in the evenings.[53] Despite the fact that the play's premiere was pushed back by four days (thus cancelling the first four performances, much to the Royal Court's ire),[54] Stafford-Clark felt there were not enough rehearsals and noted gloomily in his diary, 'I think we're sliding towards a disaster.'[55]

Stafford-Clark dealt with the pressures of this rehearsal period and the challenges of guiding Wertenbaker through the redrafting and editing process by treating rehearsals as a continual discussion about the play's themes and aims; in doing so, he maintained a sense of structure and purpose during this period without being too authoritarian in his approach and inhibiting Wertenbaker's creativity. Although the process was not without conflict, Wertenbaker,

Stafford-Clark and the performers seem to have avoided any serious disagreements or stalemates that might have impinged upon the production. For example, when Wertenbaker wanted to include a dream sequence for Ralph, which Stafford-Clark felt would not be effective (preferring she expressed his dreams and anxieties through a diary entry), instead of resorting to using his ultimate authority as the director by cutting the scene immediately, he negotiated with Wertenbaker and allowed the scene to be tested throughout the rehearsal period.[56] In one rare instance, Stafford-Clark looked to improvisation in order to work out a dramaturgical issue, relying on the performers' instincts to find a solution. Wertenbaker had not written any scenes that intimately addressed the hangings that were carried out in the book, so Stafford-Clark instructed the performers to improvise the preparation for the hanging of Liz Morden. Bassett played the scene completely silently, but later telephoned Wertenbaker to say that if the scene had continued she would have broken the silence; Wertenbaker noted that she found both the improvisation and the comment Bassett made later to be useful in her rewrites of the script.[57] Production notes from the rehearsal period show that the episodic structure of the play, with varying lengths and rapid changes in location, while providing the company with a flexible dramaturgical framework for their representation of the newly colonised, eighteenth-century Sydney, also proved to be difficult practically, in terms of the necessitation of quick costume and set changes, adding another stressful element to the process.[58] Being an experienced playwright with several professional credits to her name, Wertenbaker was not unsympathetic to the plight of the company, understanding both the nature of stagecraft and the difficulty in staging her own writing. She noted:

I find that I get a lot from actors if they are in tune with the play. [. . .] Stafford-Clark and quite a few others are incredibly sensitive to the audience. [. . .] Because my plays are complicated enough anyway I am grateful for other people's contributions, for a director who can tell me when I am losing the audience.[59]

The writer understood the need for continual discussion of the text with the director and performers and the rewrites she was asked to make throughout rehearsals, recognising the play's daunting complexity and its potential for alienating audiences. As she had already cemented a relationship with the company throughout the workshop process by researching and exploring the world of the play with them, she trusted them to appreciate what she had worked so hard to achieve in the two months of writing afterwards.[60]

Conclusion: The Writer–Director Relationship

The working relationship between Stafford-Clark and Wertenbaker was a highly successful one (successful enough to result in a second collaboration for the Royal Court in 1991, *Three Birds Alighting on a Field*), but not entirely without conflicts and anxieties. As Stafford-Clark was mounting *The Recruiting Officer* at the same time as he was helping Wertenbaker develop *Our Country's Good*, the process was more stressful for him than previous Joint Stock productions. Although being able to work with the same group of performers and being able to engage in the same research process on the Georgian period was highly beneficial to both productions, the strain of staging both a Restoration classic and a new play simultaneously was overwhelming for the director. In his diary entries from the period, he commented regularly on his frustrations with *The Recruiting Officer* and *Our Country's Good*, the limited budget from the Royal Court, the pressures from the box office to produce two productions that would be popular and lucrative, the too-short rehearsal period, and his general exhaustion.[61] He wrote:

> The whole background to *The Recruiting Officer* and *Our Country's Good* was one of financial despair. Through the eighties, the Royal Court's subsidy had been continually cut back. By the end of the decade the Royal Court was able to produce about half the work we had been able to do fifteen years earlier.[62]

The director's entry demonstrates not only the pressure he was under to make the pairing of Farquhar's and Wertenbaker's plays commercially successful, but also the conviction with which he created *Our Country's Good*. The play was not only a product of Wertenbaker's agenda to dramatise the redemptive power of theatre, but also Stafford-Clark's to prove that government subsidy of the arts was as crucial for the production of new work in the 1980s as the support of the colonial government of New South Wales for the convict production of *The Recruiting Officer* was in the 1780s. Fortunately, *Our Country's Good* was hugely successful, garnering rave critical reviews and healthy box office returns and later being produced in various theatres around the world.

The nature of Stafford-Clark and Wertenbaker's relationship fluctuated throughout the process, responding to the small successes and challenges of the workshop and rehearsal period. In a moment of candour, Stafford-Clark admitted that while the workshop was 'a honeymoon', once rehearsals began, he and Wertenbaker, 'drew the bile from each other's personalities', saying Wertenbaker, 'defended her script with pugnacious and inflexible stubbornness while [he] sometimes exposed its shortcomings with malice and a certain cruelty'.[63] The director confessed, 'I don't always get on well with playwrights. Their obsessions are the banner we directors fight under and this doesn't always make for an easy relationship';[64] the writer admitted, 'we did have a lot of fights'.[65] These statements belie both Stafford-Clark and Wertenbaker's ambivalence about the close relationship between the writer and director necessitated by the production of a new play. Although the two did not need to be in perfect agreement during the entire process, and debate and negotiation was often productive, the constant need to be diplomatic about each other's opinions and requests was exhausting for both. Bassett, however, maintained that the two worked well together because Wertenbaker's plays 'go very deep' and Stafford-Clark was committed to the project and the company enough to plumb the depths of *Our Country's Good*, finding out how to make it work on stage. During the process, Bassett felt she could trust the two to create a production worthy of the company's time and efforts.[66]

Wertenbaker herself felt that the director acted alternately as a supporter and a provocateur with respect to her writing, in that he was 'responsive' to the decisions she made, being honest about what in the script worked and what did not, without interfering with the overall content, which was important to Wertenbaker: 'it was wonderful working with him [. . .] because I'm quite defensive, and he's quite ruthless about cutting'.[67] Although the process of developing *Our Country's Good* was an enormously pressurised one that tested the limits of everyone in the company, the groundwork laid by the research and exercises in the workshop allowed Wertenbaker to adapt Keneally's novel in a way that indirectly addressed the politically sensitive issues of the ethos surrounding the criminal justice system and those involved in it, and the decline of government subsidy for the arts; it also enabled Stafford-Clark and the performers to come to understand the writer's process and her aims for the play, and to support her professionally and emotionally throughout the rehearsal period.[68]

Our Country's Good in Melbourne
Roger Hodgman

I read about *Our Country's Good* when the Royal Court first announced it. I immediately asked for a copy. I had read Thomas Keneally's *The Playmaker* and was intrigued to see how Timberlake Wertenbaker had adapted it. I had also enjoyed *The Fatal Shore*, Robert Hughes sprawling and enthralling book about the early days of the Australian colony and, when I read Wertenbaker's script, I wondered whether that had influenced her as well (as indeed it had). I loved the play and thought it perfect material for my company, The Melbourne Theatre Company, one of the two largest subsidised companies in Australia.

When we enquired about the rights, it turned out that the other large company, The Sydney Theatre Company, was already negotiating with the Royal Court to bring its original production out to Sydney. Max Stafford-Clark and his theatre were understandably keen to present the play in the STC's Wharf Theatre, which is located so near to the play's setting. However, I thought it was important to mount an Australian production as well, as I thought then, and still do, that the play captured something quite profound about the Western settlement of Australia. While the play's theme of the redemptive nature of art and its practice was obviously important and immensely appealing, Wertenbaker, wittingly or otherwise, had also provided a chance to explore theatrically and simply the remarkable event that was the founding of that first colony. It is perhaps worth mentioning that, after many decades of feeling ashamed about Australia's convict heritage, it is now a matter of, perhaps defiant, pride to be able to say that one has a convict ancestor. A brief standoff ensued, before it was agreed that we could present our own production of the play to open a couple of days after the Sydney production. Wertenbaker agreed to join us for many of the rehearsals, an experience the cast and I enjoyed immensely.

In preparation for the production I made two decisions that were seen later to set it apart from the Royal Court production, which I had not seen and about which I knew very little. The first, made in consultation with my designer Tony Tripp, was to attempt to suggest the vastness and strangeness of the continent that greeted this small band of Europeans in 1788. Tony designed a beautiful large blue box, subtly painted to suggest a sea and sky, with a row of cell-like openings high along the walls. There were three entrances and a sand-coloured floor. Towards the back stood a tattered flagpole with an English flag hanging limp and a pile of boxes and luggage at its foot. Occasionally a few chairs or a rowing boat broke up this epic space, but in general it remained a vast empty landscape in which the events played out. As Rosemary Neill, writing in *The Australian*, noted:

> Tripp lines the perimeters of the cavernous Playhouse with an imposing modern prison wall. But for the seemingly random assembly of simple props, the stage is bare. Thus – through the specificity of history and the timeliness of metaphor – Tripp alludes to a cell-like confining within the yawning space we call Australia.[69]

My lighting designer, Jamie Lewis, provided the bright clear light that must have seemed so strange to those first English immigrants. A key moment in the production followed the prologue, in which the convicts were closely huddled together in a dimly lit group behind a scrim. At the end of Wisehammer's opening speech, the scrim was flown out, the unique sounds of the Australian landscape were heard, and the convicts stumbled to their feet and emerged, blinking, into that vast set (and continent) and startling bright sunlight.

A second, for me important, decision concerned the aboriginal character, which seemed somewhat underwritten in the playtext. We were considering the production a few months after the Bicentenary celebrations that commemorated the establishment of this first colony. To many Australians it had been brought home to us that, while we were celebrating the European settlement of the country of

Melbourne Theatre Company's *Our Country's Good*. Set designed by Tony Tripp.
Photography: Jeff Busby.

which we were all so proud, the original inhabitants of the continent saw the occasion as the anniversary of an invasion and the beginning of a threat to their ancient civilisation. Even as recently as 1962, the notable (left-wing) historian Manning Clark had started his lauded *A History of Australia* with the words 'Civilization did not begin in Australia until the last quarter of the eighteenth century.'[70] Anyone who has had even a passing experience of the complex culture of the aboriginal people rebels against that idea, and the character called The Aborigine in Wertenbaker's play seemed to provide an opportunity to at least touch on this vital strand of our history.

I invited the distinguished indigenous actor Tom E. Lewis, who had come to prominence playing the title role in Fred Schepisi's fine film *The Chant of Jimmy Blacksmith*, to join the cast. With Timberlake's enthusiastic assistance and support, the character became a memorable part of the production, on stage throughout, observing and commenting. *The Nation Review* critic Barry Oakley reported that the actor was omnipresent and unforgettable: 'Tom Lewis becomes a positive force – still a spectator and victim, but one who makes haunting comment with his didgeridoo, giving a howling, growling dimension.'[71] Tom's didgeridoo was also used to assist scene changes and was the only non-verbal sound in the production apart from naturalistic bird and sea noises and the horrifying sounds of an off-stage flogging. It was, however, vital that this powerful strand of the production did not detract from what I saw as the central life-affirming story of this disparate group of largely uneducated convicts achieving pride and self-respect through the mounting of the play. I believe this balance was achieved by Tom E. Lewis's character developing a rapport and empathy with the convicts, whom he recognised as being oppressed by the same group and class that was invading his country.

The very distinguished cast adored working on the play, embraced all its elements with enthusiasm, and were magnificent. Rosemary Neill records observing 'an awesome dramatic range, straddling emotions from stomach-knotting anticipation to jagged pathos and boisterous humour'.[72] Each scene was rewarding to explore and the actors relished the opportunity to switch from the sympathetically drawn convict characters to the large range of officers and soldiers. Timberlake's supportive presence in the room, the beautiful writing and our familiarity with the historical background of the play all contributed to a feeling that we were working on something special. When I directed another production of the play, with a partially new cast, a year later for the South Australian Theatre Company the same feeling was there.

I believe it was the *story* of the play and what it seemed to be saying that had the greatest impact on those of us who worked on it. We never saw it as being about civilizing the artistically impoverished convicts, but about the redemptive power of artistic practice and pursuit. I had a personal anecdote that informed my attitude to this theme. When I was Artistic Director of the Vancouver Playhouse in the early 1980s, I had received a surprising visit from a social worker who ran a drop-in centre for the large number of juvenile prostitutes in the city's West End. A group of them wanted to put on a play: would I help? With Diane D'Aquila, an actor friend, I directed them in a production of *The Jones Boy* by Tom Walmsley, a well-known Canadian play about prostitution and drugs that the group had found and chosen. I found the group remarkable: mostly victims of abuse or neglect, but with an optimism and sense of camaraderie not unlike Wertenbaker's convicts. None were experienced actors but their enthusiasm and sense of truth and pride in what they were doing combined to make a successful and much praised production. A year later, the social worker visited me again. He told me that of the twenty or so teenagers (most of whom were under sixteen) who had worked on the production, only one was still on the streets and many had returned to education or found rewarding jobs. He thought that the pride and thrill they had felt through working on the play had had an enormous effect on their sense of self-worth. This had a profound effect upon me and the experience informed my approach to the rehearsals of *Our Country's Good*. I am certain that personal experiences such as these connect with why rehearsing the play was such a moving experience for us all. The play seemed to validate the importance of what we do, not just by reinforcing and celebrating our roles as 'playmakers' but by exploring and emphasising the power of collective creation and celebrating the redemptive nature of making art.

Many of the original Melbourne cast still remember *Our Country's Good* with pride and affection. The fine actor Helen Morse (who played Liz Morden) recently cited it in a rare interview as one of the highlights of her career. Bob Hornery (Ketch), when honoured by Actors Equity with a Lifetime Achievement award, also mentioned it as one of his favourite roles. Hornery, an admired veteran of the Australian stage, had approached me with a plea to play Ketch and I had agreed, neglecting to tell him that the character was meant to be in his teens. I worried what Timberlake would think when she arrived, but she proved supportive and enthusiastic, as she was throughout the rehearsal period.

Timberlake did not really tell us how different our production was from the fine Royal Court version, something I only discovered when I travelled to Sydney to see it (as Max Stafford-Clark had

Melbourne Theatre Company's *Our Country's Good*. Cast from left to right: Bob Hornery (Ross), Kim Trengrove (Dabby), Helen Morse (Liz), Robert Menzies (Wisehammer), Tom E. Lewis (Aborigine), and Phillip Holder (Ralph). Photography: Jeff Busby.

done to Melbourne to see ours). Two critics, Rosemary Neill and Barry Oakley (both unusually respected in the theatre community) reviewed both productions and commented on the very different approaches. Significantly, they were equally enthusiastic about both. The fact that the play can bear such different approaches (and I believe it has had many more since then) surely indicates a great play, a classic even.

Our Country's Good in the Classroom
Debby Turner

As outlined in the previous chapter, *Our Country's Good* has been embraced by teachers (predominately, but not exclusively, of drama and theatre studies) at secondary, further and higher education level, as well as education workers in a range of social and cultural institutions. Its appeal is manifold: the wealth of rewarding roles provided by its epic, ensemble structure; the depth of its historical, social and political contexts; the compelling nature of its central argument. I first met Max Stafford-Clark in 2000, two years after the triumphal revival of *Our Country's Good* at the Young Vic. My overpowering memory of that production was the use of a great wooden swing in the centre of the stage that became different locations such as the ship. It was an iconic design for an iconic play, illustrating physically the enormous shifts of opinion for and against the humanising qualities of theatre and its importance in society. In 2013, when theatre in schools is again under attack from government changes in education policy, this play is still so relevant and ready to ignite yet another generation to question and understand the importance of theatre. While observing the rehearsals for Out of Joint's 2012 production of *Our Country's Good* as preparation for the creation of a scheme of work for teaching the play at A level, it felt like part of the zeitgeist. Yet this has also become a classic play, now in its third revival by Stafford-Clark alone. Some of the actors voiced their fears over having so much to live up to, but as John Hollingworth's blog states:

Timberlake's response to this feeling of baggage and predecessors was 'don't be so respectful of the text, enjoy yourself
more'. Max's response came from his past at the Royal Court,
the mission statement of which had been articulated by his
predecessor Lindsay Anderson as 'presenting new plays as
classics and classics as new plays'.[73]

The play is a classic but a classic because of its continuing relevance
in our society and its universal themes.

The following exercises reflect Max Stafford-Clark's techniques
and some of my own that I hope complement his in guiding students
through the text. While these were designed to cover most A level
syllabuses' requirements for practical and exam study of text, they
can be adapted for other levels or abilities by simplifying or intensi-
fying the degree of discussion and reflection applied to each task.

Introducing the Play

In introductory lessons, it is important to gauge what students view
as 'good' theatre and how they see the role of theatre in society.
Later, this can be used as a reference point when exploring the scene
'The Authorities Discuss the Merits of the Theatre'. Students should
be challenged to think about whether theatre's function in society
is purely to entertain, or whether it can, or should, educate. This
discussion should lead to further explorations into what elements
are needed to create 'good' theatre and how the actor–audience
relationship is constituted.

Example exercise: What is 'good' theatre?

*In groups, students create a short scene that they believe uses all the
elements of 'good' theatre. After they have presented these to their peers,
they discuss what they have learnt about their own views on theatre.
To challenge them further, introduce them to Peter Brook's famous
statement, 'A man walks across this empty space whilst someone else is
watching him, and this is all that is needed for an act of theatre to be
engaged'.[74] Discuss the relevance of this statement, and whether they
believe it to be true. Test it by asking one person to sit opposite the other*

members of the group and do nothing. Discuss whether this is theatre, whether theatre can be placed anywhere, or whether it needs a realistic stage to make it believable.

When asked to create 'good' theatre, some students often try to recreate an elaborate scene with a lot of costume, setting and with mostly comic or musical theatre overtones. Others might create a piece with lots of freeze-frames and physical theatre. However, most tend not to focus on the meaning or themes of their scenes, which are usually relationship based and very personal. Therefore, it is important to guide them towards the importance of text, language and the broader themes of a play, and to facilitate them to recognise how little may be needed in the way of setting or location to form theatre in non-theatre settings. This can feed into conversations about *Our Country's Good* in a number of ways. Firstly, the students should be encouraged to think about how the prisoners in the play had to put on their production of *The Recruiting Officer* in a non-theatre environment in Australia in 1789. Secondly, it may help them make sense of the design of a number of productions of *Our Country's Good*, the majority of which do not use a realistic set.[75] The Out of Joint website contains a number of photographs and a trailer from their 2012 production of the play, which can be used to provoke a discussion about this and about the students' first impressions of what the play is about and what the characters might be like.

To cement the ideas explored in these exercises and discussions, students can write an essay exploring 'What is theatre?' This can prove a useful reference point later in the course when the students can reread what they put and monitor how far their ideas have changed after studying the play.

Social, Cultural, Historical and Political Contexts

As detailed in Sigal's essay, one of the key elements of Stafford-Clark's rehearsal process is research. Before the actors begin rehearsing they are expected to have read Robert Hughes's *The Fatal Shore*, a book that describes the transportation of 160,000 men, women and children, often for petty crimes, and how they proceeded to found a new nation. Stafford-Clark quotes L. P. Hartley, 'The past is a foreign country; they do things differently there', to emphasise the role research must have in understanding the play and its characters.[76] In rehearsals for his 2012 production, the actors brought examples of their own research about their characters and the social, historical and political contexts of their lives to share with their fellows in between working on the text.

As well as *The Fatal Shore*, a work pack available from Out of Joint and Stafford-Clark's *Timberlake Wertenbaker's Our Country's Good: A Study Guide* can be used to introduce students to historical information, such as the details of the Georgian judicial system that created the Transportation Act, which allowed the displacement of criminals to Australia to happen. Students can be set research tasks, leading to presentation and discussion, on topics such as 'What were the rules of the Georgian judicial system?'; 'What did John Locke believe about punishment and why was this so important in the way prisoners were treated?'; 'What types of crimes could someone be transported for?'

Example exercise: The transportation game
Working in pairs, students are given three playing cards, the numbers on which denote the severity of the crimes they have committed. A king can be used for a pardon and a queen means a woman is pregnant, which can save her from hanging, but not from transportation. The pairs must imagine the crimes they have committed with a severity that corresponds with the number on the card. For example, an eight may mean they have stolen a sheep: a hangable offence. Students should be encouraged to research the sorts of crimes that did occur at the time of the First Fleet. The teacher then draws a card and if it is higher than the students' card, they are caught, hanged and out of the game. If lower, the students get the points value of their card and get away with it. The aim of the game is to get the most points and therefore money and avoid hanging or transportation.

This exercise can be used to explore what the students have learnt about the fairness of sentencing. In the 2012 rehearsals,

Stafford-Clark was especially keen to make sure that the crime the actors chose fitted the number on their card and would only accept suitably appropriate crimes, not over-exaggerated or impossible ones. The actors became quite inventive and at the same time learnt a lot about what types of petty crimes could lead to transportation.

In 1988, when the play was written, Margaret Thatcher's Conservative government had ushered in an era of 'popular capitalism' based on individual consumerism and the commodification of all social provision. Thatcher once said, 'There is no such thing as society: there are individual men and women, and there are families.'[77] Any collective view of the world or a sense that there could be socialised provision of welfare was anathema. Additionally, in the mid 1980s, the crime prevention world was paying close attention to the writings of the right-wing American criminologists James Q. Wilson and George Kelling. Wilson and Kelling urged the police to concentrate on policing disorder and minor criminality to prevent the social decay of an area and the eventual increase in serious crime. They believed in zero tolerance and that education in schools should adhere to moral values and promote social control. Little interest was paid to the potential causes of criminality, with Thatcher claiming, 'Crime is crime is crime, it is not political.'[78] One of the main themes in *Our Country's Good* meets these views head on by presenting the argument over whether the rehabilitation or the punishment of prisoners is paramount. Students should be asked to consider how contemporary views on the punishment, rather than the rehabilitation of, prisoners, might have affected the writing of *Our Country's Good*.[79]

Example exercise: Campaign adverts

Divide students into two groups. One group creates a political campaign advert for the punishment of prisoners, the other creates one for their rehabilitation. This can be done with reference to the present day, the 1700s or the 1980s.

The letters between Joe White and Timberlake Wertenbaker regarding the rehabilitating qualities of theatre for prisoners, published alongside most copies of the playtext, are a valuable resource for these debates. The Out of Joint website also features a video about the research the actors did by speaking to modern-day prisoners. All these resources and exercises help the students understand the world of the play and its relevance to modern society. Encourage them to refer back to their original ideas about theatre and its function to see whether they have changed.

In Stafford-Clark's rehearsal room, research helped the actors understand the world of the characters and more about the characters themselves. It also became a part of their bonding as a company. I watched as the actor playing Ralph read from Ralph Clark's diaries about how watching the women being flogged is a necessary part of his job. The actors then discussed Ralph's character together, establishing a common frame of understanding. Stafford-Clark uses this sharing of research and ideas as a way to help form an ensemble and avoid actors learning their roles in isolation.

Actioning

Stafford-Clark spends the first two weeks of a rehearsal process 'actioning' the script. 'An action has to be expressed by a transitive verb and gives the character's intention or tactic for that particular thought.'[80] In the 2012 rehearsals, Stafford-Clark asked the actors to read from the script, stating the action before each line. Next they acted the scene speaking the actions and the lines and, finally, playing the lines with the actions but without voicing them. This process gave a very detailed ensemble understanding of each character's motivations for saying each line and the under-lying meaning of the scenes. It helps actors and students gain an understanding of the subtext. While actioning the whole text is not feasible in the limited time available to teach students, this method should be applied to key scenes. In rehearsal, Stafford-Clark intersperses actioning with the reading out of character research done by the actors. More detailed information on actioning can be found in the study guide by Stafford-Clark and Maeve McKeown.[81]

Example exercise: Actioning tableaux
In fours, students create four tableaux to show the shifts in status during Act I, sc. viii. They choose one action (a transitive verb, for example, 'humiliates') for each tableau. Discuss what these tell us about the relationships between the women and Ketch, how the women change towards each other when he enters the scene and how the women use language to gain status over him. Act the scene using one or all of the tableaux as well as the dialogue.

Example exercise: Actioning Act I, sc. vi
Work with the students to find transitive verbs to action the text. Play the scene with no lines and just the actions, using body language and non-verbal communication to communicate the verb. This makes the actors think about using their whole bodies to communicate meaning. Next, act the scene using actions and lines and, finally, act the scene as written, noting how the students' understanding of the scene and subtext has changed.

This method is at the heart of Stafford-Clark's techniques, working to establish a common frame of reference and discover subtext and underlying objectives for the characters within a scene. For students, it is an excellent tool to use when preparing scenes for public performance or practical examination, or for understanding the subtext and meaning of the lines and themes of the play for written exams and essays.

Language
As Bush has discussed in detail, Wertenbaker explores the power of language in society and how social status is affected by the characters' understanding of, and love for, language. The convicts and officers are set apart by their use of language, especially their choice of words or slang. The ability to read gives Mary Brenham access to social status, allowing her to gain the lead in the play and eventually the recognition and love of Ralph and Wisehammer. Students often find it difficult to discuss language in essays and the following exercises can help them identify how the use of language

in precise scenes from the play reveals the development of characters and their function in society.

Example exercise: The ten commandments

This is essentially a writing exercise. Each student writes down the spoken or unspoken rules of behaviour of their own family: their 'ten commandments'. Next they write the ten commandments of the criminals, and finally, those of the officers. Sharing these lists should prompt discussion about the hegemonic ideas of society and how they affect individuals.

When I tried this exercise out at a training day for fellow teachers, we rediscovered a lot of negative rules that participants had subsequently broken from their own families, as well as some they had continued to follow and were often shocked they still believed in. When considering the rules of the officers, many participants find the need to define which officers they are referring to, as different officers have such opposing beliefs, but some common ground can still be found. The exercise provokes great debate and is always a valuable tool for creating a response from students.

Example exercise: Vocabularies

Give out a list of slang used by the convicts and another of words used by the officers. In pairs, the students create a short dialogue as either criminals or officers. Encourage the students to concentrate on communicating the social class of the characters through body languages and proxemics as well as language. Present the scenes and discuss what has been learnt about the importance of language in communicating character and social class.

Example exercise: Exchanging words

In pairs, students read through Act I, sc. x. Discuss what the ability to read and write and the knowledge of language gives Mary and Wisehammer in this society and situation. Now give each student a playing card; the higher the card the more they love words. Perform the scene again and discuss how this affects our views about the characters.

At the training day, the teachers acting out this scene found it immediately clear which number worked for Mary and Wisehammer and it was extremely difficult to play the scene with any other combination of values. The discussion then explored how useful this exercise was in helping students to understand the subtext and underlying emotions of the scene. Stafford-Clark also uses playing cards to explore how much Wisehammer and Mary like each other in this scene.

Developing Characters

There is often so little time to explore character and text effectively within lessons, so I have developed exercises that ask fundamental questions about the characters students are to play in a performance or discuss in an exam, in a practical way that allows them to utilise their research and connect it to the scenes directly. The students' individual research and creation of character biographies will help guide these exercises.

Example exercise: Objects

Students are asked to imagine an object that is in their character's possession, either in their bedroom, tent or pocket. They write down what that object means to their character, where they got it from, who gave it to them or where they bought or stole it, as well as the emotions it makes them feel, the memories attached to it and how they would feel if it was lost or taken from them.

This exercise enables students to connect more fully with their character and understand the emotional intensity an object can evoke. As the prisoners were allowed so few possessions, this becomes an even more poignant exercise.

Example exercise: Five steps

Each student takes one of the play's main characters and stands with their eyes closed. When directed, they step into five important events in their character's life. For example, the day they were sentenced to transportation, the day they got to Australia, or the day they discovered that there was going to be a play. For each step, ask them the questions: Where are you? What is happening? How do you feel? Discuss what this reveals about the characters.

This off-text exercise prompts students to delve into their imagination and learn a lot very quickly about events that may have happened to the characters before the play, in an emotional, as well as factual, capacity. This makes the characters' lives more accessible and reminds students that the characters' lives do not begin and end with the timeframe of the playtext, but that they are rounded human beings and their pasts influence how they behave within the play.

Example exercise: Duckling's vows
Working on Act II, sc. viii in pairs, give each actor playing Duckling a playing card; the higher the card, the stronger Duckling feels about losing Harry, and the more convincing her vows become. If she is convincing enough, Harry wakes and lives. Present the scenes and discuss how the differences in interpretation of the strength of Duckling's emotions change the meaning of the scene and the relationship between Harry and Duckling. This may be led into a discussion about the importance of a relationship with an officer for a convict's quality of life and what will happen to Duckling and Harry's possessions when Harry dies.

In the 2012 rehearsals, the actress playing Duckling was able to revive Harry with a high card. Her strength of feeling resonated anger towards him but also exhibited that she did have feelings for him. When the scene was played again, her strength of feeling made his death more moving and the loss more profound. In the Out of Joint blog, Wertenbaker discusses this scene and the mixture of anger and love that can accompany losing someone.

Visual Elements
Stafford-Clark has now produced this play three times with extremely different sets, lighting and sound. This is a great opportunity to explore how a play can be interpreted visually. The following exercises ask students to investigate the choices Stafford-Clark has made and how they have informed the meaning of the play.

Example exercise: Set
Research the set design of Stafford-Clark's 1988, 1998 and 2012 produc-
tions of the play. Photographs of the first two versions are available from
the Theatre Museum, now part of the Victoria and Albert Museum in
London, and the Out of Joint website contains many images of their most
recent production.[82] *(You may also wish to consider Tony Tripp's design for*
Roger Hodgman's Melbourne Theatre Company production, detailed in
the previous essay.) Discuss the choices for set, considering how each reacted
to different design styles and budgetary constraints. Compare similarities
and differences, thinking about: the use of representational, rather than
naturalistic sets; the differences of a set designed for a tour and one that will
stay in one theatre; examples of symbolism or cyphers for meaning within
the design; the use of colour; whether materials appear distressed or new;
the actor/audience relationship the design facilitates.[83] *Next students create*
their own set design for Our Country's Good *and explain their choices.*

Stafford-Clark discusses how the convicts' clothes had so disinte-
grated before the end of the voyage that they had to be re-clothed
in sack cloth to avoid them being naked.[84] Therefore, their costumes
had to be basic and appear dirty, a huge contrast from their costumes
for *The Recruiting Officer*. This also showed how clothes could create
status and well-being.

Example exercises: Costume
1. Look at Act II, scene xi. Remembering the development of the
characters through the play, discuss how much importance costume plays
in the change in their behaviour, language, relationships and future
hopes. Using authentic or representational costume, ask the students to
act out the scene with costume and without, exploring the difference it
makes to their body language and status.
2. Look at Act I, sc. vi, in which the women in the company wear parts
of officer uniforms to become officers in the debate. Discuss how the
representational costume choice changes the actor–audience relationship
and the role of the officers in this scene. Consider whether the focus of this
scene is the debate about theatre and its role in society, or the individual
stories of the characters.

Lighting should communicate the emotions and meaning of the story as well as the environment and atmosphere of a piece of theatre.

Example exercise: Lighting
Look at the production photos on the Out of Joint website and discuss the choices of lighting in different scenes. See if it is possible to tell from the lighting what is the setting of the scene, whether it is night or day, or good or bad weather. Consider also what atmosphere and emotions the lighting creates and how it can affect the meaning of the scene.

Example exercise: Sound
Andy Smith writes about designing the sound for the 2012 production in the Out of Joint blog.[85] After reading this, choose one scene from the play and create sound effects that will create atmosphere, emotion and environment, without detracting from the dialogue. Present the scenes with and without the sound effects, and discuss which is the most effective and why. Discuss what difficulties surround this task.

Rehearsing Scenes for Presentation
It can be helpful to follow some of Stafford-Clark's rehearsal techniques to bring student productions up to the standard required for practical assessment or public performance. In the 2012 rehearsals, the focus was always on detail and clarity in terms of developing and communicating the character and their actions and relating to the other characters on stage. Here are a few of the techniques used. If lighting, sound and costumes are available, try to involve students in making decisions about the use of these visual elements and the staging of their final presentation.

Example exercise: Status
Use playing cards, chosen at random, to determine characters' relative statuses within a scene. Different combinations, for example, playing a ten for Mary and a three for Ralph within their love scene on the beach, will change the interpretation of the scenes dramatically. By experimenting with different statuses, the actors are able to determine the correct status for each character within a scene.

Example exercise: Actioning
Towards the end of the rehearsal period, return to this technique,
challenging the actors to become more detailed in their choice of actions
for each line. See if any previously defined actions need changing to
clarify the development of the characters and the scene.

In one of the later rehearsals for Stafford-Clark's 2012 production, William Gaskill (former director of the Royal Court and fellow founder of Joint Stock) ran a workshop on rhythm and tempo: a Stanislavski technique. He made the actors work on a small part of a scene over and over again, concentrating on bringing all the elements of their work together in a communion of techniques that bring the scene alive. He emphasised the need to listen to the other characters in the scene and to play an action with strength from the beginning to the end of a line and beyond, never losing it from the body language and voice, while still focusing on practical considerations, such as proxemics, and the status of the character and their relationships with others in the scene. The actors found the slow movement of this work and repetition of scenes very difficult and frustrating, but it eventually helped them to communicate their actions more clearly and to really listen to the other actors as though they were hearing the lines for the first time. Students can be guided towards the same level of detail, working in shorter bursts of time to allow them to process the notes given and avoid losing confidence in their own performance. It is important to reassure them of the importance of communication through the body, language and relationships between the characters and the audience. This type of complex, detailed work can only be done towards the end of rehearsals.

Our Country's Good is a play that is easily accessed by students, who often feel an affinity with its themes of justice and the right to have a voice and improve one's place in society. They also enjoy the historical aspects of the play and respond well to the political debate. The clarity of the writing and its structure help the students to write coherently about themes and meaning, and the wealth of research material available on the play makes finding quotations and working on the text more accessible.

Conclusions

As Sigal, Hodgman and Turner have demonstrated, *Our Country's Good* has had a huge impact on the theatrical landscape, in the United Kingdom and far beyond. While Wertenbaker has yet to repeat this level of critical success or wide-reaching influence, we will now see how her next plays are equally engaged with (in Turner's words) 'themes of justice and the right to have a voice'.

CHAPTER 5
'THE LONGING TO BELONG': ON CULTURAL GENEALOGIES

It's strange that most of the people I know in London are 'mixed' in some way, Brazilian, Italian, Greek, French, American, Polish and even the English are Scottish and yet all the plays are about 'the English' – and pretend no one else lives in England or lives at all. Boring. When this country-lessness is very much a sense of our time, and the longing to belong somewhere and its impossibility.[1]

Wertenbaker has a long-standing suspicion of the parochial 'state-of-the-nation' play. A 'state-of-England piece will [not] tell you much about England or about anything else', she explains, 'it's naïve and arrogant to assume so'.[2] As we have seen, her major plays of the 1980s avoided this genre by assuming historical or mythical settings, but during the 1990s and the first years of the new millennium, she wrote a series of plays with (at least partly) contemporary British settings. However, these plays are far from insular; Wertenbaker knew what it was to feel a cultural outsider and the 'longing to belong somewhere and its impossibility' is a theme that appears particularly strongly in her work in the run up to the millennium. While these plays centre on modern British life, they take care to situate the state of the nation within an international context. Immigration, trans-racial adoption, economic migration, the fall of Eastern European communism and the plight of refugees all feature prominently in one or a number of these texts, and are shown to be tightly interwoven with the lives and concerns of the plays' more 'properly English' characters.[3]

This chapter focuses on the way Wertenbaker writes the influence of nation, ethnicity and environment on to personal and group identities. Alongside the individual stories of her characters, Wertenbaker shows a constant awareness of the historical and political factors affecting cultural identity. Her plays reveal how the countries featured within them have been physically and ideologically shaped by global forces such as colonialism, postcolonialism, tourism, conflict, cultural imperialism, and continually shifting borders. Wertenbaker examines the impact of voluntary and forced relocation, and the consequences of remembering, discovering, abandoning or creating cultural histories. All the texts feature a sustained discussion about bi/multiculturalism, demonstrating not only that our countries are becoming increasingly diverse, but that they were never as monolithic as we might assume. Wertenbaker seems to propose that cultural and national identities are less rigid than is frequently asserted. Call it 'countrylessness', call it a 'floating identity'; embracing this fluidity is presented as a source of hope, just as fluidity within gendered identities is privileged in her earlier works.

Alongside these discussions runs a parallel strand, concerned with genealogy and reproduction. This is very apparent in *The Break of Day* (1995), which centres on two women's struggles to become mothers. In *After Darwin* (1998), Wertenbaker moves back from this personalised study of the desire to procreate, to consider the phenomenon on a mass scale. *Credible Witness* (2001) settles partway between these extremes, with far-reaching themes of migration and survival, pivoting on an intense mother–son relationship. Exploring these themes alongside issues of international relations allows Wertenbaker to suggest that, like the nation, the family is a structure that can either reproduce or resolve conflict. *The Ash Girl* (2000) is different in style from these three plays: a family Christmas show that draws on fairy-tale and pantomime. However, by characterising the Prince and his family as wealthy refugees from an unspecified and exoticised Eastern land, Wertenbaker continues to examine the theme of cultural dislocation. Furthermore, the traditional characters of stepmother and stepsisters extend discussions about the potentially oppressive qualities of the family unit.

In the gap between her two plays of 1988 and *The Break of Day* (1995), Wertenbaker's only 'original' stage play was *Three Birds Alighting on a Field* (1991). Although this play contains many similar themes to those discussed in this chapter, I have omitted it from consideration here, due to its inclusion in the final chapter. During the period 1989 to 1994, Wertenbaker was also busy with tours and revivals of *Our Country's Good*, a radio adaptation of Maeterlinck's *Pelleas and Melisande*, a film adaptation of Edith Wharton's *The Children* (1990), her television play *Do Not Disturb* (1991) and her RSC translation of *The Theban Plays* (1991).

Filiation and Affiliation

Sheila Rabillard has used Edward Said's essay 'On Repetition' (which draws on Giambattista Vico's theory of history as recursion) as a 'guide to Wertenbaker's dramatic recursions' in *The Break of Day*. Rabillard cites the 'ceremonies that frame [the play's] action' and the 'doublings and re-doublings' of themes and characters from Chekhov's *Three Sisters* as examples of the 'gesture of repetition'.[4] She also refers, more briefly, to Said's distinctions between filiation and affiliation, offering these as a way to view the alternative routes to motherhood taken by the play's central characters, Tess and Nina. I argue that this is a key concept not only within *The Break of Day* but in all the plays discussed in this chapter, principally because Said relates the dual concepts of filiation ('natural bonds and natural forms of authority – involving obedience, fear, love, respect, and instinctual conflict') and affiliation ('transpersonal forms – such as guild consciousness, consensus, collegiality, professional respect, class, and the hegemony of the dominant culture') to the pain of cultural dislocation and exile, and to the inability to reproduce.[5]

Speaking of the creation of Erich Auerbach's *Mimesis*, written while its German-Jewish author lived in Turkey to escape Nazi persecution, Said describes 'the concrete dangers of exile: the loss of texts, traditions, continuities that make up the very web of a culture', but which he believed Auerbach had been able to convert 'into a positive mission, whose success would be a cultural act of great importance'.[6] Said quotes Auerbach's assertion that the 'most priceless and indispensable part of a philologist's heritage is still his own nation's culture and heritage. Only when he is first separated from this heritage, however, and then transcends it does it become truly effective.'[7] Auerbach's description positions cultural heritage as the property of nations. It assumes a filial relationship between subject and culture, invoking an image of the coming of age of the child: painful separation, which, if endured, allows the boy to become a man. Said complicates the picture, acknowledging that while the 'readiest account of place might define it as the nation [...], this idea of place does not cover the nuances, principally of reassurance, fitness, belonging, association, and community, entailed in the phrase *at home* or *in place*'.[8] In other words, although national heritage may be filial – one is born German, Greek, Macedonian, or a relatively definable mixture of such – affiliative processes bear strongly on one's experience of cultural heritage and the concept of being 'at home'.

Said positions culture, in its broadest sense, as that which 'creates the environment and the community that allows people to feel they belong'. Although this may sound a comforting function, inherent within the seemingly benign idea of 'belonging' is the need to define, by contrast, that which does not belong: the Other. Thus, culture can play a positive, nurturing, identifying role in our lives, but it can also condition us to reproduce its beliefs, social structures and prejudices to the detriment of the Other. Yet all this is not hopelessly predetermined, Said argues, as 'the individual consciousness is not naturally and easily a mere child of the culture, but a historical and social actor in it'. Consequently, 'knowledge of history, a recognition of the importance of social circumstance, an analytical capacity for making distinctions: these trouble the quasi-religious authority of being comfortably at home among one's people'.[9] Said does not suggest that cultural dislocation is the only way to achieve the distance necessary to master this critical attitude. However, it is clear that, if following his model, the process of exile, while traumatic, could facilitate one's progression away from 'quasi-religious' allegiance.

Filiation and affiliation are both capable of producing positive and negative systems, but while the filiative is fixed, innate and immutable, the affiliative is constructed. It must be sustained by human action, and can therefore be disrupted by alternative human action; ensuring that affiliative systems are constructed in a way that is not abusive or repressive is within our control. In order to challenge one's culture, it must be recognised as affiliative, man-made and socially constructed, not accepted as filiative, natural, and self-perpetuating.[10] Consequently, when constructed with thoughtfulness and compassion, affiliation can be a source of hope and resistance.

Although she never uses Said's terminology, these concepts are prominent in Wertenbaker's plays. In *After Darwin*, the playwright Lawrence (an academic at an American University) reveals that he teaches a course entitled 'The Metaphysics of Cultural Genealogy'. According to Raphael Falco's essay, 'Is there a Genealogy of Cultures?':

> Cultural genealogy is best understood as simultaneously a conviction and a practice – a conviction regarding the link to past civilizations and the practice of selecting suitable origins. It is a form of narrative construction conceived as nature and remythicization conceived as rational knowledge. Its continuing presence reflects a desire to believe in hereditary intellectual authority, a hunger for cultural descent.[11]

This definition places cultural genealogy very close to affiliation. While undoubtedly a construct (something we are able, to an extent, to select), it is often perceived as natural, predetermined and filial. *After Darwin* is as much about the cultural genealogies we automatically inherit and purposefully create as it is about Darwin's theories on natural genealogies.

Connected to the hopefulness of affiliation is the fact that it is open to all. Contrastingly, despite being vital to the continuation of the human race, filiation is not always possible. Lawrence has been ripped from the land of his fathers by historical forces; Tess and Nina are unable to conceive children. Said also cites a number of literary works that dwell on such themes:

Childless couples, orphaned children, aborted childbirth [...] populate the world of high modernism with remarkable insistence, all of them suggesting the difficulties of filiation [...], the pressure to produce new and different ways of conceiving human relationships. For if biological reproduction is either too difficult or too unpleasant, is there some other way by which men and women can create social bonds between each other that would substitute for those ties that connect members of the same family across generations? [...] The only other alternatives seem to be provided by institutions, associations and communities whose social existence was not in fact guaranteed by biology, but by affiliation.[12]

The 'pressure to produce new and different ways of conceiving human relationships' is a particular imperative in *The Break of Day*, which offers the possibility of creating affiliative ties not just within smaller communities but across international borders.

The Break of Day (Out of Joint, 1995)

The Break of Day saw Wertenbaker collaborate once more with Max Stafford-Clark, this time with his company Out of Joint. The play premiered at the Haymarket Theatre, Leicester, before transferring to the Royal Court. Its central concerns of motherhood and adoption were present from its conception and, for a time, Wertenbaker thought to model it on David Rudkin's *Ashes*.[13] However, the work developed to encompass issues of gender, nationality and cultural history, as well as incorporating a recognisable metatheatrical vein.

Inspired by the previous success of the new play/old play twin productions of *Our Country's Good* and *The Recruiting Officer*, Wertenbaker began to imbue her play with echoes of Chekhov's *Three Sisters*. This device places Wertenbaker, as a dramatist, and the character of Tess's husband Robert, as an actor, within a certain line of cultural genealogy. Rabillard has noted that 'Chekhov in a genealogical sense has produced Robert. Within

Wertenbaker's dramatic fiction, Chekhov's work at the turn of the twentieth century has shaped the theatrical world in which the character Robert finds his present career.'[14] Likewise, Wertenbaker admits, 'I adore Chekhov, and although it is not obvious, he has influenced me very much.'[15] There are traces of this influence in others of Wertenbaker's plays, but in *The Break of Day* she creates clear thematic, narrative, atmospheric and character-based links with Chekhov's drama, particularly *Three Sisters*. The first act is played in real time and a single locale, with little action and much conversation, during which everyone becomes increasingly melancholy. Tess, like Irina, is 'celebrating' her birthday (name day). She is joined by her two oldest friends, Nina and April, creating a sisterhood of three, in the feminist sense. Also present are Nina's husband Hugh and April's reluctant boyfriend (and Tess's brother) Jamie, who, as a disheartened surgeon, evokes the disillusioned Chekhovian doctor. Visually, the setting – a '*garden of a small country house in the middle of summer. Lawn, some flowers. Nothing grand, but beautiful and peaceful*'[16] – invokes the quiet, natural beauty of the second act of *The Cherry Orchard* or the first of *Uncle Vanya*. The perpetual drinking of coffee furthers this atmosphere:

> **Tess** It's not even lunchtime and we're all depressed sitting talking around a cafetière.
> **Robert** The Russians sat around their samovar, talking –[17]

As in much of Chekhov's work, conversation is frequently directed at the failings of society. April complains about the bureaucracy and lack of funding in the education system; Jamie has the same concerns for the National Health Service. Their anxieties are contemporary, but their paralysing sense of apathy is highly Chekhovian. Robert relates the lethargy of the *Three Sisters*, 'suspended in an odd paralysis at the end of their century, with a cataclysm already in formation', to his own moment: 'There's something familiar about that paralysis, feeling outside history.'[18] Wertenbaker's dialogue is also Chekhovian in its expositionary style:

Tess When we first met you were writing those types of songs.
You'd formed your band.
Nina That's right ... you came to interview us.[19]

A number of reviewers questioned whether these allusions enriched
Wertenbaker's play. Some failed to grasp that Wertenbaker's characters
'tell each other biographical details that they must already know'[20]
not because, as Jack Tinker assumed, she was 'a playwright in deep
trouble',[21] but because this is what Chekhov's sisters do. Yet it is
not possible to dismiss all the play's critics so easily. Some reviewers
were well aware of the Chekhovian resonances, but found that these
only encouraged unfavourable comparisons. Several suggested that,
where Chekhov's genius lay in his 'ability to delineate character
through what is not said rather than what is', Wertenbaker was
guilty of overwriting.[22] Louise Doughty, although one of the play's
least hostile critics, considered it 'more of an interesting dinner party
debate than a drama'.[23] As the play's first act contains little 'action'
beyond the entrance and exit of new characters, such criticisms are
perhaps understandable. However, the play's second act is markedly
different.

All the plays discussed in this chapter suggest the need to remain
in dialogue with our cultural heritage, remembering the histories
that shape us, but questioning traditions that stifle our ability to
adapt. Wertenbaker's attitude to the cultural genealogy of Chekhov
is no different. The atmosphere established in Act One is torn apart
by Act Two: a montage of short scenes, which move rapidly forward
through time (spanning approximately nine months) and place
(most set in Eastern Europe, some back in England). While the first
act is largely static, the second opens chaotically. As Hugh and Nina
wait in the airport, they are approached by a succession of salesmen
and beggars: twelve new characters (none of whom appear again)
within four pages of dialogue. Here, Wertenbaker seems indebted
to other dramatic ancestors: both Aston and Roth have described
this act as Brechtian.[24] If this play ended with Act One, it might
have been possible to accuse Wertenbaker (as Chekhov himself has
been accused) of creating an atmosphere of stasis and placing the

ability to change outside her characters' control. Shirking any sense of responsibility, Nina suggests that 'England [...] sort of makes you silent' and is a country in which 'you're not encouraged to look'.[25] April is similarly disillusioned, commenting that 'Dictatorships use force. Democracies convince you you are wrong.'[26] In contrast, the second act follows Brechtian precedents, demonstrating that change is not only necessary but possible, as Tess and Nina become engaged in action designed to bring them the children they desire.[27]

Nina cites another cultural ancestor when she evokes the Greek myth of Demeter and Persephone to describe her feelings for the child she is trying to adopt.[28] As well as signalling a link to Wertenbaker's interest in Greek mythology, this passage highlights the common cultural genealogy between Anglo-American couples and the Eastern European children they adopt: the classical mythology so highly esteemed in the West, but geographically, and perhaps spiritually, closer to Eastern Europe.[29]

The brief third act of *The Break of Day* returns to a calmer English setting, but restates how this contemporary drama has evolved from its Chekhovian roots. At the end of *Three Sisters*, Irina and Olga express the belief that they will someday *know* what their 'lives and sufferings are for', that the 'answer will be known one day, and then there will be no more mysteries'.[30] In direct contrast, Tess explains that she and her friends 'want to try and *understand* what we've done' (my emphasis).[31] While the Prozorovs (characterised throughout by their passivity) seem to expect understanding to fall into their laps, Wertenbaker's characters understand that it is something they must actively struggle towards. They also see their lives in terms of their own previous actions ('what we've done') and their consequences, rather than a part of an abstract plan in which they might be living 'for' some greater purpose.

It is also interesting to consider Wertenbaker's play in terms of its most recent ancestry. Coming less than a decade after the best-known collaboration between its writer and director, there was an extent to which Wertenbaker and Stafford-Clark fell victim to their previous success. The foreknowledge that this was the team behind the much lauded twin productions of *The Recruiting Officer* and *Our*

Country's Good set many critics up to be disappointed.[32] This added to the endless number of shadows the play fell under: it was not as good as Chekhov, not as good as *Our Country's Good*; Benedict Nightingale even felt compelled to state that it was not as good as *Top Girls*.[33] At times, Wertenbaker's work has been deeply enriched by its metatextuality and historical resonances but, in this instance, critics felt her play was dwarfed by the comparisons it provoked.

Critical reservations aside, rooting her play in two somewhat opposing theatrical traditions (Chekhovian realism and Brechtian epic) allowed Wertenbaker to retain some distance from what is, nonetheless, a deeply personal exploration of the desire for motherhood. The idea that even established career women could be overwhelmed by their yearning for children caused some to consider *The Break of Day* post-feminist, or even illustrative of an anti-feminist backlash. Aston sees this reaction as evidence of 'how hard it is to engage in a debate around reproduction without it being read as advocating a biologically deterministic view of women's lives'.[34] Through the presence of the third 'sister' April, who is content to remain childless, Wertenbaker refutes Nicholas de Jongh's assessment that 'for all the cut and thrust of feminism, Miss Wertenbaker believes women need motherhood'.[35] Rather, her play explores the ethics involved in the different options available to women who find themselves unable to conceive. That is not to say that the work moralises – either over Tess's series of exhausting and consistently unsuccessful IVF attempts or Nina's trans-racial adoption – but neither does it present these choices as equally appealing. Rabillard sees the differing paths taken by Tess and Nina as examples of the filiative/affiliative distinction:

> Tess's raw desire simply to reproduce seems an embodiment of the kind of generation involving struggle; it is filiative and potentially Oedipal in its imposition of self as Tess asserts her right to the maternity a prior generation of women enjoyed. Nina and Hugh's part in creating ties across national and ethnic boundaries suggests the ameliorative, 'affiliative' role of institutions such as marriage and adoption in the cycle of history.[36]

Tess's privileging of filiative motherhood is evident in her blanket refusal of Nina's suggestion:

Nina There are so many children in the world. Lost. Waiting. Why don't you look into that? [...]
Tess I couldn't cope with a child who's been abused in different foster homes for years. You have to know your strengths. I want my own child, in here.[37]

When Tess's IVF hopes are reduced to the possibility of carrying an embryo created from a donated egg, she restates the importance of filial parentage: a concern echoed by the priorities of her doctor:

Dr Glad [...] We like to match hair colour and skin.
Tess What about –
Dr Glad Intelligence? That must be left to your husband's genes. [...] [If you decide to use] different sperm, we have very nice donors, all nationalities, Jewish, anything you need.[38]

Tess's desire for offspring supersedes the existing relationship she has with her husband. She insists that she will continue pursuing the IVF he hates, even if he withdraws his involvement, and even if it costs her the marriage. She loses her job and puts friendships at risk, effectively destroying the majority of her affiliative ties in the attempt to gain one filial one.

Wertenbaker has described her play as an exploration of the 'selfishness of the generation of Tess and Nina', and this egotism is most evident in Tess.[39] She reacts petulantly when Nina receives good news from her adoption agency,[40] and there is an implication that her desire for a child has been magnified by the ease with which she has got everything else.[41] Tess admits to holding a sense of entitlement, which she connects, uncritically, to imperialism: 'I felt I had a right to what I wanted. It goes with the empowerment I felt all my life. Born into this heroic empire – that's what they taught us – educated, national healthed.'[42] Although there is some irony here, there is no real critique. Tess speaks about her 'right' (in this case to Robert, who she decided she 'wanted' after hearing Nina describe him during 'consciousness-raising' sessions) without any sense of how this might affect her 'sisters'. Although it is with a greater sense of her own failings that she acknowledges, 'Women used to be my sisters. Now they're objects: egg vessels', she makes no attempt to change this outlook.[43]

Tess's self-centredness is apparent in her lack of interest in her maid Natasha, who she 'assumed [...] was from Bosnia'. Natasha appears at numerous points throughout the play's first act – bringing coffee or croissants for the guests – but is ignored by everyone except April and barely speaks. Her only interaction is when, having misunderstood April's talk of her research on Sappho, she '*lunges at April and kisses her*'. Tess's single-faceted notion of a refugee is shattered by Natasha's attraction to April, causing her to conclude that Natasha is 'probably from Cardiff'. April is more aware of the multiplicity of identity, rebuking Tess, 'You can't be gay and a war victim?' When Tess questions April's desire to apologise to Natasha for their 'cultural misunderstanding', April is stern about the casual way the group have been treating Natasha's presence: 'her life has ceased to interest us, although we cry for her on television, because our imagination has been depleted by this terrible century'.[44] This theme of compassion fatigue is touched on in a number of the plays discussed in this chapter. Here it helps shift our attention from Tess's lack of concern for others on a personal level, to the wider issue of how the empowerment of Tess's generation of white, middle-class feminists has been achieved with little concern for the advancement of other classes and races of women. In Aston's view, Wertenbaker's play presents feminism 'as a rather fragile source of energy, that to survive must aim to be inclusive rather than exclusive; must move beyond the bourgeois feminist model of privilege and look to the transformation of family and nation'.[45]

In the play's first act, Nina behaves almost as selfishly as Tess, but in Act Two, she develops into a more sympathetic character. While Tess becomes increasingly hostile and embittered, Nina is personally and artistically reinvigorated, a hint that Wertenbaker sought to privilege the latter's choices. This impression is reinforced by the play's structure. Act Two gives Nina's story twice the number of scenes, and almost three times the amount of stage time, as Tess's. The host of Eastern European characters Hugh and Nina meet, while caricatured to an extent, are richly drawn. Mihail, who is instrumental in helping the couple obtain their child, is an especially powerful and positive force. By contrast, Tess's only interaction is with the eerily insensitive Dr Glad. Where Mihail constantly questions his place within the systems in which he works (see below), Dr Glad reveals no personality, acting as a mouthpiece for his profession: 'we've performed another miracle. Best of luck. You pay as you go out.'[46] There was also some critical consensus that Nina's story is the better written of the two women's. Benedict Nightingale referred to Nina's 'emotionally authentic passages'[47] and Michael Billington felt that they were the only 'genuinely emotional area' in which Wertenbaker seemed to be 'writing from the heart rather than to a prescribed plan'.[48] Elsewhere, many critics found the play overloaded, a persistent criticism being that 'too many themes are conceived but too few are brought to term'.[49] Similar complaints had been levelled against *The Grace of Mary Traverse* and would be repeated over *After Darwin* and *The Ash Girl*, but while these plays had their fair share of defenders, even Billington (who looked favourably on the majority of Wertenbaker's work) felt that while any one of *The Break of Day*'s themes 'alone might make a fascinating evening: hurled together, they make for thematic confusion'.[50]

It is not simple to pronounce whether the play's profusion of themes is a fault or a crafty device. Wertenbaker believed that most critics did not 'make the effort to understand' this play, suggesting she felt it had a level many failed to grasp.[51] It is possible to argue that the proliferation of ideas within the piece is an accurate reflection of late-twentieth-century life, in which people deal with multiple issues at all times. The first image of the play is Tess *'sitting with a huge pile of newspapers, which she is scanning very fast'*.[52] Later, Jamie rifles through the same papers to find news of his hospital's closure. Before he enters, we are told he is on his mobile phone; Nina and Hugh receive the news that their little girl is waiting via Tess's mobile;

Hugh's son Nick expresses surprise that his girlfriend Marissa has been able to find and call him. In short, everyone is contactable all the time; news is received immediately and simultaneously. In an earlier draft, Wertenbaker considered having April proclaim that the 'mobile is the final blow to public space'[53] and a draft of *Three Birds Alighting on a Field* (1991) includes a passage that almost predicts the response to *The Break of Day*:

> This play, which I haven't seen, is reproached for being set against a background of Sudanese starvation, but not being about that. But that is how we lead our lives, I think, here in London, oh dear, all those starving Sudanese and shall I buy blue or red towels?[54]

Even if Wertenbaker's thematic confusion is an accurate depiction of real life, not to mention consistent with her ongoing struggle not to be boxed or labelled, some would argue that art must distil and structure that chaos into something more meaningful. Perhaps this would have been a 'better' play if, as several critics recommended, it had explored Nina's emotional journey without the distractions of Tess's IVF, Jamie's hospital closure and Natasha the Bosnian maid. But perhaps, that we, as critics, have difficulties identifying precisely what Wertenbaker is doing, and how she is doing it, may point to our inadequacies rather than hers. Wertenbaker clearly aimed to explore much more than the personal trauma of adopting an Eastern European baby. Benedict Nightingale cites the fact that he did not cry as a criticism of the piece, but if Brecht is as strong an influence as Chekhov in this work, it would seem likely that Wertenbaker was not out to tug on heart strings. Instead, her play explores the social and ethical issues surrounding the choices women make when they adopt children or undergo IVF, making the personal political in the most literal way.

By adopting from Eastern Europe, Nina commits to a long-term affiliative relationship that crosses not only familial but international boundaries. While there are many ethical questions at play here, some of which are explored, Wertenbaker focuses on the positive aspects of this process. The strongest cases for forging such links are put forward in two compelling monologues: a dramaturgical decision that highlights the ideas contained within them. One monologue falls at the end of Act One and is delivered by Tess's neighbour Mr Hardacre. The English widower of a Macedonian Jew, his life has embraced the cross-border ethics the play seems to advocate. He claims to feel an affiliation not only to his wife's race but to all oppressed peoples, suggesting the connections we make from family to family can begin an engagement that crosses national and cultural boundaries:

I watch the television all the time now. And I see them. I think I see her. People with suitcases, walking, walking with their suitcases. I thought we'd never see those images again. Do you remember in Denmark how everybody wore a Star of David as a protest against the Nazis? To say we are all one. This suitcase is my Star of David. I'm going to march with my suitcase every day for the rest of my life.[55]

The second monologue is delivered by Mihail, the Eastern European who helps Hugh and Nina locate their adoptive daughter. It occurs towards the end of Act Two, and is spoken directly to the audience. Speaking of his hope for the children he has found international parents for, he declares:

I still believe in history. Now, it will be in the hands of the children, possibly most of all, these cross-border children I have helped to get out. Born in one country, loved and raised in another, I hope they will not descend into narrow ethnic identification, but that they will be wilfully international, part of a great European community. I hope that they will carry on history with broad minds and open hearts. They have complexity from their childhood: change, migration, indifference and uncertainty came to them early. Now cherished, secure, educated. Is it unfair of me to place the responsibility of history onto them? We must not go into the next century with no ideal but selfishness.[56]

Mihail acknowledges that his philosophy places a great responsibility on the shoulders of children as yet too young to understand the processes he describes. However, the issue of bi/multiculturalism (discussed in greater detail in the following sections) is presented less problematically here than in *After Darwin* and *Credible Witness*, both of which deal as much with 'the stresses of biculturalism' as with its value.[57]

Mihail's rousing and compassionate ideals place him closer to Chekhov's Vershinin than to *The Break of Day*'s more disillusioned British characters. In Act One, Robert says that he does not 'believe Chekhov intends to mock' Vershinin's vision of a better future, but Wertenbaker's attitude to *her* characters was another thing that provoked critical confusion. Does the play parody Chekhovian sentiment? Does it mock Mihail for not moving on from these ideals? Or does it deride the British for having given up on them? Aleks Sierz felt that the play seemed 'unable to decide whether it [was] a light-hearted satire or a serious examination of the pain of childlessness'.[58] Nicholas de Jongh considered that it 'emerge[d] as an unintentional satire upon liberal trendies' and its 'self-righteous, preachy tone verge[d] on parody'.[59] That de Jongh was so sure these qualities were unintended implies that the play was staged with sincerity, but perhaps these elements of parody were not so much an unintended as an *unexplored* quality of the writing. Only one review suggested that a 'more highly stylised form of acting from all concerned might make some kind of virtue of Wertenbaker's artificial writing'.[60] This seems highly plausible, particularly if one compares the middle-class angst of this play's British characters with a clearly parodic draft scene (discussed in the next chapter) for *Three Birds Alighting on a Field*, in which a fictionalised Wertenbaker and her husband discuss the Gulf War over breakfast. Given Wertenbaker's close working relationship with Stafford-Clark, it seems likely that she would have had some influence over the tone of the production. However, there is some suggestion that Stafford-Clark found more gravitas in Wertenbaker's work than did others.[61] Although it is difficult to establish the degree of sincerity with which Wertenbaker intended her British characters to be played, it seems unlikely that she intends to mock Vershinin/Mihail. David Nathan, in the play's one really positive review, praised Wertenbaker's Chekhovian 'ability to combine an honest account of a coarse and hopeless present with an unshakeable belief in a shining future'.[62] While her next plays would complicate Mihail's optimistic outlook on cross-border citizenship, she would never abandon the sense of possibility captured in his speech. The same sentiment inspires her 2001 article 'Everyone comes to Café Europa', which imagines a response to the concept of 'Fortress Europe':

> Of course cafés can be irritating: you get jostled, bumped, so many different conversations and languages can give you a headache, your bag might get stolen, and sometimes you can't find a table because there are too many people. But isn't that better than looking down from the battlements in fear and solitude? I don't want to be imprisoned in the silence of Fortress Europe. Let me walk out into the pavements and sit somewhere, maybe to talk about history, maybe just to watch a city teeming with stories, interest, languages and cultures. Let's not build high, expensive and hostile towers, let's put up instead with the noise, the life, the annoyance, the openness and the music of our Café Europe.[63]

Looking at *The Break of Day* in its historical context, it appears markedly different in tone from the plays that were becoming 'fashionable' in the 1990s, particularly at the Royal Court. There is even a sense that it is Wertenbaker's response to the tide of introverted, hopeless, angry plays that characterised the decade. Wertenbaker felt alienated by the fashion for 'male violence [and] homoerotica',[64] and *The Break of Day* seems intentionally polarised from the work of the 'in yer face' generation: girls not boys; middle classes not working classes; large and rambling not small and contained; emotional detachment not intense and violent involvement; a cast of characters still trying to find the answers not giving up and assuming there are none; engaged debate rather than the feeling that '[t]he best we could hope to do was construct our own private dreams and tell each other stories'.[65] Opening in November 1995, it closed a year that began with Sarah Kane's *Blasted*. While Wertenbaker's reviews are less hysterical than those that accompanied Kane's play, they are almost as hostile, and Wertenbaker remembers being 'extremely upset and quite shocked' by them.[66] At times, it appears her work was derided for the opposite reasons to Kane's, as is most apparent in Aleks Sierz's review, which sounded angry that Wertenbaker's play had not embraced the new style: 'With its improbable plot, lacklustre songs and didactic tone, it is a scandal that the Royal Court – which should be promoting new writers – has given space to this ludicrous play'.[67] Jane Edwardes looked more sympathetically at the prospect of Wertenbaker's piece – 'After a succession of plays for the boys, it's quite like old times to have a play by a woman' – but concluded that 'Wertenbaker is running behind the pack when she should be ahead.'[68] Neither critic entertains the possibility that Wertenbaker might be deliberately flouting and rejecting the contemporary trend.

Despite Wertenbaker's self-professed distrust of the 'state-of-the-nation' play, many critics referred to her piece in those terms.[69] According to Dan Rebellato, this genre had become increasingly rare in the 1990s, as it gave way to plays that set their political discussion in vague or unspecified locales (such as those by Sarah Kane and Philip Ridley, or Caryl Churchill's *Far Away*). Rebellato reads this as a response to 'a growing sense that territory is no longer an adequate focus for political aspiration, that the forces that threaten us require the bursting of national boundaries in favour of a more cosmopolitan sense of ourselves as global citizens with rights and obligations that span the world'.[70] Wertenbaker's play is clearly engaged with such ideas yet, unlike the dramatists mentioned above, she chooses to locate her play with the specificity of more traditional 'state-of-the-nation' pieces. In doing so, Wertenbaker created a hybrid form, both ahead of and behind its times and, as a result, pleased almost no one with it. While older reviewers (with what Rebellato describes as 'outdated dramaturgical models')[71] condemned Wertenbaker's failure to refine her multi-issue play into something that would allow them to 'remain in judgement',[72] a younger generation, exemplified by Aleks Sierz, saw the piece as a 'tedious lecture' from a bygone era.[73]

After Darwin (Hampstead Theatre, 1998)

After Darwin takes the desire for offspring, presented in personal terms in *The Break of Day*, and reframes it on a broader, ideological level. Featuring a Bulgarian theatre director (Millie), two English actors (Ian and Tom) and a black American playwright (Lawrence), *After Darwin* is also about cultural interactions. The play is deepened by metatheatre as these characters are working on their own play, which follows Charles Darwin and Captain Fitzroy of *The Beagle* at various stages throughout the development of Darwin's theories. The juxtaposition of these two storylines highlights the history and geography inherent in the state of our nation; our place in the wider world is constantly emphasised by this play-within-the-play, set during the age of British expansion, mapping and colonisation.

Surprisingly, the majority of *After Darwin's* critics chose to view the play-within-the-play as the piece's primary component. Susannah Clapp saw the modern-day episodes as 'a nervous tic, [...] springing from [Wertenbaker's] anxiety to free her discussions from the taint of costume drama'.[74] Robert Butler complained that there was 'enough going on' in the scenes between Darwin and Fitzroy, before 'Wertenbaker turns this into a play-within-a-play',[75] and Charles Spencer recalled a 'lowering of the spirits' as he recognised 'yet more art about art'.[76] Even the less condemnatory Sheridan Morley wrote with an assumption that the Darwin/Fitzroy narrative was Wertenbaker's main focus: '*After Darwin* only ever gets into logistical trouble when the latterday drama of the actors in the pub threatens to become rather more interesting than the original conflict between Fitzroy and Darwin.'[77] These assumptions are perplexing. The play-within-the-play is a common device. Reviewers do not treat *The Recruiting Officer* as the first order of drama within *Our Country's Good*, or the mechanicals' play as more important than *A Midsummer Night's Dream*.

Admittedly, *After Darwin* gives more stage time and focus to its play-within than *A Midsummer Night's Dream* does. Likewise, where *Our Country's Good* focuses on rehearsal, *After Darwin* requires the scenes of the play-within to be delivered at performance level, although, in narrative terms, they are depictions of rehearsals.

This discrepancy was criticised by Butler, who was sceptical about 'actors [...] rehearsing in full costume while [the director] watches from outside the door'.[78] However, Butler's reliance on the codes of realism prevents him from appreciating the levels on which this play works. At least to begin with, the two layers of *After Darwin* have more in common with Tom Stoppard's *Arcadia* (in which characters from two time periods occupy the same space) than with the metatheatrical pieces mentioned above. This comparison is still not entirely accurate as, in *After Darwin*, contemporary characters consciously create scenes from the past, which unfold the way they do because of choices made by the living. Conversely, in Stoppard's play, which depicts a number of modern-day academics trying to piece together the history of a country house, its gardens and former inhabitants, the past unfolds independently and in spite of their attempts to interpret it, as highlighted when scenes from the past directly contradict their 'discoveries' and theories.

As *After Darwin* progresses, its two time frames become less distinct. In the play's first half, scenes i, ii, iv, vi, viii and x depict only Fitzroy and Darwin, and scenes iii, v, vii, ix and xi feature only the contemporary characters. Sc. xii, which closes the first act, is the first in which nineteenth-century and present-day characters appear simultaneously: an interaction between Darwin and Fitzroy with the stage direction '*Lawrence and Millie, watching*'. When Lawrence stops the action, claiming, 'Something's missing', it does not seem coincidental that this first direct intervention comes from the 'playwright'. During Act Two, such interjections become more frequent. In Act II, sc. i, Lawrence and Millie dress the set, occasionally interrupting Tom and Ian's rehearsal to highlight certain properties. Most scenes in Act Two begin with dialogue between Darwin and Fitzroy that is later disrupted by the intrusion of the modern day. Echoing the fate of the whole production (within), these scenes of rehearsal usually descend into bickering and sometimes chaos. We witness the opposite trajectory to that in *Our Country's Good*, where the disparate group of convicts coalesces over the course of the play. By the final scene of *After Darwin*, the play's two initially distinct time periods have merged completely:[79]

Darwin's study as it is now in Down House, some of it cordoned off. Darwin comes on, an old man, with a cane and beard [...]. Fitzroy comes on with his razor, in full admiral's jacket. Millie and Lawrence come on, dressed for the outside. They look around, like tourists.[80]

Thus, Wertenbaker's play combines two theatrical devices: the dramatic style of dual or multi-period plays like *Arcadia*, and the self-consciousness of metatheatre. Elaine Aston has commented that as 'a spectator, I found that the metatheatricality of this jolted you backwards and forwards between past and present, in a way that mirrored the shifts in perception that the characters are forced to make about their own lives and the lives of others'.[81]

If the two periods in *After Darwin* are equally weighted, this does not explain why the majority of critics showed more interest in the Darwin than the After. Perhaps they found it easier to engage with conflicts that are safely in the past, but dramaturgical factors may have contributed to this tendency. The play opens powerfully with a scene between Darwin and Fitzroy, not the contemporary characters. Some critics seemed unaware that the play possessed another level until Millie's first entrance in sc. iii. If Wertenbaker had opened her play with a scene between the modern-day actors, perhaps those who saw the contemporary storyline as an unnecessary intrusion on the nineteenth century might have re-angled their perspectives.

In *The Break of Day*, transnational adoption marks the start of a process of bi-culturalism for the unnamed child adopted by Hugh and Nina. The cross-border child is presented as a positive, hopeful force in a world that must embrace international communication and collaboration. In *After Darwin*, we meet the cross-border adult, a more troubled species, dealing with a range of threats and challenges. Millie, a Bulgarian economic migrant to the United Kingdom, provides the most obvious example of this phenomenon. Her interest in evolution prompts her to describe her migration in Darwinian terms: 'I thought [...] I could thrive in the West because I have something you do not have – intellectual energy and passion'.[82] Millie is keen to appear '[m]ore British than the British',[83] a desire that can also be linked to Darwinism, as highlighted by Ian and Tom's discussion on the value of camouflage to survival.[84] Millie believes she must eliminate all outward indications of her foreignness, such as her accent. Tom urges her not to 'lose the passion in [her] vowels', but Millie is adamant:

> **Millie** I can't pass for British unless I get rid of them.
> **Tom** What a sacrifice.
> **Millie** Not for survival.
> **Tom** (*correcting the 'u' of survival*) Survival.[85]

Sacrificed also was Millie's Bulgarian name, in favour of the English-sounding Amelia.[86] When the actors question her about her heritage, she replies, 'It is not my history any more, this is my history.'[87] While her confidence in claiming ownership of English culture demonstrates strength of purpose, Millie's belief that she must renounce her own heritage is damaging and ultimately unachievable. She cites passion, fear and anger as central to Bulgarian identity, and these characteristics appear in her working methods. She '*throws herself down at Ian's feet*' to implore him to follow her direction. When he rebukes her, 'This is no way to direct', she replies, 'It is in Moscow.' Over the course of the play, Millie becomes disillusioned with British life. Like Natasha in *The Break of Day*, she is a victim of compassion fatigue. On her arrival in the United Kingdom, Millie benefited from 'the spare rooms of those who found Eastern Europe exotic', but over time 'the rooms have got smaller' and she is 'becoming less fashionable'. On top of this, she finds the British so underhand and apathetic that she comes to consider her 'intellectual energy and passion' a 'disadvantage'.[88] This disenchantment is mirrored by a re-attachment to Bulgaria.[89] She tells Ian a story about the Bulgarian army with such a sense of personal investment that he asks, 'Was your family in that army?' 'Perhaps', Millie replies, 'It happened in the year one thousand and fourteen.' As a result of this ancient battle (in which the entire Bulgarian army was defeated and blinded), Millie claims '[l]ike most Bulgarians', to 'feel in my blood the ardent desire for conquest combined with a terrible fear of being blinded'.[90] Millie's reference to her bloodline invokes the idea of an inescapable filial genealogy, which her story links to notions of war and conquest. The connection between these concepts is expanded and critiqued more thoroughly in *Credible Witness*.

Millie's confused identification with Bulgarian and English culture is echoed in the Darwin/Fitzroy storyline. Fitzroy has previously captured four Tierra del Fuegans, returning one, Jemmy Button, as part of a 'civilising mission'. Unsurprisingly, Jemmy's influence is rejected by his tribe, but although he is badly treated by them, he declines Fitzroy's offer for him to return to Western 'civilisation'. As Lawrence explains, Jemmy 'adopted Englishness with total enthusiasm, but had then readopted the customs of his tribe with equal commitment, thus becoming perhaps one of the first people to suffer the stresses of biculturalism, a condition which was to reach endemic proportions in the late twentieth century'.[91] Millie suffers from just such a contemporary malaise.

Although *After Darwin* is more concerned with the struggle for individual survival than the reproduction of the species, the latter is an underlying theme. In the play's opening lines, Fitzroy bemoans, 'No more like me. [...] No more now. I leave nothing behind.'[92] Towards the end of the play, Tom, who – footloose and gay – represents a certain type of childlessness,[93] confesses to have 'absorbed enough about this to want to profligate – promulgate my genes'.[94] He is attracted to the medium of film, largely because of its ability to keep you 'there for ever. Fixed': a possible substitute for preserving oneself through future generations.[95] These examples provide a somewhat theoretical take on the issues of parenting so personally portrayed in *The Break of Day*, but there are also a number of crucial parent–child relationships between characters and offstage characters, and pseudo-parental relationships among the onstage characters of *After Darwin*.

Fitzroy is positioned in a pseudo-paternal role toward Darwin (and toward the offstage character Jemmy Button). When the two first meet, Fitzroy takes responsibility for helping Darwin choose pistols and other essentials for the long voyage. Darwin places himself in the role of obedient son: 'I shall follow your guidance in all matters'.

This contrasts with Darwin's earlier comment that he 'did not feel compelled to obey his [actual father's] wishes' that he 'follow him into' the medical profession, and that his father had initially 'opposed the idea' of his joining *The Beagle*.[96] The parent–child relationship is reinforced in Act I, sc. iv: 'Tenderness'. Here, Fitzroy tends a seasick Darwin in a way reminiscent of a parent with a sick child. Stage directions specify that he *'gently adjusts a pillow'* for Darwin, before settling down to 'read [him] the next chapter of *Persuasion*'.[97] As the men's relationship deteriorates, one can read elements of the rebellious child wishing to shake off parental control, and the strict father attempting to keep his offspring in check. Fitzroy cites the need to 'protect' Darwin among his arguments to dissuade him from publishing his theories, and claims to 'feel responsible for the misery you bring to yourself'. Darwin's response – 'you will have to allow me to look after myself' – is straight from the teenager's guide to parental comebacks (nineteenth-century edition).[98] Immediately following this line, the play-within is interrupted by the sudden imposition of two more parent–child relationships, as Ian's absent daughter's Tamagotchi beeps for attention. This intrusion causes us to shift our attention from Fitzroy as pseudo-father to Darwin, to Ian as actual father to a hitherto unmentioned daughter, and to both Ian and his offstage daughter as joint pseudo-parents to an electronic device that Ian describes as a 'virtual baby. You get very attached.' Throughout the rest of the scene, Ian is repeatedly distracted by the Tamagotchi, each time showing genuine concern for its welfare. Several reviewers were put off by this incident, which Patrick Marmion felt 'woefully cheapens the production'[99] and David Nathan saw as an 'entirely irrelevant' disturbance on a par with those from audience members' mobile phones.[100] The tendency to view this episode as simply a 'modish joke' misses the point.[101] Ian's fixation with the Tamagotchi suggests his 'relationship' with it has become a substitute for the relationship he is unable to have with his daughter: 'She comes every other weekend and I look after it the rest of the time. If something happens, she'll never trust me again.'[102] Michael Coveney understood this, calling the interruption a 'wonderful moment', 'which shows how far we have crept out of the slime that such technological confections are now capable of being endowed with human responses'.[103] This episode provides an extreme (and not particularly positive) case of affiliative ties superseding the filiative, but Ian, it seems, has spent his life privileging such relationships:

> I saw a great actor when I was a child. When I met him years later I went over to him and hugged him. You're my father, I said to him, you put me into this world. I never hugged my real father. I want spiritual sons. I'll do what I have to to get them.[104]

Most of the parental relationships this play alludes to are those between fathers and children. This is perhaps unsurprising in a play that seems focused on genealogy: a filiative process traditionally associated with the male ancestor. In contrast, mothers are almost uniformly absent. Both Darwin and Fitzroy lost their mothers as small children. Ian and Tom, who each make one (negative) reference to their fathers, never mention their mothers, and Millie simply refers once to her 'parents'.[105] The exception to this maternal void is the important role played by Lawrence's offstage mother in terms of the play's plot, themes and character development. As well as giving the audience their greatest insight into Lawrence's background (see below), when the play-within is threatened, it is only Lawrence's invocation of his mother that convinces Tom to stay long enough to perform it once. The consequent bearing Lawrence's mother has on the plot of the drama causes her to feature almost as strongly within it as the onstage characters.

Lawrence grew up amid racial tensions in Washington, DC. Rather than have him drawn into a gang of angry, dissatisfied black youths, his mother took him out of school and 'locked [him] up with books'. He was isolated not only from his peers but from the canon of his ethnic heritage, as his mother's curriculum included 'No black writers. No writing on slavery.' Even *The Tempest* was torn from his collected Shakespeare when he began to show an interest in Caliban. 'Here, she said to me, here's your friends, Shakespeare,

Milton, Moby Dick, that's the only gang you're ever going to hang out with.'[106] Lawrence acknowledges that, due to this unusual upbringing, 'Blind kings, barren women, runaway children and castaways peopled my childhood – [...] they became my ancestors, these loved figures carved from the crooked timber of humanity – [...] lining the shelves of my memory – a parallel evolution, where imagination multiplies... [...] Their legacy: empathy, complexity'.[107] Thus, Lawrence created his own alternative 'cultural genealogy' from the world of literature available to him. He shows no anger at his mother's regime and, although there is some critique implicit in his comment that he 'wouldn't do it to [his] children', concludes that it 'worked' for him.[108] This concept is problematic, echoing the colonial education of black children, which ignored their own heritage and oppression, seeking to create falsely pacified young people who identified against themselves and with a Western canon, much akin to the one Lawrence cites. Postcolonial theorist Ngugi wa Thiong'o remembers a similar immersion in English Literature, which jarred with the characters and stories from the oral tradition of his early childhood: 'Jim Hawkins, Oliver Twist, Tom Brown – not Hare, Leopard and Lion – were now my daily companions in the world of imagination. [...] Thus language and literature were taking us further and further from ourselves to other selves, from our world to other worlds.'[109] While Wertenbaker seems to champion the universal power of 'great' literature, even suggesting that it can provide a sense of cultural identity when one's ethnic identity has been denied, for Thiong'o, who actually experienced a similar educative process to the one undergone fictitiously by Lawrence, this sense of humanistic idealism does not bear weight:

> From the point of view of alienation, that is of seeing oneself as if one was another self, it does not matter that the imported literature carried the great humanist tradition of the best in Shakespeare, Goethe, Balzac, Tolstoy, Gorky, Brecht, Sholokhov, Dickens. The location of this great mirror of imagination was necessarily Europe and its history and culture and the rest of the universe was seen from that centre.[110]

Of course, in Lawrence's case, it was not a white schoolmaster but his own black mother who insisted on this programme of studies. Just as Millie voluntarily eradicates her own accent, Lawrence's mother is complicit in erasing her family's cultural heritage in the hope that they will thrive better in the West. Yet, unlike Millie, Lawrence does not seem to suffer 'the stresses of biculturalism'. By presenting Lawrence as a largely contented character, does the play implicitly condone the process Thiong'o criticises? Does the absence of a voice that critiques Lawrence's upbringing suggest that Wertenbaker is uncritical of such practices, even that she endorses them? Elsewhere in the play, Ian advises Tom, 'You have to be very lucky or very stupid to survive in two environments at once.'[111] Ian is referring to Tom's desire to branch into film work, and because Tom's interest in such work causes him to break his theatrical contract and jeopardise the play, Ian's comment seems to hold some truth. However, the desirability, or even the necessity, of being able to survive in two (or more) environments at once is a recurrent theme in Wertenbaker's work, appearing in all the plays in this chapter, as well as *New Anatomies, Our Country's Good* and *The Love of the Nightingale*. Far from dismissing the practice as stupidity, the sensitivity with which Wertenbaker writes of bi/multiculturalism shows a deep under-standing of the complex processes of loss, gain and renegotiation involved. [112] In *After Darwin*, although Lawrence's detachment from black history is left uncriticised, Tom's disinterest in the forces that have shaped Europe is not:

Tom [...] some things that maybe didn't happen, like the Holocaust.
Ian *moves to seize* **Tom**, *quick and violent.*
Ian Don't you ever say that, ever!
Tom OK, sorry. Don't get so emotional.
Ian Even your stupidity doesn't excuse a statement like that.
Tom I'm only repeating what I hear. I don't care one way or the other.
Ian Don't you?
Tom I wasn't there. Were you?

Ian We all carry the luggage.

Tom Not me. I live in the present. I travel light.[113]

If Wertenbaker's failure to condemn the actions of Lawrence's mother remains problematic, this is balanced by the merit evident in Lawrence's ability to make conscious choices and piece together his fictional heritage of 'empathy' and 'complexity' from the sources available to him.[114] Yet again, we see processes of affiliation privileged over the filiative. Perhaps too, the success with which Lawrence has created his own cultural genealogy stems, in part, from his awareness of the process he has undergone. He does not employ the contradiction that Falco cites in his definition of cultural genealogy, that is, he does not attempt to naturalise the construct but recognises his part in its creation. Lawrence's final lines speak of the 'failed characters we are and create', reminding us that his ability to reconstruct his own cultural genealogy is akin to his ability to construct believable characters for the stage.[115] This is something he shares with 'fellow' playwright Wertenbaker, who recognises the value her complex background has in her chosen career. 'I don't know why people can't accept that you can have several cultures', she explains, 'The whole thing about being a writer is that you have a floating identity anyway.'[116] As Rabillard has noted, *The Break of Day* links processes of theatrical, biological and historical reproduction, and through these nuances, so too does *After Darwin*. Lawrence's creation of his own cultural genealogy is similar to the way in which the convicts in *Our Country's Good* and Philomele in *The Love of the Nightingale* re-establish their identities through theatrical acts. The ability to live in two or more environments at once can also be linked to theatrical activity, invoking the concept of actors' duality: their ability to inhabit two realities, two worlds, simultaneously. Perhaps Wertenbaker sees the theatre not just as a place where lost voices (and consequently lost identities) can be regained, but as a space for practising the increasingly vital art of bi/multiculturalism.

Credible Witness (Royal Court, 2001)

Credible Witness was produced by the Royal Court's Theatre Upstairs. Set largely in a British detention centre for refugees awaiting a verdict on their right to remain in the country, and with migration and exile as key themes, this play is overtly about cultural identities. Issues of bi/multiculturalism, compassion fatigue, cultural genealogy and postcolonialism feature heavily, and the concept of filiation and affiliation is developed. Again, we are presented with the intense power of the maternal bond, this time through the relationship of Petra Karagy (a Macedonian Greek) and her son Alexander, who has fled to England following a beating from the Greek police (for teaching local children about their Macedonian heritage). The drama is set in motion when Petra travels to England in search of her lost son. Attempting to enter the United Kingdom with a false passport, she is immediately detained, thereupon meeting a host of asylum seekers from around the world. Alexander also comes into contact with fellow 'exiles' at a community centre where he helps refugee children come to terms with their cultural dislocation.

Credible Witness addresses the complicated process of retaining elements of cultural identity in exile. At its start, when Macedonian history means everything to Alexander, he warns his pupils that losing their history will make them 'poor, and flat'.[117] Later, he begins to question his own cultural obsessions, but gives a similar warning to Anna, a young refugee from Eastern Europe, who finds comfort in the seeming stability of English history. Alexander urges her to have the 'courage to be complicated',[118] but for some, such as the Algerian Aziz, the weight of such a complex past causes mental disorder, including hallucination and paranoia. 'Algerian history is making my head come off', he complains.[119]

In the hope of avoiding such anguish, Alexander teaches refugee children to find a balance between remembering and honouring their roots and respecting and appreciating their host nation: 'An exile learns to love and respect his new country. But this will not happen until the exile has lamented his loss [...]. One day Ali will remember his home, his friends, the food he liked, the good times.'[120] Alexander's insight and objectivity have been achieved through a similar process to that discussed by Said: his physical detachment from his homeland having caused him to question the way his people hold on to their history, often to the detriment of their future. '[F]rom here, it looks like madness this obsession with Macedonia', he tells his mother, 'Here I've felt light, free.' This is the essence of the debate in the pivotal scene in which mother and son are reunited. Although Alexander once championed the importance of Macedonian identity, he comes to resent the extent to which it has consumed his life. He blames his mother for this filial reproduction of conflict, accusing her of singing him to sleep with 'lullabies of blood and hatred'. His judgement seems correct as Petra maintains, 'If you [lose] Macedonia you will lose everything.'[121] Petra is fixated with ideas of genealogical heritage. She believes Alexander is descended from Alexander the Great and that he has 'inherited' his intelligence. This relates to Falco's assessment that 'genealogy retains its force only by sustaining the myth that a particular blood tie somehow preserves the original magic of the charismatic founder of the line, movement, or institution'. Falco asserts that this myth makes genealogy

> antithetical to evolution or to the evolutionary assessment of history because the strength of a line of descent is in the fiction (or myth) that the original magical element remains intact despite the passage of generations. To contend that this magical element evolves is to suggest that it is subject to mutability, being both transformable and unstable. But mutability, transformability, and instability are patently threatening to genealogy, in particular to any notion of the genealogical preservation of an original or essential charisma from generation to generation, stretching back *ad fontes*.[122]

As previously demonstrated, Wertenbaker's work places great value on mutability, transformation and evolution. Petra's fatal flaw is her inability to accept these things and her attachment to the myths of which Falco speaks. Alexander develops a wider worldview, questioning his mother's over-reliance on cultural heritage: 'Why should I die for your obsessions? You dripped them into my food, the water I drank. You called it history, maybe it's only your anger.'[123]

Petra seems to associate filiative ideas of genealogy, nation and conflict with masculinity. She privileges the male line, acknowledging that mothers 'hold [our sons] more tightly than our daughters'[124] and, when asking whether Alexander has been tortured, shows particular concern for his reproductive parts. Her hope that he will continue their blood line seems almost as great as her fear for his well-being. After Alexander renounces his passion for Macedonian heritage, Petra feminises him: 'What kind of a life is there when you're a nobody, without a past, without a name, [...] when maybe you're not a man anymore?'[125] When he describes helping refugee children to 'lament' (a means of putting to rest cultural trauma), Petra replies that lamenting is 'for women'.[126] Later she retells a dream in which she was abandoned by Alexander the Great, and recalls that Alexander 'was at the back of the procession, dancing like a girl'. However, this vision seems to raise Petra's awareness of the paradox created by the association of masculinity with the responsibility to carry and defend cultural heritage: 'We tremble when they're sick, we would die to protect them, but then we ask them to be men. Our history tells us to make sons that will fight – if that's not right, what have we been doing for hundreds of years?' The dream prompts Petra to repent her denial of Alexander ('I wouldn't open my arms to the person in front of me, maybe if I had, my son would have come back'), demonstrating that she has learnt to be less absolute.[127]

Despite Petra's obstinacy, she does open her arms, not at first to Alexander, but to her fellow detainees. During the course of the play, both she and Alexander come to value the affiliative if not over, at least alongside, the filiative. As Aston has noted, Petra's 'maternal role needs to shift from a reproduction of the nation to having a care for others outside of her own history, her own family. Significantly, both Alexandra and Petra come to care for children who are not their biological children, but children in exile.' As a teacher, Alexander has always nurtured other people's children, but once in England, his role shifts 'out of his authoritative position as teacher, and now serves as a facilitator in a participatory mode of "instruction" in which the children are encouraged to find their own voices'.[128] He progresses from training native children to discover their own history to helping exiled children accept a new future. The children he becomes responsible for have all lost their own parents, making his position *in loco parentis* even more vital. This is emphasised by the 'abandoned child' resonances of Anna's anger after Alexander is forced to leave his position: 'We thought we'd done something. [...] [W]hy did you desert us?'[129]

Petra develops a pseudo-parental role towards fellow detainee Ameena, a young Somali woman and victim of a brutal rape. At first, another refugee, Shivan, has to draw Petra's attention to Ameena's need but, once alerted, Petra's motherly reaction and language seem instinctual:

> **Petra** Oh, child.
> *Then quickly moves to hold her.*
> Ameena…
> **Ameena** *subsides. Sobs continuously.*[130]

Wertenbaker situates this compassion based on circumstance, rather than familial ties, as a vital commodity in our rapidly changing world.

Credible Witness suggests that the need to adopt a fluidity of cultural identity is equally imperative for the host nation. Wertenbaker reinforces and challenges the concept of England as a historically stable, monolithic culture (contrasted with the volatile regions of Africa, Eastern Europe and Asia, from whence the refugees have fled). Alexander validates the idea, telling Petra, 'They've only had one civil war in England, and an endless parade of kings and queens, they speak one language, they don't even use the word history, they call it heritage.'[131] Elsewhere, however, this image is questioned. Alexander later admits it is 'interesting here',[132] and Wertenbaker employs a number of devices to reveal the country's underlying complexities. When Petra misremembers Simon's name, he corrects her, explaining that 'Le Britten' is a Norman name, deriving from 'Le Breton'.[133] Thus Simon, who would never consider himself anything but British, reveals that his own heritage has a French root. This highlights the intricacy of Britain's cultural heritage. You may have to delve further into British history to find its civil wars, invasions and conquests, but they are there.

The play's other Briton, Paul (a guard at the detention centre), was among the first generation of Indians to immigrate to England. This gives him a connection to, and sense of alienation from, the modern-day asylum seekers: 'we never behaved like that. We did everything to fit in. [...] I can't make my son understand that, he's always in trouble, but he says he's British.'[134] Paul and Simon highlight the fluidity of the term 'British', as both are, in a sense, immigrants themselves, whether that immigration occurred fifty or nine hundred and fifty years ago. Implicitly, the play asks whether Britain might be a more open nation if Britons acknowledged more readily the complexity of their own cultural past.

The power of language, a crucial theme in the plays discussed in Chapter Three, is closely related to this chapter's focus on cultural identity. Said's 'On Repetition' discusses Marx's *The Eighteenth Brumaire of Louis Bonaparte*, explaining that 'Marx reflects in his language an understanding of the way in which language itself, while genealogically transmitted from generation to generation, is not simply a fact of biological heredity but a fact as well of acquired identity.'[135] In Wertenbaker's play, it is Petra who expresses the importance of linguistic identity:

Then the bridegrooms asked the women to kneel and swear never to speak Bulgarian again because now they were Greeks and their children would be Greek. [...] From that day, we became known as the women who refuse to kneel. Because we still speak Bulgarian and we never kneel to anything or to anyone.[136]

Just as the adoption of Greek would mean a loss of identity for Petra's great-grandmother, so the adoption of English, at times, presents a loss of surety for the refugees. Alexander bemoans that 'translating all those certainties into English made them crumble'.[137] However, the play is ambiguous about whether this is a wholly negative process. In a later scene, Petra advises Ameena that words are 'like medicine, they taste bad, but they help after. With every English word, you will tell your story more.'[138] This statement, which begins with a general endorsement of the value of language, somewhat unexpectedly locates this power within the English language. A similar assertion is made by Shivan, who is 'reading *Paradise Lost* for the third time to help endure the humiliation [of the detention centre] and also to share the power of this language'. Here is another seeming endorsement of the universal comfort provided by a great work of English literature. Like that cited by Lawrence in *After Darwin*, it carries problematic implications of the prioritising of the Western canon. Wertenbaker has sought to de-politicise the concept of language within both plays:

> I think in terms of Lawrence and Shivan having the *English* language, I think that's just the way it is. You know, these sorts of people who fall in love with the English language [...], and I don't make a judgement on it. [...] I don't write political plays as such. I'm not making a point. [...] I just try to do it character by character, without really judging where they are [...] – it's just the way these characters function. [...] I do feel very strongly about language, but I think I just feel very strongly about the right to speak and to be believed. That's important and that's the only point I'm trying to make in *Credible Witness* – that if you don't even believe what someone is saying then everything breaks down.[139]

These assurances seem somewhat disingenuous. Wertenbaker's comprehensive understanding of the politics of language is evident throughout her oeuvre. It is particularly apparent in this play's portrayal of the value of names as emblems of cultural and professional identities, which can be used or withdrawn as a form of cultural oppression and/or resistance. For example, Alexander's pupil

'Ali' took on a French name to facilitate his entry into England. Later, he was given a succession of English names, because no one could pronounce the French one. Eventually, he forgot his real name. One day, Alexander tells us, 'Ali will remember his name. Until then we will cry for Ali.' Another child, 'Henry', does remember his name, but will not reveal it, as his 'secret name is all he has left'.[140]

Alexander defines himself as a teacher who 'respected the emotive force of names', having grown up in the 'complex, bitterly fought over name: Macedonia'. He too entered England with a false identity, confident he could soon retrieve his 'true name', but later finds his loss of name translates into a loss of identity on the most literal of levels:

[T]oday, your teacher has been told the name Alexander Karagy does not exist, never existed. It seems the name is on no records, nowhere – and there will be no papers giving your teacher back the name Alexander Karagy. And because you can't have a no name – an imposter – teaching vulnerable children, he has been told – very politely – he has until five o'clock this afternoon to leave. It is nearly five o'clock. The name Alexander Karagy will now dance out of this room into silence and disappear.[141]

Thus Alexander also loses the name 'teacher'. When Henry sees him sweeping the streets and excitedly recognises his 'Teacher!' *Alexander shakes his head, shows his broom and orange overcoat*. Henry invites Alexander into the imaginary game he is playing, offering him the title 'Minesweeper' and introducing himself as 'Freedom fighter'. However, in his interaction with Henry, Alexander slips back into his role as teacher, challenging Henry's wish to 'Kill them all' with the question 'Who'll be left to run the village?' He offers Henry a strategy for coping with his unhappiness: 'find one thing you like here, and like that one thing a lot'.[142] Henry reinforces Alexander's role by continuing to call him 'teacher' whenever they meet. In the play's final scene, Henry reveals that the one thing he likes about England is its parks, and Anna admits to having done 'hours of crying homework' after his lessons, until she 'began to unfreeze'.[143] Thus, Alexander's status as teacher outlives his official position. Teaching, Wertenbaker suggests, is a process as much as a formalised profession.

Shivan also suffers a loss of identity stemming from a failure to have his professional title (Doctor) recognised. Initially, Paul refuses to take Shivan's medical advice and seems not to believe he is qualified to give it. Shivan is emphatic about the danger of such a denial: 'If we do not share the truth of language, what then? You don't believe I am a doctor, why should I believe you are a guard? If language disintegrates, there's nothing left.'[144] By their final scene, Paul has bought a range of exotic foods so the detainees can try to coax Petra to eat by making their favourite dishes. This, he explains, is 'Doctor Rajagopal's idea'.[145] As with Alexander's refusal to stop *being* a teacher after that name has been withdrawn from him, Shivan succeeds in remaining a doctor when others deny him that title. His determination provokes a change of attitude in those around him. The play highlights that, despite our obsessions with titles and labels, what we do is more important than what we are called.

In a small redressing of the British disregard for the names of immigrants, Petra repeatedly misremembers Simon Le Britten's name, calling him a range of alternatives, from 'Mr England' to 'Mr Great Britain'.[146] It is no coincidence that Petra's first use of Simon's correct name follows his promise to reopen Ameena's case for asylum. Petra returns this favour by making the effort to appreciate Simon's name and history. Thus, Wertenbaker shows the immigration process as requiring a two-way understanding. Petra concedes, 'I've been walled, like you. History shifts, we can't hold it': a huge change in a woman formerly so fixated with her Macedonian heritage. Her efforts must be matched by a similar openness in the host nation, as she instructs Simon, 'don't cover your eyes and think of the kings and queens of England. Look at us: we are your history now.'[147] This ability to move forward, crucial to the play as a whole, can be linked to the concept of language, once again using Said's assessment of Marx:

In language, as in families, Marx implies, the past weighs heavily on the present, making demands more than providing help. [We] will produce a disguised and semi-monstrous offspring [...] unless the past is severely curtailed in its power to dominate the present and the future.[148]

Perhaps because language is such a highly charged concept, *Credible Witness* explores non-linguistic ways in which its exiles can communicate with new cultures *and* preserve a sense of identity. Two of the play's most striking scenes occur when the refugees engage in certain 'rituals', which remember and express their native identities. In one, this is achieved through music:

> **Leon** *has finished his flute and starts playing.* Aziz *joins in, singing, drumming on chairs. The music is jazzy, Afro-Algerian Rai. The singing is for* **Petra** *and* **Ameena***, who holds herself next to* **Petra** *but can't help drumming the beat.*[149]

The second involves the detainees cooking their favourite national dishes. The mood is immediately lifted. Ameena, who has barely spoken, expresses delight at the 'smells of my country', and Shivan is proud to create the 'special Tamil brew', 'Rusam'.[150] In both scenes, a strong sense of cultural identity is established by the evocative power of music and food, not by linguistic communication. Thus, the play suggests that there are a range of methods through which cultural identities can be preserved, enjoyed and shared, without the need for translation. Consequently, such alternative 'languages' may prove easier and less ideologically charged elements of cultural identity to retain in a foreign country. 'I was trying to look at identity [...] beyond language', Wertenbaker explains, 'which may be why you find that they do get together when they are doing something which is non-linguistic'.[151]

Throughout the play, Wertenbaker redeems accounts of extreme suffering with these moments of hope. Morley described a 'lightness of touch which lifts a distressing catalogue of immigrant ills into a curious affirmation of the life force itself',[152] and John Nathan found 'a refreshingly optimistic antidote to nationalism' in Wertenbaker's depiction of 'London's melting pot where no nation is an island'.[153] An image for this delicate balancing act is provided by Petra:

> When my mother came out of the camps in the 1950s, she didn't talk, she only painted. She gave me a painting of a flag: red, white and black. She called it the flag of history and labelled it red for blood, black for grief, white for hope. I measured the colours. They were all the same. Except white looks bigger.[154]

This pattern continues to the play's final scene. Alexander is shown *'wrapped in a blanket. He looks rough'*, but his former students Anna and Henry have come a long way: Henry has a gardening job; Anna has five A Levels and is wanted by the 'best university in England'. As is so often the case in Wertenbaker's plays, the element of hope is thus positioned firmly with the younger generation. It is refreshing that a play that has discussed our obsessions with our histories turns at its end to look toward the future. Also common to many of Wertenbaker's optimistic endings is the idea that our future must be more about what we share than what divides us. In *Credible Witness*, this idea is eloquently expressed by Anna's academic ambitions to find 'Not this country's history, or the one I came from, but the common mechanism'.[155] It is to these common mechanisms of humanity that Wertenbaker's future looks. This is not a call for assimilation or the levelling of national and ethnic variety, but a celebration of our potential to use the very nature of cultural difference to make such connections.[156] The final image of the play is Anna's request: 'teacher, come and walk with us in an English park'.[157] Like the characters in *The Break of Day* staying up to 'wait for the dawn',[158] we are left with a tentatively hopeful invocation of human solidarity and natural beauty.

Critics reviewing *Credible Witness* were anxious to signal its immediacy. This was nowhere more apparent than in Nicholas de Jongh's reminder that Wertenbaker's play opened only a 'few hours' after his paper, the *Evening Standard*, broke a story claiming that 'Britain is being overwhelmed with bogus asylum-seekers'.[159] De Jongh was not alone: most reviews opened with similar references.[160] The impression of the play's topicality was increased by the simultaneous run of Kay Adshead's *The Bogus Woman* at the Bush, with some critics writing joint reviews.

Expectations set by these factors led some to be disappointed by the obliqueness of Wertenbaker's writing. Charles Spencer complained that Wertenbaker's characters were overly symbolic, that she seemed 'more interested in archetypes of suffering than individuals, and the piece smells of the library [...] rather than real life'. John Peter agreed that the play 'contains no life'[161] and Jonathon Myerson felt it 'simply lacks sufficient, breathing, human content to carry the core of the debate'.[162] Others felt that Wertenbaker's play was an inaccurate reflection of immigration issues, with de Jongh accusing Wertenbaker of having 'not read up enough' on her topic. A number of factors may have contributed to this critical scepticism, which seems partly motivated by the media's hysteria towards the 'crisis over asylum-seekers'. This is evident in several reviewers' surprise that Wertenbaker's immigrants are all 'so obviously decent and deserving'[163] and 'improbably, have good cause to stay'.[164]

Reviewers' emphases on the play's timeliness overlook the reality that Wertenbaker had been working on it long before its opening. That its premiere coincided so exactly with newspaper front pages was essentially that: a coincidence. Of course Wertenbaker was exploring issues she knew were of immediate relevance, but the impression that her play responded to news that broke the day it opened is clearly illusory. It is understandable that reviewers and audiences made these connections. As Georgina Brown commented, '[t]he government's recent move to get tough on bogus asylum seekers is the stuff publicity officers dream of'.[165] However, it is vital to remember that Wertenbaker never set out to create a 'living newspaper' or agitprop response to the asylum question, and her treatment of the theme is as philosophical as it is topical.

Some critics understood this. Sheridan Morley remarked that anyone expecting *Credible Witness* to be a 'searingly topical documentary' would receive 'something of a shock', as the play was 'more concerned with the mythical nature of exile than with any actual case history'.[166] Alastair Macaulay also recognised that the play was 'larger than mere topicality' and Michael Billington saw that it 'raises philosophical questions'.[167] Myerson and Benedict Nightingale gave similar descriptions of the play as 'a muted chamber opera on the themes of memory and history'[168] and a 'meditation on the merits and demerits of culture and history'. While Nightingale felt that because the play was 'partly a particularised critique of British immigration policy, partly an over-arching debate about human identity', it lacked dramatic tension, he concluded that Wertenbaker achieved a remarkably 'rounded [...] account of so immediate yet permanent a topic'.[169] Macaulay described 'a completely "now" play', that simultaneously made 'superb' points about the nature of history. '[O]ne thinks of it in the same breath as certain Greek tragedies', he wrote in the play's most glowing review.[170] Spencer also spotted these parallels, concluding that Petra was 'required to act as a chorus on her own predicament'.[171] Petra also bears a resemblance to matriarchs such as Hecuba, as has been productively explored by Sara Freeman.[172]

Credible Witness is the last of Wertenbaker's plays to have an unambiguously contemporary setting. As Freeman argues, and several critics recognised, the play contains allusions to ancient Greek tragedies such as *Hecuba* and *The Supplicants*. However, these resonances are subtler than the metatheatrical devices and historicisation employed in Wertenbaker's earlier works, and went unappreciated by many. After this piece (and alongside it, in the case of *The Ash Girl*), Wertenbaker did not cease her interrogation of present-day issues, but returned to the use of more apparent historical and mythical frames.

The Ash Girl (Birmingham Rep, 2000)

An adaptation of the *Cinderella* story commissioned as a family Christmas show for the Birmingham Rep, *The Ash Girl* draws on elements of fairy-tale and pantomime. Its narrative remains close to the version by the Brothers Grimm (1812), retaining friendly animal characters and their magical transformation by a benevolent fairy, as well as more disturbing elements of the story. In addition, Wertenbaker invents a collection of malevolent anthropomorphic characters that represent the seven deadly sins and include Angerbird, Greedmonkey and Pridefly.

The Ash Girl shares many themes with the other plays discussed in this chapter. As it opened in December 2000 and *Credible Witness* premiered in February 2001, it is probable that Wertenbaker worked on the two plays simultaneously. There is certainly much correlation of concern between the two, which both explore issues of racial prejudice and cultural dislocation. The combination of these serious 'adult' themes with talking otters and a silvery ball gown 'spun from the belly of a giant spider'[173] makes *The Ash Girl* a strange hybrid that perplexed reviewers. Jeremy Kingston called the show 'a right old mess', 'burdened with Message', 'Preachiness' and 'Lessons We Must Learn'.[174] Paul Taylor thought the piece was 'too busy being preachy and politically correct' to be an entertaining children's show,[175] and Dominic Cavendish considered it 'a thesis, not a treat'.[176] Michael Billington, however, while recognising that the play was 'ambitious' and 'a bit overloaded', reported that the show 'kept a packed house so quiet you could hear a pin drop' and praised both its 'visual magic' and a 'subversiveness that should appeal to children'.[177] Yet even the more positive reviews questioned Wertenbaker's balancing of the play's disparate elements. Jonathon Gibbs felt there was 'not enough mindless wish-fulfilment to counteract the darker motifs'.[178] The subsequent production history of the play (predominately in educational establishments) suggests it is more appealing to those wishing to explore its complex themes and challenging roles than those engaged in making work for children in a professional capacity.

The Ash Girl plays heavily on ideas of filial heredity. Within the play's opening lines, Ashgirl's stepsisters (Ruth and Judith) bemoan, 'Mother says we must be thin. [...] Because girls are thin', highlighting how the family structure can support and perpetuate oppressive ideologies, bolstered by the received notion that one should obey one's parents.[179] The stepsisters' lines evoke the phenomenon of daughters 'inheriting' their mothers' eating disorders. Ruth's and Judith's mother has a devastating effect on her daughters, stifling their attempts to be creative, individualistic or adventurous. Ruth professes, 'I'd like to paint, but mother says it makes me look a mess.'[180] Although Ruth and Judith are given names and characterised as individuals, 'Mother' takes a more symbolic, generalised role and is named accordingly. She is never physically violent but exerts complete psychological control over her daughters. 'When Mother is disappointed I feel like I'm going to shrivel into a speck of dust', admits Ruth. 'With me it's more like being strangled', agrees Judith.[181]

The most graphic example of the harm Mother causes her daughters is her instruction to them to cut off parts of their feet to fit the Prince's slipper. This is clearly one of the elements that Wertenbaker found most compelling in the *Cinderella* story, as she also references it in *Three Birds Alighting on a Field*.[182] Wertenbaker does much to emphasise the sisters' reluctance and Mother's insistence on this act, which is positioned within a pattern of filial duty by Mother's command: 'You have to! Girls don't disobey their mothers.' This scene draws attention to historical and, more alarmingly, to contemporary mutilations of the female body in an attempt to make it more desirable. This is charted from the country 'where young girls have all the bones of their feet broken to look beautiful' (presumably a reference to the ancient Chinese custom of foot binding) to the 'woman on the edge of the forest who knows how to add a little flesh here, take away a few bones there, all for the sake of beauty': an apparent allusion to the contemporary trend for cosmetic surgery, de-familiarised by its relocation within a fairy-tale context.[183]

In Grimm's *Cinderella*, as in Wertenbaker's, the mother suggests her daughters' self-mutilation. Even so, it is the girls who are punished for it, having their eyes picked out by Cinderella's bird friends. In Wertenbaker's version, the girls are let off with a stern lecture from the good fairy: 'when someone, even your mother, asks you to do something stupid and harmful, have the courage to say no. It is difficult, I know, and I won't be harsh.' Mother is treated with less benevolence. The fairy rebukes her with ideas based not on filial obedience but filial care – 'These are your daughters: where was your love and your compassion?' – and decides she has 'to change [her] into something horrid'. But Wertenbaker allows Mother to question this judgement:

> Love? Compassion? Whoever had love and compassion for me? Keep up appearances, that's what I was taught, crave power, grasp riches, I was told. Love and compassion rotted underneath. I only ever did what was done to me.
> *The* **Mother** *lifts her skirts to reveal her own stumps. The* **Father** *bows his head.*[184]

While Mother's explanation cannot excuse her actions, the theme of the self-perpetuating quality of violence is as clear here as in the final scenes of *The Love of the Nightingale*.[185] Mother explains, 'I followed the rules. They were the wrong rules, but I had no way of knowing that. Do what you want with me, I no longer care.'[186] These lines are strikingly similar to Procne's: 'I obeyed all the rules: the rule of parents, the rule of marriage, the rules of my loneliness, you. [...] There are no more rules. There is nothing. The world is bleak. The past a mockery, the future dead. And now I want to die.'[187] Procne, like Mother, is not wholly responsible for the harm that befalls her child, but she does contribute to it by her failure to question these rules. In *The Ash Girl*, Angerbird tries to ensure this cycle is perpetuated, goading Judith, 'What is there left for you now but hatred and revenge? Make someone else suffer as you have, that's the kind of anger I like, an anger that spreads like a forest fire.'[188] Whether Judith has the strength to resist this temptation and break this cycle is not clear.

Despite her failings, Mother is not the evil stepmother of traditional fairy-tales. In early scenes, she tries to include Ashgirl in family life, emphasising that the invitation to the ball 'is to all my daughters'. It is Ashgirl who rejects this affiliation, responding, 'I am not your daughter!'[189] However, given the misguided nature of Mother's parenting, and its reproduction of oppression, Ashgirl's refusal to be affiliated could be seen as a positive stand. Additionally, Mother's inclusion of Ashgirl lasts only as long as it does not threaten her filiative offspring. When she discovers that Amir wants to marry Ashgirl, she adopts the tone more usually associated with the 'wicked stepmother': 'She's the embarrassment of the family, we take pity on her and feed her, she's full of tricks, her father's a criminal who ran away into the forest – Go. Disappear! Shamed child of a shamed father. She won't deny her father's shame!'[190] Mother's implication that Ashgirl should suffer for the sins of her father highlights another level of harm that can be passed along filial lines. In this play, fathers are a source of trauma for their children not through their presence but through their absence. When Ashgirl remembers her father, she is tormented by the personification of Sadness, who taunts her, 'He abandoned you, no one there for you.'[191] When she meets Prince Amir, they bond over their shared lack:

Amir I don't know where my father is…
Ashgirl Mine told me he had to leave…[192]

Ashgirl is not the only one who suffers from her father's disappearance. Mother complains repeatedly about the financial hardship his abandonment has brought. We may have little sympathy for her mercenary concerns, but Wertenbaker presents, more subtly, other ways in which Father's absence deprives his daughters. In the play's opening scene, Ruth and Judith discuss ways to entertain themselves. Judith wants 'a good gallop over the fields', but this option is unavailable as 'Father took away the last horse': a symbolic representation of a young girl's desire for adventure denied because a man has taken it for himself. Next, Judith wishes to dissect insects under a magnifying glass, but the glass is locked 'in Father's study' and 'Mother keeps the key'. This image of female potential, locked away by men and guarded by female collaborators, is a potent one. The girls' plan to steal this key is thwarted by Ashgirl's threat to 'tell Mother'.[193] Although, in the following scene, Ashgirl shows no loyalty to Mother, her filial allegiance to her father is clear throughout. This prevents her forging affiliative links with her stepsisters, even though they are young women who, like herself, have been denied the opportunity for adventure.

The most disturbing representation of a father's potential to harm his daughters is in the play's allusion to incest. After Ashgirl has fled the Prince's ball, she becomes lost in the forest and is caught by a man who is struggling against the personification of Lust. Lust '*laughs*' and '*curls around*' the man who sees with horror that Ashgirl is 'so young' and asks Lust to '[h]ave pity'. He begins to realise '[s]he looks like –' and eventually '*pushes Lust away*', defying her, 'I won't let you drag me down – not to this'. Not until he '*runs off, screaming*', with Lust '*laughing*' in pursuit, does Ashgirl allow herself to realise: 'Father?'[194] The lack of resolution to this storyline is one of the play's most troubling elements. Father returns in the final scenes to defend himself and his daughter against Mother's accusations of his criminality, declaring that there have been 'no crimes'. At the end of the play, he starts to follow Lust off, but is convinced to stay by Ashgirl ('Father, I need you') and Amir's friend Paul ('A father's place is here').[195] A family Christmas show can hardly resolve issues of lust and potential incest more decisively than this, leaving a number of questions hanging in the air.

Alongside themes of filiation and heredity, Wertenbaker's preoccupation with cultural dislocation and assimilation is dramatised through the family of Prince Amir. These characters are given greater depth than in traditional versions of the story. The relationship between Prince Amir and his mother, Princess Zehra, is a reversal of the mother–son relationship at the centre of *Credible Witness*. That is, Zehra voices the need to 'become part of this country and learn to love it' and Amir is obsessed with his former homeland and the need to find his father. 'If he is a prisoner, I'll free him', he insists, 'If he is dead, I'll avenge him and take back our pastures.' Some of Zehra's lines, and her strategies for coping with exile, resemble those of Alexander. '[O]ur hosts are not welcoming, so we must become generous guests', she maintains, 'We haven't yet learnt to find beauty in this country, we will.' At Amir's invocation of his filial duty to find or avenge his father, Zehra offers the alternative of affiliative ties in their new land: 'You will marry here and that will root you in this country.'[196] Urging him to choose a wife, she acknowledges that such ties may be more about making connections than love: 'I said marry, I wouldn't pry into your heart.'[197] In direct contrast to Petra's willingness to risk her son's life through her obsession with the past, Zehra declares, 'I am a mother. I owe my son a future.' Like Alexander, she warns against becoming overwhelmed by anger. She advises Amir to follow the example of Paul, another young man from their country, who has 'relinquished his anger and [...] is happy'. Paul's assimilation is evident from his Western name and his keenness for 'this country's dances'. 'If we want to get on here', he tells Amir, 'we have to show off.' When Amir resists this suggestion his mother gently admonishes, 'We're only asking you to dance.'[198] In an article entitled 'Dancing with History', published shortly after these plays, Wertenbaker writes:

> Human beings are no longer sleeping beauties, waiting for the prince charming of history to tap them on the shoulder and invite them to greatness [but] we must not turn away in confusion; on the contrary, we must join the dance, because that's the most interesting place to be. [...] And what happens when we go into the dance is a new mystery. Do we go in as French and come out as English? Do we go in weighted by the anger of one history and in the pleasure of the dance throw it off? I think that's what the playwrights of the twenty-first century are discovering. It is an invitation to a new dance.[199]

A similar sentiment is implicit in Zehra's invitation to Amir, which urges him to throw off his anger and the weight of his history.

Although Paul is more content than Amir, Wertenbaker does not make this a simple (and politically dubious) case of homesickness being bad and assimilation proving advantageous. Both men make valid points concerning their position:

> **Amir** You've changed your name, you imitate the manners of the people here, you forget where you came from.
> **Paul** What's wrong with that? Life is life. Land is land.
> **Amir** How can you say that? The land you come from, the land where your ancestors were born, is not the same as this.[200]

When Amir invokes the land of his ancestors, he brings the issues of filiative genealogy and cultural belonging directly in line. His attachment to his homeland is problematised, as it is not merely a connection to a sense of place but to a sense of privilege. As Pridefly (an observer to this scene) notes, 'Only the best of us have ancestors, most only have grandparents.' Paul detects this air of arrogance, accusing Amir, 'No one knows you here, no one bows down to your great family, maybe that's what you don't like.' As the boys begin to fight, Amir is the first to pull away, exclaiming, 'No! Paul! My friend!' Paul is soon to follow, admitting, 'You've been more than a brother.'[201] With these invocations of affiliation – friend, *more than* a brother – the filiative processes by which Paul is made to feel inferior and Amir experiences the bitter loss of his former status and land are dispelled.

The need for adaptation and change are made manifest in *The Ash Girl*. As with the conscious invocation of metamorphosis in *The Love of the Nightingale*, *The Ash Girl* plays on fairy-tale notions of magical transformation. This is most evident in Wertenbaker's version of the well-known scene in which Cinderella and a number of assorted creatures and vegetables are transformed into glittering socialite, footmen, coach and horses. A number of factors disrupt our expectations of this scene. Firstly, although Wertenbaker positions the transformation of Ashgirl as positive and necessary, she highlights that the transformation of the animals, not for their own benefit but to assist the progress of the heroine, is essentially exploitative. It requires the only things below Cinderella in the pecking order to serve her, not unlike the way she has been forced to serve her stepmother and sisters. Wertenbaker's play draws attention to the problematic nature of this episode, forcing us to think about its significance, rather than merely accept it as part of the story. Otter, chosen to become a footman, is far from keen on the idea. 'You've turned me into a human! That's degrading! What have I done to deserve such a punishment', he wails. His opinion that this transformation is degrading (a reversal of the tendency for traditional stories to turn people into animals as punishments) creates a defamiliarising effect, highlighting the propensity for dominant cultures to see the

Other (or in this case the Otter) as inferior. When Ashgirl tells Otter he looks beautiful, he replies, 'I looked beautiful before. I'm cold', calling into question pseudo-philanthropic policies aimed at bettering the culturally Other. The exploitative nature of this scene is further endorsed by the brutal nature of the transformation, during which Otter is graphically flayed with a scalpel. This is a clear distancing from ideas of benign magic. Not all the animal transformations are portrayed with such negativity. The Fairy intends to turn a couple of young mice into silver ponies, but confronted with a ferociously intelligent, confident little girl mouse who would 'rather be a silver dragon', she contends that 'we don't always have to do what everyone else does', and obliges.[202] This line can be applied both to Wertenbaker's attitude to adapting traditional stories, and to her portrayal of the importance of self-determination.

The impossible metamorphosis that prevents further bloodshed at the end of *The Love of the Nightingale* makes it implicit that, in the real world, other solutions must be sought. In *The Ash Girl*, this point is made explicit. At the end of the transformation scene, which falls directly before the interval, the Fairy warns Ashgirl that 'Magic cannot last because it is a chance and chance is short and fleeting. There is another magic that might last, but it depends on you.' When Ashgirl asks if, at midnight, she must return to her 'old life', the Fairy is clear: 'If you let chance change you, no.'[203] Additionally, the Fairy is not a 'Disneyfied' Fairy Godmother but a 'Fairy in the Mirror': 'the one you find when you see yourself clearly'.[204] This description highlights (perhaps more cloyingly than is usual in Wertenbaker's writing, but perhaps this whole play can be seen as a pastiche of the pantomime style) that we are agents of our own change. While keeping an element of magical intervention, crucial to the atmosphere of the story, Wertenbaker does not allow this to become an easy way out of hardship. This is reinforced at the play's end, when the Fairy asks Prince Amir and Ashgirl (and the audience), 'Will you have the courage to change this circle of cruel convention?'[205] This line would hardly seem out of place in a Brechtian *Lehrstücke*. Zehra tells her son and his bride, 'We have stilled the forest. It is your time now.'[206] The only characters left on stage that Zehra's 'we' could allude to are Father and the Fairy. This suggests a generational element to this statement, a passing down of responsibility, and an instruction to children not to continue the conflicts of their parents but to build on what they have achieved. Our inheritance is what we make of it, the play proposes.[207]

The ending of *The Ash Girl* endorses the human capacity for hope, generosity, friendship, energy, pity and love, and suggests that these qualities constantly thwart the encroachment of the 'deadly sins' upon our lives. A fairy story must have a 'happy ending', and Wertenbaker complies with this tradition, leaving us with the lines:

Fairy The rare flash –
Ashgirl I searched, and I found –
Amir I knew I could find –
Ashgirl You –
Amir You –
Fairy Of happiness.[208]

However, this is not a simple fairy-tale ending. Disturbing questions have been raised and not answered. Ashgirl may have succeeded, but her sisters (who, in this retelling, cannot be dismissed as ugly or evil) have not been so lucky. Throughout, Wertenbaker has asserted that fairy stories are more complex and troubling than Disney cartoons and contemporary pantomimes depict. She has reminded us of more disturbing versions such as the Brothers Grimm account, which concludes not with Cinderella and her Prince living 'happily ever after' but with the fate of the blind and mutilated sisters. The suffering of Ruth and Judith is not the final image of Wertenbaker's play, but it has barely left the stage before Ashgirl and Amir profess their newfound contentment. This juxtaposition forces us to look more closely at how our culture apportions punishment and happiness, and by what factors it chooses to define a 'happy ending'. The passage quoted above may seem to embrace some of the saccharine sentiment the play largely avoids, but this overemphasis jars with the more critical attitude the audience have been encouraged to take.

Conclusions

The plays discussed in this chapter draw attention to the reproduction of the species and of human cultural identities. They
demonstrate the problematic replication of conflict and oppression
on a familial and a national level, but also offer the possibility of
breaking such cycles: to 'repeat in order to produce difference, not
to validate'.[209] The figure of the child, whether an onstage character
or an offstage presence, is a recurrent trope, which evokes Carl Jung's
discussion of the child archetype. Jung believed any archetype 'has
always to do with a picture of belonging to the whole human race'
and asserted that one of the 'essential features of the child-motif
is its *futurity*. The child is potential future.' Describing life as 'a
flux, a flowing into the future, and not a stoppage or a back-wash'
(potentially another floating identity), Jung explained that it was
'not surprising' that the child had become the model for 'so many
of the mythological *saviours*'. He considered it a '*uniting symbol*
which unites the opposites, a mediator, bringer of healing, that is,
one who makes whole'.[210] In *The Break of Day*, the cross-border child
Hugh and Nina adopt is presented as a source of hope on two levels.
Firstly, the couple's decision to raise a child is positioned as an act of
faith in the future. Earlier in the play, Nina says of the creative act
of song writing: 'To sing, you have to believe someone will be there
to listen to you, not only now – in the future.'[211] At the end of the
play, she describes her adoption in a similar way: 'I brought my child
to this country, I have to believe in it.'[212] Additionally, as Mihail
proposes, such children carry a responsibility to 'not descend into
narrow ethnic identification, but [...] be wilfully international' and
to 'carry on history with broad minds and warm hearts'.[213] *The Ash
Girl* places a similar responsibility onto the shoulders of the young,
contrasting the potential each generation has to move forward with
the harm and misery that occur if they do not.

Rabillard notes that 'Wertenbaker repeatedly uses the image
of a child's life threatened to suggest entrapment in the past, an
inability to see a generative pattern in experience.'[214] We see this
threat averted in *The Grace of Mary Traverse* and carried out in *The

Love of the Nightingale, where Itys' death is witnessed moments after we are told 'A child is the future.'[215] In Wertenbaker's later plays, these threats are more metaphorical: not poison or swords, but the potentially crushing effects of history and genealogy, so apparent in *Credible Witness* and *The Ash Girl*. This phenomenon is also voiced in Wertenbaker's radio play *Dianeira* (1999), produced during the same period as these stage plays. Wertenbaker creatively adapts Sophocles' *Women of Trachis*, a tragedy which focuses on Heracles' wife Deianira. After years of dedication and anxiety, Deianira poisons (perhaps accidentally) her husband, in an attempt to prevent him from taking the young and beautiful Iole as a second wife. This plot contains resonances of *Medea* – the archetypal tale of infanticide – but in Wertenbaker's play, Dianeira and Heracles destroy their offspring more subtly. We are introduced to their son Hyllos with the words 'He is a son, a promise of hope.' Shortly afterwards, we are told ominously how 'His father's shadow begins to cover him, merges with his own shadow.'[216] At the end of the play, the dying Heracles secures the lasting presence of his shadow by commanding Hyllos to marry Iole, calling on 'the law that orders sons to obey their fathers'. Hyllos pleads, 'please, let me decide: give me back my life', but Heracles dismisses him: 'We must look to my death'. The stark implications of this hopeless destruction of the potential for life and future, because of a fixation on the past and the dead, are re-emphasised by the storyteller: 'fathers do eat their sons if they can, there is no other myth that rings so true. [...] You do what your fathers tell you in the end, one way or another, even now, you'll die by their order.'[217] While Hyllos fails to escape his father's shadow, this chapter has shown that in Wertenbaker's contemporaneous stage plays, several characters are better able to cast off filial ties.

The pressures and complexities of filial relationships, alongside other now-familiar concerns, such as the fluidity of gender roles, the danger of absolutes and the value of the arts, remain noticeable as we move forward to consider Wertenbaker's most recent plays, discussed in the next and final chapter.

CHAPTER 6
'LANDSCAPES WITH FIGURES IN THEM': ON PITY AND TENDERNESS

I'm doing landscapes with figures in them. We are made to look at each other, Suzanne. Our responsibility is to show, in detail, a few people with their aspirations and their frailties. If we don't look at human beings, at their bodies, where will pity and tenderness come from? Isn't that what the world needs? Who will love human beings if we stop painting them?[1]

When England began doubting itself, why did it have to stop loving itself? It keeps gashing its own limbs.[2]

The Line, produced by the Arcola in November 2009, focuses on the relationship between Edgar Degas and his pupil Suzanne Valadon. The need 'to look at each other' is a crucial statement of this play, which adapts Wertenbaker's tendency towards theatrical self-reflexivity, recognisable from *Our Country's Good* (1988), *The Love of the Nightingale* (1988), *The Break of Day* (1995) and *After Darwin* (1998). *The Line*, however, uses the frame of visual art as a synecdoche that allows Wertenbaker to explore the social function of the arts and the artist. This device is hinted at in Degas's instruction 'You'll have to read if you want to be an artist, just as writers need to look at paintings.'[3] Degas's insistence that we must look at each other becomes, therefore, more than just a mantra for the painter. What do plays such as Wertenbaker's do, if not study the human figure? As a dramatist, she has never strayed too far into the abstract: her plays are peopled with recognisable human beings in recognisable human situations. They are also filled with the 'pity and tenderness' of which Degas speaks, even alongside their criticism and doubt. Wertenbaker has emphasised that Degas's 'Who will love human beings if we stop painting them?' is 'a line that I really felt myself'.[4]

A similar theme is apparent in *Three Birds Alighting on a Field* (1991), a study of the contemporary art scene, which predates *The Line* by almost two decades. *Three Birds* features a formerly successful painter, Stephen, who has fallen out of fashion and lives a reclusive existence, shunning the art world with which he has become disillusioned. Yet, despite his cynicism, Stephen is one of the more positive forces within the play. Where Degas's drawings demonstrate his love for human beings, Stephen's landscapes represent a similar commitment to England. Although *Three Birds* differs from *The Line* in terms of narrative, style and scope, the plays share many themes, and Stephen and Degas display similar characteristics. These parallels make it productive to examine the two alongside each other: an analysis that forms the main thrust of this chapter and leads towards tentative conclusions about Wertenbaker's most pronounced and long-standing concerns. In particular, I foreground her plays' persistent hope for the future, which often connects to natural beauty, the human imagination and the human capacity for pity and tenderness. Firstly, however, I turn briefly to the other plays Wertenbaker has written in the last decade.

Wertenbaker's recent output is varied in subject and style, consisting of a new play about Galileo's relationship with his beloved daughter, which warns of the danger of absolutes ('The Laws of Motion', 2004); an adaptation of a nineteenth-century Czech play about the anxieties of motherhood and the stifling nature of small communities (*Jenufa*, 2007); and a youth theatre piece based on *As You Like It*, which highlights the importance of the natural world and the mutability of gender roles (*Arden City*, 2008). These plays do not bear much resemblance to one another, but all suggest links with previous phases of Wertenbaker's writing. 'The Laws of Motion', for example, presents a debate between religion and science, recognisable from *After Darwin* (1998), 'Monads' (c.1979) and 'The Vigil' (c.1977), and re-examines a woman traditionally excluded from history, in a way reminiscent of Wertenbaker's plays from the early 1980s. *Jenufa* is more in keeping with Wertenbaker's

1990s plays, continuing her exploration of the anxieties of filiative and affiliative relationships and the propensity for unbending families and communities to damage the future of their offspring. *Arden City* has an environmental focus: a long-standing concern for Wertenbaker, as is evident from early drafts such as 'Near Miss' (c.1979) and 'A Year on Exmoor' (c.1976), and an underlying preoccupation of more recent works such as *The Break of Day* and *Three Birds Alighting on a Field* (1991). It also features transvestism, as previously explored in Wertenbaker's early 1980s 'trilogy': *New Anatomies* (1981), 'Variations' (c.1981) and 'Inside Out' (c.1982).

Arden City (NT Connections, 2008)

A contemporary reworking of Shakespeare's *As You Like It*, *Arden City* was written for the National Theatre's 2008 Connections Festival.[5] The play is set in contemporary London and the Forest of Arden is a patch of inner city allotments under threat from Olympic redevelopment. Here we find Valerie (a female Duke Senior) and assorted others living off the land. In the late 1970s, when Wertenbaker was drafting 'Near Miss', she had sought to resist writing 'a let's all go back to the land play'.[6] At face value, this contemporary piece seems to exhibit that naivety, but an education pack that accompanied the play explains that these allotments are 'a magical world with a more sensible way of life. An alternative to the Urban Jungle.' They exist not as a 'geographical notion' but as 'an idea, a feeling and a state of being passed on from one resident to the next'.[7] Life in them is not supposed to be presented as 'a pastoral idyll, but a challenge'.[8]

Wertenbaker has, at times, expressed a reticence towards writing for teenage audiences and/or performers, and this play confirms that it is not her strongest genre.[9] The play's main stumbling block is its attempt to be current. Modern language does not help Wertenbaker imbue the allotments with a sense of magic ('Arden City? I've heard about it. I was researching this project on wilderness in the cities, remember, and they talked about these allotments in London and they were going to be destroyed'),[10] and some of her attempts to draw contemporary parallels (wrestler Charles becomes Che the kick-boxer) take on the patronising quality of a grown up trying to appeal to 'the kids'.[11] Without the distancing effect of Shakespearian language, the instant infatuation between characters strains credulity and the improbability of the narrative is left exposed. This is exacerbated by the play's brevity (Connections pieces are one act) and the fact that Wertenbaker attempts to retain nearly every character and narrative element of Shakespeare's already crowded play. This gives little time for themes or relationships to develop convincingly.

Despite its theatrical flaws, the play raises a number of interesting issues, albeit ones it does not have time to explore rewardingly. Retaining the cross-dressing element of Shakespeare's narrative returns Wertenbaker to a theme that occupied much of her earlier writing. Jay (Jacques) recognises Rosie/Garry (Rosaline/Ganymede) as one of the liminal figures so often peopling Wertenbaker's plays: 'What he was I don't know, I'm not even sure he was a he, I don't ask questions any more than I answer questions. If nobody labels you, you can be what you want. Maybe even who you truly are.'[12] Although this theme is not explored here with the depth and subtlety of *New Anatomies*, *The Grace of Mary Traverse*, 'Variations' and 'Inside Out', *Arden City* provides Wertenbaker with the opportunity to bring some twenty-first century openness to Shakespearian transvestism. For example, just before the reveal, Orlando admits, 'I really like you as Garry. So, maybe I'm gay, which is fine, but what about Rosie? And also, I don't know what you feel about that... I know you like pretending to be a girl, this is a bit confusing, you know.'[13] In a final address to the audience, Rosie explains, 'I don't know whether to speak as a boy or a girl or whether there is much difference. I leave that for you to decide.'[14] Thus, Wertenbaker avoids the wholehearted resolution of transgression that accompanies the end of many Shakespearian comedies.[15]

Jenufa (Natural Perspective/Arcola, 2007)

Adapted from the Czech play *Její pastorkyňa*, by Gabriela Preissová, *Jenufa* begins with a love triangle in a small village.[16] Jenufa loves wealthy, profligate mill owner Steva, but his jealous stepbrother Latsa has loved her since childhood. Convinced of the superficiality of his brother's affections, Latsa scars Jenufa's 'perfect round and rosy cheeks'[17] and, as expected, Steva loses interest. The tragedy ensues as Jenufa has already 'sinned' with Steva and, concealed by her draconian stepmother Kostelnichka, bears his child. Racked with shame at her stepdaughter's disgrace, Kostelnichka murders the child, telling Jenufa he died of a fever. Broken, Jenufa agrees to marry Latsa, but their wedding day is disturbed by the discovery of the child's body and the revelation of Kostelnichka's crime.

As in the plays discussed in Chapter Five, *Jenufa* is highly conscious of filiative and affiliative relationships. Kostelnichka emphasises that Jenufa's 'own mother wouldn't have done as much for' her, a claim Jenufa accepts with gratitude and respect, calling Kostelnichka 'Mama'.[18] Other characters reiterate their bond, suggesting Jenufa has 'inherited' Kostelnichka's intelligence and piety.[19] That people 'think Jenufa will take after' her stepmother seems to reinforce arguments for nurture over nature,[20] but the villagers still remind Kostelnichka she is 'only' a stepmother.[21] Although these voices seem to question the authenticity of Kostelnichka's motherhood, her influence over Jenufa, and the obedience she demands, are as harmful as that of the filial parents in *The Love of the Nightingale, The Ash Girl, Credible Witness* and *Dianeira*. In forging an emotionally compelling link between the importance of religious and parental authority, she cripples Jenufa's capacity for independent action: 'God doesn't like disobedience, and he'll punish you severely if you don't do what I say.'[22] In one of the play's most striking lines, which echoes the sentiment of the plays discussed in the previous chapter, Jenufa pleads, 'Can't we find a way forward?'[23] Here, as in *Dianeira*, the younger generation's hope and possibility are murdered by the older generation's prejudices and rigidity, metaphorically for Jenufa and literally for her baby son. At the end of the play, Jenufa seeks to break the bond with her stepmother, calling her 'Kostelnichka, like a stranger' and rebuking her with words that echo the village gossips: 'I'm not your daughter. You're only my stepmother.' However, the strength of their bond remains visible in the play's final lines, in which Jenufa resolves to marry Latsa: 'After all, it's […] what Mama wanted'.[24]

Wertenbaker's introduction to *Jenufa* consciously links the play's theme of parentage to the methods of its creation. Writing of the process of adaptation, she describes Preissová as the 'common parent' her work shares with its 'original'. However, like Jenufa herself, the play owes much to the 'nurture' it received, in this case from Natural Perspective Theatre Company, who developed and produced it, with director Irina Brown, music and movement specialist Christopher Sivertsen and a group of professional and student actors. Although Wertenbaker had worked collaboratively before, with companies such as the Women's Theatre Group and Out of Joint, with Natural Perspective she claimed to have found 'another way of working', which she describes as 'objective':

> That is, we'd created the society in which the play took place before looking at the individuals in it. We'd done this with movements, rhythms, dances, music, research, and thought. Once the actors understood the world they were living in, they had the framework with which to explore their characters. We all live in communities, however fragmented. A community is a character as complex and nuanced as the individuals in it. Always present, always in some kind of dialogue with the individual. It needs as much work as the characters in it.[25]

Although Wertenbaker claims not to 'want to sound like Brecht here', the debt still seems apparent.

The Laws of Motion (Peter Hall Company/Bath Theatre Royal, 2004)

This play was first produced as 'Galileo's Daughter', having been inspired by Dava Sobel's well-researched account of that name. However, where Sobel writes to reveal historical 'truths' about Galileo's marginalised daughter (the nun Maria Celeste), Wertenbaker's play is fictionalised to suit her 'own polemical purpose'.[26] This is not to say that Wertenbaker neglects to point (as in her drafts of 'Agamemnon's Daughter' and 'Don Juan's Women') to the significance of a woman excluded from previous histories.[27]

Perhaps most crucially, in her play, Galileo's work survives not because a faithful pupil smuggles it into Europe (as in Brecht's *The Life of Galileo*) but through the actions of his daughter.[28] The play also demonstrates the struggle Maria undergoes to gain recognition, indicating how easily she will be forgotten. Her attempts to show an active interest in Galileo's work are repeatedly ignored or patronised:

> **Maria** Father, please, let me help you.
> **Galileo** Sister Luisa liked my music? Is Sister Teresa's back pain better?
> [...] I have a book to finish. How can my own son show no interest?
> **Maria** I have that interest, Father.
> **Galileo** Yes, you do. It ought to shame him.
> [...]
> **Maria** Why could I not assist you, father? With your book.
> **Galileo** Send your pure prayers to heaven that I may finish it quickly.[29]

This tendency to disregard women is pervasive. Galileo did not marry his children's mother because she 'would have ruined the name of Galilei' and Maria not only accepts but extends this misogyny.[30] She regards her lowly mother as 'not interesting' and tells her sister Arcangela she 'must never think about her', and instead 'be content with the most noble flesh and blood father'.[31] However, this play is not a feminist 'herstory' and gender is not its primary concern. Rather, the relationship between Galileo and his daughter offers a personal echo of the play's main political theme: 'Living with absolute world systems degrades everyone.'[32] Following his time with the Inquisition, Galileo learns that it is possible to hold two 'imperfect' and 'contradictory truths', and 'two contradictory loves'. 'It may not be a heroic stand', he admits, 'but it is more human. If we see both nature and God through a glass darkly, where is the ground for absolutes? To insist on one absolute truth leads only to ignorance and a fanatical humour.'[33] The play accepts that the loss of absolutes is unsettling. The 'universe you reveal in your books is vast and changing, imperfect and frighteningly unknown', recognises Maria, having felt the same devastation at the revelation of her father's imperfection.[34] In her darkest hour, she rails: 'I don't believe in anything anymore, God is arbitrary, the Church slippery, laws crumble like sand, there is no order, no truth, there is nothing, nothing, only darkness, and my empty heart.'[35] Her descriptions bear some resemblance to the cruel post-Darwinian world of 'struggle, disorder, despair, horror [and] chaos', which Fitzroy fears in *After Darwin*. Yet Fitzroy has already reconciled himself with Galileo's world, almost ridiculing the suggestion that this was ever a concern: 'It does not matter whether the Earth revolves around the Sun or the Sun around the Earth, there is still order and harmony.' With hindsight, both he and Darwin can see that the world and 'the notion of God' have been able to 'recover quite easily' from Galileo's discoveries, just as a contemporary audience knows it has once more since Darwin.[36]

The idea that the world is 'frighteningly unknown' and essentially unknowable is a recognisable theme in Wertenbaker's work (see *The Grace of Mary Traverse*). Yet here, as before, it is coupled with the suggestion that a lack of certainty is no reason to despair: accepting that we can never know the answers is no reason to abandon the questioning. Galileo explains that 'Nature is so complex we will never understand it but we must look',[37] as our 'world is too interesting to remain ignorant of'.[38] Although Father Anthony fears the 'poisoned apple of doubt',[39] Wertenbaker embraces it, not as poison but as possibility.

Maria's convent provides a picture of how religion can function alongside rationality, intelligence and humanity, providing a microcosm through which the play makes another of its central arguments: that faith and knowledge need not be in conflict. Wertenbaker presents the reasons they collide so violently in Galileo's story as twofold. Firstly, she suggests the Catholic Church had purposefully endeavoured 'to weave faith and reason together, Scripture and Aristotle', in order to appeal 'both to the simple minded who rely on faith' and 'the intricately minded who rely on logic'. These false parallels force those in disagreement with scientific authority into conflict with religious authority. Secondly, Galileo's troubles result not from religious intolerance but from the need for socio-political order. As in Brecht's *Galileo*, the Church fears that, without Aristotle, more sophisticated citizens 'will play with all kinds of other theories, Luther, political ideas, who knows'.[40] This gives the impression that the Church is more concerned with the breakdown of political stability than with religious orthodoxy. The Papacy is depicted as a political institution and while the play argues that religion and science are capable of renouncing absolutism and remaining open to one another, it does not show the same hope for conventional politics. Thus the Pope argues that 'Political stability requires intellectual stability' and because in seventeenth-century Europe 'intellectual stability is based partly on Scripture and partly on Aristotle', the domains of religion and science become politicised and must succumb to the same totalitarian principles.[41] Ambassador Niccolini regrets: 'We are living in a different world, it is a world of extremes and it has no use for diplomats. Or mathematicians. We seem to be moving back to the dark ages although some no doubt will call it a new dawn.'[42] A politics based on absolutes rather than diplomacy is a contemporary concern. We hear the familiar Anglo-American rhetoric 'if you're not with us, you're against us' in Father Anthony's indictment that 'we are in a different world now and the Church must opt for clarity and take strong action. Those who are not with us are traitors: they are our enemies.'[43] This play opened in 2004, a year after the American-led invasion of Iraq and three years into the conflict in Afghanistan, about which both George Bush and Hillary Clinton had used similar phrases.[44]

Unlike many of the parents in Wertenbaker's work,[45] Galileo is aware of the potential harm he could cause his daughter, especially through obstinacy and inflexibility. In contrast, Galileo hurts his daughter through his ability to compromise and adapt, and it is she who wounds him with her pride and rigidity. Maria worries that her love for her father has been 'too human' and she has not been 'enthusiastic enough about God',[46] but her words reveal that she has, in fact, loved her father as a God:

I love you more than myself. I only place you after God. (*She looks up.*) And sometimes I love you more than –? No, I can't say that – even if it's true. (*She reads/writes on.*) I recognize in you the most important being in my life. I would give my life for you and accept any torment. Sometimes I am transported by such emotion... (*She shakes herself out of this.*)[47]

Even in dedicating her life to God, she chose the name Maria Celeste (Maria of the Sky) in acknowledgement of her father. This love is reciprocal, with Galileo citing 'an almost religious intensity in the love of a parent for a child, a love so immense it hurts the very sinews of the heart',[48] but having spent the first half of the play worshipping her father, Maria rejects him completely after his recantation. Galileo recognises that her affections need to settle somewhere between these two absolutes. 'I do not ask for your devotion', he explains, 'only a little tenderness.'[49] Tenderness: a now familiar word. In loving her father as a God, Maria lacked the human tenderness needed to understand human fallibility. Father Anthony is similarly curtailed by his belief that as 'the love of God transcends anything personal', 'Human beings are expendable.' It is the Abbess who demonstrates the deepest degree of humanism, insisting, despite her dislike of Anthony, that no 'human being is expendable. Not even you.' Her humanism is not naïve or idealistic but remarkable in its ability to withstand her realisation that all 'human beings disappoint in the end'. Even so, she insists, we must 'resist this trend' to become narrow, closed and unforgiving when we feel under threat. 'This means refusing to be overcome by disappointment and the anger that accompanies disappointment', she explains.[50] Refusing to be overcome by disappointment is a central tenet of Wertenbaker's work, indeed of her whole career. The Abbess's words echo Robert's report of his director's interest in the question of 'how much evidence you needed to stop being a humanist' (in *The Break of Day*)[51] and Mary Traverse's desire to 'forgive the history of the world'.[52] They also pre-empt Degas's insistence on the need to look at and love the human figure.

The Need to Look at Paintings

Principally concerned with the relationship between Edgar Degas and Suzanne Valadon, *The Line* (Arcola, 2009) has only one other character: Degas's long-serving housekeeper Zoe Clozier. The narrative starts with the first meeting of Degas and Suzanne, follows the ups and downs of their constantly renegotiated relationship and ends with Degas's death. This covers a thirty-year time span (1888–1917), and the intervals between scenes range from a few months to several years. Some critics considered this breadth a disadvantage. Kate Bassett wrote that 'Wertenbaker's writing feels stilted, and the storytelling is jerky'[53] and Lloyd Evans called it 'uncomfortably vast', 'choppy and fragmented'.[54] If the play is vast in its temporal dimension, it is spatially compact. Apart from two scenes that occur in Suzanne's studio, all the action takes place in Degas's rooms (predominately his studio).[55] Yet despite John Nathan's puzzling assertion that 'the play makes no connections outside the time in which it is set, and few connections outside the studio in which most of the action takes place',[56] its scope reaches considerably further; not perhaps in narrative terms (where it touches on wider issues of its period, such as the Dreyfus Affair and the First World War, only to reveal the characters' attitudes to them),[57] but certainly in its examination of the role of the artist. Although set on the cusp of the nineteenth and twentieth century, *The Line* poses still pertinent questions about the present role and condition of the arts, through its discussion of issues such as commercialisation, celebrity, the position of women in art, the economic pressures on artists and the respective values of tradition and innovation. With little narrative beyond that of Degas and Suzanne's fluctuating relationship, it is the philosophical examination of these topics that give the play its substance.

As with many of Wertenbaker's later works (particularly *The Break of Day*), a lack of action led to criticisms that *The Line* is more debate than drama. While Quentin Letts found it 'agreeably wordy',[58] Michael Billington considered it 'decent, if somewhat undramatic'.[59] The Arcola's production did not perhaps take full advantage of the play's self-conscious artistry. It is structured as a series of snapshots or paintings. Each scene is titled, either with the name of a Degas painting ('Two Women'),[60] something that sounds like one ('Young Woman with an Envelope'),[61] or an artistic technique or genre ('Soft Ground Etching',[62] 'Self-Portrait').[63] Thus, Wertenbaker assumes the aesthetics of painting in a highly conscious manner. Highlighting this in production could have given the play its defining theatricality, but the device is more evident on the page than it was on stage.

The play's third scene, entitled 'Zoe I', is a 'portrait' without words: '**Zoe** *discreetly tidies the studio* [...]. *Continuous movement with some stops in different positions. Something elegant and fluid in the movement and great stillness in the stops, like music*'.[64] Such a scene must be treated with exactly the right attitude or *geste* if it is to appear more than an inefficient scene change. If its importance is lost, there are further repercussions, as the scene needs to be viewed in relation to sc. xi: 'Zoe II', a monologue revealing more of Zoe's character.[65] By creating two versions of Zoe's 'self-portrait', as well as two scenes for Zoe and Suzanne ('Two Women I'[66] and 'Two Women II'),[67] Wertenbaker's structure mirrors Degas's artistic process:

> Repetition makes the good artist. Art does not branch out: it concentrates. They say I repeat myself, but they don't understand I've narrowed my subjects because I'm looking for a truth, layer by layer. It's not pretty or exciting, only real.
>
> A narrative carries you along easily, but where's the truth? [...] I give people glimpses, but they have to stand still and pay attention. It's too hard for them so they clamour for a story. Something noisy and emotional.[68]

However, even critics who recognised this device did not necessarily appreciate it:

> [L]ine is more truthful than painting that's stuffed with narrative; artists become good by repetition. Wertenbaker has

taken it all to heart. Her play is a series of small scenes, in each of which [...] Valadon rushes into the artist's studio, shows herself to be both talented and unrecognised, squawks the name of a famous man [...] and scarpers, leaving Degas with art. Then she does it again. Good actors are stuck in poses.[69]

The feeling that the play was too repetitive was shared by many, perhaps suggesting that the writing failed to create a fully engaging drama out of formal experimentation.[70] However, while *The Line* was not Wertenbaker's greatest theatrical success, it has considerable value as a text that illuminates her persistent interrogation of the nature and role of the arts and the artist.

As the play's title implies, the theme of (cultural) genealogy, so deeply explored in the plays discussed in Chapter Five, also features here. Degas speaks reverently of 'the line' of art history, which has influenced him more than familial ancestry.[71] He believes it his duty to take a 'place in history',[72] by painting not 'what you want but what you must'.[73] Suzanne disagrees, claiming that the twentieth-century painter does not 'need an education'.[74] Degas complains that there is 'no history' in Suzanne's paintings, a term he uses synonymously with the phrase 'hierarchy of excellence', and thus is far from neutral. His subservience to tradition is connected to an unquestioning allegiance to the state of France. Although he speaks passionately about the need to paint and draw with truth, he has a very subjective understanding of this concept. He understands that truths are created and do not exist in any abstract or objective state, but does not seem to find this problematic. He is happy to conclude that Dreyfus 'can't be [innocent] because he was found guilty',[75] and that women are beautiful because the 'history of painting tells us that women are beautiful'.[76] Essentially, he respects authority to such an extent that he cannot conceive that history or the French military could have been mistaken. Again we see Wertenbaker playing with the meaning of words, demonstrating that concepts like truth, justice and freedom have no stable meaning.

Suzanne is wary of Degas's deference to tradition, telling him she 'never went for hierarchies'. In response, he patronises her, asserting that hierarchy is one of the few things women are unable to understand. What Degas identifies as a lack of understanding could equally be read as a lack of respect, which allows Suzanne to make artistic innovations. Degas warns Suzanne that in refusing to occupy her place in 'the line', she risks being forgotten, as 'no one will know how to judge your work'.[77] This risk is one that Wertenbaker is familiar with. As early as 1984, she had begun 'to feel that, unless critics feel very secure with [a play] and that they are really being carried away, they don't make an effort to see what the playwright is trying to do and they dismiss it out of hand'.[78] Similarly, Sara Freeman suggests that the tendency for critics to try to 'remain in judgement of a piece of theatre rather than in dialogue with it' may have led to poor reviews of Wertenbaker's 'most mature and complex plays', which are 'difficult to "translate" in a first watching'.[79]

Suzanne represents the artist who rebels against convention, but it is unfair to suggest that Degas stands entirely within it. Rather, he presents two illuminating metaphors to illustrate the intermediate path he has taken:

An artist works the way a horse ploughs a field, not looking to left or right, obeying the tradition, and fitting into it the way the horse fits into the groove and then moves forward, breaking up new ground.

[...]

I left [tradition] the way a son might leave his father's house, but he continues the family values and he respects his inheritance.[80]

Suzanne finds these metaphors meaningless as they invoke privileges she lacked: 'I never had a father. I don't have an inheritance. I made my own way. I learned by myself and I'm going to do it differently.' Her own metaphors are more brutal and universal: 'we'll sweep tradition out of the door like the dust it is'.[81] Suzanne's powerful rhetoric might prompt us to assume that a contemporary female writer is voicing her own ideas through this feisty, progressive female character. However, it is arguable that, as an artist, Wertenbaker has more in common with Degas. While her writing is by no means staid, neither has she made the extreme formal and structural innovations of writers such as Caryl Churchill or Sarah Kane. When it comes to her work as a translator, she recognises a great allegiance to the cultural and linguistic traditions in which she is working,[82] and many of her 'original' plays show a classical influence, or employ elements of earlier traditions of playwriting, albeit inventively reworked.

Of the traditions Degas feels compelled to follow, the most apparent is his preoccupation with the human figure. When, towards the end of the play, Suzanne reports painting landscapes, Degas reminds her of the importance of placing 'figures in them'. His insistence that we 'are made to look at each other' is one of the play's most crucial statements.[83] Although, at times, Suzanne appears a warmer, livelier, friendlier character than Degas, in contrast to his call for 'pity and tenderness', she muses, 'tenderness belongs to the last century. The war ripped it out of us. I'm modern. I don't like humanity.'[84] If pity and tenderness belonged to the nineteenth century, and the twentieth century did not like humanity, the play implicitly asks where this leaves us as we enter the twenty-first.

Degas and Suzanne do not merely argue about what they should paint and how it should be painted, they disagree over the way to *be* an artist. Degas believes artists must sacrifice everything for their work: not marry, have children, or if (as with Suzanne) this is already unavoidable, be prepared to ignore such 'details' and focus all their love, creativity and dedication on artistic creation. In contrast, Suzanne lives a life full of lovers, responsibilities and worries for her son, her relationships and her finances. In a rather Brechtian way, she provides a number of down-to-earth reminders, which disrupt Degas's assumptions and aesthetics. When Zoe tells her that Degas never takes models from the Place Pigalle because 'they look too eager', Suzanne exclaims, 'Well, they're hungry aren't they.'[85] While Degas seems embarrassed by any mention of commerce ('Americans turn everything they touch into a commodity. I sell to them too, but

I don't boast about it'),[86] Suzanne mentions money in most scenes, whether concern for her poverty or surprise at her later wealth.[87] Her material concerns root the play, providing a contrast to Degas's detached ideals.

Wertenbaker does not disguise the very real presence of financial pressures on the artist, but neither does she glorify their effect. A genuine question is posed as to whose art will be truer: those who can represent life because they have lived it, or those who have removed its distractions to study it. The text provides no clear answer and, while Wertenbaker makes it clear that this ambiguity is deliberate, she has conceded that 'having to earn a living is a strain, you know, it really is. Because you can do things you don't really want to do, and that can be very damaging. I mean, I speak from experience. [...] I think patronage would be perfect.'[88] Like Suzanne, Wertenbaker was not wealthy enough as a young artist to concentrate solely on writing. In the late 1970s, she juggled a job at the Camden Plaza cinema with journalism and playwriting. Her need for an income required her to write to commission for companies such as the Women's Theatre Group, and these experiences, and the artistic compromises she felt they forced her to make, may be the 'things you don't really want to do' to which she alludes. In 1981, she approached David Sulkin at the Royal Court about the possibility of becoming their 'Theatre Attaché'. Correspondence suggests that Sulkin tried to reassure Wertenbaker that non-theatrical work could benefit her writing, but she remained unconvinced:

> I took to heart what you said about having an independent income [but] I think theatre work would be more useful. [...] [T]he only job open to me at the moment is a motor-cycle messenger and I don't think tearing around London at 100mph will give much insight into humanity[89]

Even after Wertenbaker achieved significant success as a writer, her financial position was far from secure. 'I've a play at the RSC, a play at the Royal Court and I still can't afford West End theatre tickets', she complained in 1988.[90] In 1991, she described being visited by bailiffs during the West End run of *Our Country's Good*[91] and, in 1997, she sold her archive to the British Library, having initially considered selling it to Texas, which she 'really didn't want to' do, because she 'desperately needed money'.[92] In 2010, she developed some un-commissioned work while living 'for four weeks, on a tiny stipend' from the National Theatre Studio. Her attitude towards this grant – 'But it's a stipend, you know, it's not nothing' – demonstrates how rare even such small opportunities for her to work without pressure have been.

As well as financial concerns, there are social barriers to Suzanne assuming the same artistic focus as Degas. She brings a gendered aspect to the debate, reminding him that he 'has the permission of society to be an artist', which she, as a woman, does not.[93] In the early 1980s, Wertenbaker had commented on a number of occasions on the unequal access women had to the arts and culture:

> As America enters the 1980's, it is clear that here at least, and despite ten years of feminism, history continues to be made and written by men.[94]

> [M]y feeling is that feminism has had this tremendous intellectual strength and success but has failed practically to put women into any kind of power and that WIE [Women in Entertainment] should concentrate on that.[95]

Although today's theatre may be more accessible to women than that of the early days of Wertenbaker's career, Suzanne's concerns do not seem purely historical. That she questions nineteenth-century attitudes to female artists is unsurprising, but that she does so in Wertenbaker's twenty-first-century play suggests that Wertenbaker does not feel confident such problems have been entirely eradicated by modern feminism. Suzanne recognises that she would be labelled self-indulgent, unfeminine and irresponsible if she assumed the qualities that, in Degas, are admired as dedication. Suzanne admits to being a 'bad mother', torn between devotion to her son Maurice and desire for 'time to draw in peace'.[96] Her concern for Maurice's welfare fluctuates between her being 'too busy to notice' that he is malnourished, to her marrying a respectable banker in an attempt to give Maurice a stable future. Degas is contemptuous about this decision:

Degas A future husband – in a carriage. My dear, you must still have a fever. [...] I taught you, I nourished you, I even loved you. You insult me, you betray art, you threaten France! **Suzanne** [...] I don't want to argue, I came to get your blessing, please, Maître.
Degas My curse. You won't paint. Ducks and geese are not conducive to good art. [...] The bourgeoisie exists to dull the sharp edges of the soul. I'm the one saw your spirit, your talent. I treated it like the precious thing it is [...]. Go then, wallow in the torpor of your new-found comfort.[97]

Three Birds Alighting on a Field exposes a similar double standard in the relationship between Stephen and Fiona, a younger artist who was once his pupil and his lover. Although Stephen is not an unsympathetic character, he abuses his position of waning power over Fiona. In this extract, in which he mocks Fiona's desire to marry, we find many similarities with the passage quoted above:

Fiona [...] I'd like some stability. I know that sounds Victorian.
Stephen No, worse: new age. You're having your first show in a glitzy gallery. Isn't that enough? You don't want babies as well, do you?
Fiona Why not? You did.
Stephen It's not the same. Fiona, you won't paint. I know it. I'll have wasted my time. [...] Is he an aromatherapist? [...] A medium? A social worker? No, even you wouldn't fuck a social worker.[98]

Stephen and Degas express the worry that their pupils will stop painting after marriage, not as an altruistic concern but a mark of personal 'investment'. It follows that, if these men see their pupils' failure to achieve their full potential as a devaluation of their own 'stake' in them, they would be equally likely to take credit for any success the women achieve.

Stephen and Degas profess to be happy to accept women into their profession. Degas expresses no reluctance to take on female pupils and we are told he 'never talks about men or women artists but about good and bad ones'.[99] However, his apparently progressive attitude is not extended to women in general. '[W]hen women get together it's not to talk about art', he remarks, implying that Suzanne is tolerated among the artists of Montmartre only while she is a single, transgressive figure. She is seen as an oddity, who sits among men and has learnt to paint almost as well as them, but has not opened the doors to women being accepted as artists on a wider scale. This level of 'acceptance' requires the few tolerated female artists to be artists in a way defined and demonstrated by male artists: the familiar theme of women having to ape masculine behaviours to achieve success appears again. The same attitude is present in *Three Birds*. Stephen cannot believe that a liberated woman like Fiona, achieving a level of career success denied women of previous generations, could possibly want to return to the traditional feminine roles of wife and mother. His own desire to promulgate his genes has been achieved with minimal involvement from himself and without the need to sacrifice anything of his art. The desire for motherhood, explored so thoroughly in *The Break of Day*, is touched on briefly here, but the episode draws attention to the expectations still placed on women to take a more active role in child-raising, and the difficulty of pursuing a creative career (or any career) alongside these commitments.

Connected to wider issues of gender inequality is a debate around the concepts of artist and model. Both Wertenbaker's 'art plays' ask whether these roles are dichotomous or whether fluidity exists between them. In *The Line*, Suzanne argues the latter. As is historically accurate, Suzanne has much modelling experience, a favourite of Renoir, Puvis de Chavannes and Toulouse Lautrec. Her two roles complement each other productively, enabling her to imitate a pose required by Degas to finish a drawing because, as an artist, she 'could see from the drawing' how she needed to position herself. Likewise, Degas remarks that her artwork demonstrates the ability to 'understand women's backs from the inside', presumably aided by her experience of modelling them.[100] Towards the end of the play is a scene that underlines Suzanne's joint artist/model status. She paints her self-portrait, an act which, even for artists who do not normally straddle this divide, necessitates that artist and model become one. Suzanne's speech (a monologue) draws attention to her dual role as subject and creator of the painting, at the same time challenging received conventions of what a model should be:

> I remember when Renoir painted me, all soft curves, shimmering face, minute hands. What's left of that red-haired fifteen-year-old full of grace? Does strength wipe out beauty in a woman? [...] The face of success. They call me the best woman painter of the century. [...] The ageing woman. No, the ageing painter. I'm at the height of my powers so why am I sad if my face is in decline? [...] Not a face to be looked at. This is a face that sees.[101]

Suzanne's straddling of the artist/model divide reflects a more general ability to inhabit multiple roles. She treats labels as unfixed and interchangeable, as is evident in her search for the right phrase to describe her self-portrait. 'The ageing woman' becomes 'the ageing painter', the second term superseding but not erasing the first. In some respects, the label 'woman' frustrates her ('They call me the best woman painter of this century. They wouldn't say "best painter", would they, they always have to put "woman" in there'), yet in adding a necklace to the portrait 'in homage to the woman', she recognises the need to acknowledge that part of her identity.[102]

Suzanne's appreciation of the fluidity of roles and terms is a rarity within this play. She recalls how Puvis de Chavannes, on finding her drawing, 'was impressed but [...] tore it up and said I was a model not an artist'. In contrast to this chauvinism, Degas's insistence that Suzanne's beautiful arm is 'for doing work [...], not for modelling' seems more enlightened, but his single-mindedness is almost equally restrictive.[103] Throughout the play, Degas places rigid distinctions between things that he believes are mutually exclusive, telling Suzanne she may be model or artist, pupil or mistress, artist or wife and mother. When Suzanne returns as a married woman, he turns away 'Madame Mousis', instructing her, 'if that artist I used to know, that Suzanne Valadon, if I'm mistaken and she's not dead, tell her she is always welcome here.' Suzanne protests, 'We are one and the same', but Degas insists otherwise.[104] He embraces absolutes in the way Wertenbaker warns against in 'The Laws of Motion', and shows the same inability to adapt as Petra Karagy or Captain Fitzroy. Not until his deathbed does he even consider Suzanne's suggestion that she could have been both his pupil and lover: 'Both? Do you think so? [...] We could have been both? I don't think so... you wouldn't have respected... Both?... We'll never know.' This is too little, too late and Degas's realisation that he is 'ending [his] life without ever having tasted happiness' is the clearest condemnation of his absolutism.[105]

In *Three Birds Alighting on a Field*, it is Stephen who is shown as both artist and model. Although his identity as an artist is established by others before he appears, in his first scene, 'The Artist's Model', the 'Artist' is apparently Fiona and the model, Stephen. He is revealed '*lying on the bench, very still. He is naked under a toga-like sheet, which covers odd parts of his body, and he wears a crown of leaves on his head.*' While this seems to reverse the typically gendered roles of artist and object, it soon becomes apparent that Stephen has far from relinquished his role as artist. As Fiona sketches, he constantly instructs, 'You won't get the curve of my back if you're so tentative. [...] Assurance and speed. [...] Will it be my back or a generalised back? Do it again.'[106] This language not only establishes his role as artist but as teacher or 'master', in the same position of authority over Fiona as Degas holds over Suzanne. Suzanne is good at being an artist and a model because she understands that the two positions require different skills and attitudes, and is capable of floating her identity between the two. Stephen can never simply be a model because he refuses to stop being an artist while he does it.

While drafting *Three Birds*, Wertenbaker experimented with a semi-autobiographical character, simply called 'the playwright': the literary equivalent of a self-portrait. This role is edited out of the final text, but one of her speeches is replaced by Fiona's final monologue, also titled 'Self-Portrait'. Through this device, Wertenbaker played with the potential of being artist and model on the most direct level. That she eventually abandoned the device to hide herself more subtly among characterisations like Fiona's might suggest that even she struggled with this duality. Alternatively, she may simply have feared the added exposure that seeming to put 'herself' on stage would bring. Wertenbaker believes that 'from the first day of rehearsal [a play] moves from the private to the public'. She describes this as 'the most public art, possibly the most public act'.[107] This might seem to contradict her private nature, but should prompt us instead to make the distinction between product and producer. The acknowledgement that art is public should not mean the artist must live a public life. Wertenbaker's Degas is highly suspicious of the fame and commerce that can surround art. He perceptively divides the desirability of artistic success from the less attractive fame, remarking, 'I don't want to be famous, I want to be renowned but unknown.'[108] He thinks art and not the artist should be the object of scrutiny, bemoaning, 'In my day artists were never "successes" and certainly not on the strength of their biography.'[109] Wertenbaker's stated resentment to 'the idea that you have to look into a writer's life in order to explain their work, because that assumes there is no transformation, no creative process involved' is very prominent in this line.[110]

If late-nineteenth-century society was already intrigued by the artist's biography, by the late 1980s – when *Three Birds* is set – this had become an obsession. Advising her clients on the type of artist to commission, gallery consultant Alex specifies, 'Make him big. He can drink, but I can't have him smoke', '[from] The North, that's good', 'Angry. I like that. That's real sexy. Constable with Balls. He's not political, is he?'[111] In contrast, Alex shows no regard for the quality or content of artwork. Like Degas, Stephen finds this mentality abhorrent and has become similarly reclusive, even refusing to show his work. When Fiona reminds him that he taught her 'art was public', Stephen replies that now the 'world has changed', the 'public doesn't deserve art'.[112] His journey in the play involves finding a way to give his art back to the public without completely (re)embracing the vapid, commercial world from which he fled.

Degas predicts the cut-throat business art will become with the line 'Soon there will be no art, only commerce.'[113] Again, this process peaks in *Three Birds*. The opening scene presents a fantasy auction. The first lot, a 'totally flat, authentically white' canvas, is sold for over a million pounds. The second lot is an illuminated billboard, reading, 'ART IS SEXY, ART IS MONEY, ART IS MONEY-SEXY, ART IS MONEY-SEXY-SOCIAL-CLIMBING-FANTASTIC'.[114] As well as these incidences, demonstrating how art has become commerce – the business itself, making itself millions – *Three Birds* deals with issues of private sponsorship. Wealthy businessman Yorgos donates a million pounds to a London Opera House. For some, such as Lady Lelouche who receives this cheque, this is a wonderful arrangement. 'What better than Art – fine, delicate and often wayward – looked after by powerful and hard-headed Business', she enthuses, 'let us wish this marriage long and lasting happiness'. The darker side to this 'happy marriage', hinted at in the word 'wayward', is highlighted when Lelouche confides, 'I hope some of these art people got my word of warning, we can't have too much waste and irresponsibility anymore.' Her colleague David encourages Yorgos to 'state a preference for tunes' in the new opera his money will fund. 'Don't let them intimidate you with all this artistic independence nonsense', he adds, 'You paid the money, you call the tune.'[115] The idea that a business could 'call the tune' to any artistic venture it sponsored was deeply troubling to Wertenbaker. In 1991, the year *Three Birds* was produced, the Royal Court decided to approach private sponsors to support its commissioning fund. Wertenbaker was horrified by this prospect, writing to the Court's Associate Director Lindsay Posner about her 'great concern' for their 'dangerous proposal'. 'I believe it will put writers in an awkward position', she explained:

If I know that a contributor to the commissioning fund is a company I have worries about, I will feel I am accepting a commission I am not comfortable with and at the very least I will have to waste a lot of time finding out what the company does exactly. [...] [I]t is [my responsibility] to know who might be paying directly for my play. [...] How can you guarantee that the theatre will not try to 'please' its sponsors by commissioning certain writers rather than others? Or that sponsors won't exercise discreet pressure to see more of some writers, less of others, by threatening to stop supporting the fund? [...] Surely the Royal Court should be in the forefront of those asking new and important questions about sponsorship, not finding new ways to get it.[116]

Three Birds was written towards the end of a Thatcherite administration that had tried to strangle the arts, forcing many organisations and artists further towards embracing potentially compromising sponsorship deals. *The Line*, with its similar concerns, was produced in 2009, perhaps indicating that Wertenbaker feared a return to such difficult times: a fear that has been realised by current funding cuts, which now threaten the arts as severely as those of the 1980s.[117]

That Wertenbaker reports feeling compelled to research the ethical standing of any company that might indirectly fund her work shows how seriously she took her own social responsibility. However, *The Line* warns against placing too much expectation on artists as the carriers of cultural and social values. In its final scene, the dying Degas muses, 'Why should artists think better than anyone else? All those passionate opinions, for what?'[118] This sense of fallibility is also present in *Three Birds*, when Fiona tells the audience:

I work very hard. I am not happy, but I don't think I ever expected that. I wake early every morning. Some days the world is at war, some days that doesn't matter. Sometimes I paint the darkness of it all, sometimes I paint the light. Sometimes I paint laughter. I know you, you're waiting for the sentence that is going to click it all into place. I don't have it. This is the nineties. I'm not going to pretend I have it.[119]

The idea that artists are not necessarily better placed than the rest of humanity to provide answers to social problems seems both obvious and provocative. Elsewhere, Wertenbaker has argued that providing answers is a job for politicians, and playwriting is about posing questions. 'You write with questions, not what you would have liked to be the case',[120] she explains, 'I don't have a firm opinion of how things should be, or what things are like. I think that's why I'm a playwright.'[121] She speaks unfavourably about more didactic forms of theatre, which she connects, tellingly, to masculine cultural imperialism:

[I]f you are looking for the leader, *he* is not there. The theatre does not have one voice, one dominant voice, one megablock of thought […]. It has the hidden structure of a greenham common: no leaders, things happen, people communicate, but you wouldn't know how. No symbols of power.[122]

Fiona's 'Self-Portrait' monologue gains added weight when studied in relation to the play's development. In early drafts, the direct address to the audience that occurred at this stage in the play was delivered by a character called 'the playwright'. This character had a number of monologues, which offered a metanarrative of the writing process, based at least partially on Wertenbaker's own preoccupations:

I read a review this morning of a new play and it said it was about too many things and I immediately thought oh, that's what they'll say about this and then I thought, well, perhaps they won't notice it's about lots of things, maybe they won't think it's about anything and then the old fears start, what will people think? Will I be loved? And it's enough to make you stop writing. Because I would love to be brave and write what I want, but I want to be loved too, and that can be a contradiction.[123]

Many of these episodes are concerned with topical global events:

> Let me explain the difficulties of writing this play. As I write
> various scenes, turn over the questions of art, its values, its
> purposes, we are in the first days of the Gulf War. [...] It is hard
> to think about anything else. [...] What was the play supposed
> to be about? It was supposed to be a look at the art world. [...]
> But now I believe other questions have to be asked. [...] I want
> to think about this war. I want to place this play in that context.
> I can only do it in this way, by being here, now, revealed.[124]

Because Fiona's 'Self-Portrait' replaces a monologue originally written
for 'the playwright', Fiona's pleas to the audience seem to become a
surrogate for those Wertenbaker wished to make; Fiona's admittance
that she cannot provide any words to click meaning into place may
also be Wertenbaker's.[125]

Another draft contains a scene for two characters called simply
'T' and 'J'. In the context of the playwright who appears in
other drafts, it seems probable that T is a fictionalised version of
Timberlake and J represents her husband (the writer John Man).[126]
Although comic and largely self-mocking, this scene touches on
many genuine concerns and dilemmas crucial to *Three Birds* and
other of Wertenbaker's plays:

> **T** *and* **J** *at breakfast.* **J** *is reading several newspapers intensely,* **T**
> *is brooding darkly.*
> **T** I can't write.
> **J** Oh, darling, what's the matter now?
> **T** The Gulf War.
> **J** Yes, it's very worrying. They've just confirmed Turkish bases
> are being used.
> **T** It's the end of the world. Israel will retaliate with a nuclear
> bomb, Pakistan will drop a bomb on Israel, India will get
> involved, Turkey, Nato, all the oil will burn up, the sky will
> go black, we'll be foraging for roots and then we'll all die.
> Where's God?

J I don't think it will be quite that bad.

T I can feel it. I know it. I see the darkness. I was on Hampstead Heath yesterday and I thought, this is the last of this gentle English world, the slopes and ponds. How can I write?

J All the more reason.

T That's facile. I want to write about the war. I can't. I don't know anything. Why are intellectuals so irresponsible in England? So disregarded. I've got to call some women friends, see what they think.

J Why don't you try to do a little writing first?

[...]

T How come you can work? I'm so miserable. The house is a mess. We need some rations, you know, tins of sardines and hearts of Palm or something, why is this war like a movie? Why is death so distant and so close? America will be impossible after this. Why can't I be more intelligent and get to grips with things?

J Courage, my darling, it's not so bad. I think this war will be over very soon.

T You would think that. It won't. It's the end. I can't write. Where's the opposition? Where are the moral questions?

J They're on both sides.[127]

That Wertenbaker was concerned about the Gulf War is evident in the playwright's monologue. Here, with exchanges such as 'Oh, darling, what's the matter now? /The Gulf War. /Yes, it's very worrying', this concern – or at least the middle-class-liberal-Royal-Court-audience expression of it – becomes parodied. Wertenbaker seems to be struggling with the need to acknowledge the international events that were disturbing her world as she tried to create a play about art, but all the more so with the need to do so in a meaningful way. There is a sense of the inadequacy of the artistic medium to deal with these things. The idea that we can 'write away' such problems is, in T's words, 'facile'. There are, however, points in the passage above where T moves towards more meaningful articulations: 'why is this war like a movie? Why is death so distant and so close?' Significantly, all these points are phrased as questions, supporting Wertenbaker's belief that good drama must find 'moral questions', but not necessarily answer them. Tellingly, all T's questions are left unanswered, or are answered unsatisfactorily by J.

Although Wertenbaker found ways to place her play, more subtly, in the context of international relations, she made no specific reference to the Gulf War in the final version of *Three Birds*. Perhaps this is a case where the medium did fail to provide an adequate means of expression. Yet elsewhere, in a draft article questioning the necessity of theatre, Wertenbaker urges us not to see theatre's limited potential to bear political statements as a failure in general terms: 'oh yes, the theatre must be ill, last night I went to a play and my life wasn't changed. But whoever said the theatre should do that? [...] Yes, that idea has died – the theatre that saves the world has died, but the theatre has not died with it.'[128] The primary concern that emerges from T and J's breakfast scene is for the environmental consequences of war: the fear that 'this is the last of this gentle English world, the slopes and ponds'. Although in this short parodic scene, the sincerity of this statement is unclear, the value of nature is a recurrent theme in Wertenbaker's works and remains central to the finished text of *Three Birds*. Elsewhere, Wertenbaker links her environmental concerns to other fears: 'It is my belief that the attitudes that allow a planet to decay, that neglect the environment, also neglect the theatre and allow the mental health of a country to come low down on the scale of priorities.'[129] This correlation emphasises the importance of both these areas within Wertenbaker's thinking.

Degas's focus is the human figure, but he emphasises the need to place these figures in landscapes. Stephen's focus is primarily on landscape painting. Stephen responds disparagingly to the suggestion that he paint someone's portrait, perhaps reflecting his loss of faith in humanity at the start of the play.[130] Stephen's interest in landscape painting is shared by Wertenbaker. In an article about Salomon van Ruysdael's painting 'A View of Deventer', she recalls, 'When I was a child, I saw a film in which someone walked into a painting and began to live in that landscape. I've been pursued by this possibility ever since.' This anecdote invites the notion that landscapes fire the imagination. Later in her article, Wertenbaker reinforces this by noting, 'I think it was Pascal who once said it was important to look at wide horizons from time to time to remember the powers of one's spirit. This sky-bathed painting offers the same sensation of boundlessness and adventure.'[131] As well as sky, the defining image of Ruysdael's painting is water, which Wertenbaker elsewhere cites as crucial to the imagination: 'I like watery books [...]. [T]oo much of modern fiction and theatre is dry. I'm for those watery regions of the imagination which you're so close to as a child. The saddest thing about growing up is the threat of desiccation to the imaginative skin of the mind.'[132] In *Three Birds*, Stephen makes a similar endorsement: 'We drool over the aborigines because they hold their land sacred. But we must have all done that once. Even the English. Particularly the English. Islands are mysterious ... our land is so watery, that is its beauty'.[133] Wertenbaker suggests that 'at the bottom of it all – in the play – there was something about beauty and love and landscape. A country that was very beautiful. Those are values, and it's an attempt to celebrate that.'[134] Stephen's interest in the English landscape has allowed him to retain a faith in England as a country, which many of the play's characters have lost. This does not prevent him being critical but, he maintains, 'When England began doubting itself, why did it have to stop loving itself? It keeps gashing its own limbs.' This sentiment echoes that of the Abbess in 'The Laws of Motion', who recognises the need to love human beings in spite of their tendency to disappoint. Biddy, the other principal character in *Three Birds*, learns from Stephen to take pleasure from the natural world. In the play's final scene, she recalls the moment in her adolescence when she started 'noticing beautiful things. The Kent spring, the oasts', and then admits that for a long time she 'stopped looking'. Her happiness at being 'painted among the daffodils' at the play's end, emphasises her re-awakening to these things.[135]

Three Birds also touches on the threats to England's natural beauty. Stephen sees his landscapes in relation to work by war painters 'who were sent […] to record England before the Germans invaded'.[136] He paints 'what is vanishing. As it vanishes' and sometimes has to make do with painting 'the memory of something that was there long ago'.[137] The greenhouse effect[138] and air pollution[139] are referenced and when Alex shows an interest in paintings that show England 'as it looks now', she is told that it 'doesn't look like anything now. It's mostly motorways.'[140] These concerns are equally apparent in *The Break of Day*, in which Nina bemoans the fact that 'more than eighty per cent of England is within hearing distance of a busy road';[141] Hugh loves the greenery of England but is worried that 'it's not as green as it used to be' and Tess's gardener states:

> If it doesn't rain soon, this lawn is going to die, all the lawns of England will die, all the gardens will wither. We'll have to do what they do in California and create desert gardens, but California is yellow anyway, whereas England is deep green. That would make me unhappy, if England became yellow.[142]

Gardens are important in a number of Wertenbaker's works. The one in which Act One of *The Break of Day* is situated is described as '[n]othing grand, but beautiful and peaceful'.[143] In *Three Birds*, we see Stephen and his daughter working in his garden, where Stephen is planting an avenue of horse chestnuts that take fifty years to grow. This act demonstrates a belief in the future not shared by his ex-wife, who asks, 'What's the point?'[144] In *Credible Witness*, the one thing refugee Henry likes about England is its parks, and we are left with the image of Alexander and the two young people he has taught about to walk together 'in an English park'.[145] The final scene of *The Grace of Mary Traverse* shows the play's central characters finding a sort of hope in the beauty of Mary's father's garden,[146] a scene Wertenbaker has described as:

> a resolution, a discovery that the world is beautiful despite it all. There is a redemption, because ultimately – however much we want to destroy the world – we have created wonderful things, in art, music, architecture, whatever. So I

think the play has hope. Personally, I have great love for the world. I get pretty depressed about it, but some things give me great pleasure. So I'm hopeful, but I'm not sure if I'm an optimist.[147]

There has been some debate about the proportion of cynicism to optimism in Wertenbaker's writing. Peter Buse recognises this in his assessment that, in most of Wertenbaker's plays, 'there are two competing forces: a generous utopian impulse and a strong satirical drive'.[148] Buse believes that 'it is the regular mixing of these two normally incompatible elements which marks out Wertenbaker's dramaturgy and makes it so challenging for audiences'. David Lister proposes that Wertenbaker is 'at first sight cynical about her chosen subject; but always underlying it is an optimism and celebration of values that transcend temporary, material considerations and the vagaries of fashion'.[149] However, there is no critical consensus as to where *Three Birds* sits on this spectrum. Buse himself, while citing *Our Country's Good* as a work in which 'the optimistic, utopian strain prevails', considers that at 'the other extreme, in her treatment of the London art scene of the late 1980s, [...] biting satire wins out'. The majority of those reviewing *Three Birds*, whether hostile or complimentary, made similar assumptions. Jan Stuart describes *Our Country's Good* as a 'glorious valentine to the redemptive power of art', but found *Three Birds* to be 'its negative: A Bronx cheer for the corruptive nature of the art world. The cynicism may be valid, but its expression feels [...] curiously empty'.[150] Stuart was commenting on the New York version of the play, which was heavily criticised.[151] Several critics pronounced (or implied) that the production's failings could 'be laid squarely at Ms Wertenbaker's feet' and many expressed their disappointment that *Three Birds* did not live up to the expectations set by *Our Country's Good.*[152] Wertenbaker's greatest defender was Hilton Kramer, who, in an article for the *New York Observer* entitled 'Dimwitted Playgoers Miss Wit in Art Show', blamed unperceptive New York audiences (unaided by what he considered over-sentimental direction from Stafford-Clark) for failing to recognise the play's satirical qualities:

It would certainly have been a better play – and a more consistent one, too – if, in keeping with the sardonic comedy of the first act, Biddy's surrender to the loud mouthed artist-hero in the second act had been dealt with in the same cold-blooded comic vein, as sheer satire.[153]

Kramer asserted that Wertenbaker had intended the idea of Biddy 'finding her significant form' as a joke. Kramer's assessment is well intended, but is not the only way to read the play. An alternative interpretation was provided by Michael Billington (reviewing the original production), who made a case for placing the play more towards the 'generous utopian' side of the spectrum, and considers Wertenbaker 'that rare thing: an optimist. [...] [S]he suggests that visual art is not just a commodity but something with the capacity to enrich us morally and spiritually. That's fighting talk in these cynical times.'[154] Wertenbaker's text seems to support Billington's 'optimistic' reading more strongly than Kramer's cynical one. At one point, Stephen describes his painting as 'an affirmation and in an age of cynicism, that requires some courage'.[155] These words bear a striking resemblance to Billington's. If Stephen painting Biddy's 'significant form' is meant to be viewed with cynicism, where is the pity and tenderness with which, according to Wertenbaker's Degas, an artist must study the human figure? We know Stephen shares something of Degas's mentality as he complains that Fiona's portrait of him does not 'love my skin. When Degas drew his old tired washerwomen, their skin was still sensual.'[156] Speaking to Sally Kent, Wertenbaker admitted that although her play is 'a comedy that mocks everything', it 'takes painting and a particular painter, Stephen, very seriously': a statement which seems in tension with Kramer's assessment of the piece. However, the paradox that Wertenbaker places at the root of her play – 'I think art is wonderful and important, but it got perverted by the consumerism of the market and became risible' – goes some way towards explaining why opinions have been so divided.[157]

Through Stephen's ideals, Wertenbaker reminds us that finding and representing beauty is as important a part of the artist's role as faulting and challenging society. Once again, she found a like-minded ally in Stafford-Clark, who commented in the programme for *Three Birds* that 'Theatre without a picture of Utopia is scarcely worth working for.'[158] In a letter drafted in the mid 1980s, Wertenbaker acknowledged that such concepts might now be considered naïve and unfashionable: 'Do we think much about beauty anymore? Why not? Was this a Greek thing, or just Socrates? Have we lost that sense of wonder?'[159] 'Wonder' is another word that, like 'pity' and 'tenderness', catches us out when Wertenbaker uses it, because, as her statement suggests, we are not used to hearing such concepts discussed. Stephen uses it in response to Biddy's enquiry as to whether he ever thinks about the word 'good': 'Look at a Titian. A Velasquez. A Turner. Maybe it's not the good, but it's wonder, and that's a start.'[160] In 'The Voices we Hear', Wertenbaker discusses the possibility (which emerges in a number of her plays) that truth and self-knowledge 'may be out of reach, forever out of reach'. She acknowledges that this realisation can lead to anger. 'And yet, beyond anger, there is wonder', she consoles, quoting the ode from Sophocles' *Antigone*:

> Wonder
> at many things
> But wonder most
> at this thing:
> Man[161]

Wertenbaker re-endorses these seemingly outmoded concepts by virtue of her own work, which is never without such qualities. 'Indeed', Buse acknowledges, 'the word "hope" makes an appearance in virtually all Wertenbaker's plays.'[162] In 1987, Wertenbaker had considered herself 'hopeful' but was unsure whether to admit the label 'optimist'.[163] By 1991, she accepted the term with uncharacteristic directness:

> I'm a guaranteed optimist. I think theatre is by its nature optimistic. One thing I believe in is the importance of every

little contribution. If one person can get one prisoner out of the prison mill, it makes an enormous contribution. We've been taught to think in big numbers. We're seeing the death of these big ideologies that were going to save Everyone. As a playwright I have to think smaller.[164]

CONCLUSIONS

Stories don't end, you simply take them through different transformations. I like to leave people's lives open, characters' lives open.[1]

Acts for the Past

Timberlake Wertenbaker's playwriting has spanned over three decades. It has engaged with a vast array of themes, topics and styles, and has resisted attempts to be labelled or defined. It contains few instantly recognisable traits and has never been heralded as the start of a new movement: the term 'Wertenbakeresque' is unlikely to be added to any dictionaries. Perhaps these are some of the reasons why Wertenbaker has been less celebrated than some of her contemporaries in the years since *Our Country's Good* made her famous. If Wertenbaker's career tells us anything, it is that critics (academics and journalists alike) want to define plays and people, and those who resist definition risk, like Suzanne Valadon, the possibility that 'no one will know how to judge [their] work'.[2] This said, Wertenbaker's work does display patterns and trends, particularly at certain points in her career, which often occur around times of increased productivity. This is most noticeable in her 'women on quests' narratives of the early 1980s and her *fin-de-siècle* pieces about filiation and cultural genealogy. Recognition of these patterns has dictated the structure of my analyses.

Unsurprisingly, Wertenbaker's earliest writings are her most varied. Occasionally finished plays, more often drafts, and sometimes merely fragments, they show a young writer experimenting with techniques, styles and subjects. Some ('This is No Place for Tallulah Bankhead', 1978; 'Near Miss', c.1979; 'Act for Our Times', c.1978; 'Breaking Through', 1980; and 'Second Sentence', 1980) show a more didactic political streak than Wertenbaker is known for, others ('The Third' and 'The Vigil', 1977) explore personal, romantic and sexual relationships with an intimacy not often found in her later plays. Other characteristics are more recognisable. We see the emergence of several strong female characters (including Claire in 'Monads', Electra in 'Agamemnon's Daughter', all three protagonists in 'Don Juan's Women', Martha in 'The Vigil' and Helen in 'The Third'), some of whom respond to the need to hear female voices excluded from the male-dominated canon, and all of whom are constituted as actively desiring subjects rather than passive victims. In this period's most theatrically interesting drafts ('Agamemnon's Daughter', c.1978; 'Don Juan's Women', c.1979 and 'Monads', c.1979), Wertenbaker turns to historical and mythic settings, often to reassess traditional stories from a female perspective. Alongside these feminist-inflected practices, we find Wertenbaker questioning not only patriarchal structures but feminist responses to them.

The interrogation of the male-dominated world and the varied feminist reactions to it continues into Wertenbaker's next, more developed plays, written in the early 1980s. These works build on many of the more successful elements of her former explorations, including the use of mythic and historical settings and the inclusion of strong-willed female protagonists. This phase produced a number of plays that represent what I term 'women on quests' narratives (*The Grace of Mary Traverse*, 1985; *New Anatomies*, 1981; 'Variations', c.1981; and 'Inside Out', 1982). They explore women's potential to redefine themselves, and suggest that women will not discover the objects of their quests without embracing new and self-authored (not masculine) methods of seeking. During this period, Wertenbaker was starting to relate the oppression of women to the oppression of whole nations, races and classes of people ('Case to Answer', 1980), and these ideas were developed through the plays she wrote in the late 1980s (*Our Country's Good* and *The Love of the Nightingale*, 1988). These plays show that the dominant members of society (usually upper class white men) can define and control language to the detriment of less privileged groups (including women, the working classes and racial minorities), and suggest alternative linguistic strategies that may be available to suppressed peoples. The potential for artistic involvement to provide alternative discourses is offered, and such 'languages' are positioned in contrast to the more fixed, literal and rational languages that dominate daily life. This argument gains a particularly contemporary relevance in relation to the present day (and perhaps equally 1980s) mentality, which seems to privilege scientific and economic disciplines over the arts.[3]

A common theme emerges across all these plays: the need to create new structures, new languages and new ways of living that avoid the systems of oppression on which the current world still relies. In the 1990s, as Wertenbaker herself became a mother, she returned to a metaphor recognisable from *The Grace of Mary Traverse* and *The Love of the Nightingale*: the child as a chance either to reproduce repressive structures, or break away from these and create a more hopeful world. Her *fin-de-siècle* plays (*The Break of Day*, 1995; *After Darwin*, 1998; *Credible Witness*, 2001; and *The Ash Girl*, 2000) consider reproduction on a variety of levels, from an individual and personalised longing for children to a Darwinian struggle to continue a species. In all these works, Wertenbaker asks whether it is possible 'to repeat in order to produce difference, not to validate',[4] to recognise the roots from which we have evolved, but to allow our present environments to shape us as much as our pasts. Essentially, these plays, which acknowledge the multicultural nature of contemporary life, highlight the importance of creating affiliative links based on circumstance, rather than relying on rigid notions of filiation, genealogy and history. While all seem deeply rooted in history, they look equally firmly towards the future.

Mutability, fluidity, the ability to adapt, change and evolve: these qualities are celebrated across Wertenbaker's oeuvre and manifest in her own life. She has no fixed sense of her own nationality: American parents, a Basque nanny, German teachers, a classical education, a 'Greek Adventure', a British address and husband, an adopted Bulgarian daughter, a multi-national, 'translatorial consciousness',[5] all of which, she suggests, have given her a 'floating identity'.[6] Over the years, the reception of her work has likewise mutated and evolved. Her plays have been labelled feminist,[7] state-of-the-nation,[8] melodramatic,[9] romantic comedy,[10] Chekhovian,[11] Shavian,[12] Rabelaisian,[13] intellectual,[14] intelligent,[15] silly,[16] cartoon,[17] lyrical,[18] witty,[19] optimistic,[20] sardonic,[21] satirical[22] and compassionate.[23] She herself has sought to shirk any label except that of 'playwright'.[24] As a writer, she has been inspired by history, mythology, fairy-tale, literature, 'research, conversations overheard, newspaper articles, the messy material of life',[25] preferring the word 'writer' to 'adapter', but proposing that 'if you must have another word, I would call him or her a Hoover (of experiences and other books and history and newspapers. Isn't that what a good writer does? Tries to get rid of the dust?)'.[26] She uses every part of her own inherited cultural genealogy (Chekhov, Brecht, the Greeks, Goethe, Hogarth, Shakespeare, to name but a few), but never without critique and innovation, or with an overly deferent attitude to any sort of 'hierarchy of excellence'.[27]

Acts for Our Times

In *The Love of the Nightingale*, an impassioned chorus argue for the necessity of asking questions; this is something Wertenbaker's work has never failed to do.[28] Could women run the world any better than men? If women reject traditional definitions of femininity, how should they re-model themselves? Why do the strong seek to silence the voices of others, and how can those who have been silenced learn to speak again? How can one move forward and settle in a new land without forgetting or abandoning one's cultural background? What role can and should the arts have in society? Overriding all these questions is another: should artists be expected to have the answers to such questions? As we have seen, by leaving this last question open, Wertenbaker justifies her tendency to resist providing her audiences with definitive answers to the others. Instead, what is celebrated time and time again is the potential for art to *ask* difficult questions that are often avoided.

Questions without answers create doubt, but rather than considering this a negative attribute, Wertenbaker embraces it as a healthy mentality. However, she also recognises the need for something that might counteract the almost paralysing sense of uncertainty, loss of ideals, disillusionment with grand narratives and general millennial angst, which were monopolising new writing in the 1990s. Wertenbaker did not succumb to this mood and her plays of this period seem consciously to reject it. She balances doubt and scepticism with the equally forceful presence of hope and redemption, demonstrating that there is still room for 'pity and tenderness' in artistic works. While it is not unexpected that a playwright may surprise us by her selection of a word such as 'pity', 'tenderness' or 'wonder' in place of a more commonly used term, Wertenbaker's choices demonstrate not only a sense of aesthetics but of ethics too. In an article on her favourite works of literature, she comments, 'I find Dostoevsky was one of the best novelists of redemption. Redemption is an extraordinary concept, particularly at the end of the twentieth century, when the word could just disappear, along with the word humane.'[29] By attempting to keep such words in parlance, Wertenbaker is not simply ensuring her audience maintains a rich and complex vocabulary in linguistic terms but in emotional ones too.

Just as Governor Phillip wants to be clear that he is interested in redeeming Liz Morden's 'humanity' rather than her soul,[30] Wertenbaker uses the word 'redemption' in a secular context, and her choice of the word 'humane' is equally crucial. A slightly old-fashioned but uplifting humanism pervades Wertenbaker's oeuvre, which makes an impassioned case for the continued need to look at and love human beings, however much they disappoint, as individuals or as a race. This notion has never left Wertenbaker, who insists that 'we have to continue examining human beings and not despair'.[31]

Acts for the Future

Wertenbaker's belief in humanity imbues her writing with the sense that, however much we suffer and however much we question our governments, our societies and our very existence, we must not lose the faith that it is possible to create a better future. In this, we see Wertenbaker's self-stated debt to Chekhov. The world she presents is not set on course to get better in one 'big bang of bliss',[32] but it just might make small advances if we interrogate the way we live, forge connections between each other and actively seek to leave something behind for the benefit rather than the limitation of future generations.

The need to leave something positive behind is prominent in many of Wertenbaker's plays, where it is often positioned as an act of faith in the future of humanity, which Wertenbaker also describes as 'a future with language'.[33] Writing a song in the belief people will still be around to hear it after you are gone, raising a child, and planting trees that will not grow in your lifetime are all examples of such acts. This theme appears most clearly in Wertenbaker's later work, perhaps as she herself grew older, as she raised her own daughter, as she began to see her writing not just as individual plays but as a body of work, as she sold her archive to the British Library in the knowledge that she had become an author others will study, define and judge. However, her whole career can be seen as just such an act of faith, from her first rash move to London to try and become a professional playwright to her continued commitment to a medium that has never brought her wealth but to which she attaches the greatest social importance. '[A]lthough the theatre seems to preserve the past, it is in fact a guarantee of the future', she maintains. 'To write a play is itself a commitment to the future: not just to the immediate future of its production but also to the other more nebulous sense of marking something down.'[34] Like redemption, the notion of an 'act of faith' has religious overtones, in that it requires belief without proof. Although Wertenbaker's work does not speak on behalf of any orthodox religion, it does recognise the need for human beings to engage with their spiritual side – to sit in the Dionysian café as well as the Apollonian one – and the interplay of logos and mythos can be found in many of her plays.[35] The search for knowledge (be it self-knowledge or knowledge of our world) occupies many of her characters, and while these quests are often presented in a positive light, their objects always remain elusive. At the end of *The Grace of Mary Traverse*, Mary proposes: 'I'm certain that when we understand it all, it'll be simpler, not more confusing. One day we'll know how to love this world.'[36] Most of Wertenbaker's writing suggests that, to the contrary, the more we understand, the more confusion is generated, but Wertenbaker does not imply that this is reason to despair. She repeatedly demonstrates the need to think and to question, to try to understand, but ultimately, to accept we may often fail in this, and that it is still possible to 'love this world' without ever fully *knowing* it.

In this book, I have aimed to present the full scope of Wertenbaker's theatrical works. While some plays are not discussed in the detail they deserve, this foregrounds the overall shape of Wertenbaker's writing, her themes and concerns, and her career as a constantly fluctuating process. The potential for Wertenbaker's work to have a continued impact, both on theatrical production and theatrical scholarship, is significant, not only because Wertenbaker continues to write for the stage. Her consistently varied interests make it impossible to predict where the next decade of her work will take us.

NOTES AND REFERENCES

Introduction

1 Timberlake Wertenbaker cited in Hilary de Vries, 'This "Angry Young Man" is a Woman', *LA Times*, 10 September 1989. Wertenbaker's name should be pronounced phonetically and not Germanicised.
2 Suzie Mackenzie, 'A play for life', *Guardian*, 4 September 1991.
3 John Barber, Review of *The Grace of Mary Traverse* at the Royal Court, *Daily Telegraph*, 24 October 1985.
4 Robert Crew, 'Timberlake Wertenbaker: Taking On the World', *Toronto Free Press*, Winter 1987.
5 Anon, 'The art of love', publication unknown, 30 August 1991 (Timberlake Wertenbaker Archive, British Library Manuscripts Collection, Add 79383), hereafter TWA, BLMC.
6 Wertenbaker, interview with Sophie Bush, London, 11 February 2010.
7 Wertenbaker, undated draft/copy of letter to Clive Tempest, c.1981, TWA, BLMC, Add 79218.
8 Wertenbaker, undated draft/copy of letter to Terry Hands, c.1985, TWA, BLMC, Add 79217.
9 Wertenbaker, untitled draft article, date unknown, TWA, BLMC, Add 79382.
10 Unless otherwise indicated, quotations are taken from the latest complete draft of an unpublished text contained in the archive. Where drafts are undated, I assume they have been placed in chronological order, or use drafts that indicate that they have been used for performance.
11 Judy Simons, *Diaries and Journals of Literary Women from Fanny Burney to Virginia Woolf* (Basingstoke: Macmillan, 1990), 202.
12 Claire Wright, draft/copy of letter to Susan Carlson, 6 June 1990, TWA, BLMC, Add 79213.
13 Simons, *Diaries and Journals*, 196.
14 Wertenbaker cited in Mackenzie, 'A play for life'.
15 Wertenbaker, interview with Bush.
16 Wertenbaker cited in Mackenzie, 'A play for life'.
17 Wertenbaker cited in John L. DiGaetani, *A Search for a Postmodern Theatre: Interviews with Contemporary Playwrights* (Westport, CT: Greenwood Press, 1991, pp. 265–73), 268–9.
18 Wertenbaker, interview with Bush.
19 Wertenbaker cited in Sheridan Morley, 'Gender is not the case', *The Times*, 7 November 1988.
20 Wertenbaker, interview with Bush.
21 Lael Tucker Wertenbaker, *Death of a Man*. London: Pan Books, 1959.
22 Wertenbaker cited in Mackenzie, 'A play for life'.
23 Wertenbaker cited in Harriet Devine, *Looking Back: Playwrights at the Royal Court 1956–2006* (London: Faber and Faber, 2006), 273.

24 Wertenbaker, interview with Bush.
25 Wertenbaker cited in Devine, *Looking Back*, 274.
26 Wertenbaker, interview with Bush.
27 Wertenbaker, 'The Three Musketeers'. Unpublished article, c.1990, TWA, BLMC, Add 79382.
28 Wertenbaker, *Plays One* (London: Faber and Faber, 1996), 296.
29 Wertenbaker cited in Malcolm McGivan, 'Breaking Through', publication details unknown, c.1984, TWA, BLMC, Add 79383.
30 Wertenbaker, interview with Bush.
31 Wertenbaker cited in Mackenzie, 'A play for life'.
32 Wertenbaker cited in Mackenzie, 'A play for life'.
33 Wertenbaker, 'Kicking city habits in Lorna Doone country', *CLASSIC*, Oct/Nov 1976.
34 Wertenbaker, 'A Year on Exmoor' (unpublished prose work, c.1976, TWA, BLMC, Add 79379), 8.
35 Wertenbaker, 'A Year on Exmoor', 3.
36 Wertenbaker, 'A Year on Exmoor', 7.
37 The first draft novel is likely to be 'Rites of Entry', drafts of which are found in TWA, BLMC, Add 79380. Drafts of the gothic novel are found in Add 79381.
38 Wertenbaker, 'A Year on Exmoor', 154.
39 Wertenbaker, 'A Year on Exmoor', 98.
40 Wertenbaker, 'A Year on Exmoor', 106.
41 Wertenbaker, 'A Year on Exmoor', 155.
42 Wertenbaker, 'A Year on Exmoor', 112.
43 Wertenbaker, draft/copy of letter to Laurens van der Post, 25 February 1977, TWA, BLMC, Add 79216.
44 Dominic Shellard, *British Theatre since the War* (New Haven and London: Yale University Press, 1999), 148.
45 Shellard, *British Theatre*, 156.
46 Michael Billington, *State of the Nation: British Theatre since 1945* (London: Faber and Faber, 2007), 204.
47 Ann Jellicoe, one of the few female playwrights to be produced in major venues such as the Royal Court during the 1960s, recalls the intimidating atmosphere she encountered there, in which 'men didn't really take a woman seriously'. Cited in Ruth Little and Emily McLaughlin, *The Royal Court Theatre Inside Out* (London: Oberon Books, 2007), 238.
48 Wertenbaker, draft/copy of letter to Dr Woof at the Arts Council, 24 March 1984, TWA, BLMC, Add 79210.
49 Graham Whybrow, cited in Little and McLaughlin, *The Royal Court*, 294.
50 Wertenbaker, undated draft letter to *The Stage*, TWA, BLMC, Add 79209.
51 Billington, *State of the Nation*, 273. Billington refers, in particular, to the plays of Simon Gray, including *Butley* (1971) and *Otherwise Engaged* (1975); Harold Pinter's *No Man's Land* (1975) and *Betrayal* (1978); Alan Ayckbourn's *Just Between Ourselves* (1976); and Alan Bennett's *The Old Country* (1977).
52 Billington, *State of the Nation*, 302.
53 Shellard, *British Theatre*, 188.
54 Richard Luce cited in Billington, *State of the Nation*, 283.
55 Shellard, *British Theatre*, 199.
56 Shellard, *British Theatre*, 207.

57 Billington, *State of the Nation*, 320.
58 Max Stafford-Clark cited in Little and McLaughlin, *The Royal Court*, 238.
59 This fact is disguised by David Edgar's assessment that women's 'work had dominated the decade'. Edgar's choice of words is odd given that his next sentence reports that 38 per cent of Royal Court plays in the 1980s were by women. David Edgar (ed.), *State of Play: Playwrights on Playwriting* (London: Faber and Faber, 1999), 8.
60 Billington, *State of the Nation*, 322.
61 Graham Whybrow cited in Little and McLaughlin, *The Royal Court*, 294.
62 Edgar, *State of Play*, 22–8.
63 Wertenbaker cited in Edgar, *State of Play*, 75.
64 Simon Stephens cited in Little and McLaughlin, *The Royal Court*, 336.
65 Wertenbaker cited in Heidi Stephenson and Natasha Langridge, *Rage and Reason: Women Playwrights on Playwriting* (London: Methuen, 1997), 137.
66 Milton Shulman cited in Shellard, *British Theatre*, 196.
67 James Macdonald cited in Little and McLaughlin, *The Royal Court*, 304–5.
68 Stephen Daldry cited in Little and McLaughlin, *The Royal Court*, 292.
69 Whybrow cited in Little and McLaughlin, *The Royal Court*, 295.
70 Billington, *State of the Nation*, 361.
71 Wertenbaker, draft/copy of letter to Mark Lamos, 31 December 1991, TWA, BLMC, Add 79216.
72 Wertenbaker, *The Line* (London: Faber and Faber, 2009), 54.
73 John Major's Conservative government created the Department of National Heritage in 1992. Tony Blair's first Labour government changed its name to the Department for Culture, Media and Sport in 1997.
74 Shellard, *British Theatre*, 228.
75 Wertenbaker, draft/copy of letter to Lord Gowrie, 27 June 1995, TWA, BLMC, Add 79210.
76 Billington, *State of the Nation*, 404.

Chapter One: 'Good enough to go on': The Beginnings of a Playwright

1 Wertenbaker, draft/copy of letter to Dr Woof at the Arts Council, 24 March 1984, TWA, BLMC, Add 79210. The quotation continues, 'the second was to write well enough to go on at the [Royal] Court'.
2 Wertenbaker, interview with Bush.
3 Wertenbaker, interview with Bush.
4 Fowles had also spent time on Spetse, upon which he based his novel's fictional island of Phraxos. An anonymous article about these connections, which appeared in the *New York Times* on 24 August 1975, is preserved in TWA, BLMC, Add 79390.
5 Wertenbaker, interview with Bush.
6 Wertenbaker, undated draft/copy of letter to David Sulkin, c.1981, TWA, BLMC, Add 79217.
7 'The Third' was first produced in April 1977 at the Old Bar Studio. In June 1977, The Spetsai Players performed 'The Vigil' at the Karnayo.

8   Wertenbaker, interview with Bush.
9   Anne Morley-Priestman, Review of 'This is No Place for Tallulah Bankhead' at the King's Head, *The Stage*, c.1978, TWA, BLMC, Add 79383.
10 Wertenbaker, undated draft/copy of letter to Leda Hughes, c. 1979, TWA, BLMC, Add 79216.
11 Wertenbaker, draft/copy of letter to Verity Bargate, 30 October 1977, TWA, BLMC, Add 79218.
12 Wertenbaker, undated draft/copy of letter to Bargate, c.1979, TWA, BLMC, Add 79218.
13 Rosalie Swedlin, letter to Wertenbaker, 7 March 1979, TWA, BLMC, Add 79209.
14 Wertenbaker, interview with Bush.
15 Wertenbaker, interview with Bush.
16 Wertenbaker, draft/copy of letter to Rob Ritchie, 3 April 1980, TWA, BLMC, Add 79216.
17 Charles Plumley, Review of 'Second Sentence' at the Sea House, Brighton, *The Stage*, 4 May 1980.
18 Kay Weston, letter to Wertenbaker, 29 April 1980, TWA, BLMC, Add 79209.
19 Wertenbaker, draft/copy of letter to Weston, 6 May 1980, TWA, BLMC, Add 79209.
20 This was also the year in which Wertenbaker left Anthony Sheil Associates Ltd for the agent Michael Imison.
21 Wertenbaker, 'The Third'. Unpublished play, c.1977, TWA, BLMC, Add 79225.
22 Wertenbaker, 'The Third', 17.
23 Wertenbaker, 'The Third', 1.
24 Wertenbaker, 'The Third', 1.
25 Wertenbaker, 'The Third', 4.
26 Anon, undated letter to Wertenbaker, TWA, BLMC, Add 79218.
27 Anne Morley-Priestman, Review of 'The Third' at the King's Head, *The Stage*, c.1980, TWA, BLMC, Add 79383.
28 Wertenbaker, interview with Jenni Murray, *Woman's Hour*, BBC Radio Four, 5 July 2004, http://www.bbc.co.uk/radio4/womanshour/ 2004_27_mon_01.shtml (accessed 3 May 2011).
29 Helene Cixous, 'Sorties' in Julie Rivkin and Michael Ryan (eds), *Literary Theory: An Anthology* (Oxford: Blackwell, 1998, pp. 578–84), 583.
30 Sue Morrow Lockwood, Review of 'The Third' at the King's Head, *Spare Rib*, July 1980.
31 Wertenbaker, 'The Third', 6.
32 Wertenbaker, 'The Vigil'. Unpublished play, c.1977, TWA, BLMC, Add 79226.
33 Wertenbaker, 'The Vigil', cover page.
34 Wertenbaker, 'The Vigil', 5.
35 Wertenbaker, synopsis for 'Rites of Entry', undated, TWA, BLMC, Add 79380.
36 Wertenbaker, 'Rites of Entry' (unpublished, undated prose work, TWA, BLMC, Add 79380), 166.
37 Wertenbaker, 'The Vigil', first draft, 5.
38 Wertenbaker, 'The Vigil', final draft, 8.
39 Wertenbaker, 'Rites of Entry', 201.
40 Wertenbaker, synopsis for 'The Upper World', undated, TWA, BLMC, Add 79302.

41   *Equus* by Peter Schaffer is also concerned with the loss of the spiritual from everyday life.

42   Wertenbaker, synopsis for 'The Upper World'.

43   Wertenbaker, 'Rites of Entry', 202.

44   No one person is credited with coining the phrase 'personal is political'. Carol Hanisch's 1969 article 'The Personal is Political' explores the concept in relation to feminism, as does Robin Morgan's 1970 anthology *Sisterhood is Powerful*. C. Wright Mills's 1959 book *The Sociological Imagination* discusses a similar concept but is not a feminist text.

45   Wertenbaker, 'A Year on Exmoor', 35.

46   Wertenbaker, 'Learning to live with the English'. Unpublished article, c.1978, TWA, BLMC, Add 79382.

47   Leda Hughes, letter to Wertenbaker, 9 May 1978, TWA, BLMC, Add 79216.

48   Wertenbaker, undated draft/copy of letter to Hughes, c.1978, TWA, BLMC, Add 79216.

49   Wertenbaker, 'This Is No Place for Tallulah Bankhead'. Unpublished play, c.1978, TWA, BLMC, Add 79227.

50   Wertenbaker, 'This Is No Place', 11.

51   Wertenbaker, 'This Is No Place', 25.

52   Wertenbaker, 'This Is No Place', 16.

53   Wertenbaker, 'This Is No Place', 22.

54   Wertenbaker, 'This Is No Place', 18.

55   Wertenbaker, 'Act for Our Times'. Unpublished play, c.1978, TWA, BLMC, Add 79235.

56   Wertenbaker, 'Act for Our Times', 42.

57   Wertenbaker, 'Act for Our Times', 1.

58   Wertenbaker, 'Act for Our Times', 6.

59   Wertenbaker, 'Act for Our Times', 34.

60   Wertenbaker, 'Act for Our Times', 42. Several of Wertenbaker's later plays (notably *Credible Witness*) expand Nicole's notion of history as a tangible, almost conscious presence, and Wertenbaker's 2002 article 'Dancing with History' explores the idea further. In an early draft of *The Break of Day*, Tess tells her goddaughter, 'I can't teach you much about God, but I can tell you a little about history, and that may be the same thing', TWA, BLMC, Add 79299.

61   Wertenbaker, 'Act for Our Times', 43.

62   Anon, undated reader's report on 'Act for Our Times', TWA, BLMC, Add 79235.

63   Caissa Willmer, letter to Wertenbaker, 24 July 1980, TWA, BLMC, Add 79218.

64   Wertenbaker cited in Mackenzie, 'A play for life'.

65   Plays by Samuel Beckett, Harold Pinter, Caryl Churchill and Howard Barker (to name but a few) had long made use of the open-ending.

66   Wertenbaker, 'Near Miss'. Unpublished play, c.1979, TWA, BLMC, Add 79234. In an undated draft/copy of a letter to Rosalie Swedlin, c.April 1979, Wertenbaker wrote that 'Near Miss' was 'definitely a television play – if anything [...] because of some change in the language. [...] I've already written a rough sketch of this, but as a stage play and it doesn't work as a stage play', TWA, BLMC, Add 79209.

67   Wertenbaker, draft/copy of letter to Swedlin, 30 March 1979, TWA, BLMC, Add 79209.

68 Wertenbaker, undated draft/copy of letter to Swedlin, c.1979, TWA, BLMC, Add 79209.

69 Wertenbaker, synopsis for 'Near Miss', c.1979, TWA, BLMC, Add 79234.

70 Wertenbaker, undated draft/copy of letter to Swedlin, c.1979, TWA, BLMC, Add 79209.

71 Wertenbaker, 'Near Miss', 8.

72 Wertenbaker, 'Near Miss', 15.

73 Wertenbaker, 'Near Miss', 3.

74 Wertenbaker, 'Near Miss', 3.

75 Contrastingly, Wertenbaker often connects abject hopelessness with infanticide (see *The Grace of Mary Traverse* and *The Love of the Nightingale*). In the synopsis for 'Near Miss', Nigel advises Cathy to abort her child because she has been exposed to radiation: an episode which fits this pattern.

76 Wertenbaker, 'Near Miss', 29–30.

77 Wertenbaker, 'Near Miss', 32.

78 Wertenbaker, 'Second Sentence'. Unpublished play, c.1980, TWA, BLMC, Add 79237.

79 Wertenbaker, 'Second Sentence', 11–3.

80 Wertenbaker, 'Second Sentence', 29.

81 Wertenbaker, 'Second Sentence', 20.

82 Wertenbaker, 'Second Sentence', 18.

83 Wertenbaker, 'Breaking Through', unpublished play, c.1980, TWA, BLMC, Add 79238–19240.

84 Wertenbaker, 'Breaking Through', 25–6.

85 Wertenbaker, 'Breaking Through', 75.

86 Wertenbaker, 'Breaking Through', 54–9.

87 Wertenbaker, 'Breaking Through', 63.

88 Wertenbaker, 'Breaking Through', first draft, 55.

89 Wertenbaker, 'Breaking Through', final draft, 66.

90 Wertenbaker, draft/copy of letter to Mark (surname unrecorded), 20 November 1980, TWA, BLMC, Add 79207.

91 Wertenbaker cited in Morley, 'Gender is not the case'.

92 Wertenbaker cited in Stephenson and Langridge, *Rage and Reason*, 143.

93 Other playwrights taking a 'herstorical' approach at this time included Caryl Churchill (*Top Girls*, 1982) and Pam Gems (*Piaf*, 1978; *Queen Christina*, 1977; *My Name is Rosa Luxemburg*, 1976).

94 Wertenbaker, 'Agamemnon's Daughter'. Unpublished play, c.1978, TWA, BLMC, Add 79234.

95 Wertenbaker, draft/copy of letter to Verity Bargate, 17 November 1977, TWA, BLMC, Add 79218.

96 Wertenbaker, 'The Three Musketeers'. Wertenbaker also discusses this point in her 2004 article 'The Voices We Hear'.

97 Wertenbaker, draft/copy of letter to Bargate, 17 November 1977. Robert Graves published a collection of *The Greek Myths* in 1955.

98 Wertenbaker, 'Agamemnon's Daughter', 19.

99 Wertenbaker, draft/copy of letter to Bargate, 17 November 1977.

100 Wertenbaker, 'Agamemnon's Daughter', 19.

101 Wertenbaker, draft/copy of letter to Bargate, 17 November 1977.

102 Wertenbaker, 'Agamemnon's Daughter', 19.

103 Wertenbaker, draft/copy of letter to Bargate, 17 November 1977.
104 Wertenbaker, 'Agamemnon's Daughter', 17.
105 Wertenbaker, 'Agamemnon's Daughter', 15.
106 Wertenbaker, 'Agamemnon's Daughter', 19.
107 Wertenbaker, 'Agamemnon's Daughter', 24.
108 Wertenbaker, 'Agamemnon's Daughter', 25.
109 Wertenbaker, 'Agamemnon's Daughter', 26–8.
110 This play was read by Out of Joint at the St James Theatre, London on 6 March 2013.
111 Wertenbaker, draft/copy of letter to Mark Everett, c.1981, TWA, BLMC, Add 79210.
112 Wertenbaker, 'Don Juan's Women'. Unpublished play, c.1979, TWA, BLMC, Add 79234. The archive contains only the fourth and sixth drafts of the play. For ease of reference, I cite the earlier (fourth) draft as the 'first draft' and the latter (sixth) draft as the 'final draft'.
113 Wertenbaker, draft/copy of letter to Rosalie Swedlin, 19 March 1979, TWA, BLMC, Add 79209.
114 Wertenbaker, undated draft of letter to Swedlin, c.April 1979, TWA, BLMC, Add 79209.
115 Wertenbaker, 'Don Juan's Women', first draft, 2.
116 Wertenbaker, 'Don Juan's Women', final draft, 1.
117 Wertenbaker, 'Don Juan's Women', final draft, 2.
118 Wertenbaker, 'Don Juan's Women', final draft, 5.
119 Wertenbaker, 'Don Juan's Women', final draft, 18
120 Wertenbaker, 'Don Juan's Women', final draft, 18.
121 Wertenbaker, Plays One, 73.
122 Wertenbaker, 'Don Juan's Women', first draft, 36.
123 Wertenbaker, 'Don Juan's Women', final draft, 6.
124 Wertenbaker, 'Don Juan's Women', final draft, 11.
125 Wertenbaker, 'Don Juan's Women', final draft, 26. The antagonism between Anna and Zerlina echoes the difficulties feminist movements have encountered when working across social and racial groups. In the earlier draft, Anna exclaims, 'Now I understand why they say it's bad for women to talk together. The whole order of society could crumble' (first draft, 27).
126 Wertenbaker, 'Don Juan's Women', final draft, reverse of 12.
127 Wertenbaker, 'Don Juan's Women', first draft, 5.
128 Wertenbaker, 'Don Juan's Women', first draft, 14.
129 Wertenbaker, 'Don Juan's Women', first draft, 25.
130 Wertenbaker, Plays One, 293–4.
131 Wertenbaker, 'Don Juan's Women', first draft, 35.
132 Wertenbaker, 'Don Juan's Women', final draft, 12.
133 Wertenbaker, 'Don Juan's Women', final draft, 26.
134 Wertenbaker, 'Monads'. Unpublished play, c.1979, TWA, BLMC, Add 79228. This title may refer to the complicated metaphysical treatise by the philosopher Leibnitz, entitled Monadology. Wertenbaker cites Leibnitz's theories in early drafts of The Grace of Mary Traverse and 'Don Juan's Women'. However, the term was also used by German ethnologist Leo Frobenius, whose concept is cited in C. G. Jung and C. Kerényi's Introduction to a Science of Mythology. Kerényi reports that Frobenius's term refers to cultural differences that cannot be easily explained by environmental

factors. He gives the example of the association some cultures make between the sun and man, and the moon and woman, which is reversed in other cultures. Kerényi writes that 'a monad means an *inability to see otherwise*, a "possession"' caused by 'the gripping world of *Nature* and something in the history of *culture* that is as manifold as it is variable, that fixes the characteristic "monadic" features of each and every view of the world.' (C. G. Jung and C. Kerényi, *Introduction to a Science of Mythology* (London: Routledge, 1951), 17). Given Wertenbaker's interest in Jungian analysis, it is possible that this is the concept her title references. As we will see, themes of cultural difference and 'possession' are crucial to the text of 'Monads'.

135 Carole Woddis, 'New Voice among female writers', *The Stage*, 15 October 1981. Resentment towards tourists is also voiced by the Greek character Niko in 'Case to Answer' (1980).

136 'The subtheme of the play is obviously tourism as the new colonialism, but the main theme is more complicated', wrote Wertenbaker in one synopsis for the play, TWA, BLMC, Add 79244.

137 Wertenbaker, 'Monads', 2–3.

138 Wertenbaker, 'Monads', 8.

139 Wertenbaker, 'Monads', 17–18.

140 Wertenbaker, 'Monads', 19.

141 Wertenbaker, 'Monads', 2.

142 Wertenbaker, 'Monads', 26.

143 Wertenbaker, 'Monads', 30.

144 Wertenbaker, 'Monads', 49.

145 Wertenbaker, 'Monads', 7.

146 Wertenbaker, 'Monads', 33.

147 Wertenbaker, notes accompanying 'Monads', c.1979, TWA, BLMC, Add 79228.

148 Wertenbaker, 'Monads', 16.

149 John Fowles, *The Magus* (A Revised Version) (London: Triad/Granada, 1977), 339.

150 Fowles, *The Magus*, 410.

151 Fowles, *The Magus*, 408–9. Catastasis is the third part of a Greek drama, during which the action is heightened, leading into the catastrophe.

152 Fowles, *The Magus*, 442.

153 Fowles, *The Magus*, 413.

154 Fowles, *The Magus*, 411.

155 Wertenbaker, 'Monads', 11.

156 Wertenbaker, 'Monads', 7.

157 Wertenbaker cited in de Vries, 'This "Angry Young Man"'.

158 Wertenbaker, notes accompanying 'Monads.'

159 Lecture given 28 February 2001 and published as Wertenbaker, 'The Voices We Hear' in Edith Hall et al. (eds), *Dionysus Since '69* (Oxford: Oxford University Press, 2004), pp. 361–8.

160 Wertenbaker, 'The Voices We Hear', 362.

161 Wertenbaker, undated draft/copy of letter to Michael Imison, c.1981, TWA, BLMC, Add 79209.

Chapter Two: 'They never went on quests': The Gender of Identification

1 Wertenbaker, 'The Three Musketeers'.
2 Wertenbaker cited in Stephenson and Langridge, *Rage and Reason*, 137.
3 Annette Kobak, *Isabelle: The Life of Isabelle Eberhardt* (London: Chatto and Windus, 1988).
4 Wertenbaker, *Plays One*, 5.
5 Wertenbaker, *Plays One*, 7.
6 Wertenbaker, undated draft/copy of letter to Clive Tempest, c.1981, TWA, BLMC, Add 79218.
7 Wertenbaker, *Plays One*, 5.
8 Wertenbaker, *Plays One*, 7.
9 Wertenbaker, *Plays One*, 11.
10 Wertenbaker, *Plays One*, 12.
11 Wertenbaker, *Plays One*, 17–18.
12 Wertenbaker, *Plays One*, 8.
13 Wertenbaker, *Plays One*, 21–2.
14 Wertenbaker quotes Aristotle's phrase in 'The Playwright's Plea'. Unpublished, undated article, TWA, BLMC, Add 79382.
15 Wertenbaker, *Plays One*, 8.
16 Wertenbaker, *Plays One*, 24.
17 Wertenbaker, *Plays One*, 26.
18 Wertenbaker, *Plays One*, 26.
19 Wertenbaker, *Plays One*, 38.
20 Wertenbaker, *Plays One*, 55–6.
21 Wertenbaker, 'New Anatomies', fourth draft (TWA, BLMC, Add 79247), 1.
22 Wertenbaker, *Plays One*, 45-7.
23 Wertenbaker, *Plays One*, 49.
24 Wertenbaker, undated draft/copy of letter to Rosalie Swedlin, c.April 1979, TWA, BLMC, Add 79209.
25 Wertenbaker, 'The Playwright's Plea'.
26 Wertenbaker, *Plays One*, 234.
27 Wertenbaker, 'New Anatomies'. Unpublished radio play, c.1984, TWA, BLMC, Add 79250.
28 Susan Carlson, *Women and Comedy: Rewriting the British Theatrical Tradition* (Ann Arbor: University of Michigan Press, 1991), 219.
29 Wertenbaker, synopsis for 'New Anatomies' (radio play), c.1984, TWA, BLMC, Add 79248.
30 Wertenbaker, 'New Anatomies' (radio play), 54.
31 Lindsay Patterson, Review of *New Anatomies* at the Edinburgh Fringe Festival, *The Scotsman*, 4 September 1981.
32 Rosalind Carne, Review of *New Anatomies* at the ICA, *Financial Times*, 2 October 1981.
33 Ann McFerran, Review of *New Anatomies* at the ICA, *Time Out*, 2–8 October 1981.
34 Woddis, 'New Voice among female writers'.

35 Denise Marshall, Review of *New Anatomies*, publication unknown, c.1981, TWA, BLMC, Add 79383.
36 Wertenbaker, 'Dancing with History' in Marc Maufort and Franca Bellarsi (eds), *Crucible of Cultures: Anglophone Drama at the Dawn of a New Millennium* (Brussels: Peter Lang, 2002, pp. 17–23), 20.
37 Wertenbaker cited in McGivan, 'Breaking Through'.
38 Wertenbaker, *Plays One*, vii.
39 Wertenbaker, 'Variations'. Unpublished play, c.1981, TWA, BLMC, Add 79242.
40 Wertenbaker, undated draft/copy of letter to Clive Tempest, c.1981, TWA, BLMC, Add 79218.
41 Wertenbaker, 'Variations', 1.
42 Wertenbaker, 'Variations', 2.
43 Wertenbaker, 'Variations', 7.
44 Wertenbaker, 'Variations', 12.
45 Wertenbaker, 'Variations', 18.
46 Wertenbaker, 'Variations', 18.
47 Wertenbaker, 'Variations', 36.
48 Wertenbaker, 'Variations', 20.
49 Wertenbaker, 'Variations', 37–8.
50 Wertenbaker, 'Variations', 61–2.
51 Wertenbaker, 'Variations', 62.
52 Wertenbaker, 'Inside Out'. Unpublished play, c.1982, TWA, BLMC, Add 79252–4.
53 Kenneth Rexroth and Ikuko Atsumi, Women Poets of Japan (New York: New Directions, 1977).
54 Wertenbaker, 'Inside Out', 9.
55 Jenny Howe, undated letter to Wertenbaker, c.1982, TWA, BLMC, Add 79216.
56 Wertenbaker, draft/copy of letter to Mark Everett, 2 June 1982, TWA, BLMC, Add 79210.
57 Wertenbaker, 'Inside Out', 18.
58 Wertenbaker, 'Inside Out', 19.
59 Wertenbaker, 'Inside Out', 52.
60 Wertenbaker, 'Inside Out', first draft, 37.
61 Wertenbaker, 'Inside Out', first draft, 22–4.
62 Helen Craig McCullough, Kokin Wakashū: The First Imperial Anthology of Japanese Poetry (Palo Alto: Stanford University Press, 1985).
63 Komachi cited in Anon, 'Ono No Komachi's Poetry', *Gotterdammerung.org*, 2009, http://www.gotterdammerung.org/japan/literature/ono-no-komachi/ (accessed 30 July 2010).
64 Wertenbaker, 'Inside Out', 9.
65 Wertenbaker, draft/copy of letter to Everett, 7 September 1981, TWA, BLMC, Add 79210.
66 As discussed in the next chapter, Wertenbaker returned to this theme in *The Love of the Nightingale* (1988).
67 Wertenbaker, 'Inside Out', 17.
68 Billington, Review of *The Grace of Mary Traverse* at the Royal Court, *Guardian*, c.1985, TWA, BLMC, Add 79383.
69 John Barber, Review of *The Grace of Mary Traverse* at the Royal Court, *Daily Telegraph*, 24 October 1985.

70   Anon, Preview of *The Grace of Mary Traverse*, *Toronto Tonight*, c.1987, TWA, BLMC, Add 79383.
71   Wertenbaker, synopsis for 'Grace Note' (*The Grace of Mary Traverse*), undated, TWA, BLMC, Add 79260.
72   Wertenbaker, undated draft/copy of letter to Jules Holledge, c.1981, TWA, BLMC, Add 79216.
73   Wertenbaker, 'The Grace of Mary Traverse', undated draft, TWA, BLMC, Add 79260.
74   Wertenbaker, undated draft/copy of letter to Clive Tempest, c.1981, TWA, BLMC, Add 79218.
75   James Walker, unpublished notes, c.1981, TWA, BLMC, Add 79214.
76   Wertenbaker, *Plays One*, 67–8.
77   Wertenbaker, *Plays One*, 74.
78   Wertenbaker, *Plays One*, 80.
79   This paralleling of the exclusion of women within patriarchal societies and the exclusion of the 'foreign' or culturally Other from Western societies is a recurrent trope in Wertenbaker's work, featuring strongly in *The Love of the Nightingale* (1988) and the unpublished play 'Case to Answer' (1980). This is discussed in more detail in the following chapter.
80   Wertenbaker, *Plays One*, 83.
81   This concept is discussed in Laura Mulvey, 'Visual Pleasure and Narrative Cinema' in Rivkin and Ryan (eds), *Literary Theory*, pp. 585–95. This influential article was originally published in 1975: a decade before *The Grace of Mary Traverse*.
82   Wertenbaker, *Plays One*, 89–90.
83   Wertenbaker, *Plays One*, 91–3.
84   Wertenbaker, *Plays One*, 83.
85   In the play's opening scenes, Mary explains, 'It was the dolls who gave me my first lesson. No well-made doll, silk limbed, satin-clothed, leaves an imprint. As a child I lay still and believed their weightlessness mine. [...] You must become like air. Weightless. Still. Invisible' (Wertenbaker, *Plays One*, 71).
86   Wertenbaker, *Plays One*, 93.
87   Wertenbaker, *Plays One*, 100.
88   Wertenbaker, *Plays One*, 109.
89   Wertenbaker, *Plays One*, 112.
90   Wertenbaker, *Plays One*, 129.
91   Wertenbaker's play shows Mary and Mr Manners manipulating large numbers of common people into starting the anti-Catholic 'Gordon Riots' of 1780.
92   Wertenbaker, undated draft/copy of letter to Michael Imison, c.March 1982, TWA, BLMC, Add 79209.
93   Wertenbaker, 'The Grace of Mary Traverse', undated draft, TWA, BLMC, Add 79264.
94   Wertenbaker, *Plays One*, 157.
95   Wertenbaker, *Plays One*, 150.
96   The desire to raise a child is presented as a symbol of hope within a number of Wertenbaker's plays. The act of killing a child often represents the complete loss of hope. See, in particular, *The Break of Day* (1995), *The Love of the Nightingale* (1988) and *Jenufa* (2007).
97   Wertenbaker, 'The Grace of Mary Traverse', undated first draft (TWA, BLMC, Add 79260), 1.

98 Wertenbaker, *Plays One*, 153.
99 Wertenbaker, 'The Grace of Mary Traverse', undated first draft (TWA, BLMC, Add 79260), 65.
100 Wertenbaker cited in Bob Pennington, Review of *The Grace of Mary Traverse* at the Toronto Free Theatre, publication unknown, c.1987, TWA, BLMC, Add 79384.
101 Wertenbaker, *Plays One*, 93–4.
102 Wertenbaker, *Plays One*, 92.
103 Martha Ritchie, 'Almost "Better to Be Nobody": Feminist Subjectivity, the Thatcher Years, and Timberlake Wertenbaker's *The Grace of Mary Traverse*', *Modern Drama*, Vol. 39, No. 3 (1996), pp. 404–20: 411.
104 Wertenbaker, 'Is theatre necessary? Three wishes, three curses'. Unpublished article, c.1994, TWA, BLMC, Add 79382.
105 Wertenbaker, undated draft/copy of letter to Jenny Howe, c.1982, TWA, BLMC, Add 79216.
106 Wertenbaker, 'Is theatre necessary?'
107 Wertenbaker cited in Mick Martin, 'Sloane Square savages', *Guardian*, 31 August 1988.
108 Wertenbaker, 'The Grace of Mary Traverse', undated first draft (TWA, BLMC, Add 79260), 69.
109 John Peter, 'The shock of the new', publication unknown, c.1985, TWA, BLMC, Add 79383.
110 Michael Coveney, Review of *The Grace of Mary Traverse* at the Royal Court, *Financial Times*, 24 October 1985.
111 Martin Cropper, Review of *The Grace of Mary Traverse* at the Royal Court, *Time Out*, 24 October 1985.
112 Mackenzie, Review of *The Grace of Mary Traverse* at the Royal Court, *Time Out*, 31 October–6 November 1985.
113 Wertenbaker, undated draft/copy of letter to Clive Tempest, c.1981, TWA, BLMC, Add 79218.
114 Billington, Review of *The Grace of Mary Traverse*.
115 Peter, 'The shock of the new'.
116 Milton Shulman, Review of *The Grace of Mary Traverse* at the Royal Court, *Evening Standard*, c.1985, TWA, BLMC, Add 79383.
117 Wertenbaker, undated draft/copy of letter to Tempest, c.1981, TWA, BLMC, Add 79218.
118 Wertenbaker cited in Stephenson and Langridge, *Rage and Reason*, 139.
119 Wertenbaker cited in Morley, 'Gender is not the case'.
120 Wertenbaker cited in Martin, 'Sloane Square savages'.
121 Wertenbaker cited in Crew, 'Timberlake Wertenbaker'.
122 Wertenbaker, undated draft/copy of letter to Tempest, c.1981, TWA, BLMC, Add 79218.
123 Wertenbaker cited in Mackenzie, 'A play for life'.
124 Wertenbaker, 'Case to Answer'. Unpublished play, c.1980, TWA, BLMC, Add 79229–33.
125 Wertenbaker, undated draft/copy of letter to Leda Hughes, c.1978, TWA, BLMC, Add 79216.
126 In early drafts, the couple's communication problems are positioned as a mutual failing, but by the final text, Niko has become a far less sympathetic character and is shown to be at fault.

127 *Cloud Nine* addresses similar issues by juxtaposing a first act set in colonial Africa with a second act set in 1970s Britain, and casting against race and gender.
128 Wertenbaker, 'Case to Answer', 41.
129 Wertenbaker, 'Case to Answer', 40.
130 Wertenbaker, 'Case to Answer', 3.
131 Wertenbaker, 'Case to Answer', 48.
132 Wertenbaker, 'Case to Answer', 42.
133 Wertenbaker, 'Case to Answer', 45.

Chapter Three: 'To speak in order to be': On Language and Identity

1   Wertenbaker, 'Is theatre necessary?'
2   Susan Carlson, 'Language and Identity in Timberlake Wertenbaker's Plays' in Elaine Aston and Janelle Reinelt (eds), *The Cambridge Companion to Modern British Women Playwrights* (Cambridge: Cambridge University Press, 2000, pp. 134–50), 134.
3   Wertenbaker, undated draft/copy of letter to Terry Hands, c. 1985/6, TWA, BLMC, Add 79217.
4   Wertenbaker, *Plays One*, vii.
5   Wertenbaker, *Plays One*, viii.
6   Wertenbaker cited in Mackenzie, 'A play for life'.
7   Sara Freeman, 'Adaptation after Darwin: Timberlake Wertenbaker's Evolving Texts', *Modern Drama*, Vol. 45, No. 4 (2002), pp. 646–62: 646.
8   Philomele becomes a nightingale; Procne, a swallow; and Tereus, a hoopoe.
9   Jennifer A. Wagner, 'Formal Parody and the Metamorphoses of the Audience in Timberlake Wertenbaker's *The Love of the Nightingale*', *Papers on Language and Literature*, Vol. 31, No. 3 (1995), pp. 227–54: 228.
10 Sheila Rabillard, 'Threads, Bodies and Birds: Transformation from Ovidian Narrative to Drama in Timberlake Wertenbaker's *The Love of the Nightingale*', *Essays in Theatre/Etudes Theatrales*, Vol. 17, No. 2 (1999), pp. 99–110: 102–3.
11 Anne Varty, 'From Queens to Convicts: Status, Sex and Language in Contemporary British Women's Drama' in Katie Wales (ed.), *Essays and Studies 1994: Feminist Linguistics in Literary Criticism* (Cambridge: The English Association, 1994, pp. 65–89), 65–70.
12 Joe Winston, 'Recasting the Phaedra Syndrome: Myth and Morality in Timberlake Wertenbaker's *The Love of the Nightingale*', *Modern Drama*, Vol. 38, No. 4 (1995), pp. 510–19: 513.
13 Laura Monros-Gaspar, 'Voices from the Cave: The Chorus and the figure of echo in Timberlake Wertenbaker's *The Love of the Nightingale*', *BELLS: Barcelona English Language and Literature Studies*, Vol. 15 (2006), pp. 1–13: 2.
14 Wertenbaker cited in Mackenzie, 'A play for life'.
15 Paul Arnott, Review of *The Love of the Nightingale* at the Barbican, *Independent*, 23 August 1989.
16 Charles Marowitz, 'A Classic Tale of Man's Inhumanity to Woman', *Guardian*, 10 July 1990.

17   Nicholas de Jongh, 'A Violent Silence', *Guardian*, 23 August 1989.

18   Robert Hewison, Review of *The Love of the Nightingale* at the Barbican. *Sunday Times*, c.1989, TWA, BLMC, Add 79383.

19   D A N Jones, Review of *The Love of the Nightingale* at the Other Place, Stratford, *Sunday Telegraph*, 13 November 1988.

20   Wertenbaker, *Plays One*, 291.

21   Ovid, *Metamorphoses* (Books I–VIII), trans. Frank Justus Miller (London: William Heinemann, 1977), 319–21.

22   Wertenbaker, *Plays One*, 292–4.

23   Wertenbaker cited in Carlson, *Women and Comedy*, 245.

24   Sue Ellen Case, *Feminism and Theatre* (Basingstoke: Macmillan, 1988), 6.

25   Wertenbaker, *Plays One*, viii.

26   Wertenbaker, *Plays One*, 315.

27   Wertenbaker, *Plays One*, 330.

28   In Howard Brenton's *Romans in Britain* (1980), similar links are made between sexual and colonial violence when an invading Roman soldier attempts to rape an Anglo Saxon priest. Brenton's choice of a male rape victim detaches this act from some of its gender connotations and thus had the potential to foreground the equation of the rape of a person with the rape of a nation more clearly than Wertenbaker's play. However, the controversy surrounding Brenton's depiction of male rape somewhat eclipsed its political intent.

29   Frantz Fanon, *Black Skin, White Masks*, trans. Charles Lam Markmann (London: MacGibbon and Kee, 1968), 17–18.

30   Ngugi wa Thiong'o, 'Decolonising the Mind' in Rivkin and Ryan (eds), *Literary Theory: An Anthology* (Second Edition) (Oxford: Blackwell, 2004, pp. 1126–50), 1126.

31   Wertenbaker, interview with Bush.

32   Thiong'o, 'Decolonising the Mind', 1130–5.

33   Wertenbaker, *Plays One*, 337.

34   Wertenbaker, *Plays One*, 336.

35   Wertenbaker, *Plays One*, 342.

36   Wertenbaker, *Plays One*, 343.

37   Wertenbaker, *Plays One*, 299.

38   Wertenbaker, *Plays One*, 339.

39   Wertenbaker, *Plays One*, 316–18. These phrases resemble those Niko uses to dismiss Sylvia's speech in 'Case to Answer'.

40   Wertenbaker, *Plays One*, 337.

41   Wertenbaker, *Plays One*, 328. In sc. v, Tereus and the Athenians watch a version of Euripides' *Hippolytus*.

42   Wertenbaker, *Plays One*, 303–5.

43   Wertenbaker, *Plays One*, 328–9.

44   Varty, 'From Queens to Convicts', 69.

45   Wertenbaker, *Plays One*, 334.

46   Wertenbaker cited in Mackenzie, 'A play for life'.

47   Wertenbaker, *Plays One*, 305.

48   Wertenbaker, *Plays One*, 301–2.

49   Wertenbaker, *Plays One*, 207.

50   Wertenbaker, *Plays Two* (London: Faber and Faber, 2002), 23.

51   Wertenbaker, *Plays One*, 303–4.

52 In *The Line*, Degas connects the qualities of 'pity and tenderness', suggesting they should both be explicit in artistic representations of the human figure. Wertenbaker, *The Line* (London: Faber and Faber, 2009), 54.

53 Wertenbaker, *Plays One*, 311.

54 Wertenbaker, *Plays One*, 339.

55 Wertenbaker, *Plays One*, 349.

56 Wertenbaker, *Plays One*, 351.

57 Additionally, there are two further choruses in the play-within-the-play.

58 Wertenbaker, *Plays One*, 304.

59 Wertenbaker cited in Paul Taylor, 'The talking heads', *Independent*, c.1988, TWA, BLMC, Add 79383.

60 Wertenbaker, *Plays One*, 308.

61 Wertenbaker, *Plays One*, 315.

62 For examples, see Act I, sc. x of *Our Country's Good*: 'John Wisehammer and Mary Brenham Exchange Words' (Wertenbaker, *Plays One*, 224–6); Act III, sc. i of *The Grace of Mary Traverse*: 'Is a daughter not a daughter when she's a whore? Or can she not be your daughter? Which words are at war here: whore, daughter, my?' (Wertenbaker, *Plays One*, 117); 'The Laws of Motion': 'Do you know what I look forward to most when I come face to face with God? There will be no more disputes over the meaning of words' (Wertenbaker, 'Laws of Motion' (unpublished play, c.2004), 43). This is also a prominent theme in Wertenbaker's recently completed 'Jefferson's Garden'.

63 Wertenbaker, *Plays One*, 318–19.

64 Wertenbaker, *Plays One*, 321.

65 Rabillard, 'Threads, Bodies and Birds', 103.

66 The character of Echo is discussed in Monros-Gaspar, 'Voices from the Cave'.

67 Wertenbaker, *Plays One*, 298–300.

68 Rabillard, 'Threads, Bodies and Birds', 103.

69 Procne and Philomele do subscribe to such rules, which Philomele describes to the Captain thus: 'I'll prove it to you now, I once heard a philosopher do it. I will begin by asking you a lot of questions. You answer yes or no, but you must pay attention'. Wertenbaker, *Plays One*, 310.

70 Wertenbaker, *Plays One*, 335.

71 Wertenbaker, *Plays One*, 343.

72 Wertenbaker, *Plays One*, 317.

73 Wertenbaker, 'Case to Answer', 48.

74 Margarete Rubik, 'The Silencing of Women in British Feminist Drama' in Gudrun M. Grabher and Ulrike Jessner (eds), *Semantics of Silences in Linguistics and Literature* (Heidelberg: Universitatsverlag C, 1996, pp. 177–80), 183.

75 Rubik, 'The Silencing of Women', 177.

76 Rabillard, 'Threads, Bodies and Birds', 103.

77 Wertenbaker cited in Mackenzie, 'A play for life'.

78 Wertenbaker, *Plays One*, viii–ix.

79 Wertenbaker cited in Judy Clifford, 'Judy Clifford talks to Timberlake Wertenbaker', *The Australian*, 24 May 1989.

80 Anon cited in de Jongh, 'Our prison's good', publication unknown, 30 March 1990, TWA, BLMC, Add 79384.

81 Winston, 'Recasting the Phaedra Syndrome', 515.

82 Wertenbaker, *Plays One*, 353.

83   Wertenbaker, 'Case to Answer', 56.
84   Wertenbaker, *Plays One*, 353–4.
85   Wagner, 'Formal Parody', 240.
86   Case, *Feminism and Theatre*, 129. Case suggests that 'Monstrous Regiment's search for a new form proceeding from women's experiences', 'the plays of Adrienne Kennedy' and 'women's performance-art pieces' could be studied in relation to this notion. She also acknowledges that feminist 'opponents to this kind of thinking point out that what begins to emerge in this idea of feminine morphology is the sense that the female gender is real, rather than an invention of the patriarchy' and that 'by valorising the feminine' these ideas may 'keep women in the ghetto of gender' (128–30).
87   Thiong'o, 'Decolonising the Mind', 1131.
88   Wertenbaker, notes for *Our Country's Good*, 17 June 1988, TWA, BLMC, Add 79272.
89   See Ann Wilson, '*Our Country's Good*: Theatre, Colony and Nation in Wertenbaker's adaptation of The Playmaker', *Modern Drama*, Vol. 34, No. 1 (1991), pp. 23–34; and Peter Kemp, Review of *Our Country's Good* at the Royal Court, *Independent*, 12 September 1988.
90   Wertenbaker, notes for *Our Country's Good*, c.1988, TWA, BLMC, Add 79273.
91   Wertenbaker, 'Our Country's Good'. Unpublished draft, c.1988, TWA, BLMC, Add 79275.
92   Wertenbaker, 'Our Country's Good'. Unpublished draft, c.1988, TWA, BLMC, Add 79277.
93   Wertenbaker, 'Our Country's Good'. Unpublished draft, c.1988, TWA, BLMC, Add 79277.
94   Wertenbaker, *Our Country's Good* INSET Day, Out of Joint, 28 September 2012.
95   Wertenbaker, notes for *Our Country's Good*, c.1988, TWA, BLMC, Add 79273.
96   Wertenbaker, notes for *Our Country's Good*, c.1988, TWA, BLMC, Add 79273.
97   Wertenbaker, *Plays One*, 197.
98   Wertenbaker, *Plays One*, 197.
99   Wertenbaker, *Plays One*, 216.
100   Wertenbaker, *Plays One*, 261.
101   Wertenbaker, *Plays One*, 267.
102   Wertenbaker, *Plays One*, 278–9.
103   Wertenbaker, *Plays One*, 273.
104   Wertenbaker, *Plays One*, 268.
105   Wertenbaker, *Plays One*, 271.
106   Wertenbaker, *Plays One*, 271–2.
107   Wertenbaker, *Plays One*, 236.
108   Wertenbaker, *Plays One*, 251.
109   Wilson, '*Our Country's Good*', 23.
110   Wertenbaker, *Plays One*, 252.
111   Wertenbaker, *Plays One*, 281.
112   Michael Leech, Review of *Our Country's Good* at the Royal Court, *The Stage*, c.1988, TWA, BLMC, Add 79384.
113   Stafford-Clark cited in Little and McLaughlin, *The Royal Court*, 262.
114   Jude Wheway, show report for *Our Country's Good* at the Royal Court, 23 August 1989, English Stage Company Archive, V&A Manuscripts Collection, THM /273/4/1/230.

115 Stafford-Clark cited in Gerard Raymond, 'Time Travellers: How the Aussie Convicts in *Our Country's Good* Came to Play Broadway', *Theatre Week*, 6 May 1991.

116 Sara Freeman, 'Wertenbaker, Timberlake (1951(?) –)', *The Literary Encyclopaedia*, http://www.litencyc.com/php/speople.php?rec=true&UID=5520 (accessed 24 January 2005).

117 Philip Roberts, *The Royal Court Theatre and the Modern Stage* (Cambridge: Cambridge University Press, 1999), 207.

118 Neil O'Malley, fax to Stafford-Clark, Graham Cowley and Bo Barton, 24 July 1989. ESCA, V&AMC, THM /273/4/6/17.

119 Anthony Vivis, Review of *Our Country's Good* at the National Theatre of Bucharest, *Bucharest EUROPE*, December 1990/January 1991.

120 Wertenbaker wrote: 'There are plays people hesitate to go and see and *Our Country's Good* was one of them – the only place it's been a roaring success is Rumania' (Wertenbaker, draft/copy of letter to Mark Lamos, 31 December 1991, TWA, BLMC, Add 79216). The negativity of this comment may reflect the recent financial failure of the Broadway production of *Our Country's Good*.

121 Wertenbaker, draft/copy of letter to Gru Rayner, 14 May 1993, TWA, BLMC, Add 79214.

122 Scenes by Shahida Siddique sent by Dolores Long, 23 March 1995, TWA, BLMC, Add 79214.

123 Prologues sent by William Ellis School, London, 6 September 1995, TWA, BLMC, Add 79214.

124 Venturers Drama Group, undated letter to Wertenbaker, c.1991, TWA, BLMC, Add 79218.

125 Wilson, '*Our Country's Good*', 23.

126 Wilson, '*Our Country's Good*', 31–3.

127 Peter Buse, *Drama and Theory: Critical Approaches to Modern British Drama* (Manchester: Manchester University Press, 2001), 161–5.

128 Carlson, 'Language and Identity', 138.

129 Wertenbaker, *Plays One*, 188.

130 Wertenbaker, 'Our Country's Good'. Unpublished draft, c.1988, TWA, BLMC, Add 79276.

131 Wertenbaker, *Plays One*, 209.

132 Wertenbaker, *Plays One*, 270.

133 Wertenbaker, *Plays One*, 205.

134 Wertenbaker, 'Is theatre necessary?'

135 Wertenbaker, *Plays One*, 245.

136 Wertenbaker, *Plays One*, 205–6.

137 Christine Dymkowski, 'The Play's the Thing: The Metatheatre of Timberlake Wertenbaker' in Nicole Boireau (ed.), *Drama on Drama* (Basingstoke: Palgrave, 1997, pp.121–35), 123.

138 Dymkowski, 'The Play's the Thing', 155.

139 Stephen Weeks, 'The Question of Liz: Staging the Prisoner in *Our Country's Good*', *Modern Drama*, Vol. 43, No. 2 (2000), pp. 147–56: 155.

140 Wertenbaker, *Plays One*, 196–8.

141 Wertenbaker, *Plays One*, 224.

142 Wertenbaker, *Plays One*, 202–10.

143 Wertenbaker, *Plays One*, 194.

144 Andrew McIntosh [Blundeston inmate], letter to Wertenbaker, 20 October 1992, TWA, BLMC, Add 79219.

145 Frances Kay [Blundeston education worker], letter to Wertenbaker, 1 February 1990, TWA, BLMC, Add 79219.

146 'Greg' [Prison inmate, surname unrecorded], undated letter to Wertenbaker, TWA, BLMC, Add 79219.

147 Joe White, 'A study on the merits, both artistically and in terms of rehabilitation, of theatre within the English penal system: focussing on productions staged in four establishments (1984–1993)' (unpublished article, c.1994), 9.

148 Wertenbaker, *Plays One*, 245.

149 Wertenbaker, *Plays One*, 272.

150 Varty, 'From Queens to Convicts', 88.

151 Theodor Adorno, *Prisms*, trans. Samuel and Shierry Weber (London: Neville Spearman Limited, 1967), 225.

152 Jim Davis, 'A Play for England: The Royal Court adapts The Playmaker' in Peter Reynolds (ed.), *Novel Images: Literature in Performance* (London: Routledge, 1993, pp.175–90), 183.

153 Weeks, 'The Question of Liz', 154.

154 Paul Bentley, 'Australian Culture 1789–2000', *The Wolanski Foundation*, http://www.twf.org.au/research/culture.html (accessed 10 March 2011).

155 Wertenbaker, *Plays One*, 274. The character of Dabby is based on the historical figure Mary Bryant, who did escape from the penal colony.

156 Wertenbaker, *Plays One*, 258.

157 Wertenbaker, *Plays One*, 261–2.

158 Buse, *Drama and Theory*, 165.

159 Wertenbaker, *Plays One*, 272. This last point is particularly troubling. However strongly one argues that the production benefits the convicts, one must accept that this is achieved at the expense of the aborigines. As Dymkowski has noted, 'the obverse side of communal identity' is the frequent presence of an 'out-group' (Dymkowski, 'The Play's the Thing', 128).

160 Susan Carlson, 'Issues of Identity, Nationality and Performance: the Reception of Two Plays by Timberlake Wertenbaker', *New Theatre Quarterly*, Vol. 9, No. 35, pp. 267–89.

161 Wertenbaker, *Our Country's Good* INSET Day, Out of Joint, 28 September 2012. That the play's serious side can be somewhat lost in performance is evident from a show report from Stafford-Clark's most recent production: 'Good show. Young audience who laughed at anything vaguely sexual! They laughed through most of the Harry and Duckling scenes. During 'A Love Scene', when Mary says to Ralph 'Let me see you', some girls screamed 'yes' and booed when the lights were brought down on the scene'. Show report for *Our Country's Good* on tour at the Birmingham Rep, 27 September 2012.

162 Stafford-Clark cited in Roberts, *The Royal Court*, 204.

163 Echoing Margaret Thatcher, Captain Tench believes a 'crime is a crime. You commit a crime or you don't. If you commit a crime you are a criminal. Surely that is logical?' (Wertenbaker, *Plays One*, 204), and considers that the hanging of a 17-year-old boy 'does seem to prove that the criminal tendency is innate' (188).

164 Wertenbaker cited in Stephenson and Langridge, *Rage and Reason*, 142–3.

165 Davis, 'A Play for England', 178.

166 Wertenbaker, undated letter to 'John' [surname unrecorded], c.1988, TWA, BLMC, Add 79280.

167 Wertenbaker, notes, 17 June 1988, TWA, BLMC, Add 79272. [?] denotes an illegible word.

168 Wertenbaker, *Plays One*, 245.

169 Hicks cited in Wertenbaker, 'Women ex-prisoners: out of the closet and on to the stage'. Unpublished article, c.1979, TWA, BLMC, Add 79382.

170 Wertenbaker cited in Martin, 'Sloane Square savages'.

171 Wertenbaker cited in Kate Kellaway, 'The play's the thing, the rest is silence: Kate Kellaway talks to Timberlake Wertenbaker on her winning Olivier Award', publication unknown, c.1988, TWA, BLMC, Add 79384.

172 Wertenbaker, draft/copy of letter to 'Greg', 6 December 1991, TWA, BLMC, Add 79219.

173 Reid cited in Wertenbaker, *Plays One*, 176.

174 Wertenbaker cited in Carlson, *Language and Identity*, 138.

175 Irene Backalenick, 'Hartford Stage opens season with *Our Country's Good*', *Westport News*, 12 October 1990.

176 David Wilson, 'Blossoming Hope', *New Haven Advocate*, 22 October 1990.

177 Stafford-Clark cited in Jim Davis, 'Festive Irony: Aspects of British Theatre in the 1980s', *Critical Survey* Vol. 3 (1991), pp.339–50: 178.

178 Georgina Brown, 'A muse in chains', *Independent*, c.1989, TWA, BLMC, Add 79384.

179 Christopher Edwards, Review of *Our Country's Good* at the Royal Court, *The Spectator*, 24 September 1988.

180 Milton Shulman, Review of *Our Country's Good* at the Royal Court, *Evening Standard*, 12 September 1988.

181 Adele Gaster, Review of *Our Country's Good* at Hartford Stage, *Connecticut Jewish Ledger*, 11 October 1990.

182 One show report records that 'Mr Wadham [Ralph] has taken to, well, grasping his willy at the moment he kisses his wife's picture. What was formerly a suggestion has developed into a reality' (Jude Wheway, show report for *Our Country's Good* on tour at the Wharf Theatre, Sydney, 1 July 1989, ESCA, V&AMC, THM/273/4/6/17).

183 Chris Pudlinski, Review of *Our Country's Good* at Hartford Stage, *The Register Citizen*, 8 October 1990.

184 Buse, *Drama and Theory*, 161.

185 White, 'A study on the merits', 12.

186 Conversely, Buse argues that '*Our Country's Good* may endorse a slightly conservative vision of culture and, in doing so, occlude the implications of culture in empire. But such is the protean nature of this play – its openness to different interpretations – that it has been successfully performed against itself' (Buse, *Drama and Theory*, 166).

187 Wertenbaker, *Plays One*, 301.

188 Dymkowski, 'The Play's the Thing', 130.

189 Wertenbaker, *Plays One*, 306.

190 For a discussion of the representation of women across these two texts, see Val Taylor, 'Mothers of invention: female characters in *Our County's Good* and *The Playmaker*', *Critical Survey*, Vol. 3, No. 3 (1991), pp. 331–8.

191 Davis, 'A Play for England', 188.

192 Sara Soncini, *Playing with(in) the Restoration* (Naples: Edizioni Scientifiche Italiane, 1999), 95.
193 Philip Gaskell, *From Writer to Reader* (Winchester: St Paul's Bibliographies, 1984), 261-2.
194 Gaskell, *From Writer to Reader*, 261-2.

Chapter Four: *Our Country's Good*: Three Professional Perspectives

1 Stafford-Clark wrote: 'Halfway through reading *The Playmaker* I began re-reading *The Recruiting Officer* and the idea took hold both of reviving *The Recruiting Officer* and of commissioning an adaptation of Thomas Keneally's novel. Like all my predecessors at the Royal Court, I longed for a more permanent acting ensemble and part of the appeal was that the two halves of the joint project were very different. To revive a major classic unseen in London for over twenty years and to collaborate with a writer in making an adaptation of Keneally's novel would draw on very different skills both from me and from the acting company.' Max Stafford-Clark, *Letters to George: The Account of a Rehearsal* (London: Nick Hearn Books, 1989), xii.
2 Wertenbaker, 'A Dialogue With One's Ghosts', Out of Joint, 28 June 2012, http://www.outofjoint.co.uk/writing/2012/06/a-dialogue-with-ones-ghosts.html (accessed 30 August 2012).
3 Max Stafford-Clark and Philip Roberts, *Taking Stock: The Theatre of Max Stafford-Clark* (London: Nick Hearn Books, 2007), 152-3.
4 Stafford-Clark, *Letters to George*, xv.
5 Stafford-Clark, *Letters to George*, xv.
6 Wertenbaker wrote: 'I could just about function by then although I found it difficult to get to the workshops without getting lost. These workshops would provide masses more information and inspiration as well as emotional support'. Wertenbaker, 'A Dialogue'.
7 Stafford-Clark, *Letters to George*, xii–xiii.
8 Stafford-Clark, *Letters to George*, xii–xiii.
9 Stafford-Clark, *Letters to George*, 33-4.
10 Stafford-Clark, *Letters to George*, xii–xiii.
11 Stafford-Clark, *Letters to George*, 4.
12 Stafford-Clark and Roberts, *Taking Stock*, 154.
13 Linda Bassett, interview with Sarah Sigal, London, 12 September 2012.
14 Bassett, interview with Sigal.
15 Stafford-Clark and Roberts, *Taking Stock*, 152-3.
16 Stafford-Clark, *Letters to George*, 24.
17 Christopher Bigsby, *Writers in Conversation with Christopher Bigsby: Volume Two* (Norwich: The Arthur Miller Centre for American Studies, 2001), 231.
18 Stafford-Clark and Maeve McKeown, *Timberlake Wertenbaker's Our Country's Good: A Study Guide* (London: Nick Hearn Books, 2010), 69.
19 Stafford-Clark and McKeown, *Timberlake Wertenbaker's Our Country's Good*, 77.
20 Wertenbaker said, 'Originally, I said no, but then I did get interested in the project

- primarily by reading about present-day projects to get prisoners involved in staging plays.' Cited in DiGaetani (ed.), *A Search for*, 272.

21 Wertenbaker, 'A Dialogue'.

22 Bigsby, *Writers in Conversation*, 232.

23 Wertenbaker explained, 'It was also the beginning of the devaluation of education [. . .] the idea that you couldn't educate certain people, that it was hopeless. I was very aware of that and keen to attack'. Cited in Stephenson and Langridge, *Rage and Reason*, 142–3.

24 Stafford-Clark and Roberts, *Taking Stock*, 151.

25 Stafford-Clark and Roberts, *Taking Stock*, 151.

26 Stafford-Clark, *Letters to George*, 115.

27 Stafford-Clark, *Letters to George*, xii–xiii.

28 Stafford-Clark, *Letters to George*, 189.

29 Wertenbaker cited in DiGaetani, *A Search for*, 272.

30 Wertenbaker 'A Dialogue'.

31 Maya E. Roth, 'Introduction' in Roth and Freeman (eds), *International Dramaturgy*, 26–7.

32 Stephenson and Langridge, *Rage and Reason*, 141.

33 Wertenbaker, *Plays One*, 165.

34 Stephenson and Langridge, *Rage and Reason*, 143.

35 In a preface to *Our Country's Good*, written in 1991, Wertenbaker recorded, 'As I write this, many Education Departments of prisons are being cut – theatre comes under the Education Department – and the idea of tough punishment as justice seems to be gaining ground in our increasingly harsh society.' Wertenbaker, *Plays One*, 164.

36 John Mahoney, 'It's all so public', *Guardian*, 30 June 2004, http://www.guardian. co.uk/stage/2004/jun/30/theatre (accessed 30 August 2012).

37 Stafford-Clark and McKeown, *Timberlake Wertenbaker's Our Country's Good*, 60–1.

38 Bassett, interview with Sigal.

39 Stafford-Clark and McKeown, *Timberlake Wertenbaker's Our Country's Good*, 14.

40 Wertenbaker, notes for *Our Country's Good*, 17 June 1988. TWA, BLMC, Add 79273.

41 Stafford-Clark, *Letters to George*, 49.

42 Stafford-Clark and McKeown, *Timberlake Wertenbaker's Our Country's Good*, 83.

43 Roth, 'Introduction' in Roth and Freeman (eds), *International Dramaturgy*, 23–4.

44 Thomas Keneally, *The Playmaker* (London: Serpentine Publishing Co. Pty Limited, 1987), 19–14.

45 Wertenbaker, *Plays One*, 185.

46 Wertenbaker, *Plays One*, 261–2.

47 Stafford-Clark and Roberts, *Taking Stock*, 159.

48 Stafford-Clark and Roberts, *Taking Stock*, 155.

49 Stafford-Clark and Roberts, *Taking Stock*, 167–8.

50 Stafford-Clark and Roberts, *Taking Stock*, 159.

51 Stafford-Clark wrote: 'Timberlake was given a total of two months to write the play, which she found a considerable struggle, working flat out from six in the morning until midnight every day. However, since there was no absolute demand for a finished play, she also felt a degree of freedom.' Stafford-Clark and McKeown, *Timberlake Wertenbaker's Our Country's Good*, 14.

52 Stafford-Clark and Roberts, *Taking Stock*, p.167.

53 Stafford-Clark wrote: 'I am beginning to feel knackered. [. . .] My most desired wish would be to dispense with food, sleep and union regulations, and have the ability and appetite to rehearse continually.' Stafford-Clark, *Letters to George*, 139.

54 *Our Country's Good* Production File, ESCA, V&AMC, 4/1/220

55 Stafford-Clark and Roberts, *Taking Stock*, 164.

56 Stafford-Clark wrote: 'Nor should a director be too authoritarian, particularly in the early days of rehearsal. If you proceed by argument and debate it's important to know which arguments to lose as well as which ones to win.' Stafford-Clark and Roberts, 160.

57 Bassett, interview with Sigal.

58 *Our Country's Good* Production File, ESCA, V&AMC, THM/273/4/1/220.

59 Bigsby, *Writers in Conversation*, 237–8.

60 Wertenbaker wrote in an introduction, 'the actors who had researched it acted it and so came to the play with a marvellous authority and commitment'. Wertenbaker, *Plays One*, viii.

61 Stafford-Clark wrote: 'I feel so tired. Two plays back to back is a killer.' Stafford-Clark and Roberts, *Taking Stock*, 159.

62 Stafford-Clark and Roberts, *Taking Stock*, 159.

63 Stafford-Clark, *Letters to George*, xv.

64 Stafford-Clark, *Letters to George*, x–xi.

65 Stafford-Clark and Roberts, *Taking Stock*, 167–8.

66 Bassett, interview with Sigal.

67 Stafford-Clark and Roberts, *Taking Stock*, 167–8.

68 'London's current tide in theatrical chic is swinging towards [. . .] entertainment rather than to provocative debate. Plays that take on public issues may no longer carry the public with them. But as a political solution to the Left's problems seems increasingly remote, so the voice of theatre becomes more important. Its value in illuminating different corners of society and in explaining ourselves to ourselves has never been needed more'. Stafford-Clark, *Letters to George*, 31.

69 Rosemary Neill, Review of *Our Country's Good* by the Melbourne Theatre Company, *The Australian*, 8 June 1989.

70 C. M. H. Clark, *A History of Australia Volume 1* (Melbourne: Melbourne University Press, 1962), 3.

71 Oakley cited in Susan Carlson 'Issues of identity', 283.

72 Rosemary Neill, Review of *Our Country's Good*.

73 John Hollingworth, 'Legacy – an actor on the pressures of making a classic new', *Out of Joint*, 26 September 2012, http://www.outofjoint.co.uk/our-countrys-good/2012/09/legacy-an-actor-on-the-pressures-of-making-a-classic-new.html (accessed 7 December 2012).

74 Peter Brook, *The Empty Space* (London: Penguin, 1990), 9.

75 Parallels can be drawn to Brecht's work if students are familiar with this, but remind students that neither Timberlake Wertenbaker nor Max Stafford-Clark intended this to be an Epic production in Brechtian terms.

76 L. P. Hartley, *The Go-Between* (London: Penguin, 1953), 5.

77 Margaret Thatcher, interview with Douglas Keay, *Woman's Own*, 23 September 1987.

78 Thatcher, cited in 'What happened in the hunger strike?' BBC, 5 May 2006, http://news.bbc.co.uk/1/hi/northern_ireland/4941866.stm (accessed 7 December 2012).

79   Disturbingly, some exam boards have warned teachers against mentioning Thatcher's policies in conjunction with the play's writing.

80   Stafford-Clark, *Letters to George*, 66.

81   Stafford-Clark and McKeown, *Timberlake Wertenbaker's Our Country's Good*, 83–6.

82   See also Stafford-Clark and McKeown, *Timberlake Wertenbaker's Our Country's Good*, 95.

83   Students may also want to consider what the theatre space would have been like for the convict production of *The Recruiting Officer*.

84   Stafford-Clark and McKeown, *Timberlake Wertenbaker's Our Country's Good*, 97.

85   Andy Smith, 'Designing the sound for *Our Country's Good*', Out of Joint, 8 August 2012, http://www.outofjoint.co.uk/our-countrys-good/2012/08/designing-the-sound-for-our-countrys-good.html (accessed 7 December 2012).

Chapter Five: 'The longing to belong': On Cultural Genealogies

1   Wertenbaker, undated draft/copy of letter to Mike Alfreds, c.January 1983, TWA, BLMC, Add 79218.

2   Wertenbaker cited in Clifford, 'Judy Clifford talks'.

3   In Wertenbaker's 1991 play *Three Birds Alighting on a Field*, Biddy describes being married to a Greek as 'not quite properly English'. Wertenbaker, *Plays One*, 363.

4   Sheila Rabillard, 'Translating the Past: Theatrical and Historical Repetition in Wertenbaker's *The Break of Day*' in Roth and Freeman (eds), *International Dramaturgy*, 139.

5   Edward Said, *The World, the Text and the Critic* (London: Vintage, 1991), 20.

6   Said, *The World*, 6.

7   Auerbach cited in Said, *The World*, 7.

8   Said, *The World*, 8.

9   Said, *The World*, 14–6.

10   Said also applies this distinction to postcolonial literary criticism; revealing the constructed nature of the Western canon by undermining the idea that such texts have been generated 'filiatively' by their writers' place in a line of white Western authors.

11   Raphael Falco, 'Is There a Genealogy of Cultures?' *BNET*, 2000, http://findarticles.com/p/articles/mi_m2220/is_4_42/ai_ 75950975/pg_3/?tag=content;col1 (accessed 6 April 2009), 3.

12   Said, *The World*, 17. The first sentence of this quotation bears much resemblance to Lawrence's line 'Blind kings, barren women, runaway children and castaways peopled my childhood'. Wertenbaker, *Plays Two*, 177.

13   Wertenbaker, draft/copy of letter to Jenny Topper, May 2 1995. TWA, BLMC, Add 79216. *Ashes* (1974) is also about the trauma of childlessness.

14   Rabillard, 'Translating the Past', 146. This links very clearly with the idea of 'spiritual sons' invoked by Ian in *After Darwin* (Wertenbaker, *Plays Two*, 170).

15   Wertenbaker cited in Carlson, 'Language and Identity', 144.

16   Wertenbaker, *Plays Two*, 7.

17   Wertenbaker, *Plays Two*, 23.

18   Wertenbaker, *Plays Two*, 19.

19   Wertenbaker, *Plays Two*, 8.

20   Robert Butler, Review of *The Break of Day* at the Royal Court, *Independent on Sunday*, 3 December 1995.

21   Jack Tinker, Review of *The Break of Day*, at the Royal Court, *Daily Mail*, 29 November 1995.

22   Clive Hirschhorn, Review of *The Break of Day*, at the Royal Court, *Sunday Express*, 3 December 1995.

23   Louise Doughty, Review of *The Break of Day*, at the Royal Court, *Mail on Sunday*, 3 December 1995.

24   See Roth, 'Im/Migrations, Border-Crossings and "Wilful Internationalism" in Timberlake Wertenbaker's *The Break of Day*' in Maufort and Bellarsi (eds), *Crucible of Cultures*, 79–90, and Aston, *Feminist Views on the English Stage*. Cambridge: Cambridge University Press, 2003. Another Brechtian device appears in the inclusion of songs. In the original production, Nina (a singer-songwriter) was played by musical theatre star Maria Freidman, who performed several numbers. The first, which is worked into the narrative at the end of Act One, is the only one mentioned in the published text. However, drafts and reviews reveal that the second half of the play contained a number of additional songs, which were incorporated less naturalistically within the flow of the drama.

25   Wertenbaker, *Plays Two*, 19–21.

26   Wertenbaker, *Plays Two*, 16. Wertenbaker knew she could succumb to such a mood, writing, 'I've been working like a fiend this winter as well as finding myself caught up in a lethargic daze more implacable than anything Tchekov [*sic*] ever wrote. One long day of snow, vagueness and effort to make an effort these three months' (Wertenbaker, undated draft/copy of letter to Leda Hughes, c.1978, TWA, BLMC, Add 79216).

27   Additionally, the Eastern European country from which Nina and Hugh adopt is in a state of flux, following the collapse of its communist system. Its instability is the far end of the trajectory of upheaval signalled by Chekhov's revolutionary student characters. This encourages us to re-contextualise our experience of Chekhov. Just as Wertenbaker's adaptations and translations of Greek texts question our identification with classical civilisation as the cradle of our own development (see Victoria Pedrick, 'Ismene's Return from a Sentimental Journey' in Roth and Freeman (eds), *International Dramaturgy*, pp. 41–59), so *The Break of Day* questions our (mis) appropriation of Chekhov as the father of middle-class British drama (see Stuart Young, 'Fin-de-siècle Reflections and Revisions: Wertenbaker Challenges British Chekhov Tradition in *The Break of Day*', *Modern Drama*, Vol. 41, No. 3 (1998), pp. 442–60).

28   Wertenbaker, *Plays Two*, 70.

29   The British interest in classical heritage is emphasised by April's position as a professor of classics, and her publication of a new translation of Sappho. April describes Sappho's writings as '[f]ragments every generation fills' (Wertenbaker, *Plays Two*, 13), highlighting our interaction with such sources. A more negative reference to our espousal of classical heritage occurs in *Three Birds Alighting on a Field*, where private medic Dr Mercer relishes in his collection of ancient Turkish statuary, but shows no compassion towards a young Turkish boy whose kidney he sells to a rich Westerner.

30   Anton Chekhov, *Five Plays*, trans. Ronald Hingley (Oxford and New York: Oxford University Press, 1977), 236–7.

31 Wertenbaker, *Plays Two*, 98.

32 Reviews of *The Break of Day* at the Royal Court by Benedict Nightingale, *The Times*, 30 November 1995; Neil Dowden, *What's On*, 6 December 1995; Charles Spencer, *Daily Telegraph*, 30 November 1995.

33 Nightingale, Review of *The Break of Day*.

34 Aston, *Feminist Views*, 157.

35 Nicholas de Jongh, Review of *The Break of Day* at the Royal Court, *Evening Standard*, 29 November 1995.

36 Rabillard, 'Translating the Past', 145.

37 Wertenbaker, *Plays Two*, 39.

38 Wertenbaker, *Plays Two*, 69–70.

39 Jozefina Komporaly, 'Maternal Longing as Addiction: Feminism Revisited in Timberlake Wertenbaker's *The Break of Day*', *Journal of Gender Studies*, Vol. 13, No. 2 (2004), pp. 129–38: 135.

40 Wertenbaker, *Plays Two*, 44.

41 Wertenbaker, *Plays Two*, 38.

42 Wertenbaker, *Plays Two*, 9.

43 Wertenbaker, *Plays Two*, 75.

44 Wertenbaker, *Plays Two*, 26–8.

45 Aston, *Feminist Views*, 154. Likewise, Roth has commented that in the 'trope of the cross-border figure [the child adopted by Nina], Wertenbaker locates hope – for a more ethnically connected internationalist consciousness, for a more multicultural, feminist ethics' (Roth, 'Im/Migrations', 89). Wertenbaker's interest in such a possibility dates at least as far back as the early 1980s when she wrote: 'I do feel [we] should communicate with other countries [...]. I think we'll be stronger as women in the theatre if we're not just stuck with English theatre but make this international, or at least European' (Wertenbaker, draft/copy of letter to 'Maggie' [surname unrecorded], 4 July 1981, TWA, BLMC, Add 79216).

46 Wertenbaker, *Plays Two*, 53.

47 Nightingale, Review of *The Break of Day*.

48 Billington, Review of *The Break of Day* at the Royal Court, *Guardian*, 30 November 1995.

49 Aleks Sierz, Review of *The Break of Day* at the Royal Court, *Tribune*, 8 December 1995.

50 Billington, Review of *The Break of Day*.

51 Wertenbaker cited in Stephenson and Langridge, *Rage and Reason*, 144.

52 Wertenbaker, *Plays Two*, 7.

53 Wertenbaker, 'The Break of Day'. Unpublished draft, c.1995, TWA, BLMC, Add 79300.

54 Wertenbaker, 'Three Birds Alighting on a Field'. Unpublished (first) draft, c.1991, TWA, BLMC, Add 79284.

55 Wertenbaker, *Plays Two*, 46.

56 Wertenbaker, *Plays Two*, 86.

57 Wertenbaker, *Plays Two*, 136.

58 Sierz, Review of *The Break of Day*.

59 de Jongh, Review of *The Break of Day*.

60 Alastair Macaulay, Review of *The Break of Day* at the Royal Court, *Financial Times*, 30 November 1995.

61 In relation to *Our County's Good*, Wertenbaker wrote: 'Max and I have different

views of the play anyway. I just want people to laugh, he thinks I've written something serious, and that should be respected. He was right, of course' (Wertenbaker, 'Out theatre's good, too', *Guardian*, 2 December 1989). Jim Davis thought Stafford-Clark's production of *Our Country's Good* failed to highlight the sense of irony he felt should be underlying the play's endorsement of the theatre (Davis, 'A Play for England'). Similarly, Hilton Kramer criticised Stafford-Clark's New York production of *Three Birds Alighting on a Field* for being overly sentimental and not capitalising on what he saw as the play's satirical potential (Hilton Kramer, 'Dimwitted Playgoers Miss Wit in Art Show', *New York Observer*, 21 February 1994).

62 David Nathan, Review of *The Break of Day* at the Royal Court, *Jewish Chronicle*, 1 December 1995.

63 Wertenbaker, 'Everyone comes to Café Europa', *Open Democracy*, 2001, http://www.opendemocracy.net/people-debate_36/article_304.jsp# (accessed 3 March 2011).

64 Wertenbaker cited in Stephenson and Langridge, *Rage and Reason*, 144.

65 Billington, *State of the Nation*, 361.

66 Wertenbaker cited in Stephenson and Langridge, *Rage and Reason*, 144.

67 Sierz, Review of *The Break of Day*.

68 Jane Edwardes, Review of *The Break of Day* at the Royal Court, *Time Out*, 6 December 1995.

69 Nathan; de Jongh; Dowden; Michael Coveney, Review of *The Break of Day* at the Royal Court, *Observer*, 3 December 1995.

70 Dan Rebellato, 'From the State of the Nation to Globalization: Shifting Political Agendas in Contemporary British Playwriting' in Nadine Holdsworth and Mary Luckhurst (eds), *A Concise Companion to Contemporary British and Irish Drama* (Malden, Oxford and Victoria: Blackwell Publishing, 2008, pp. 245–62), 258.

71 Rebellato, 'From the State', 246.

72 Sara Freeman, 'Group Tragedy and Diaspora: New and Old Histories of Exile and Family in Wertenbaker's *Hecuba* and *Credible Witness*' in Roth and Freeman (eds), *International Dramaturgy*, 280.

73 Sierz, Review of *The Break of Day*.

74 Susannah Clapp, Review of *After Darwin* at Hampstead Theatre, *Observer*, 19 July 1998.

75 Robert Butler, Review of *After Darwin* at Hampstead Theatre, *Independent on Sunday*, 19 July 1998.

76 Charles Spencer, Review of *After Darwin* at Hampstead Theatre, *Daily Telegraph*, 15 July 1998.

77 Sheridan Morley, Review of *After Darwin* at Hampstead Theatre, *Spectator*, 18 July 1998.

78 Butler, Review of *After Darwin*.

79 A similar effect is achieved by the final scene of Stoppard's *Arcadia*.

80 Wertenbaker, *Plays Two*, 175.

81 Aston, *Feminist Views*, 163. This description echoes some analyses of another 1990s science play: Michael Frayn's *Copenhagen* (1998), which 'didn't simply talk about science. It applied it through the act of performance' (Billington, *State of the Nation*, 368). Like Frayn, Wertenbaker draws attention to the impossibility of knowing exactly what may have happened between two historical figures by playing out a number of possible scenarios.

82   Wertenbaker, *Plays Two*, 159.
83   Wertenbaker, *Plays Two*, 130. This desire is similar to that of Greek immigrant Yorgos in *Three Birds Alighting on a Field*.
84   Wertenbaker, *Plays Two*, 121.
85   Wertenbaker, *Plays Two*, 131–2.
86   Wertenbaker, *Plays Two*, 155.
87   Wertenbaker, *Plays Two*, 113.
88   Wertenbaker, *Plays Two*, 159.
89   A similar process is undergone by Yorgos in *Three Birds Alighting on a Field*. After abandoning as much of his cultural heritage as possible, on his deathbed he realises that he is 'not sure England is what I thought it was', and is consoled by singing traditional Greek songs with his mother. Wertenbaker, *Plays One*, 442.
90   Wertenbaker, *Plays Two*, 162.
91   Wertenbaker, *Plays Two*, 136.
92   Wertenbaker, *Plays Two*, 105.
93   This play was first produced in 1998, four years before same-sex couples in the UK won the right to adopt children in 2002.
94   Wertenbaker, *Plays Two*, 160.
95   Wertenbaker, *Plays Two*, 116.
96   Wertenbaker, *Plays Two*, 107–10.
97   Wertenbaker, *Plays Two*, 115.
98   Wertenbaker, *Plays Two*, 146.
99   Patrick Marmion, Review of *After Darwin* at Hampstead Theatre, *Evening Standard*, 14 July 1998.
100   David Nathan, Review of *After Darwin* at Hampstead Theatre, *Jewish Chronicle*, 17 July 1998.
101   Alastair Macaulay, Review of *After Darwin* at Hampstead Theatre, *Financial Times*, 15 July 1998.
102   Wertenbaker, *Plays Two*, 147.
103   Michael Coveney, Review of *After Darwin* at Hampstead Theatre, *Daily Mail*, 14 July 1998.
104   Wertenbaker, *Plays Two*, 170.
105   Wertenbaker, *Plays Two*, 155.
106   Wertenbaker, *Plays Two*, 161.
107   Wertenbaker, *Plays Two*, 177.
108   Wertenbaker, *Plays Two*, 161.
109   Thiong'o, Decolonising the Mind', 1132.
110   Thiong'o, Decolonising the Mind', 1136.
111   Wertenbaker, *Plays Two*, 148.
112   Perhaps Ian's comment reveals his own fatal flaw: the inability to adapt, which threatens his career and his personal relationships, despite his high moral code.
113   Wertenbaker, *Plays Two*, 122.
114   Wertenbaker, *Plays Two*, 177.
115   Wertenbaker, *Plays Two*, 178.
116   Wertenbaker cited in Carlson, 'Issues of Identity', 267–8.
117   Wertenbaker, *Plays Two*, 185–6.
118   Wertenbaker, *Plays Two*, 212.
119   Wertenbaker, *Plays Two*, 206–7.
120   Wertenbaker, *Plays Two*, 188–9.

121 Wertenbaker, *Plays Two*, 221–3.
122 Falco, 'Is There a Genealogy of Cultures?'.
123 Wertenbaker, *Plays Two*, 223–4.
124 Wertenbaker, *Plays Two*, 226.
125 Wertenbaker, *Plays Two*, 223.
126 Wertenbaker, *Plays Two*, 219.
127 Wertenbaker, *Plays Two*, 226.
128 Aston, 'The "Bogus Woman": Feminism and Asylum Theatre', *Modern Drama*, Vol. 46, No. 1 (2003), pp. 5–21:15.
129 Wertenbaker, *Plays Two*, 213.
130 Wertenbaker, *Plays Two*, 211.
131 Wertenbaker, *Plays Two*, 202.
132 Wertenbaker, *Plays Two*, 224.
133 Wertenbaker, *Plays Two*, 201.
134 Wertenbaker, *Plays Two*, 208.
135 Said, *The World*, 123.
136 Wertenbaker, *Plays Two*, 202.
137 Wertenbaker, *Plays Two*, 221.
138 Wertenbaker, *Plays Two*, 234.
139 Wertenbaker, interview with Bush.
140 Wertenbaker, *Plays Two*, 189.
141 Wertenbaker, *Plays Two*, 196–7.
142 Wertenbaker, *Plays Two*, 202–4.
143 Wertenbaker, *Plays Two*, 237.
144 Wertenbaker, *Plays Two*, 209.
145 Wertenbaker, *Plays Two*, 228.
146 Wertenbaker, *Plays Two*, 201.
147 Wertenbaker, *Plays Two*, 236.
148 Said, *The World*, 123.
149 Wertenbaker, *Plays Two*, 216.
150 Wertenbaker, *Plays Two*, 227–8.
151 Wertenbaker, interview with Bush.
152 Sheridan Morley, Review of *Credible Witness* at the Royal Court, *Spectator*, 24 February 2001.
153 John Nathan, Review of *Credible Witness* at the Royal Court, *Jewish Chronicle*, 23 February 2001. Writing in the *Jewish Chronicle*, Nathan seems well positioned to comment on Wertenbaker's themes of exile and the compelling, yet potentially oppressive, weight of cultural history.
154 Wertenbaker, *Plays Two*, 201.
155 Wertenbaker, *Plays Two*, 237.
156 Wertenbaker's writing has continued to offer such a possibility. Her 2009 radio play 'What is the Custom of your Grief?' imagines a conversation between two young women – one British, one Afghan – both of whom have lost brothers in the conflict. Here, it is by sharing the very different ways of mourning each culture employs that the 'common mechanism' of shared grief emerges.
157 Wertenbaker, *Plays Two*, 238.
158 Wertenbaker, *Plays Two*, 97.
159 Nicholas de Jongh, Review of *Credible Witness* at the Royal Court, *Evening Standard*, 14 February 2001.

160 Reviews of *Credible Witness* at the Royal Court by Jane Edwardes, *Time Out*, 21 February 2001; Charles Spencer, *Daily Telegraph*, 15 February 2001; Georgina Brown, *Mail on Sunday*, 18 February 2001; Robert Gore-Langton, *Express*, 18 February; Sam Marlowe, *What's On*, 21 February 2001; Michael Coveney, *Daily Mail*, 16 February 2001; Kate Bassett, *Independent on Sunday*, 18 February 2001.

161 John Peter, Review of *Credible Witness* at the Royal Court, *Sunday Times*, 18 February 2001.

162 Jonathon Myerson, Review of *Credible Witness* at the Royal Court, *Independent*, 15 February 2001.

163 Gore Langton, Review of *Credible Witness*.

164 Edwardes, Review of *Credible Witness*. Similar comments are found in reviews by de Jongh, Brown, Marlowe and John Gross, *Sunday Telegraph*, 18 February 2001.

165 Brown, Review of *Credible Witness*.

166 Morley, Review of *Credible Witness*.

167 Michael Billington, Review of *Credible Witness* at the Royal Court, *Guardian*, 14 February 2001.

168 Myerson, Review of *Credible Witness*.

169 Benedict Nightingale, Review of *Credible Witness* at the Royal Court, *The Times*, 15 February 2001.

170 Alastair Macaulay, Review of *Credible Witness* at the Royal Court, *Financial Times*, 15 February 2001. Macaulay also asserted that the play was vital viewing for every politician and official involved in issues of immigration and asylum, and described a 'spellbound' audience on press night.

171 Spencer, Review of *Credible Witness*.

172 Freeman, 'Group Tragedy', 61–75.

173 Paul Taylor, Review of *The Ash Girl* at Birmingham Rep, *Independent*, 20 December 2000.

174 Jeremy Kingston, Review of *The Ash Girl* at Birmingham Rep, *The Times*, 14 December 2000.

175 Taylor, Review of *The Ash Girl*.

176 Dominic Cavendish, Review of *The Ash Girl* at Birmingham Rep, *Daily Telegraph*, 29 December 2000.

177 Michael Billington, Review of *The Ash Girl* at Birmingham Rep, *Guardian*, 14 December 2000.

178 Jonathan Gibbs, Review of *The Ash Girl* at Birmingham Rep, *Independent on Sunday*, 31 December 2000.

179 Wertenbaker, *Plays Two*, 245. Wertenbaker is careful not to label the sisters 'ugly'.

180 Wertenbaker, *Plays Two*, 246.

181 Wertenbaker, *Plays Two*, 285.

182 Painter Fiona tells the audience: 'I've always felt sorry for the ugly sisters. In some versions, their mother tells them to cut off part of their foot to get it into the slipper. It works and they go off with the Prince until he notices the blood, so he sends them back and eventually gets the diaphanous Cinderella, who will not bleed. Great, but what happens to the sisters with their half-foot? How do they spend the rest of their lives? Are they angry with their mother for telling them to cut off their foot? Or do they just get on with it?' Wertenbaker, *Plays One*, 443.

183 Wertenbaker, *Plays Two*, 302–3.

184 Wertenbaker, *Plays Two*, 315–18.

185 *The Love of the Nightingale* also carries the theme of change and adaptation. While

she was still working on a project that would incorporate larger sections of Ovid's *Metamorphoses*, Wertenbaker wrote: 'All of the myths are concerned with change and survival. [...] [T]he message, such that it is, is that it is when people can no longer take in new ideas, new ways of being that decay sets in.' Undated synopsis, TWA, BLMC, Add 79270.

186 Wertenbaker, *Plays Two*, 318.
187 Wertenbaker, *Plays One*, 351.
188 Wertenbaker, *Plays Two*, 309.
189 Wertenbaker, *Plays Two*, 251.
190 Wertenbaker, *Plays Two*, 314–15.
191 Wertenbaker, *Plays Two*, 264.
192 Wertenbaker, *Plays Two*, 286.
193 Wertenbaker, *Plays Two*, 246–7.
194 Wertenbaker, *Plays Two*, 289–91.
195 Wertenbaker, *Plays Two*, 319.
196 Wertenbaker, *Plays Two*, 254.
197 Wertenbaker, *Plays Two*, 298.
198 Wertenbaker, *Plays Two*, 255–6.
199 Wertenbaker, 'Dancing with History', 22–3.
200 Wertenbaker, *Plays Two*, 268.
201 Wertenbaker, *Plays Two*, 268–9.
202 Wertenbaker, *Plays Two*, 277–8.
203 Wertenbaker, *Plays Two*, 280–1.
204 Wertenbaker, *Plays Two*, 274.
205 Wertenbaker, *Plays Two*, 315.
206 Wertenbaker, *Plays Two*, 320.
207 The play as a whole is dedicated to Wertenbaker's daughter, adding an extra-textual element of filiation to the work.
208 Wertenbaker, *Plays Two*, 320.
209 Said, *The World*, 124.
210 Jung in Jung and Kerényi, *Introduction to a Science*, 111–15.
211 Wertenbaker, *Plays Two*, 23.
212 Wertenbaker, *Plays Two*, 97.
213 Wertenbaker, *Plays Two*, 86.
214 Rabillard, 'Translating the Past', 147.
215 Wertenbaker, *Plays One*, 349.
216 Wertenbaker, *Plays Two*, 331–3.
217 Wertenbaker, *Plays Two*, 371.

Chapter Six: 'Landscapes with figures in them': On Pity and Tenderness

1 Wertenbaker, *The Line*, 54.
2 Wertenbaker, *Plays One*, 444.
3 Wertenbaker, *The Line*, 23.
4 Wertenbaker, interview with Bush.

5   NT Connections works in heats, with winning productions selected regionally and
     then nationally. In its final stage, Daydreamer Youth Theatre from Warford was
     selected to perform *Arden City* at the National Theatre.
6   Wertenbaker (c.1979). Undated draft of letter to Rosalie Swedlin. Wertenbaker
     Archive, Add 79209.
7   Irina Brown and Daniel Rollings, 'Production Notes' in *New Connections 2008*,
     60.
8   Brown and Rollings, 'Production Notes', 60.
9   When Spectacle Theatre asked Wertenbaker to write a piece for their teenage
     youth group in the early 1980s, Wertenbaker replied, 'frankly I'm more interested
     in writing for 9–10 year olds, or for adults' (Wertenbaker, undated draft/copy
     of letter to Spectacle Theatre, c.1982, TWA, BLMC, Add 79218). Of 'Breaking
     Through', created for a teenage audience, Wertenbaker wrote: 'I'd like it to be at
     the bottom of the pile because it's a youth show, I mean it isn't exactly subtle, and
     [...] I don't want to write many more of them, at the moment'. Wertenbaker,
     draft/copy of letter to Mark [surname unrecorded], 20 November 1980, TWA,
     BLMC, Add 79207.
10   Wertenbaker, *Arden City*, 21.
11   Wertenbaker, *Arden City*, 12.
12   Wertenbaker, *Arden City*, 51.
13   Wertenbaker, *Arden City*, 48–9.
14   Wertenbaker, *Arden City*, 54.
15   As Penny Gay describes, these comedies are 'profoundly conservative' and 'allow
     the topsy-turvydom of carnival – the transgressions of gender and sexuality
     involved, for instance in the transvestism of some Shakespearean heroines, or even
     in their talkativeness – as a way of "letting off steam". The community or audience
     thus permitted to enjoy its fantasies of disruption will then, after the carnival
     event, settle back happily into the regulated social order of patriarchy.' Penny Gay,
     As She Likes It: Shakespeare's Unruly Women (London: Routledge, 1994), 2.
16   Wertenbaker's setting is unspecific, although she retains Czech character names.
17   Wertenbaker, *Jenufa* (London: Faber and Faber, 2007), 25.
18   Wertenbaker, *Jenufa*, 19–20.
19   Wertenbaker, *Jenufa*, 15–16.
20   Wertenbaker, *Jenufa*, 17.
21   Wertenbaker, *Jenufa*, 46.
22   Wertenbaker, *Jenufa*, 23.
23   Wertenbaker, *Jenufa*, 28.
24   Wertenbaker, *Jenufa*, 50–1.
25   Wertenbaker, *Jenufa*, unnumbered page.
26   Michael Billington, Review of *Galileo's Daughter* at Theatre Royal, Bath, *Guardian*,
     21 July 2004.
27   In Brecht's play, Galileo's daughter (Virginia) shows little intelligence and
     encourages Galileo to recant.
28   Wertenbaker, 'The Laws of Motion', 95.
29   Wertenbaker, 'The Laws of Motion', 15–17.
30   Wertenbaker, 'The Laws of Motion', 41.
31   Wertenbaker, 'The Laws of Motion', 4–5.
32   Wertenbaker, 'The Laws of Motion', 100.
33   Wertenbaker, 'The Laws of Motion', 86–7.

34   Wertenbaker, 'The Laws of Motion', 94.
35   Wertenbaker, 'The Laws of Motion', 86.
36   Wertenbaker, *Plays Two*, 164.
37   Wertenbaker, 'The Laws of Motion', 18.
38   Wertenbaker, 'The Laws of Motion', 61.
39   Wertenbaker, 'The Laws of Motion', 36.
40   These lines are from Wertenbaker's play. In Brecht's *Galileo*, an Inquisitor warns the Pope that a 'terrible unrest has come into the world' and Galileo's theories have caused people to question 'at the same time so many things which the schools and other authorities have declared to be beyond question'. His deepest concern is that people will no longer respect the concepts of 'Upper and Lower'. Bertolt Brecht, *The Life of Galileo*, trans. Desmond I. Vesey (London: Methuen, 1969), 101–2.
41   Wertenbaker, 'The Laws of Motion', 61.
42   Wertenbaker, 'The Laws of Motion', 73.
43   Wertenbaker, 'The Laws of Motion', 67–8.
44   Hillary Clinton said 'Every nation has to either be with us, or against us' during an interview with Dan Rather on CBS Evening News on 13 September 2001. Cited in Anon, 'Quotes and Facts on Iraq', Freedom Agenda, www.freedomagenda.com/iraq/wmd_quotes.html (accessed 21 March 2011). George Bush said 'Every nation, in every region, now has a decision to make. Either you are with us, or you are with the terrorists.' George Bush, 'Address to a Joint Session of Congress and the American People', *The White House*, 20 September 2001, http://georgewbush-whitehouse.archives.gov/news/releases/2001/09/20010920-8.html (accessed 21 March 2011).
45   See Petra in *Credible Witness* or Mother in *The Ash Girl*.
46   Wertenbaker, 'The Laws of Motion', 98.
47   Wertenbaker, 'The Laws of Motion', 10.
48   Wertenbaker, 'The Laws of Motion', 81.
49   Wertenbaker, 'The Laws of Motion', 87.
50   Wertenbaker, 'The Laws of Motion', 90–1.
51   Wertenbaker, *Plays Two*, 74.
52   Wertenbaker, *Plays One*, 156.
53   Kate Bassett, Review of *The Line* at the Arcola, *Independent*, 29 November 2009, http://www.independent.co.uk/arts-entertainment/theatre-dance/reviews/nation-national-theatre-londonbrthe-line-arcola-londonbrthe-priory-royal-court-london-1830348.html (accessed 11 March 2011).
54   Lloyd Evans, Review of *The Line* at the Arcola, *The Spectator*, December 2009, http://images.spectator.co.uk/arts-and-culture/theatre/page_23/5591703/degas-as-mentor.thtml (accessed 7 August 2012).
55   This emphasises the sense of displacement Degas feels when he is forced to move so his building can be demolished: 'Every inch of this studio has layers of hours worked, battles [...], discoveries, false starts, triumphs. I've paced this floor for twenty years, I can recount every painting I did from my footsteps.' Wertenbaker, *The Line*, 56.
56   John Nathan, Review of *The Line* at the Arcola, *Jewish Chronicle*, 26 November 2009, http://thejc.com/arts/theatre-reviews/22339/review-the-line (accessed 11 March 2011).
57   The Dreyfus Affair was the false, anti-Semitic conviction and imprisonment of Jewish army Captain Alfred Dreyfus for alleged treason, which led to Emile Zola's famous 'J'accuse' letter.

58   Quentin Letts, Review of *The Line* at the Arcola, *Daily Mail*, 27 November 2009, http://www.dailymail.co.uk/tvshowbiz/reviews/article-1231316/Arts-canvas-accents-ropes.html (accessed 11 March 2011).

59   Billington, Review of *The Line* at the Arcola, *Guardian*, 24 November 2009, http://www.guardian.co.uk/stage/2009/nov/24/the-line-review (accessed 11 March 2011).

60   Wertenbaker, *The Line*, 28.

61   Wertenbaker, *The Line*, 9.

62   Wertenbaker, *The Line*, 21.

63   Wertenbaker, *The Line*, 60.

64   Wertenbaker, *The Line*, 21.

65   Wertenbaker, *The Line*, 50–1.

66   Wertenbaker, *The Line*, 28–31.

67   Wertenbaker, *The Line*, 51–2.

68   Wertenbaker, *The Line*, 24–5.

69   Susannah Clapp, Review of *The Line* at the Arcola, *Observer*, 29 November 2009, http://www.guardian.co.uk/stage/2009/nov/29/nation-ravenhill-pratchett-the-priory (accessed 11 March 2011).

70   Charles Spencer, who made it particularly clear he was bored by the play, called it 'ridiculously repetitive' (Charles Spencer, Review of *The Line* at the Arcola, *Daily Telegraph*, 24 November 2009, http://www.telegraph.co.uk/culture/theatre/theatre-reviews/6644644/The-Line-at-the-Arcola-Theatre-review.html# (accessed 11 March 2011), and Benedict Nightingale, although politer, still considered it 'a bit dogged and repetitive' (Benedict Nightingale, Review of *The Line* at the Arcola, *The Times*, November 2009, http://entertainment.timesonline.co.uk/tol/arts_and_entertainmen t/stage/theatre/article6929849.ece (accessed 11 March 2011).

71   We hear only briefly about Degas's relationship with his father, who Suzanne tells us 'hurt' him by not appreciating his work (Wertenbaker, *The Line*, 60).

72   Wertenbaker, *The Line*, 54.

73   Wertenbaker, *The Line*, 37.

74   Wertenbaker, *The Line*, 59.

75   Wertenbaker, *The Line*, 42–3.

76   Wertenbaker, *The Line*, 60.

77   Wertenbaker, *The Line*, 59.

78   Wertenbaker cited in McGivan, 'Breaking Through'.

79   Sara Freeman, 'Afterword: The Translatorial Consciousness', in Roth and Freeman (eds), *International Dramaturgy*, 280.

80   Wertenbaker, *The Line*, 38-9.

81   Wertenbaker, *The Line*, 38–9.

82   Wertenbaker cited in 'In a Version By', unpublished transcript of platform discussion with Michael Frayn, Timberlake Wertenbaker and Christopher Hampton, chaired by Colin Chambers, Lyttelton Theatre, 20 October 1989, TWA, BLMC, Add 79382.

83   Wertenbaker, *The Line*, 54.

84   Wertenbaker, *The Line*, 61.

85   Wertenbaker, *The Line*, 10.

86   Wertenbaker, *The Line*, 49.

87   Wertenbaker, *The Line*, 58.

88   Wertenbaker, interview with Bush.

89   Wertenbaker, draft/copy of letter to David Sulkin, 11 November 1981, TWA, BLMC, Add 79217.
90   Wertenbaker cited in Morley, 'Gender is not the case'.
91   Wertenbaker, interview with Rosemary Harthill, 'Writers Revealed', *Kaleidoscope*, BBC Radio Four.
92   Wertenbaker, interview with Bush. For example, the wealthy Harry Ransom Center at the University of Texas at Austin houses the archives of many British writers.
93   Wertenbaker, *The Line*, 30.
94   Wertenbaker, 'American Feminism Enters the '80s'. Unpublished article, c.1980, TWA, BLMC, Add 79382.
95   Wertenbaker, undated draft/copy of letter to Maggie [surname unrecorded], c.1981, TWA, BLMC, Add 79216. Women in Entertainment was a feminist pressure/support group that Wertenbaker had some involvement with at this time.
96   Wertenbaker, *The Line*, 31.
97   Wertenbaker, *The Line*, 35–40.
98   Wertenbaker, *Plays One*, 386–7.
99   Wertenbaker, *The Line*, 30.
100 Wertenbaker, *The Line*, 17.
101 Wertenbaker, *The Line*, 60-1.
102 Wertenbaker, *The Line*, 61.
103 Wertenbaker, *The Line*, 19–21.
104 Wertenbaker, *The Line*, 49–50.
105 Wertenbaker, *The Line*, 64–5.
106 Wertenbaker, *Plays One*, 385.
107 Wertenbaker, untitled draft article, date unknown, TWA, BLMC, Add 79382.
108 Wertenbaker, *The Line*, 17.
109 Wertenbaker, *The Line*, 53.
110 Wertenbaker cited in Morley, 'Gender is not the case'.
111 Wertenbaker, *Plays One*, 368–9.
112 Wertenbaker, *Plays One*, 388.
113 Wertenbaker, *The Line*, 58.
114 Wertenbaker, *Plays One*, 361–2.
115 Wertenbaker, *Plays One*, 370–2.
116 Wertenbaker, draft/copy of letter to Lindsay Posner, 14 January 1991, TWA, BLMC, Add 79217.
117 See various articles at http://www.guardian.co.uk/culture/arts-funding (accessed 3 May 2011).
118 Wertenbaker, *The Line*, 63.
119 Wertenbaker, *Plays One*, 443–4.
120 Wertenbaker cited in Ray Conlogue, Preview of *The Grace of Mary Traverse* at Toronto Free Theatre, *The Globe and Mail*, c.1987, TWA, BLMC, Add 79383.
121 Wertenbaker cited in Martin, 'Sloane Square savages'.
122 Wertenbaker, 'Is theatre necessary?'
123 Wertenbaker, 'Three Birds Alighting on a Field' (unpublished (first) draft, c.1991, TWA, BLMC, Add 79284), 122.
124 Wertenbaker, 'Three Birds Alighting on a Field' (unpublished (first) draft, c.1991, TWA, BLMC, Add 79284), 13–15.
125 Ironically, in his review of the play, Martin Spence commented that 'even the

talented Wertenbaker has neither the courage nor the creativity to write [the sentence Fiona cannot find]'. Martin Spence, Review of Three *Birds Alighting on a Field* at the Royal Court, *Midweek*, 26 November 1992.

126 The drafts of *Three Birds* are not the only example of Wertenbaker 'appearing' in her own writing. In her radio play *Dianeira* (1999), a character called Timberlake introduces, once interrupts, and concludes the play. This sets the story within the context that 'Timberlake' claims to have first heard it: from a professional Greek storyteller called Irene. As well as providing an element of metatheatre, the multiple layers and presences of tellers in this story highlight its changing nature: its translations and adaptations, and the mutability of the myth. They also place the ancient tale within the frame of modern Greece where you can 'hear the guns of the country north of the border, where there is always a war' (Wertenbaker, *Plays Two*, 374). Ann Wilson has suggested that the inclusion of the character of 'Timberlake' 'invites the audience to receive the character as Wertenbaker's self-representation while, at the same time, [...] the playwright's creation of her own persona involves deliberate self-fashioning' (Wilson, '*Dianeira*, Anger and History' in Roth and Freeman (eds), *International Dramaturgy*, pp.209–21: 209). In other plays, this self-fashioning is more disguised, with Wertenbaker represented not by name, but by profession. Lawrence in *After Darwin* (1998) and Wisehammer in *Our Country's Good* (1988) both speak for the playwright upon occasion and we also find elements of Wertenbaker in the songwriter Nina in *The Break of Day* (1995).

127 Wertenbaker, 'Three Birds Alighting on a Field'. Unpublished draft, c.1981, TWA, BLMC, Add 79285.

128 Wertenbaker, 'Is theatre necessary?'

129 Wertenbaker, 'Health and Deficiency: Playwright Timberlake Wertenbaker on the state of British theatre', publication unknown, c.1989, TWA, BLMC, Add 79383.

130 In the final scene of the play, entitled 'Biddy in the landscape', Stephen seems reconciled with the human figure, telling Biddy, 'When I started this painting, there were three birds, and you were a vanishing figure, but you've taken over the canvas' (Wertenbaker, *Plays One*, 445). Just as Stephen has helped Biddy rediscover the beauty of the natural world, she has helped him regain his faith in mankind.

131 Wertenbaker, 'A View of Deventer by Salomon van Ruysdael', unpublished, undated article, TWA, BLMC, Add 79382.

132 Wertenbaker, 'The Three Musketeers'.

133 Wertenbaker, *Plays One*, 414.

134 Wertenbaker cited in David Lister, 'MONEY-SEXY-SOCIAL-CLIMBING-FANTASTIC: David Lister talks to Timberlake Wertenbaker and Harriet Walter', *Modern Painters*, c.1994, TWA, BLMC, Add 79383.

135 Wertenbaker, *Plays One*, 444–5.

136 Wertenbaker, *Plays One*, 380.

137 Wertenbaker, *Plays One*, 414.

138 Wertenbaker, *Plays One*, 369.

139 Wertenbaker, *Plays One*, 384.

140 Wertenbaker, *Plays One*, 367.

141 Wertenbaker, *Plays Two*, 7.

142 Wertenbaker, *Plays Two*, 10–2. In *Arden City*, Jay (Jacques) expresses a similar desire: 'Let's sing a song for disappearances, all change is not to the good. I never thought much of nature, of the planet. Now that it's disappearing, I'm falling in love with it.' Wertenbaker, *Arden City*, 47.

143 Wertenbaker, *Plays Two*, 7.
144 Wertenbaker, *Plays One*, 395.
145 Wertenbaker, *Plays Two*, 238.
146 Wertenbaker, *Plays One*, 159.
147 Wertenbaker cited in Crew, 'Timberlake Wertenbaker'.
148 Buse, 'Timberlake Wertenbaker', *Contemporary Writers*, 2003, http://www. contemporarywriters.com/authors/?p=auth138 (accessed 1 September 2009).
149 Lister, 'MONEY-SEXY'.
150 Jan Stuart, Review of *Three Birds Alighting on a Field* on Broadway, *New York Newsday*, 9 February 1994.
151 This production kept Stafford-Clark as its director and Harriet Walter in the role of Biddy, but was forced to adopt an American cast for all other roles.
152 David Richards, Review of *Three Birds Alighting on a Field* on Broadway, *New York Times*, 9 February 1994.
153 Hilton Kramer, 'Dimwitted Playgoers Miss Wit in Art Show', *New York Observer*, 21 February 1994.
154 Billington, Review of *Three Birds Alighting on a Field* at the Royal Court, *Guardian*, c.1991, TWA, BLMC, Add 79383.
155 Wertenbaker, *Plays One*, 438.
156 Wertenbaker, *Plays One*, 388.
157 Wertenbaker cited in Sarah Kent, 'Rogues Gallery', *Time Out*, 4–11 September.
158 Stafford-Clark, 'Artistic Director's Statement', programme for *Three Birds Alighting on a Field* at the Royal Court, 1992. TWA, BLMC, Add 79386.
159 Wertenbaker, undated draft/copy of letter to Maurice Podbrey, c.1985, TWA, BLMC, Add 79215.
160 Wertenbaker, *Plays One*, 414.
161 Wertenbaker, 'The Voices We Hear', 367. The ode is from Wertenbaker, trans., Sophocles, *Oedipus Tyrannos; Oedipus at Kolonos; Antigone*. London: Faber and Faber, 1998.
162 Buse, 'Timberlake Wertenbaker'.
163 Wertenbaker cited in Crew, 'Timberlake Wertenbaker'.
164 Wertenbaker cited in letter from Susanne Tighe to Wertenbaker, 17 May 1991, TWA, BLMC, Add 79209.

Conclusions

1 Wertenbaker cited in Mackenzie, 'A play for life'.
2 Wertenbaker, *The Line*, 59.
3 Anushka Asthana and Rachel Williams, 'Growing outcry at threat of cuts in humanities at universities', Observer, 28 February 2010, http://www. guardian. co.uk/education/2010/feb/28/outcry-threat-cuts-humanities-universities (accessed 5 April 2011).
4 Said, *The World*, 124.
5 Freeman, 'Afterword', 280.
6 de Vries, 'This "Angry Young Man"'.
7 Morrow Lockwood, Review of 'The Third'; Jim Hiley, Review of 'Case to Answer'

at the Soho Poly, *Time Out*, c.1980, TWA, BLMC, Add 79383; Beatrice MacLeod, Review of 'Happy Ending' ('Case to Answer') at the Central Casting Theatre, New York, *Ithaca Journal*, 24 June 1980; and many others.

8   Nathan; de Jongh; Dowden; Coveney; Reviews of *The Break of Day*.

9   Reviews of 'Abel's Sister' at The Royal Court by Billington, *Guardian*, c.1984; and Lyn Gardner, *City Limits*, c.1984, TWA, BLMC, Add 79383.

10 Lydia Conway, 'Private View: Lydia Conway talks to Timberlake Wertenbaker', *What's On*, 28 August 1991.

11 McFerran, Review of *New Anatomies*.

12 Cropper, Review of *The Grace of Mary Traverse*.

13 Pennington, Review of *The Grace of Mary Traverse*.

14 McGivan, 'Breaking Through'.

15 Billington, Review of *Three Birds*.

16 Coveney, Review of *The Grace of Mary Traverse*.

17 Coveney, Review of *The Grace of Mary Traverse*; Spencer, Review of *Three Birds Alighting on a Field* at the Royal Court, *Daily Telegraph*, 12 September 1991; and Jack Pitman, Review of *Three Birds Alighting on a Field* at the Royal Court, *Dramatic Publishing Co*, 23 September 1991.

18 Coveney, Review of *The Grace of Mary Traverse*; and Peter, 'The shock of the new'.

19 Gardner, Review of *The Grace of Mary Traverse* at the Royal Court, *City Limits*, c.1985, TWA, BLMC, Add 79383.

20 Peter 'The shock of the new'; and Billington, Review of *Three Birds*.

21 Shulman, Review of *The Grace of Mary Traverse*.

22 Shulman, Review of *Three Birds Alighting on a Field* at the Royal Court, *Evening Standard*, 11 September 1991; Stuart, Review of *Three Birds*; and Kramer, 'Dimwitted Playgoers'.

23 Peter, Review of *Three Birds Alighting on a Field* at the Royal Court, *Sunday Times*, 15 September 1991.

24 Martin, 'Sloane Square savages'.

25 Wertenbaker, 'First Thoughts on Transforming a Text' in Roth and Freeman, *International Dramaturgy*, pp. 35–40: 39.

26 Wertenbaker, 'Words and also, plugs'. Unpublished, undated article, TWA, BLMC, Add 79382.

27 Wertenbaker, *The Line*, 59.

28 Wertenbaker, *Plays One*, 349.

29 Wertenbaker, 'The Three Musketeers'.

30 Wertenbaker, *Plays One*, 245.

31 Wertenbaker, interview with Bush.

32 Wertenbaker wrote in a synopsis for 'Return to Greece' (a version of 'Monads'), 'I think we still suffer in our private and political lives from the 19th century Christian-Hegelian notion that history must end with a big bang of bliss', TWA, BLMC, Add 79244.

33 Wertenbaker, *Plays Two*, 23.

34 Wertenbaker, 'Health and Deficiency'.

35 The image of the Apollonian and Dionysian cafes appears in 'Monads'.

36 Wertenbaker, *Plays One*, 160.

CHRONOLOGY

The chronology details the opening productions of Wertenbaker's plays and important developments in her career, alongside significant political and cultural events from the period.

1940s/50s	Childhood in Basque France
1950s	Returns to New York
1964	Labour (Harold Wilson) elected; begin to increase theatre subsidy
1966	Graduates from St John's College, Annapolis
1968	Theatres Act abolishes censorship
1969	British troops sent into Northern Ireland
1970s	Working for Time Life-Life Books in New York and London
1970	Conservatives (Edward Heath) elected
1973	Women's Theatre Group established
1974	Labour (Harold Wilson) elected
	Joint Stock established
1975	Theatre subsidy frozen
	Leaves Time-Life to work at Exmoor riding stables
1976	Teaching in Spetse; drafts **'A Year on Exmoor'**
1977	**'The Third'** and **'The Vigil'**, Spetse
1978	'Winter of Discontent'
	Living between London and New York; drafts **'Agamemnon's Daughter'** and **'Act for Our Times'**; **'This is No Place for Tallulah Bankhead'**, King's Head, London
1979	Conservatives (Margaret Thatcher) elected
	Caryl Churchill's *Cloud Nine*
	Clean Break established
	More permanent move to London; working at Camden

Plaza Cinema; represented by Anthony Sheil Associates Ltd; drafts **'Don Juan's Women'**, **'Monads'** and **'Near Miss'**

1980   Moves to Michael Imison's agency
'Second Sentence', Brighton Actors' Workshop
'Case to Answer', Soho Poly, London
'The Third', King's Head
'Breaking Through', Women's Theatre Group

1981   Brixton Riots
Greenham Common Women's Peace Camp begins
Drafts **'Variations'**
Attends Clive Tempest's New Theatre Workshop
New Anatomies, Women's Theatre Group

1982   Falklands War
Caryl Churchill's *Top Girls*
'Home Leave', Wolsey Theatre, Ipswich
'Inside Out', Rodent Arts Trust

1983   Writer in Residence at Shared Experience; translates *False Admissions* and *Successful Strategies*

1984   Royal Court's subsidy threatened
Writer in Residence at Royal Court (to 1985)
'Abel's Sister', Royal Court, London
'New Anatomies', BBC Radio

1985   *The Grace of Mary Traverse*, Royal Court
Leocadia (trans.), BBC Radio

1986   The Cork Report
Mephisto (trans.), RSC, Stratford

1987   *La Dispute* (trans.), BBC Radio

1988   *Our Country's Good*, Royal Court
The Love of the Nightingale, RSC

1989   **'Pelleas and Melisande'** (trans.), BBC Radio

1990   Poll Tax riots
Margaret Thatcher's resignation
First Gulf War (to 1991)

	The Children (adapt.), Arbo Fil/Channel Four Films/ Isolde Films/Maram
1991	*Three Birds Alighting on a Field*, Royal Court
	The Theban Plays (trans.), RSC
	Do Not Disturb, BBC Television
1992	Balkan conflict begins
	Conservatives (John Major) re-elected
1994	Introduction of Heritage Lottery Fund (National Lottery)
1995	Sarah Kane's *Blasted*
	The Break of Day, Out of Joint
	Hecuba (trans.), ACT, San Francisco
1996	Mark Ravenhill's *Shopping and Fucking*
1997	Labour (Tony Blair) elected
1998	*After Darwin*, Hampstead Theatre, London
	Filumena (trans.), Peter Hall Company/Piccadilly, London
1999	*Dianeira*, BBC Radio
2000	The Boyden Report
	The Ash Girl, Birmingham Rep
2001	Attack on twin towers; US/UK led invasion of Afghanistan
	Credible Witness, Royal Court
	Hecuba (trans.), BBC Radio
2002	'Wild Orchids' (trans.), Chichester Festival Theatre
2003	US/UK led invasion of Iraq
	'The H. File' (adapt.), BBC Radio
2004	'Galileo's Daughter'/'The Laws of Motion', Peter Hall Company/Theatre Royal, Bath
2005	'Scenes of Seduction', BBC Radio
2006	'The Love of the Nightingale' (libretto), Perth International Arts Festival
2007	Start of financial crisis in US and Europe
	Jenufa, Natural Perspective Theatre Company/Arcola, London
2008	*Arden City*, NT Connections

2009	*The Line*, Arcola
	Hippolytus (trans.), Temple Theatre/Onassis Programme
	'Phaedra' (trans.), Shakespeare Festival, Stratford Ontario
	'What is the Custom of Your Grief', BBC Radio
2010	Conservatives (David Cameron) elected; austerity policies
	'Elektra' (trans.), ACT
2011	Riots in multiple UK cities
	Britannicus (trans.), Natural Perspective/Wilton's Music Hall, London
	'Possession' (adapt.), BBC Radio
2012	**'Ajax in Afghanistan'/'Our Ajax'**, Women and War, Greece
	'Das Rheingold'/'The Memory of Gold', BBC Radio

BIBLIOGRAPHY

Wertenbaker's published plays:

—*Arden City* in *New Connections 2008: Plays for Young People*. London: Faber and Faber, 2008.
—*Hippolytus*. London: Faber and Faber, 2009.
—*Jenufa*. London: Faber and Faber, 2007.
—*Plays One* (*New Anatomies, The Grace of Mary Traverse, Our Country's Good, The Love of the Nightingale, Three Birds Alighting on a Field*). London: Faber and Faber, 1996.
—*Plays Two* (*The Break of Day, After Darwin, Credible Witness, The Ash Girl, Dianeira*). London: Faber and Faber, 2002.
—*The Line*. London: Faber and Faber, 2009.

Wertenbaker's unpublished plays:

—'Abel's Sister' (stage play c.1984). Timberlake Wertenbaker Archive, British Library Manuscripts Collection, Add 79255–7.
—'Act for Our Times' (unperformed stage play c.1978). TWA, BLMC, Add 79235.
—'Act for Our Times' (unperformed radio play c.1978). TWA, BLMC, Add 79235.
—'Agamemnon's Daughter' (unperformed stage play c.1978). TWA, BLMC, Add 79234.
—'Breaking Through' (stage play c.1980). TWA, BLMC, Add 79238–40.
—'Case to Answer' (stage play c.1980). TWA, BLMC, Add 79229–79233.
—'Don Juan's Women' (unperformed stage play c.1979). TWA, BLMC, Add 79234.
—'Inside Out' (stage play c.1982). TWA, BLMC, Add 79252–4.
—'London Nights' (unperformed libretto c.1989). TWA, BLMC, Add 79378.
—'Monads' (unperformed stage play c.1979). TWA, BLMC, Add 79228.
—'Near Miss' (unperformed stage/television play c.1979). TWA, BLMC, Add 79234.
—'New Anatomies' (radio play c.1984). TWA, BLMC, Add 79250.
—'Second Sentence' (stage play c.1980). TWA, BLMC, Add 79237.
—'The Laws of Motion' (stage play c.2004). Available from Casarotto Ramsay and Associates.
—'The Third' (stage play c.1977). TWA, BLMC, Add 79225.
—'The Vigil' (stage play c.1977). TWA, BLMC, Add 79226.

—'This is No Place for Tallulah Bankhead' (stage play c.1978). TWA, BLMC, Add 79227.
—'Variations' (stage play c.1981). TWA, BLMC, Add 79242.

Wertenbaker's published articles:

—'About Then: History Plays' in David Edgar (ed.), *State of Play: Playwrights on Playwriting*. London: Faber and Faber, 1999, pp. 73–6.
—'Dancing with History' in Marc Maufort and Franca Bellarsi (eds), *Crucible of Cultures*, pp. 17–23.
—'Kicking city habits in Lorna Doone country', *CLASSIC*, Oct/Nov 1976.
—'Health and Deficiency: Playwright Timberlake Wertenbaker on the state of British theatre', publication details unknown, c.1989, TWA, BLMC, Add 79383.
—'Out theatre's good, too', *Guardian*, 2 December 1989.
—'The Voices We Hear' in Edith Hall et al. (eds), *Dionysus Since '69*. Oxford: Oxford University Press, 2004, pp. 361–8.

Wertenbaker's unpublished articles (TWA, BLMC, Add 79382):

—'American Feminism Enter the '80s' (c.1980).
—'A View of Deventer by Salomon van Ruysdael' (undated).
—'Is theatre necessary? Three wishes, three curses' (c.1994).
—'Learning to live with the English' (c.1978).
—'The Playwright's Plea' (undated).
—'The Three Musketeers' (c.1990). (A version of this article is published in Fraser, Antonia (ed.), *The Pleasure of Reading*. London: Bloomsbury, 1992).
—'Women ex-prisoners: out of the closet and on to the stage' (c.1979).

Interviews with Wertenbaker:

Bigsby, Christopher. *Writers in Conversation with Christopher Bigsby: Volume Two*. Norwich: The Arthur Miller Centre for American Studies, 2001.
Devine, Harriet, *Looking Back: Playwrights at the Royal Court 1956–2006*. London: Faber and Faber, 2006, pp. 273–82.
DiGaetani, John L., *A Search for a Postmodern Theatre: Interviews with Contemporary Playwrights*. Westport, CT: Greenwood Press, 1991, pp. 265–73.
Stephenson, Heidi and Langridge, Natasha, *Rage and Reason: Women Playwrights on Playwriting*. London: Methuen, 1997, pp. 136–45.

Comparative literature:

Barker, Howard, *The Castle; Scenes from an Execution*. London: Calder, 1985.
— *The Europeans: Struggles to Love; Judith: A Parting from the Body*. London: Calder, 1990.
Brecht, Bertolt, *The Life of Galileo*. Trans. Desmond I. Vesey. London: Methuen, 1968.
Chekhov, Anton, *Five Plays*. Trans. Ronald Hingley. Oxford and New York: Oxford University Press, 1977.
Churchill, Caryl, *Cloud Nine*. London: Nick Hern Books, 1989.
Clark, C. M. H., *A History of Australia Volume One*. Melbourne: Melbourne University Press, 1962.
Farquhar, George, *The Recruiting Officer*. Manchester: Manchester University Press, 1986.
Fowles, John, *The Magus* (A Revised Version). London: Triad/Granada, 1977.
Frayn, Michael, *Copenhagen*. London: Methuen, 1998.
Hughes, Robert, *The Fatal Shore*. New York: Vintage Book, 1988.
Keneally, Thomas, *The Playmaker*. London: Serpentine Publishing Co. Pty Limited, 1987.
Kobak, Annette, *Isabelle: The Life of Isabelle Eberhardt*. London: Chatto and Windus, 1988.
McCullough, Helen Craig, *Kokin Wakashū: The First Imperial Anthology of Japanese Poetry*. Palo Alto: Stanford University Press, 1985.
Ovid, *Metamorphoses* (Books I–VIII). Trans. Frank Justus Miller. London: William Heinemann, 1977.
Rexroth, Kenneth and Ikuko Atsumi, *Woman Poets of Japan*. New York: New Directions, 1977.
Stoppard, Tom, *Arcadia*. London: Faber and Faber, 1993.
Wertenbaker, Lael Tucker, *Death of a Man*. London: Pan Books, 1959.

On Wertenbaker:

Carlson, Susan, 'Issues of Identity, Nationality and Performance: the Reception of Two Plays by Timberlake Wertenbaker', *New Theatre Quarterly*, Vol. 9, No. 35 (1993), pp. 267–89.
— 'Language and Identity in Timberlake Wertenbaker's Plays' in Aston and Reinelt (eds), *The Cambridge Companion to Modern British Women Playwrights*, pp. 134–50.
Gömceli, Nursen, *Timberlake Wertenbaker and Contemporary British Feminist Drama*. Bethesda, Dublin and Palo Alto: Academica Press, 2010.
Mideke, Martin, 'Drama and the Desire for History: The Plays of Timberlake Wertenbaker' in Uwe Böker and Hans Sauer (eds), *Anglistentag 1996 Dresden*. Trier: WVT, 1996, pp. 223–33.
Rabey, David Ian, 'Defining Difference: Timberlake Wertenbaker's Drama of Language, Dispossession and Discovery', *Modern Drama*, Vol. 33, No. 4 (1990), pp. 518–77.

Roth, Maya E. and Freeman, Sara (eds), *International Dramaturgy: Translation & Transformations in the Theatre of Timberlake Wertenbaker*. Brussels: P.I.E. Peter Lang, 2008.

Rubik, Margarete, 'The Silencing of Women in British Feminist Drama' in Gudron M. Grabher and Ulrike Jessner (eds), *Semantics of Silences in Linguistics and Literature*. Heidelberg: Universitatsverlag C, 1996, pp. 177–80.

Sullivan, Esther Beth, 'Hailing Ideology, Acting in the Horizon, and Reading between Plays by Timberlake Wertenbaker', *Theatre Journal*, Vol. 45, No. 2 (1993), pp. 139–54.

Varty, Anne, 'From Queens to Convicts: Status, Sex and Language in Contemporary British Women's Drama' in Katie Wales (ed.), *Essays and Studies 1994: Feminist Linguistics in Literary Criticism*. Cambridge: The English Association, 1994, pp. 65–89.

Wilson, Ann, 'Forgiving Histories and Making New Worlds: Timberlake Wertenbaker's Recent Drama' in James Acheson (ed.), *British and Irish Drama Since 1960*. Basingstoke: Macmillan, 1993, pp. 146–61.

On *The Grace of Mary Traverse*:

Dahl, Mary Karen, 'Constructing the Subject: Timberlake Wertenbaker's *The Grace of Mary Traverse*', *Journal of Dramatic Theory and Criticism*, Vol. 7, No. 2 (1993), pp. 149–59.

Ritchie, Martha, 'Almost "Better to Be Nobody": Feminist Subjectivity, the Thatcher Years, and Timberlake Wertenbaker's *The Grace of Mary Traverse*', *Modern Drama*, Vol. 39, No. 3 (1996), pp. 404–20.

On *Our Country's Good*:

Bell, Michael, 'Novel and Theatre in Thomas Keneally's *The Playmaker*: Historical and Generic Models of the Self' in Wilhelm G. Busse (ed.), *Anglistentag 1991 Düsseldorf: Proceedings*. Tübingen: Niemeyer, 1992, pp. 228–36.

Bimberg, Christiane, 'Caryl Churchill's *Top Girls* and Timberlake Wertenbaker's *Our Country's Good* as Contributions to a Definition of Culture', *Connotations: A Journal for Critical Debate*, Vol. 7, No. 3 (1998), pp. 399–416.

Bligh, Kate, 'Oppositional Symmetries: An Anthropological Voyage through *Our Country's Good* and *The Poetics*' in Roth and Freeman (eds), *International Dramaturgy*, pp. 177–93.

Buse, Peter, *Drama and Theory: Critical Approaches to Modern British Drama*. Manchester: Manchester University Press, 2001.

Davis, Jim, 'Festive Irony: Aspects of British Theatre in the 1980s', *Critical Survey*, No. 3 (1991), pp. 339–50.

Bibliography

—'A Play for England: The Royal Court adapts The Playmaker' in Peter Reynolds (ed.), *Novel Images: Literature in Performance.* London: Routledge, 1993, pp. 175–90.

Dymkowski, Christine, 'The Play's the Thing: The Metatheatre of Timberlake Wertenbaker' in Nicole Boireau (ed.), *Drama on Drama.* Basingstoke: Palgrave, 1997, pp. 121–35.

Foster, Verna, 'Convicts, Characters, and Conventions of Acting in Timberlake Wertenbaker's *Our Country's Good*', *Connotations*, Vol. 7, No. 3 (1997), pp. 417–32.

Inverso, Mary Beth, 'Der Straf-block: Performance and Execution in Barnes, Griffiths, and Wertenbaker', *Modern Drama*, Vol. 36, No. 3 (1993), pp. 420–30.

Soncini, Sara, *Playing with(in) the Restoration.* Naples: Edizioni Scientifiche Italiane, 1999.

Stafford-Clark, Max. *Letters to George.* London: Nick Hern Books, 1997.

Stafford-Clark, Max and McKeown, Maeve. *Timberlake Wertenbaker's Our Country's Good: A Study Guide.* London: Nick Hern Books, 2010.

Stafford-Clark, Max and Roberts, Philip. *Taking Stock: The Theatre of Max Stafford-Clark.* London: Nick Hearn Books, 2007.

Taylor, Val, 'Mothers of Invention: Female Characters in *Our County's Good* and *The Playmaker*', *Critical Survey*, No. 3 (1991), pp. 331–8.

Weeks, Stephen, 'The Question of Liz: Staging the Prisoner in *Our Country's Good*', *Modern Drama*, Vol. 43, No. 2 (2000), pp. 147–56.

Wilson, Ann, '*Our Country's Good*: Theatre, Colony and Nation in Wertenbaker's Adaptation of The Playmaker', *Modern Drama*, Vol. 34, No. 1 (1991), pp. 23–34.

On *The Love of the Nightingale*:

Monros-Gaspar, Laura 'Voices from the Cave: The Chorus and the Figure of Echo in Timberlake Wertenbaker's *The Love of the Nightingale*', *BELLS: Barcelona English Language and Literature Studies*, No. 15 (2006), pp. 1–13.

Rabillard, Sheila, 'Threads, Bodies and Birds: Transformation from Ovidian Narrative to Drama in Timberlake Wertenbaker's *The Love of the Nightingale*', *Essays in Theatre/ Etudes Theatrales*, Vol. 17, No. 2 (1999), pp. 99–110.

Wagner, Jennifer A., 'Formal Parody and the Metamorphoses of the Audience in Timberlake Wertenbaker's *The Love of the Nightingale*', *Papers on Language and Literature*, Vol. 31, No. 3 (1995), pp. 227–54.

Winston, Joe, 'Recasting the Phaedra Syndrome: Myth and Morality in Timberlake Wertenbaker's *The Love of the Nightingale*', *Modern Drama*, Vol. 38, No. 4 (1995), pp. 510–19.

On *The Break of Day*:

Aston, Elaine, 'Geographies of Oppression – The Cross-Border Politics of (M)othering: *The Break of Day* and *A Yearning*', *Theatre Research International*, Vol. 24, No. 3 (1999), pp. 247–53.

Cousin, Geraldine, 'Revisiting the Prozorovs', *Modern Drama*, Vol. 40, No. 3 (1997), pp. 325–36.

Johnsen-Neshati, Kristin, 'Chekhovian Transformation: *Three Sisters* and Timberlake Wertenbaker's *The Break of Day*' in Roth and Freeman (eds), *International Dramaturgy*, pp. 123–33.

Komporaly, Jozefina, 'Maternal Longing as Addiction: Feminism Revisited in Timberlake Wertenbaker's *The Break of Day*', *Journal of Gender Studies*, Vol. 13, No. 2 (2004), pp. 129–38.

Rabillard, Sheila, 'Translating the Past: Theatrical and Historical Repetition in Wertenbaker's *The Break of Day*' in Roth and Freeman (eds), *International Dramaturgy*, pp. 135–53.

Roth, Maya E., 'Im/Migrations, Border-Crossings and "Wilful Internationalism"' in Timberlake Wertenbaker's *The Break of Day*' in Maufort and Bellarsi (eds), *Crucible of Cultures*, pp. 79–90.

Young, Stuart, 'Fin-de-siècle Reflections and Revisions: Wertenbaker Challenges British Chekhov Tradition in *The Break of Day*', *Modern Drama*, Vol. 41, No. 3 (1998), pp. 442–60.

On *After Darwin*:

Freeman, Sara, 'Adaptation after Darwin: Timberlake Wertenbaker's Evolving Texts', *Modern Drama*, Vol. 45, No. 4 (2002), pp. 646–62.

On *Credible Witness*:

Aston, Elaine, 'The "Bogus Woman": Feminism and Asylum Theatre', *Modern Drama*, Vol. 46, No. 1 (2003), pp. 5–21.

Freeman, Sara, 'Group Tragedy and Diaspora: New and Old Histories of Exile and Family in Wertenbaker's *Hecuba* and *Credible Witness*' in Roth and Freeman (eds), *International Dramaturgy*, pp. 61–75.

On Wertenbaker's translations:

Pedrick, Victoria, 'Ismene's Return from a Sentimental Journey' in Roth and Freeman (eds), *International Dramaturgy*, pp. 41–59.

Wilson, Ann, '*Dianeira*, Anger and History' in Roth and Freeman (eds), *International Dramaturgy*, pp. 209–21.

On feminisms and feminist and women's theatres:

Aston, Elaine, *Feminist Views on the English Stage*. Cambridge: Cambridge University Press, 2003.

Aston, Elaine and Reinelt, Janelle (eds), *The Cambridge Companion to Modern British Women Playwrights*. Cambridge: Cambridge University Press, 2000.

Carlson, Susan, *Women and Comedy: Rewriting the British Theatrical Tradition*. Ann Arbor: University of Michigan Press, 1991.

Case, Sue Ellen, *Feminism and Theatre*. Basingstoke: Macmillan, 1988.

Cixous, Helene, 'Sorties' in Rivkin and Ryan (eds), *Literary Theory: An Anthology*, pp. 578–84.

Cousin, Geraldine, *Women in Dramatic Place and Time*. London: Routledge, 1996.

Fetterley, Judith, 'On the Politics of Literature' in Rivkin and Ryan (eds), *Literary Theory: An Anthology*, pp. 561–9.

Gale, Maggie B. and Gardner, Viv (eds), *Women, Theatre and Performance: New Histories, New Historiographies*. Manchester: Manchester University Press, 2000.

Gay, Penny, *As She Likes It: Shakespeare's Unruly Women*. London: Routledge, 1994.

Gilbert, Sandra and Gubar, Susan, 'The Madwoman in the Attic' in Rivkin and Ryan (eds), *Literary Theory: An Anthology*, pp. 598–611.

Goodman, Lizbeth, *Contemporary Feminist Theatres: To Each Her Own*. London: Routledge, 1993.

Irigaray, Luce, 'The Power of Discourse and the Subordination of the Feminine' in Rivkin and Ryan (eds), *Literary Theory: An Anthology*, pp. 570–3.

Klindienst, Patricia, 'The Voice of the Shuttle is Ours' in Rivkin and Ryan (eds), *Literary Theory: An Anthology*, pp. 612–29.

Morgan, Robin, *Sisterhood is Powerful*. London, Random House, 1970.

Rich, Adrienne, 'Notes Towards a Politics of Location' in Rivkin and Ryan (eds), *Literary Theory: An Anthology*, pp. 637–49.

On British theatre history:

Billington, Michael, *State of the Nation: British Theatre since 1945*. London: Faber and Faber, 2007.

Edgar, David (ed.), *State of Play: Playwrights on Playwriting*. London: Faber and Faber, 1999.

Hall, Edith et al. (eds), *Dionysus Since '69*. Oxford: Oxford University Press, 2004.

Holdsworth, Nadine and Luckhurst, Mary (eds), *A Concise Companion to Contemporary British and Irish Drama*. Malden, Oxford and Victoria, Blackwell Publishing, 2008.

Little, Ruth and McLaughlin, Emily, *The Royal Court Theatre Inside Out*. London: Oberon Books, 2007.

Maufort, Marc and Bellarsi, Franca (eds), *Crucible of Cultures: Anglophone Drama at the Dawn of a New Millennium*, Brussels: Peter Lang, 2002.

Roberts, Philip *The Royal Court Theatre and the Modern Stage*. Cambridge, Cambridge University Press, 1999.

Shellard, Dominic, *British Theatre since the War*. New Haven and London: Yale University Press, 1999.

On biography:

Ellis, David (ed.), *Imitating Art*. London: Pluto Press, 1993.

Gaskell, Philip, *From Writer to Reader*. Winchester: St Paul's Bibliographies, 1984.

Homberger, Eric and Charmley, John (eds), *The Troubled Face of Biography*. Basingstoke: Macmillan, 1988.

Simons, Judy, *Diaries and Journals of Literary Women from Fanny Burney to Virginia Woolf*. Basingstoke: Macmillan, 1990.

Swindells, Julia (ed.), *The Uses of Autobiography*. London, Taylor & Francis, 1995.

On postcolonial studies:

Fanon, Frantz, *Black Skin, White Masks*. Trans. Charles Lam Markmann. London, MacGibbon and Kee, 1968.

Said, Edward, *The World, the Text and the Critic*. London: Vintage, 1991.

Thiong'o, Ngugi wa, 'Decolonising the Mind' in Rivkin and Ryan (eds), *Literary Theory: An Anthology* (Second Edition), pp. 1126–50.

Other:

Jung, C. G. and Kerényi, C, *Introduction to a Science of Mythology*. London: Routledge, 1951.

Rivkin, Julie and Ryan, Michael (eds), *Literary Theory: An Anthology*. Oxford: Blackwell, 1998.

—*Literary Theory: An Anthology* (Second Edition). Oxford: Blackwell, 2004.

Online sources:

Anon, 'Ono No Komachi's Poetry', *Gotterdammerung.org*, 2009, http://www.gotterdam-merung.org/japan/literature/ono-no-komachi/ (accessed 30 July 2010).

Bentley, Paul, 'Australian Culture 1789–2000', *The Wolanski Foundation*, 1999, http://www.twf.org.au/research/culture.html (accessed 10 March 2011).

Buse, Peter, 'Timberlake Wertenbaker', *Contemporary Writers*, 2003, http://www.contemporarywriters.com/authors/?p=auth138 (accessed 1 September 2009).

Falco, Raphael, 'Is There a Genealogy of Cultures? – Critical Essay'. *BNET*, 2000, http://findarticles.com/p/articles/mi_m2220/is_4_42/ai_ 75950975/pg_3/?tag=content;col1 (accessed 6 April 2009).

Freeman, Sara, 'Wertenbaker, Timberlake (1951(?) –)', *The Literary Encyclopaedia*, 2004, http://www.litencyc.com/php/speople.php?rec=true&UID=5520 (accessed 24 January 2005).

Hollingworth, John, 'Legacy – an actor on the pressures of making a classic new', Out of Joint, 26 September 2012, http://www.outofjoint.co.uk/our-countrys-good/2012/09/legacy-an-actor-on-the-pressures-of-making-a-classic-new.html (accessed 7 December 2012).

Out of Joint, http://www.outofjoint.co.uk/ (accessed 31 October 2012).

Smith, Andy, 'Designing the sound for *Our Country's Good*', Out of Joint, 8 August 2012, http://www.outofjoint.co.uk/our-countrys-good/2012/08/designing-the-sound-for-our-countrys-good.html (accessed 7 December 2012).

Wertenbaker, Timberlake, 'Everyone comes to Café Europa', *Open Democracy*, 2001, http://www.opendemocracy.net/people-debate_36/article_304.jsp# (accessed 3 March 2011).

—'A Dialogue With One's Ghosts', Out of Joint, 28 June 2012, http://www.outofjoint.co.uk/writing/2012/06/a-dialogue-with-ones-ghosts.html (accessed 30 August 2012).

Radio sources:

Wertenbaker, interview with Rosemary Harthill, 'Writers Revealed', *Kaleidoscope*, BBC Radio Four, 1991.

—interview with Jenni Murray, *Woman's Hour*, BBC Radio Four, 5 July 2004. Available online at http://www.bbc.co.uk/radio4/womanshour/ 2004_27_mon_01.shtml (accessed 3 May 2011).

—interview with Miriam O'Reilly, *Woman's Hour*, BBC Radio Four, 22 October 2007. Available online at http://www.bbc.co.uk/radio4/ womanshour/03/2007_43_mon.shtml (accessed 3 May 2011).

—'What is the Custom of Your Grief?' *From Fact to Fiction*, BBC Radio Four, 13 December 2009.

NOTES ON CONTRIBUTORS

Roger Hodgman
Roger Hodgman has directed over a hundred stage productions and many hours of television drama. He was Artistic Director for Melbourne Theatre Company for twelve years until 2000. Prior to that, he was Dean of Drama at the Victorian College of the Arts, Artistic Director of the Vancouver Playhouse, Director of the Vancouver Playhouse Acting School, and acting teacher and director at East 15 Acting School in London. Highlights in Vancouver include working with Tennessee Williams on two new plays. For MTC he directed a range of classics, contemporary work, several musicals by Stephen Sondheim, and counts working on *Our Country's Good* as one of his favourite experiences. Since leaving MTC he has pursued a busy freelance career directing numerous operas, musicals, plays and television dramas.

Sarah Sigal
Originally from Chicago, Sarah Sigal has a BA in English Literature and Theatre Arts from Gettysburg College and an MA in Writing for Performance from Goldsmiths College, University of London, where she recently completed a PhD on the role of the writer in new collaborative theatre-making in Britain. She is a freelance writer, director and dramaturg, working in text-based and devised performance, as well as physical theatre, radio, site-specific work, short films, live art and cabaret. She has had work produced at such venues as the Albany, the Arcola, the Bike Shed, Cheltenham Everyman, Theatre503, the Old Red Lion and the Edinburgh Festival. She is the writer-in-residence for Fluff Productions and a visiting lecturer at Goldsmiths College. She is currently working on a book about writing and collaboration for Palgrave Macmillan.

Debbie Turner

Debby Turner (MA) trained at Rose Bruford College of Speech and Drama and has since worked in theatre and education as a teacher, director and writer. Debby met Max Stafford-Clark while researching her MA dissertation and has since followed many of his productions and observed his techniques and working practices. She created a scheme of work for teaching *Our Country's Good* at A Level, after observing rehearsals for Stafford-Clark's 2012 production of the play. She is a freelance lecturer on the MA Ensemble course at Rose Bruford College of Speech and Drama.

INDEX

7:84 16

'Abel's Sister' 311, 314
aborigines 118–20, 133,
    163–4, 290n. 159
'Act for Our Times' 3, 24,
    37–40, 266, 310, 314
actioning 172–3, 178–9
adaptation (literary) 44, 97,
    140, 143–61, 183, 233,
    237, 292n. 1, 296n. 27,
    307n. 126, 312–13
adoption 186–98
Adshead, Kay 17, 219
Aeschylus 48
affiliation 183–6, 190–5, 205,
    208, 209, 211, 223, 224,
    225, 227, 234, 236, 268
After Darwin 2, 4, 9, 10, 15,
    97–8, 105, 107, 182,
    185, 193, 196, 199–208,
    214, 232, 233, 239, 268,
    295n. 14, 307n. 126,
    312, 314, 319
'Agamemnon's Daughter' 3,
    24, 48–52, 59, 73, 75,
    237, 267, 310, 314
'Ajax in Afghanistan'/'Our
    Ajax' 313
Anthony Sheil Associates Ltd
    25, 276n. 20, 311

Antigone 264
Apollo and Dionysus 57–8, 271
Arbour, The 17
Arcadia 200–1, 298n. 79
archives 5–7, 248, 271, 314–15
Arcola Theatre 235, 242,
    312–13
Arden City 4, 233–5,
    307n. 142, 312, 314
Aristotle 53, 66, 239–40
art (visual) 232–3, 242–64
Arts Council 15–16, 20, 55
Ash Girl, The 4, 105, 182,
    193, 220–31, 236, 268,
    304n. 45, 312, 314
Aston, Elaine 188, 190, 192,
    201, 211
As You Like It 233–5
Auerbach, Eric 183–4
Aukin, David 14, 146
Aukin, Liane 26

Bargate, Verity 26–7, 48
Barker, Howard 14, 136, 151
Basque Country/language 1,
    7–9, 96, 103–4, 114–15,
    310
Bassett, Kate 242
Bassett, Linda 119, 147, 154,
    158, 160
Bath Theatre Royal 237, 312

BBC 311–13
Beautiful Thing 18
Bent 18
bi/multiculturalism 181–231
Billington, Michael 15, 17,
  19, 21, 92, 193, 220,
  221, 242, 263
biography 5–12, 253–4, 321
Birmingham Rep 220, 312
Black Skin, White Masks 102
Blasted 19, 198, 312
Bogus Woman, The 219
Boyden Report 20, 312
'Breaking Through' 3, 24, 44–7,
  266, 303n. 9, 311, 314
Break of Day, The 4, 9, 107,
  182–3, 186–98, 199,
  201, 202, 203, 208, 218,
  230, 232, 234, 241, 242,
  250, 261, 268, 277n. 60,
  283n. 96, 296nn. 24, 27,
  29, 307n. 126, 312, 314,
  318–19
Brecht, Bertolt 51, 188–90,
  194, 228, 237, 238, 240,
  246, 294n. 75, 296n. 24,
  303n. 27, 304n. 40
Brenton, Howard 14–5, 17,
  145, 286n. 28
Brighton Actors' Workshop
  27, 43, 311
Britannicus 313
British Library 248, 271
Brothers Grimm 221–9
Brown, Georgina 219
Brown, Irina 237

Buse, Peter 126, 130, 136,
  138–9, 141, 142, 262,
  264, 291n. 186
Butler, Robert 199–200

canon/canonicity 2, 3, 24, 48,
  77, 94, 206, 214, 267,
  295n. 10
Carlson, Susan 6, 72, 97, 126,
  133, 140
Cartlidge, Katrin 79
Cartwright, Jim 17
Case, Sue Ellen 116, 288n. 86
'Case to Answer' 26–7,
  39, 70–1, 95–6, 98,
  113–16, 125, 142, 267,
  280n. 135, 283n. 79,
  286n. 39, 311, 314
Cavendish, Dominic 221
censorship 12–13, 310
Central Casting Theatre,
  Ithaca, NY 39
Chekhov, Anton 29, 183,
  186–90, 196–7, 269,
  271, 296n. 27
Cherry Orchard, The 187
children/parenthood 42–3,
  88–90, 108–9, 185–6,
  189–96, 201, 203–6,
  211–12, 222–5, 229–31,
  236, 241, 248–50, 268,
  271, 278n. 75, 283n. 96
Children, The 183, 312
choruses 51–2, 78, 82, 84,
  102, 109–13, 220, 269,
  287n. 62

Churchill, Caryl 13–14, 17,
    58, 95, 145, 148, 198,
    246, 278n. 93, 310, 311
Cinderella 220–31, 301n. 182
Cixous, Hélène 29, 99, 116
Clapp, Susannah 199
Clean Break Theatre
    Company 13, 44, 133,
    135, 150–3, 310
Cloud Nine 13, 95, 145,
    285n. 127, 310
colonialism/postcolonialism 2,
    56, 70, 95–6, 102–4,
    113–17, 121–2, 125–33,
    140–2, 182, 205–8, 209,
    321
compassion fatigue 192, 202,
    209
Cork Report 16, 311
'countrylessness' 181–2
Coveney, Michael 91, 204
Credible Witness 4, 9, 45, 72,
    105, 117, 182, 196, 203,
    209–20, 221, 225, 231,
    236, 261, 268, 277n. 60,
    304n. 45, 312, 314, 319
Cropper, Martin 91
cross-casting 66, 72, 79–82,
    146, 285n. 127
cultural genealogy 185–9,
    206–8, 244, 266, 269
cultural imperialism 96, 113,
    126, 138–41, 182, 256
cynicism 262–3

Daldry, Stephen 19

Dance of Death 63
Daniels, Sarah 17
Darwin, Charles 199–205,
    239
Das Rheingold 313
Davis, Jim 134, 140–1,
    297–8n. 61
de Angelis, April 17
Death of a Man 8
Deathwatch 9
Decolonising the Mind: The
    Politics of Language in
    African Literature 103
Degas, Edgar 232–3, 241–55,
    259, 263
de Jongh, Nicholas 15, 114,
    190, 196, 218–19
Department of National
    Heritage 20, 275n. 73,
    312
Descartes, René 53, 97
de Ségur, La Comtesse 63
Dianeira 231, 236, 307n. 126,
    312, 314, 319
docudrama 21
'Don Juan's Women' 3, 24,
    48, 52–5, 70, 73, 237,
    267, 311, 314
Do Not Disturb 183, 312
Dostoevsky, Fyodor 270
Doughty, Louise 188
Dumas, Alexander 7
Dumbarton Oaks 10, 36
Dunbar, Andrea 17
Dymkowski, Christine 127–8,
    140, 290n. 159

Eastern Europe 19, 181,
    188–9, 192–5, 201–3,
    209, 296n. 27
Eberhardt, Isabelle 64–73,
    82–3
Edgar, David 14, 17–18,
    275n. 59
Edinburgh Fringe Festival 74,
    78
Edwardes, Jane 198
Edwards, Christopher 137
*Eighteenth Brumaire of Louis
    Bonaparte, The* 213
Elektra/Electra 48, 52, 100, 313
Elyot, Kevin 18
ENRON 21
Epsom Downs 145
Equus 33
Euripides 58, 139
Evans, Lloyd 242
Evening Standard 18, 218–19
'Everyone comes to Café
    Europa' 197
evolution 10, 105, 138, 201–2,
    206, 210–11, 268–9
exile 183–4, 209–12, 217,
    219–20, 225–7
Exmoor 11–12, 40–2, 310

fairy-tales 182, 220–31
Falco, Raphael 185, 208, 210
False Admissions 311
Fanon, Frantz 102–3
Fanshen 145
Farquhar, George 117–18, 123,
    127, 130–3, 144, 147–8

Fatal Shore, The 118, 147,
    154, 161, 169–70
fathers/fatherhood 203–5,
    224–5, 231, 238–41,
    245, 75, 85–6, 108–9
Faust 84–6
feminism 2–3, 13–15, 29–30,
    33–4, 36–7, 44–50,
    52–5, 60–2, 63–153,
    190–2, 237–8, 248–52,
    267, 320
filiation 4, 109, 183–6,
    190–1, 202–5, 208,
    209–11, 221–5, 227,
    231, 234, 236, 266, 268,
    295n. 10, 302n. 207
film 3, 183, 203, 207, 312
Filumena 312
First Fleet, The 119, 147, 149,
    154, 170
Fitzroy, Captain Robert
    199–205, 239, 252
floating identities 1, 22, 62,
    63, 127, 182, 208, 230,
    252, 268
Fowles, John 24, 48, 58–60
Freeman, Sara 98, 124, 220,
    245

Galileo Galilei 233, 237–41
Galileo's Daughter 237–41, 312
gardens 52, 66, 90–1, 187,
    215, 218, 261
Gaskell, Philip 141–2
Gaskill, William 14, 145–6,
    179

Gaster, Adele 138
Gay Sweatshop 13, 18
Gems, Pam 13, 278n. 93
gender 3, 13–15, 17–18,
    29–30, 33–4, 36–7, 39,
    44–50, 52–5, 59–62,
    63–96, 98–102, 106,
    113–17, 142, 186, 190,
    211, 224, 231, 233, 235,
    237–8, 244–5, 248–52,
    256, 267–9, 275n. 59,
    283n. 79, 286n. 28,
    288n. 86, 303n. 15, 320
Genet, Jean 9
Georgetown, University of 10
Gibbs, Jonathon 221
Glad Hand, The 129–30
Goodman, Lizbeth 99
Gordon Riots 71, 88,
    283n. 91
Grace of Mary Traverse, The 3,
    42, 59, 62, 63–4, 71, 73,
    75, 84–95, 97, 114, 115,
    142, 145, 193, 230, 235,
    239, 261, 267, 268, 272,
    278n. 75, 279n. 134,
    287n. 62, 311, 314, 317
Graves, Robert 48–9
Greece 12, 24–5, 55–62, 209,
    213, 264, 268, 299n. 89,
    307n. 126
Greek mythology/tragedy
    48–52, 55–62, 98–117,
    139–40, 189, 220,
    296n. 27, 307n. 126
Greeks, The 17

Greenham Common Women's
    Peace Camp 90, 311
Grid Iron 21
Griffiths, Trevor 14
Gulf War 19, 196, 257–9, 311
Gupta, Tanika 20

'H. File, The' 312
Half Moon Theatre Workshop
    13, 26, 27
Hall, Peter 16, 237, 312
Hampstead Theatre 199, 312
Hare, David 14, 15, 17, 21,
    145, 146
Harvey, Jonathon 18
Hecuba 220, 312, 319
Herriot Watt Theatre 78
herstory 47–62, 238, 278n. 93
Hicks, Jenny 44, 135–6
Hippolytus 106–8, 139–40,
    313, 314
historicisation 47–8, 153, 155,
    181, 220, 267
history (as a force/presence)
    38–9, 110, 182–8, 195,
    202, 207–8, 209–13,
    216, 218, 220, 226, 231,
    241, 244, 268, 277n. 60
HMP Blundeston 114
HMP Holloway 44, 133, 151
HMP Wormwood Scrubs
    136, 151–3
Hodgman, Roger 4, 118, 119,
    133, 136–7, 143, 161–7,
    177, 180, 323
Holborough, Jacqueline 135

Hollingworth, John 167–8
'Home Leave' 311
hope 5, 9, 38–9, 42, 88–92,
    105, 129, 132–3,
    156, 185, 195, 197,
    201 217–18, 229–31,
    233, 261–5, 268–72,
    278n. 75, 283n. 96
Hornery, Bob 166
Howard, Michael 134
Howe, Jenny 79
Hughes, Robert 118, 147,
    161, 169
humanism 206, 241, 270

Imison, Michael 276n. 20,
    311
immigration 181–2, 195,
    201–2, 209–20
incest 65, 85, 225
infanticide 88–9, 108–9,
    113–15, 231, 236,
    278n. 75
'Inside Out' 3, 63, 74, 78–84,
    234, 235, 267, 311, 314
Institute for Contemporary
    Arts (ICA) 13
'in-yer-face' theatre 19
Iraq 240, 312
Irigaray, Luce 116
IVF 190–4

Jacobson, Lenore 134
'Jefferson's Garden' 52,
    287n. 62
Její pastorkyňa 235

Jenufa 4, 233, 235–7,
    283n. 96, 312, 314
Joint Stock 14, 16, 21, 134,
    143–61, 179, 310
Jung, Carl 11, 24, 33, 230,
    279–80n. 134

Kane, Sarah 19, 197–8, 246,
    312
Kaur Bhatti, Gurpreet 20
Keatley, Charlotte 17
Kelling, George 171
Keneally, Thomas 5, 44,
    118–19, 134–5, 140,
    143–56, 161, 292n. 1
Kent, Sally 263
King and I, The 9
King's Head Theatre Club 13,
    25, 27, 35, 310, 311
Kingston, Jeremy 221
Komachi, Ono 74, 78–84
Kramer, Hilton 262–3,
    297–8n. 61
Kwei-Armah, Kwame 20

La Dispute 311
Lan, David 58
landscape 162–3, 232–3, 246,
    259–61, 307n. 130
language 4, 8, 9, 33, 95–6,
    97–142, 173–5, 206,
    213–17, 267–71
Lavery, Bryony 17
'Laws of Motion, The' 4,
    233, 237–41, 252, 260,
    287n. 62, 312, 314

Lehrstücke 228
Leicester Haymarket 186
Leocadia 311
Les Petites Filles Modèles 63
Letts, Quentin 242
Lewis, Jamie 163
Lewis, Tom E. 164, 166
Libation Bearers, The 48
Life of Galileo, The 238,
    303n. 27, 304n. 40
Light Shining in
    Buckinghamshire 13
Line, The 4, 107, 232–3,
    242–65, 287n. 52, 313,
    314
Lister, David 262
Locke, John 170
London 12–13, 21–2, 25–8
London Labour and the London
    Poor 147, 150
Love of a Good Man, The 136,
    151–2
Love of the Nightingale, The
    3, 9, 38, 45, 52, 55, 71,
    95, 97–117, 119–20,
    125, 139–40, 142, 207,
    208, 223, 227, 228,
    230–1, 232, 236, 267,
    268, 269, 278n. 75,
    282n. 66, 283nn. 79, 96,
    301–2n. 185, 311, 312,
    314, 318
Luce, Richard 16

Macaulay, Alastair 220,
    301n. 170

Macdonald, James 19
Macedonia 209–11, 215, 216
Mackenzie, Suzie 1, 91
madness 31–2, 56–60
Maeterlinck, Maurice 183
magic 210, 227–8, 234
Magus, The 24, 48, 58–60
Mahoney, John 153
male gaze 86, 101
Man, John 257
Marmion, Patrick 204
Marx, Karl 213, 216–17
Marxism 34–5
Masterpieces 17
Mayhew, Henry 147, 150
McGrath, John 14
McIntyre, Clare 17
McKellen, Ian 18
McKeown, Maeve 172
McTeer, Janet 91
Medea 231
Melbourne Theatre Company
    161–7, 177
'Memory of Gold, The' 213
Meno, The 10
Mephisto 97, 311
Metamorphoses 97–9
metamorphosis 115, 227–8
metatheatre 9, 35, 38, 58–9,
    71, 84, 99, 106–9,
    119–42, 186–8, 199–201,
    204–5, 208, 307n. 126
Midsummer Night's Dream, A
    199
migration 181–2, 195–6,
    201–3, 209–20

Mimesis 183–4
Mnouchkine, Ariane 97
'Monads' 3, 11, 24, 48,
    55–62, 73, 233, 267,
    279–80n. 134, 311,
    314
Monros-Gaspar, Laura 99–100
Monstrous Regiment 13,
    288n. 88
Morgan, Robin 48, 277n. 44
Morley, Sheridan 199, 217,
    219–20
Morse, Helen 166
mothers/motherhood 33–4,
    41–2, 49–51, 65, 75,
    87–9, 182–3, 186,
    190–3, 205–8, 209–12,
    221–6, 233, 236, 238,
    248–50, 268, 299n. 89
Mouthful of Birds, A 58
multi-roling 64, 72, 79–81,
    109–10, 137, 146, 177,
    285n. 127
Myerson, Jonathon 219–20
My Night with Reg 18
Mysteries, The 17
myth 33, 47–51, 57–8, 75,
    83–4, 94, 98–117,
    185, 189, 210,
    219–20, 230–1, 267,
    271, 301–2n. 185,
    307n. 126

National Lottery 20, 312
National Theatre 15–17, 20,
    234, 248, 312

National Theatre Connections
    Festival 234, 312
National Theatre Studio 248
Nation Review, The 164
Nathan, David 196–7, 204
Nathan, John 217–18, 242,
    300n. 153
Natural Perspective Theatre
    Company 235, 237, 312,
    313
'Near Miss' 3, 24, 40–3, 59,
    234, 266, 277n. 66,
    278n. 75, 311, 314
Neill, Rosemary 162, 164, 167
New Anatomies 3, 9, 63–74,
    76–7, 79, 83–4, 93,
    114–15, 142, 207, 234,
    235, 267, 311, 314
New Playwrights Festival,
    Ithaca, NY 39
New Theatre Workshops 78,
    85, 311
New York 7–12, 25, 39, 262,
    310
Nicholas Nickleby 16
Nightingale, Benedict 190,
    193, 194, 220
Noh theatre 79
nuclear industry 2–3, 24,
    40–3, 44–7
Nunn, Trevor 16

Oakley, Barry 164, 167
'On Repetition' 183, 213
optimism 5, 90–2, 196–7,
    217–18, 261–5

Oresteia, The 17
Orpheus and Euridice 32–3
Other, the 184, 227–8,
    283n. 79
Other Place, The 98
'Our Ajax' 313
Our Country's Good 2, 3, 4,
    5, 9, 10, 14, 22, 43–4,
    52, 71, 95, 97–8, 107,
    114, 119–80, 183, 186,
    189–90, 199, 200, 207,
    208, 232, 247–8, 262,
    266, 267, 287n. 62,
    289n. 120, 290nn. 159,
    161, 163, 291nn. 182,
    186, 190, 307n. 126,
    311, 314, 317–18
Out of Joint 14, 94–5,
    167–79, 186, 237,
    279n. 110, 312
Ovid 97–101, 301–2n. 185
Owners 13

Page, Louise 13–14, 17
Paine, Tom 92–3
Paradise Lost 214
Pelleas and Melisande 183, 311
Permanent Way, The 21
Peter, John 92, 219
Peter Hall Company 237, 312
Phaedra 313
Piaf 13, 278n. 93
Pinnock, Winsome 17
Plantagenets, The 17
Plato 10, 11–12, 53
Playmaker, The 5, 44, 118–19,

140, 143–56, 161,
    291n. 190, 292n. 1
play-within-a-play 9, 71,
    99, 106–9, 119–42,
    199–201, 204–5, 208
Poll Tax Riots 18, 311
Posner, Lindsay 254–5
'Possession' 313
postcolonialism *see* colonialism/
    postcolonialism
Power of Yes, The 21
Pravda 17
Prebble, Lucy 21
pregnancy 31, 42, 87, 170
Preissová, Gabriela 235, 237
Price, John 95, 98, 144
prison(ers) 5, 43–4, 114,
    119–80, 264–5
Pudlinski, Chris 138–9
Punchdrunk 21
Pygmalion in the Classroom 134

Rabillard, Sheila 99, 111–12,
    114, 183, 186–7, 190,
    208, 230
radio 39, 69, 72, 183, 231,
    300n. 156, 307n. 126,
    311–13, 314, 322
Rake's Progress, The 75, 84–5,
    92
rape 55, 80, 86, 89, 99–109,
    139–40, 212, 286n. 28
Ravenhill, Mark 18, 312
Rebellato, Dan 198
Recruiting Officer, The 117–18,
    124, 126–9, 132–3, 144,

147–8, 151–60, 169,
177, 186, 189–90, 199,
292n. 1
redemption 130, 135–7,
261–2, 270–1
Rees-Mogg, William 16
refugees 181–2, 192, 209–20,
261
Register Citizen, The 138
Reid, Billy 136
reviews 27, 29, 63–4, 73,
91–3, 100, 124–5,
137–9, 160, 164, 167,
188–90, 193–4, 196–8,
199–201, 204–5,
218–20, 221, 242–5,
256, 262–3
Rita, Sue and Bob Too 17
Ritchie, Martha 90
'Rites of Entry' 31–3, 61
Road 17
Rodent Arts Trust 74, 78–9,
311
Romans in Britain 15,
286n. 28
Rosenthal, Robert 134
Roth, Maya E. 152, 155, 188,
297n. 45
Royal Court 3, 13–19, 71,
84, 91, 93, 94, 118, 124,
133–4, 140–1, 143–5,
157, 159, 161, 162, 166,
168, 179, 186, 197–8,
209, 247, 254–5, 258,
274n. 47, 275nn. 59, 1,
292n. 1, 311–12

Royal Shakespeare Company
3, 14–17, 94–5, 97, 98,
183, 247, 311–12
Rubik, Margarete 113–14

Said, Edward 4, 126, 183–6,
210, 213, 216–17,
295n. 10
Sand, George 74–8, 82–4, 94
Sappho 192, 296n. 29
'Scenes of Seduction' 312
'Second Sentence' 3, 5, 24,
27, 43–4, 266, 311, 314
self-portraits 243, 251, 253
Serious Money 17, 148
seven deadly sins 221, 223,
227, 229
Shakespeare, William 17,
205–6, 234–5, 303n. 15
Shared Experience 311
Shellard, Dominic 13, 15, 20
Shopping and Fucking 18, 312
Shulman, Milton 18, 92,
137–8
Sierz, Aleks 196, 198
Sigal, Sarah 4, 14, 98, 118,
119, 134, 143–61, 169,
180, 323
silencing 8, 43–4, 97–142,
269
Simons, Judy 6
Siren 13
Sivertsen, Christopher 237
Smith, Andy 178
Sobel, Dava 237
Socrates 53, 264

Soho Poly 26–7, 48, 311
Soncini, Sara 141
Sophocles 48, 52, 231, 264
South Africa 114
Spare Rib 29
Speakers, The 145
Spectator, The 137
Spencer, Charles 199, 219–20
Spetse 12, 21, 24–5, 35,
    55–62, 275n. 4, 310
sponsorship 20, 133–4, 254–5
Stafford-Clark, Max 4, 14,
    17, 98, 118, 124, 134,
    137, 143–61, 166–79,
    186, 189, 196, 262, 264,
    290n. 161, 292n. 1,
    293n. 51, 294nn. 53, 56,
    68, 297–8n. 61
Stage, The 26, 27, 29, 55–6
Stanislavski, Konstantin
    154–5, 179
State of Play 17–18
state-of-the-nation 181, 198
St John's College, Annapolis
    10, 310
Stoppard, Tom 200
Strindberg, August 63
Stuart, Jan 262
Stuff Happens 21
subsidy 15–16, 20–1, 133–4,
    159–61, 255, 310, 311
Successful Strategies 311
Sulkin, David 247
Supplicants, The 220
Swindells, Julia 6

Sydney Theatre Company
    (STC) 161
Sykes, Peter 78–9

Taylor, Paul 221
teaching 4, 125, 143, 167–79,
    211–12, 215–16
television 3, 40, 183,
    277n. 66, 312, 314
Tempest, Clive 78, 85, 311
tenderness 5, 107–8, 204,
    232–3, 241, 246, 263–4,
    270, 287n. 52
Thatcher, Margaret 15–19, 90,
    133–4, 150–1, 171, 255,
    290n. 163, 295n. 79,
    310, 311
Theatre in Education 44–7
Theatre Museum, London 177
Theatres Act 12, 310
Theban Plays, The 183, 312
Thiong'o, Ngugi wa 103–4,
    117, 206–7
'Third, The' 2, 12, 24, 25, 27,
    28–30, 267, 310, 311,
    314
'This is No Place for Tallulah
    Bankhead' 3, 10, 24,
    25–6, 35–7, 38, 70–1,
    266, 310, 315
*Three Birds Alighting on a
    Field* 2, 4, 9, 159, 183,
    194, 196, 222, 233–4,
    249–64, 295n. 3,
    296n. 29, 297–8n. 61,

299n. 89, 306–7n. 125, 312, 314
Three Musketeers, The 7, 63
Three Sisters 183, 186–9, 196
Timberlake Wertenbaker's Our Country's Good: A Study Guide 170
Time-Life 7, 10, 36, 310
Tinker, Jack 188
Top Girls 17, 190, 278n. 93, 311
translation 52, 97, 183, 213–14, 217, 245, 246, 268, 296n. 27, 307n. 126, 311–13, 319
Transportation Act 170
Transportation Game, The 149, 170
transvestism 66–8, 70, 72–7, 80–4, 234–5, 303n. 15
trials 35–6, 52–4, 69–72, 75, 121–2, 244
Tripp, Tony 162–3, 177
Trotter, Mary Kate 89
Trueman, Pat 78
Tucker Green, Debbie 20
Turner, Debby 4, 118, 125, 143, 149, 167–80, 234

Uncle Vanya 187
'Upper World, The' 32–3, 61

Valadon, Suzanne 232, 242–52, 266
Vancouver Playhouse 165

van Ruysdael, Salomon 259–60
Variations 3, 63, 74–8, 82–4, 114, 234, 235, 267, 311, 315
Varty, Anne 99, 106
verbatim theatre 21
verfremdungseffekt/ de-familiarisation 100, 222, 227–8
Vico, Giambattista 183
victims (women as) 53–5, 62, 83–4, 91–2, 94, 267
'View of Deventer, A' 259–60
'Vigil, The' 2, 11, 24, 25, 30–4, 61, 233, 267, 310, 314
Vinegar Tom 13
Vivis, Anthony 125
'Voices We Hear, The' 61–2, 264, 315

Wagner, Jennifer A. 99, 116–17
Waka poets 82
Walsh Jenkins, Linda 99
'War on Terror' 21
Weeks, Stephen 128
Wertenbaker, Charles 7–8
Wertenbaker, Lael Tucker 7–10
Wharf Theatre, Sydney 162
Wharton, Edith 183
'What is the Custom of Your Grief' 300n. 156, 313, 322

White, Joe 130, 139, 153,
    171–2
Whybrow, Graham 17, 19
'Wild Orchids' 312
Williams, Faynia 27
Willmer, Caissa 39–40
Wilson, Ann 123, 126, 130,
    136, 138–9, 141, 142,
    307n. 126
Wilson, James Q. 171
Wilson, Snoo 129–30
Winston, Joe 99, 114–15
Woddis, Carole 73
Wolsey Theatre, Ipswich 311
Women in Entertainment
    (WIE) 248

Women in Love 9
Women of Trachis 231
women on quests 3, 73, 84–5,
    87, 89–90, 94, 266–7,
    271–2
Women's Theatre Group
    (WTG) 6, 13, 44, 64,
    73, 93, 237, 247, 310,
    311
wonder 264, 270

'Year on Exmoor, A' 11–12,
    34, 234, 310
Young Vic 167

Zecora Ura/Para Active 21